The Thrales of Streatham Park

The Thrales of
Streatham Park

MARY HYDE

HARVARD UNIVERSITY PRESS
CAMBRIDGE, MASSACHUSETTS
LONDON, ENGLAND
1977

Library of Congress Cataloging in Publication Data

Piozzi, Hester Lynch Salusbury Thrale, 1741–1821.
　The Thrales of Streatham Park.

　Annotated journal of Hester Thrale.
　Includes index.
　1. Piozzi, Hester Lynch Salusbury Thrale, 1741–1821 — Biography.　2. Thrale family.　3. Salusbury family.　4. England — Social life and customs — 18th century. I. Hyde, Mary Morley Crapo.　II. Title.　PR3619.P5A827　1977　828'.6'09 [B]
77–24922　　ISBN 0–674–88746–8

FOR OUR GODCHILDREN

Peter Depew Whitman · John Spencer Gordon
Deborah Farwell Field · Rolf Christopher Ainsworth Christophersen
Frances Gwenllian Hamblin · Anne Stuart Hinshaw
Elizabeth Noble Goodenough · Suzette de Marigny Dewey
Carter Boardman Alsop · Sarah Bullard
Sara Kent Paterson · Deborah Billings Vander Poel
Duncan Ely Jones · Halsted Billings Vander Poel, II
Emma Louise Hobson · Sarah Willis-Bund Curtis
Julia Willcox Crapo · Elizabeth Jean Lucinda Cameron
Louise Gabrielle Austin

PREFACE

The story which follows surrounds a journal of Hester Lynch Thrale, one which gives a rare insight into the life of an eighteenth-century family that was to have both typical and unusual experiences — the most unusual experience being its close friendship with one of the great men of English literature.

In 1766 Mrs. Thrale began the journal as a record of the growth and education of her children. She gave it the title of "The Children's Book." It was to be an account of the Thrale nursery, but in short order it became, as will be seen, a record of much larger scope.

Hester Thrale began with the facts one finds in a family Bible, and added observations upon each child's progress. This kind of book is an accepted part of baby equipment today, but for the eighteenth century it is apparently unique.

Since the undertaking was so unusual, one wonders how the idea came to Mrs. Thrale. Perhaps because she was fond of diaries (she had been keeping them since she was a young girl), and the birth of her first child was an event which made her want to start a separate record. If so, why did she not begin the journal at the child's birth, the logical starting point? Did Dr. Johnson launch the project? He was forever advising his friends to keep records for one purpose or another and, at the time of the baby's birth in 1764, he had not yet been introduced to the Thrales. By 1766, however, he was a virtual member of the family, and it is in this year that the diary begins. Johnson may well have thought that the infant Hester Maria Thrale deserved a nursery record. He was much taken with this extraordinary little creature, a prodigy, pert and pretty, amusing and imperious. "Queeney," he called her, after Queen Esther, and by this apt nickname H. M. Thrale was to be known for many years.

It was most likely a combination of influences that prompted Mrs. Thrale to start the journal: the importance of a first child in the household, the remarkable qualities of Queeney herself, Mrs. Thrale's own addiction to diary keeping, and Johnson's persuasion. The account certainly begins in Johnsonian style — on Queeney's second birthday. Johnson was on hand for this, as she was on hand for his fifty-seventh, the next day; they were to celebrate their birthdays together many times in the years to come.

Mrs. Thrale diligently continued this special journal for thirteen years, recording facts about Queeney and the eleven children who followed. Mrs. Thrale also recorded much about herself, her mother, her husband, and Dr. Johnson. In time she realized that the diary had became a great deal more than just "The Children's Book" and, amending the title, she wrote on the cover: "or rather Family Book" — which is the proper description of this fascinating journal.

The little brown calf volume of 187 pages traveled for years with Mrs. Thrale from town to country, from Southwark to Streatham. For a while, at the beginning of her second marriage to Gabriel Piozzi, the book was mislaid and forgotten, but it was found again and kept with her manuscripts at Brynbella, the Piozzis' house in Wales.

After Mrs. Piozzi's death, the *Family Book* came to her heir, John Salusbury Piozzi Salusbury, and the journal remained in the Salusbury family until 1908, when it was sold by Major Edward Pemberton Salusbury, to Mrs. Salusbury Kynaston Mainwaring. It was inherited by her son, Colonel Sir Watkin Randle Kynaston Mainwaring, and in turn by his son, Brigadier Hugh Salusbury Kynaston Mainwaring, who sold it at Sotheby's in 1969. The journal had been only in Salusbury and Mainwaring hands until it crossed the Atlantic and came to Four Oaks Farm.

As I read the *Family Book* I became increasingly curious. How did two people so opposite in temperament as Hester Salusbury and Henry Thrale happen to marry? How deep was the influence of Hester's mother, the dominating Mrs. Salusbury? What happened to the Thrale children who lived to maturity? What happened to the houses associated with members of the family? The journal was the middle part of the story. What was the beginning, and what was the end? These questions led to research and four Thrale journeys to England, Scotland, and Wales.

From the start I owed a special and personal debt to the late Dr. Robert F. Metzdorf for his unfailing concern and counsel. Another such debt I owe to Professor W. Jackson Bate, who at every stage has given just the right help and encouragement at just the right time.

A major problem I faced in editing Mrs. Thrale's journal was the subject of illness. Mrs. Thrale's journal records the symptoms and treatment of many diseases and afflictions, but latter-day comment on her notes is not easy. I have been guided in this thorny field by medical authorities in England. My special thanks go to Dr. John Edgcumbe, of Exmouth. He has been indefatigable. I am also grateful for consultation with two distinguished pediatricians, Sir Douglas Hubble of Newbury and Professor J. P. M. Tizard of Oxford. In this country I have had most helpful suggestions from Dr. James Nelson of Schenectady and Dr. Gordon Jones of Fredericksburg.

The Thrale family was plagued not only by medical problems but by legal ones as well, and in this area much assistance has come from Mr. A. M. Kenny, a London barrister. He has carried on investigations for me in London, Brighton, and Oxfordshire. In North Wales, Mr. David Hooson, a solicitor in Denbigh, has furnished information about Cecilia Thrale Mostyn and her children, and in Scotland Mr. E. D. Buchanan, Writer to the Signet, has found answers to questions about Queeney Thrale and the Elphinstone family into which she married.

I am deeply grateful to Professor James L. Clifford for having written the fine biography of Hester Lynch Thrale Piozzi. This book has been a constant guide, as has Professor Katharine C. Balderston's invaluable edition of *Thraliana*, from which I have quoted extensively, by kind permission of the Oxford University Press and the Henry E. Huntington Library.

Many libraries in England have extended courtesies but particular thanks must go to the John Rylands Library in Manchester for attentions given during my working visits there. I am especially grateful to Dr. Frank Taylor, the Principal Keeper, and to Miss Glenise Matheson, Keeper of Manuscripts, for help far beyond the call of duty.

In Oxford, research has been made a pleasant task by Dr. Robert Shackleton, Bodley's Librarian, Dr. David G. Vaisey, now Keeper of Western Manuscripts in the Bodleian Library, and Mr. David Cox, Senior Fellow of Henry Thrale's University College.

In London, investigation has been much facilitated by staff members at the libraries of the Courtauld Institute, The Greater London Council, the Guildhall, the National Maritime Museum, the Public Record Office, the Royal College of Physicians, Somerset House, and the Wellcome Library. I am indebted to Mr. Leslie Cook, Mr. Hugh Whitwell, and Miss Elizabeth McDonald for many kindnesses extended at Courage, Ltd., the brewery once owned by Henry Thrale. The tradition of hospitality continues there.

It is impossible to name all those in England who have taken trouble to help me, some are kind friends of many years standing, and some are recent friends, introduced by the Thrales. I wish to express special appreciation to the Earl of Shelburne, who has given me information about Susan Thrale as well as Queeney, and to Mr. Francis Burne and Mrs. Peter Burne, who have helped me follow the career of Sophia Thrale Hoare, and have found the answers to many questions about other characters in the story, an activity which they refer to as the "paper chase."

For information, guidance, and other kindnesses, visits to houses, churches, memorials, and other buildings, also for access to letters, cuttings, pictures, pedigrees, and baptismal records, I wish to thank: Mrs. Josephine Birchenough, Captain Oliver Burton, Mrs. P. C. Chamberlain, Mr. Hubert Chesshyre, Mr. and Mrs. Derek Chittock, Mr. Hugh Cobbe, the late Viscount Cobham, the late Earl of Crawford and Balcarres, Mr. Frank Crome, Mr. Simon Crome, Mr. Brooke Crutchley, Admiral Sir Victor Crutchley, Miss E. M. R. Ditmas, Mrs. Gerald Draper, the Very Reverend Sydney Evans, Viscount and Viscountess Garnock, Mr. Peter Glazebrook, the Reverend C. P. Gordon-Clark, Mr. and Mrs. David Hambro, the Reverend Michael Hamilton-Sharp, Lady Hoare, Mr. H. P. R. Hoare, Mr. and Mrs. Peter Holdcroft, Mr. G. A. Holleyman, Lt. Commander Thomas Hornyold-Strickland, the late Sir Gyles Isham, Mr. Morley Kennerley, Miss M. S. Kerrich, Mrs. N. C. Kerrich, Mr. D. M. Laverick, Mr. and Mrs. Cedric Maby, the late Brigadier Hugh Mainwaring, Mr. and Mrs. Lloyd Mainwaring, the Reverend William Meiklejohn, Mr. and Mrs. C. A. Miller, Sir Richard Miller, Lady Mitchell, Lady Moran, Mr. and Mrs. G. E. Morris, Colonel Robert Parker, Dr. L. M. Payne, Mr. and Mrs. Arthur Pennant, Mrs. C. A. C. Perkins, Miss Kathleen Reynolds, Mr. Lionel Robinson, Dr. M. W. B. Sanderson, Lord Sandys, Mr. Alan Savidge, Mr. A. Llewellyn Smith, Miss Janet Taylor, Mr. Michael Streatfeild, Mr. and Mrs. Richard Thrale, Mrs. Beryl Whitaker, Mr. W. R. Williams, and Mr. Richard Woollett.

For assistance in gathering illustrations I am indebted to Mr. John Kerslake of the National Portrait Gallery and to Sir Geoffrey Agnew, Miss Anna Mitchell, and Mr. Clovis Whitfield. Individual acknowledgments are given in the list of illustrations and I am grateful for the generosity of each owner in letting me have permission for reproduction. A particular debt of gratitude must go to Mr. Felix Kelly for his kind counsel and for the gift of an original illustration as well as for the design of the book jacket.

In the United States, I owe a debt to Mrs. Douglas Bryant and Mr. Edwin E. Williams, my sympathetic *Harvard Library Bulletin* editors, also to their associate, Miss Deborah Smullyan. I am grateful for the many kindnesses of Professor William H. Bond and others at the Houghton Library. And I wish to thank all those at the Princeton University Library who have helped me, in particular Professor Richard Ludwig and Mr. Charles Greene. Among the many friends and scholars who have assisted and answered a wide range of questions, I wish to thank: Mrs. Gabriel Austin, Dr. Julian P. Boyd, Mrs. Katherine Bruner, Dr. Wolfgang M. Freitag, Professor Philip H. Highfill, Jr., Professor Louis A. Landa, Mr. Herman W. Liebert, Mr. Kenneth Lohf, Mr. and Mrs. Howard S. Mott, Mr. John C. Riely, Mr. Eric Sexton, and Mr. James Wells. And how can I ever acknowledge the patience and good nature of Miss Rose McTernan, who has typed and retyped the manuscript and done so much besides?

During the years I have spent with the Thrales anguishing over the children, I have thought about our nineteen godchildren — Don's and mine — and to them I dedicate this book, with the salute that they are exceedingly lucky to have been born in the twentieth century!

Mary Hyde

Four Oaks Farm
17 April 1977

		Born	*Died*	*Age*
1.	Hester Maria (Queeney)	1764: 17 September (Southwark)	1857: 31 March (London)	92
2.	Frances	1765: 27 September (Southwark)	1765: 6 October (Southwark)	9 days
3.	Henry Salusbury	1767: 15 February (Southwark)	1776: 23 March (Southwark)	9
4.	Anna Maria	1768: 1 April (Streatham)	1770: 20 March (Dean St., London)	1
5.	Lucy Elizabeth	1769: 22 June (Streatham)	1773: 22 November (Streatham)	4
6.	Susanna Arabella	1770: 23 May (Southwark)	1858: 5 November (Knockholt)	88
7.	Sophia	1771: 23 July (Streatham)	1824: 8 November (Sandgate)	53
8.	Penelope	1772: 15 September (Streatham)	1772: 15 September (Streatham)	10 hours
9.	Ralph	1773: 8 November (Streatham)	1775: 13 July (Brighton)	1
10.	Frances Anna	1775: 4 May (Streatham)	1775: 9 December (Streatham)	7 months
11.	Cecilia Margaretta	1777: 8 February (Streatham)	1857: 1 May (Brighton)	80
12.	Henrietta Sophia	1778: 21 June (Streatham)	1783: 25 April (Streatham)	4

CONTENTS

ILLUSTRATIONS

I. HESTER LYNCH SALUSBURY AND HENRY THRALE

In October 1763, three years before the journal began, Hester Lynch Salusbury, an attractive young woman of twenty-two, was given in marriage by her uncle, Sir Thomas Salusbury, to Henry Thrale, more than ten years her senior, an Oxford man, handsome, worldly, and rich, owner of the Thrale Brewery in Southwark and the adjoining residence; owner of a pack of fox hounds and a hunting box near Croydon; owner of Crowmarsh Battle, a farm in Oxfordshire; and owner of Streatham Park, a country house and property of nearly a hundred acres in Surrey, about six miles from London.

Sir Thomas Salusbury, a judge of the Admiralty Court, and a Hertfordshire country squire, had been furthering the match for some time. He had met Henry Thrale in London and later had hunted with him. He found Thrale an exceedingly personable and agreeable man and he wished to introduce him to his niece — when the time was right, when things would be pleasant at his house and there would be no chance of a disagreeable scene.

Hester Salusbury, with her mother and father, had been visiting Sir Thomas at Offley Place, near St. Albans, all summer. Indeed, for the last four years, since the death of Sir Thomas' wife, Anna Maria, these relations had been with him most of the time. At first, life had been agreeable enough for the three adults, who were in their fifties, and for Hester, in her late teens, the only child of the John Salusburys, a young lady whom everyone in the Offley area treated with respect, for they presumed that one day she would inherit the property. Hester was pretty, vivacious, and sweet-tempered; also, because her mother had spent so much time tutoring her, she was a near prodigy.

Mrs. Salusbury, apart from being a devoted and dominating mother, was a forceful and attractive woman in her own right. She still had a trim figure, was extremely handsome and polished, charming and witty. And though she had no fondness for Sir Thomas, she was self-disciplined enough to mind her manners and appear cheerful. Sir

Thomas seemed contented enough. He was a lazy, good-natured man, with simple tastes.

John Salusbury was the disruptive member of the family: indolent, overbearing, full of complaint, and quick to take offense. His foul temper soon became a torment to the others. He was critical of his daughter. He quarreled with his wife (though he adored her and she him). He argued incessantly with his brother, a year his junior. He harped on Tom's lack of appreciation for his early sacrifices. They had gone to Cambridge — Trinity Hall — together, and after John had stayed the usual time, Tom had remained (at his brother's expense) for eleven years! Even after the plodder had finally received his law degree, John continued to support him at Doctors' Commons in London, with money which he needed more than ever himself, for by then he had married his cousin, Hester Maria Cotton (at St. Paul's Cathedral). The Salusburys would have liked to live in London, for they enjoyed elegant society more than anything else, but they could not afford to stay. They moved to Caernarvonshire, and there, near Pwllheli, John leased Bodvel Hall, a seventeenth-century gatehouse, recently converted into a dwelling; the house being near a property from which John received a little annual income. Brother Tom did not slacken his demands, and Lucy Salusbury, their mother (who had insisted upon the Cambridge education for her sons) was as improvident as ever, running up debts at Bach-y-Graig, the family property, and letting the house fall into ruin. Bach-y-Graig had rightfully belonged to John for many years (since the age of seven), but he had willingly allowed his widowed mother to stay on. With her, was her youngest son, Harry, whom an early accident had rendered something of an idiot, so John was financially responsible for him, as well as Tom, who was now in London, living "from Lord to Duke, & from Bishop to Baronet, making himself agreable," while waiting for a "lucrative Place" (*Thraliana*, p. 280).

In order to support all these dependents, John and his wife lived a very restricted life in Wales, their situation made more uncomfortable when their child, Hester Lynch, was born in 1741.[1] Her sec-

---

[1] Hester Lynch Salusbury was born on 27 January 1741. Her grandmother, the former Lady Cotton, was the daughter of Sir Thomas Lynch, who had amassed a fortune when governor of Jamaica. Lady Cotton's husband, Sir Thomas Cotton (the infant's grandfather), had died in 1715, and Lady Cotton had married again. With

BODVEL HALL

ond name honored Mrs. Salusbury's mother, Philadelphia Lynch, the former Lady Cotton, but though Hester's grandmother was pleased by the gesture, she offered no hoped-for assistance, and none came from any other source.

After eight years John Salusbury was forced to abandon his wife and little daughter and go to Nova Scotia in a desperate attempt to improve his fortune. This excursion, as well as a second to Nova Scotia, was a dismal failure, despite John's important commission and his close friendship with the colonizer, Lord Halifax.

2.

Now, in 1762, John's privations were long since past, but he was still complaining about the hardships and unhappiness he had suffered. Over and over Sir Thomas admitted that he was grateful, deeply grateful, for support in years gone by, but in his own defense, he insisted that he had done everything in his power to repay his brother — after he had succeeded Sir Henry Penrice as an Admiralty judge, obtained a title, and married Sir Harry's daughter, Anna Maria. He had begged money from his heiress wife to pay off the mortgage on John's Welsh property, and had also begged money from Anna Maria to provide his brother with a fine small house in London, in Dean Street. Thus, Tom said, his debt was repaid in full. But John's recriminations continued, his attacks made more violent by heavy drinking.

As the atmosphere grew increasingly unpleasant at Offley Place, Hester tried to comfort her mother, to control her father (at which she was better than anyone else), and to enchant her uncle. Hester was well trained in the last art because the twenty-one years of her life had been a round of visits to rich relations, the length of stay depending upon how long she and·her mother were able to make themselves agreeable. During John Salusbury's long absences in Nova Scotia they had stayed for months at Offley Place with Sir Thomas Salusbury and Anna Maria, and months at East Hyde with Mrs. Salusbury's mother, and they had also passed months in the houses of Mrs. Salusbury's brother, Sir Robert Cotton — Llewenny in Flint-

Lynch money she had built and now lived in a lovely house, "East Hyde," a few miles distant from Offley Place.

This house, now called "The Hyde," still looks very much as it did in the eighteenth century. The property belongs (1975) to Mr. and Mrs. David Hambro.

EAST HYDE

shire, Combermere Abbey in Cheshire, and the London house on Albemarle Street.[2] These were all havens because Mrs. Salusbury was tactful and Hester was entertaining.

There was a sad change when the genial Sir Robert Cotton, a child-less widower, died in 1748, for everything was inherited (to the Salusburys' bitter disappointment) by Sir Robert's brother, Sir Lynch, a crusty eccentric, a penny-pinching man with a large family. Hester had no success in charming him. Her mother, however, became important in the life of Sir Lynch's timid, provincial wife, who began to ask her guidance in every major decision. But this did not help the Salusburys with practical matters. It was Sir Thomas (with his wife's money) who had taken care of his brother's family for the last ten years. And Hester had charmed her aunt. Now, in the summer of 1762, three years after Anna Maria's death, Hester was confident that she remained her uncle's favorite:

Sir Tho[s] [had] No Joy except in his Dogs, his Horses and myself ... and I never in my Life did ask a Favour of [him] which he refused: all this made me love him very tenderly, & if he fell from his Horse or had any Accident befall him I was his true & affectionate Attendant: if I wrote Verses it was about his Park, or his Possessions; and to my dear Offley I did rivet my poor foolish Heart. I kept tame Fawns, fondled favourite Hounds, got up in the Morning to make Breakfast, & then followed the Hunters in a Post Chaise — for I was not to be trusted a'Horseback forsooth ... (*Thraliana*, pp. 296–297)

Sir Thomas did not feel quite as his niece imagined. He was naturally fond of her. With the passage of time, however, he had not only tired of his brother's family, but he had developed an interest of his own. He had met a smiling widow of forty-one, who lived in nearby Wellbury, Sarah Burroughs King, "whose first Husband L[d] Kingston's Bro[r] had lived with her but three Weeks" (*Thraliana*, p. 303). Sir Thomas in his mid-fifties was still a handsome man, tall, and though his dark hair was greying and his face and figure were somewhat fat and bloated with drink, he was as charming and affable as ever. He wished to marry the widow King, and she was more than willing.

The problem which faced Sir Thomas was how to extricate himself from his responsibilities. The first move, obviously, was to present a suitor for his niece's hand, someone who could not be refused.

[2] All these houses still exist, and the first two come into the later story.
Sir Robert's Albemarle Street house, between Stafford St. and Grafton St. on the East side, is now number 15, a place of business.

Over the last few years, a number of suitors had made their appearance, but whenever a match was offered, or a proposal even mentioned, Hester's father had thrown himself into a violent passion and turned the fellow out. John Salusbury seemed to hope secretly that his daughter would never marry. This time Sir Thomas was not going to take chances with his candidate, and he waited for the proper moment of introduction. It came when he and his brother had made a journey through Wales with Lord Halifax, on his way to assume the Lord-Lieutenancy of Ireland. After the Earl had left them, John Salusbury stayed in the Vale of Clwyd to discuss property problems with Edward Bridge, his agent. Thomas, however, hastened back to Offley, and there, as soon as he was alone with Mrs. Salusbury and Hester, he delivered a paean of praise on the subject of someone called Henry Thrale:

... what an excellent, what an incomparable young Man ... [he] was in short a Model of Perfection: ending his Panegyric by saying that he was a *real Sportsman*. Seeing me disposed to laugh, he looked very grave, said he expected us to like him, — & that — scriously. The next Day Mr. Thrale follow'd his Eulogist ... (Fellowes, p. 18)

Thrale came to Offley with his aunt, Anne Thrale Smith, of St. Albans, an ordinary and talkative person, Hester thought, though good humored. Hester was amused by the deference Thrale showed his aunt, and by the great courtesy he showed her mother, who, it was quite obvious, liked the visitor. Thrale was tall and gentlemanly in appearance, with an agreeable countenance, steady eyes of the deepest blue, and very elegant hands. He was exceedingly well-mannered, though shy and reserved; however, when he was drawn out, his personality was delightful, totally unaffected and good humored. He was intelligent and thoughtful. Mrs. Salusbury, who drank no wine or spirits herself, noted his moderation with approval. Thrale's conversation was free of oaths, ribaldry, and profanity; and he attended church without urging. He was a sound, sensible person.

Though Henry Thrale devoted much attention to her mother, he took less notice of Hester "than any other Man I had ever seen come to the House almost" (*Thraliana*, p. 301). He conversed with Mrs. Salusbury, admired Sir Thomas' horses and hounds, and enthralled the neighborhood by telling everyone that his father, the rich brewer, Ralph Thrale, had come from these parts; in fact the family cottage was located on the property, a small building now used as a dog kennel. Young Thrale spoke with affection and reverence of his father (who had died in 1758), and delighted Mrs. Salusbury by "giving five Shillings to a white headed Lad who was lying on a Bank, because he could conceive his Father to have been such a Boy he said" (*Thraliana*, p. 299).

Thrale's connections were not entirely humble. His great-uncle, Edmund Halsey, the seventeenth-century owner of the Southwark brewery, had had an only child, a daughter, who married Viscount Cobham of Stowe, who laid out the gardens there. It was not fitting for a peer to be in trade, and so Halsey had gone back to St. Albans to seek out his nephew, who, he had heard, was a promising, level-headed young man. Halsey found that Ralph Thrale lived up to all reports; he was able, had an easy and pleasant manner, and for good measure was exceedingly handsome. Halsey offered him employment in the brewery, and Ralph accepted the offer without hesitation. He removed to Southwark, settled there, worked hard, and prospered, though he fell out with his uncle by marrying "a Wench that Halsey wanted to have for his own Pleasure"[3] (*Thraliana*, p. 300). Halsey considered himself something of an old beau.

Despite this humiliation, Halsey allowed Ralph Thrale to remain at the brewery — he had become indispensable. Upon Halsey's death, with some accumulation of capital, and with the power of borrowing, Ralph Thrale was able to purchase the brewery — and in subsequent years he grew rich through it.

[3] Mary Thrale's unmarried surname is not known, but a study has been made of Ralph Thrale's coffin plate by the College of Arms. Its "Gules 5 mullets of 6 points Or between 2 flaunches checky argent and sable" suggest that her last name may have been Dabbins, Dobbins, or Dobbinson. An interesting project for further research.

Ralph Thrale and his descendants, incidentally, had no right to use arms, but they did so. Their long line of Hertfordshire yeoman farmers was not apparently related to the armigerous "Threeles" of Sussex (whose pedigree was the subject of Herald visitations in 1634 and 1662). But these were the arms they assumed.

Recently, the matter has been corrected; on 4 April 1972 arms were granted to the descendants of Ralph's kinsman, Ernest Norman Thrale of Wheathampstead (1866–1909). These arms resemble those of the "Threeles," but there are several differences, including the addition of two tuns (barrels), one on either side of the oak tree in the crest.

Richard Thrale of St. Albans, a grandson of Ernest Norman, is the family genealogist and has published *A New Thraliana, a Chronicle of the Thrale Family of Hertfordshire*, Falconer Press, St. Albans, 1973.

RALPH THRALE
BY HUDSON

He carefully maintained his family ties with the Cobhams, even arranging for William Henry Lyttelton, a Cobham relation four years older than his son, to act as a sort of tutor for him on a Grand Tour of the Continent. This was after Henry left Oxford,[4] and his father, it was said, paid all of Lyttelton's expenses for he was eager that his son should avail himself of his aristocratic connections and make a place for himself in the world.

Henry Thrale's first and only visit to Offley Park was brief and decisive. Sir Thomas' "scheme" succeeded: Thrale was definitely interested in a match with Hester, and both Sir Thomas and her mother were "mad" for it, Sir Thomas saying "he saw no young Fellow upon the plan of that young Fellow," and Mrs. Salusbury saying "*this* was the Man for [her daughter] to *marry*, the only man She had ever said so of . . ." (*Thraliana*, p. 300).

Hester was not attracted to Thrale and was sure her father, who had "sole Right to dispose of [her]" (*Thraliana*, p. 303), would never tolerate him. When John Salusbury returned from Wales, the expected explosion occurred: they had brought in behind his back a man of unspeakably low birth and flashy dress and "*fashionable* Manners too, wearing [his mistress, Polly] Hart's Portrait *out*side his Snuffbox; boasting of Gallantrie" (Conway, I, 2). His daughter would not be sold "for a Barrel of Porter" (*Thraliana*, p. 302) to a whoring fop, who would give her the pox. There were scenes of great acrimony, with John Salusbury perpetually shouting that "*if the* Child does marry that Puppy, I know he'll be a Bankrupt" (*Thraliana*, p. 804).

In a furious temper, John Salusbury gathered up his wife and daughter and took them back to London, to his house in Dean Street. This was an impetuous, irrevocable, foolhardy decision — only Hester would ever see Offley Place again, and she would see it but once.

Back in the Dean Street house, Mrs. Salusbury's opinion of Thrale was not changed by her husband's diatribes. She had experienced the bitter hardships of poverty, and she wished her daughter to escape them. Henry Thrale, she maintained, was a fine, courteous man and he had a great deal to offer. His lack of birth was compensated for

---

[4] According to the Buttery Books of their respective colleges, Lyttelton entered St. Mary Hall when he was eighteen (June 1742) and he remained there until January 1744.
    In June 1744, Thrale arrived at University College, aged fifteen. He stayed until December 1745.

by his wealth; and as for his bachelor life, this period was about to be over. He was a basically serious-minded person, eager to settle down to a conventional family life. John Salusbury agreed in no point and continued to rage. Hester did not concern herself much with the battle. She was more interested in studying Latin with her tutor, Dr. Arthur Collier.

This short-sighted, erudite Oxford man, a sentimental bachelor in his fifties, was a friend of Sir Thomas Salusbury, a fellow advocate. He enjoyed teaching the Classics on the side and had tutored Hester on his frequent visits to Offley Place. Now he saw her in London, and mixed with the parsing of Latin was talk of Henry Thrale. Collier was not enthusiastic about the match, but he soon sensed the force of Mrs. Salusbury's determination and, considering opposition a lost cause, he tried to prevail upon Sir Thomas to make his niece a proper marriage settlement. Collier's efforts succeeded only in irritating Sir Thomas; as he continued to meddle, Collier aroused the hostility of Mrs. Salusbury. For some time he and Hester had been carrying on a secret correspondence in Latin, concerning her settlement and the frightening possibility that Sir Thomas might marry the widow King.

A letter from Collier toward the end of December 1762 caused final tragedy for John Salusbury:

... A Note came sent in a sly Manner from Dr. Collier to tell me — (it was written in Latin) that Sir Thomas would certainly marry Mrs King the Sunday following — and beg'd I would not say a Syllable till the next Day, when *he* would come, & break the dreadful Tydings to my Father.

My Countenance however shew'd — or his Acuteness discerned, something he did not like: an Accusation follow'd, that I received clandestine Letters from Mr Thrale, a Circumstance I had certainly every just Reason to deny, & felt extremely hurt, of Course at seeing myself disbelieved. After a fruitless & painful Contest for many Hours of this Cruel Evening — my Spirits sunk, I fainted — & my Father — gaining possession of the fatal Billet — had to ask *my* Pardon — poor unhappy Soul! & in this fond Misery spent we the Hours till 4 o'clock in the Morning. At 9 we rose — He to go cross the Park in search of my Maternal Uncle Sir Lynch Salusbury Cotton, from whom, & from Dr. Crane [5] Prebendary of Westmr. he meant to seek Counsel & Comfort; — Me, to the Employment of calling our Medical Friend Herbert Lawrence to Dinner by a Billet of earnest Request — *All of us* were *Ill* — but by the Time he came, my Father died — & was brought us home a Corpse — before the Dining hour.
This was December 1762 ... (Fellowes, pp. 20–21)

[5] Dr. Crane: tutor to the family of Lord Halifax and a close friend of John Salusbury.

3.

The sudden death of John Salusbury was a shattering blow to his wife and daughter, and even Sir Thomas was grief stricken. He at once promised his niece a marriage bond of £10,000, and he promised a yearly allowance to Mrs. Salusbury of £200. These eighteenth-century figures should be multiplied by twenty to give an idea of present value — that is to say in the 1960s, before escalating inflation.

Time passed, however, and Sir Thomas did nothing. Dr. Collier continued to press for Hester's marriage bond, even preparing a suitable draft. Sir Thomas scorned Collier's effort, and Mrs. Salusbury stopped Hester's lessons and forbade her to have any further correspondence with her tutor (over 200 letters had been exchanged during the year). Collier meant a great deal to Hester, he was her mentor, guide, and dearest friend. But she was always obedient to her mother, and she did as she was told.

On 28 June 1763 Henry Thrale wrote a note to Mrs. Salusbury and Hester jointly, saying that he wished to meet with them and discuss a "very interesting subject." At the appointed time, he saw the two ladies and asked for the hand of Hester. After a conventional pause, her affirmative answer was given with filial docility. Hester Salusbury promised herself to Henry Thrale without ever having been alone with him for five minutes (*Thraliana*, p. 692).

Hester wrote to Sidney Arabella Cotton, one of her maiden aunts in Bath, telling of the engagement. Her decision was based, she said, not "on Passion but on Reason," which gave her "some Right to expect some Happiness." Thrale's regard for her mother, she believed, was "no small proof of his Understanding — nor ought lightly to be esteem'd by me. I somehow can add no more" (Rylands 533.1).

Sir Thomas and Henry Thrale were soon discussing the marriage contract, and in contrast to the bumbling attempts of Dr. Collier, negotiations were now business-like and easy. Hester's marriage bond for £10,000 was drawn up on 9 and 10 October 1763, and on 11 October, Hester Lynch Salusbury and Henry Thrale were married at St. Anne's Church, Soho,[6] close to the house in Dean Street. After

---

[6] St. Anne's, Soho, was bombed during World War II. Now, only the bell tower remains; the churchyard is a park.

the nuptials, Mrs. Salusbury and Sir Thomas made the six-mile journey with the bride and groom to their country house. It was the
first time Hester — now Mrs. Thrale — had ever set foot in Streatham
Park. This property was on part of Tooting Common, and according
to rumor had been leased by the Duke of Bedford on long term to
Ralph Thrale in exchange for a constant supply of ale and porter at
Woburn Abbey, his Bedfordshire seat (Clifford, p. 34).

The Streatham Park residence was not an impressive great house
but a good, substantial dwelling, and Mrs. Thrale was satisfied with
what she saw. Sir Thomas stayed the night, and next day, in tears,
she bade her uncle farewell. Mrs. Salusbury, also present, was not
similarly moved; she was delighted to see Sir Thomas go. She had
grown very tired of being tactful, and was thoroughly out of sympathy with his continuing infatuation for the widow King. She was
glad to have the newlyweds to herself and to be free of Sir Thomas.
She stayed on with the Thrales — in fact, for the rest of her life she
was to be at Streatham whenever they were there.

4.

The hours passed quietly at Streatham Park. Hester read to her
mother in the morning, played backgammon with her in the afternoon, and worked carpets with her in the evening.

Mr Thrale profess'd his Aversion to a *Neighbourhood*, in wch my Mother
perfectly agreed with him, so we visited nobody; he sometimes brought a
Friend from London . . . His Sisters each came once in a formal way, my Mother
charged me not to be free or intimate with 'em, & none of them pleased me
enough to make me *wish* to break her Injunction. Mean Time my Husband
went every day to London & returned either to dinner or Tea, said he always
found two agreable Women ready to receive him, & thus we lived on Terms
of great Civility & Politeness, if not of strong Alliance and Connection. Miss
Hetty Cotton the youngest of Sir Lynch's Daughters too used to be much with
me, Mr Thrale grew passionately fond of her, so fond indeed that I was not
much pleased with the partiality . . . (*Thraliana*, pp. 306–307)

Hetty Cotton, a pretty cousin, still in her teens, was the first of
several young women, relations or friends, whom Mrs. Thrale, in
this case abetted by her mother, introduced into the family circle
and urged to remain for long periods of time. When Thrale's courteous treatment of such a lady turned into what Hester believed was

HENRY THRALE
BY REYNOLDS

HESTER LYNCH SALUSBURY THRALE
BY COSWAY

too strong a regard, her reaction was always pique against others; she never thought of blaming herself for having brought about the situation in the first place. Usually her complaint was fanciful, and in this instance certainly so, for the eagle eye of Mrs. Salusbury saw nothing to fear from Hetty Cotton's behavior — she was just a saucy little minx.

On 8 November 1763, less than a month after the Thrales' wedding, the dreaded marriage of Sir Thomas and the widow King took place. The world at large thought well of the lady but Mrs. Salusbury considered her a scheming harpy. She was outraged and aggrieved, for Hester was no longer an heiress — the fine estate of Offley Place had been snatched from her. She despised the usurping Lady Salusbury and made it clear to her brother-in-law that she would have nothing further to do with him and this woman. Sir Thomas answered Mrs. Salusbury's scorn by refusing to pay her annuity, but this was no longer a humiliating necessity. Thrale's support made her independent.

Hester had very different feelings about her uncle, and she did not dislike the new Lady Salusbury, but she was used to thinking as her mother told her to think. And she obeyed orders not to send her uncle "Letters Newspapers &c. as usual" (*Thraliana*, p. 304, n. 4).

... if I offered to think of paying him a Visit or a Compliment of any Sort [my Mother] would be out of humour & cry for whole Days ... as She was the only Creature that I saw; & if She was not in Spirits, what a Life I must lead! Mr Thrale was in his Counting house all Morning, at Carlisle House [7] perhaps, or the Opera, or some public Place all Evening, and if I did not keep my Mother in good humour what Chance had I for Comfort? (*Thraliana*, pp. 307–308)

By January 1764, alterations in the "Town house" were completed, and Thrale could now avoid the long, dark ride from Streatham. Accordingly he and his wife moved to Deadman's Place, off Dirty Lane, in Southwark. (Noxious and oderiferous trades were confined to the south bank of the Thames.) Mrs. Thrale had not been consulted about the alterations, and now saw her city residence for the first time, a bleak, four-storeyed, stone building; the Thrale counting office was attached, with rooms above. The house stood at the entrance gate to the cobblestoned brew yard, in which were the clerks' quarters, storehouses, vaults, thirty-eight great vats, stables for almost

[7] Carlisle House, Soho Square. From 1763 to 1772, balls, masquerades, and other pleasures were provided at this fashionable place of entertainment, under the direction of the notorious Mrs. Cornelys.

a hundred horses, dung pits, and so on. It was a nine-acre compound; part of the property had once been a Quaker meeting-house and burying ground, and on another part Shakespeare's Globe Theatre had once stood.

When the Thrales moved to Southwark, Mrs. Salusbury withdrew to her quiet, airy, little house on Dean Street. Mother and daughter were now separated by several miles, but this did not mean they saw much less of each other; one of Thrale's two coaches was always at Hester's disposal for visits to her mother, and these were daily, from twelve to five.

By the spring of 1764 it was apparent that Hester was pregnant. Thrale was delighted. His wife had been an only child, which is often a danger signal, and she recorded the fact herself, that "Mr Thrale had somehow a Notion we were to have no Children, & even doubted of my Pregnancy till it became quite past all Question" (*Thraliana*, p. 308). The summer was spent at Streatham, Mrs. Thrale and Mrs. Salusbury making plans for the baby's arrival. When the time for lying-in approached, the Thrales moved back to Southwark.

On 17 September 1764, Hester Maria Thrale was born, a sound and healthy baby. Thrale made no complaint at not having a boy, in fact, he seemed overjoyed with "his beautiful Daughter." He visited his wife's chambers "two or Three Times a Week in a sort of formal Way, which my Mother said was *quite right*, — & therefore I appeared to think so too" (*Thraliana*, p. 308).

Thrale believed that a wife's place should be confined to the drawing room, bedchamber, and nursery; he himself supervised all the domestic arrangements, including the kitchen. This was not surprising, for he relished food, and had become a fine host in his bachelor days. He was far more experienced in this role than either of his ladies, for they had spent their lives as visitors at relations' tables or faring economically at home. Mrs. Salusbury lived almost wholly upon vegetables and water, and would never touch a glass of wine (*Thraliana*, p. 290). Her daughter, used to following her mother in everything, never had much interest in food.

For the moment, quite naturally, her chief interest was in her child. Queeney was, incidentally, the only baby she nursed,[8] and she grew

---

[8] Other babies were to have wet-nurses, procured by her physician from the Lying-In Hospital (Rylands 590.428).

so thin in the process that a goat had to be purchased, so that she could restore her own health by drinking quantities of goat's milk. Mrs. Thrale liked life in the country, the fresh air and the walks, and she took over the dairy and the poultry yard as special projects. She was proud of her farm animals and was constantly fussing over them, and fussing over the house pets, particularly the dogs; there was always a favorite one to be fondled.

She saw hardly anyone but her mother and her husband. They did not encourage her to form friendships with neighbors, and they did not approve of her attendance at public gatherings. Reading was her greatest diversion, and occasionally she tried her hand at verses for her husband, of the kind that had once received warm praise from her Uncle Thomas. Thrale was not responsive. He valued his wife's literary talents, but he was not one to give effusive compliments. He was always civil to her, good humored, and correct, but he was totally unresponsive. She never felt close to him or at ease with him.

One reason for this was certainly the constant presence of Mrs. Salusbury, and her pervasive influence. The only visitors who occasionally came to the house were some of Thrale's old bachelor cronies, "amis de famille," as Mrs. Salusbury and Hester dubbed them. There was Simon Luttrell, "the king of Hell," and Arthur Murphy, the entertaining playwright, who could hold his own with scholars, delight people of rank with his decorous behavior and keep low company in an uproar, and George Bodens (Captain, though he was called Colonel), an enormous weight of a man, with a limp and a stammer, witty, immoral, and good natured. There was old Dr. Fitzpatrick, a hanger-on, agreeable when sober, well-bred, well-traveled, trained to be a doctor, but not practicing; and there were the chemists, Henry Jackson and his brother, Humphrey. The last was Thrale's "real Bosom Friend & Adviser; who ruled all his Actions" (*Thraliana*, p. 307).

One day Hester asked Humphrey Jackson the reason why Thrale had wanted to marry her, something she had been at a loss to understand, and Jackson told her straight out that other well-born young ladies had refused to live at the brewery even for a day. This matter of part-time residence in Southwark had never been a point of contention between Thrale and Mrs. Salusbury, though the latter avoided residence there herself. Humphrey Jackson told Mrs. Thrale something else, that he was the person who had "made the Match between *us*, which I little dreamed of at the *Time*, God help me" (*Thraliana*, p. 307).

Mrs. Salusbury, though she kept quiet about it, despised all of Thrale's bachelor friends, and she particularly disliked Humphrey Jackson. She did not trust him. Hester had no liking for Jackson, nor any of the other cronies except Arthur Murphy, and she was right in liking him, for although he had a rakish side Murphy was also a serious and cultivated man. He appreciated her possibilities, and he did her a great service. He introduced her to a sympathetic companion and adviser other than her mother.

On 9 January 1765 Murphy brought the celebrated Dr. Samuel Johnson to dine with the Thrales at Deadman's Place. Johnson was fifty-five, two years younger than Hester's father would have been, a year younger than her uncle. The great disparity in age between Johnson and the Thrales was, however, no obstacle. They were immediately attracted to each other, and the custom was soon established that Johnson came every Thursday for dinner. In short order he put Mrs. Thrale to work translating odes of Boethius, warmly applauding her talents and criticizing her faults with equal force. In a way, though he was a very different character, he took the place of her old mentor, Dr. Collier. And Johnson's warm, human qualities soon made Hester Thrale feel as much at ease with him as she was with her mother.

Johnson and the Thrale family were together a great deal in 1765, but during the first part of 1766 he no longer came regularly to Southwark or to Streatham, and soon he did not come at all. Johnson, always prone to melancholy, had been in a period of anxiety and depression for over a year, and now his situation became worse. For weeks on end he did not leave his house, nor even his room. He was unable to concentrate on any project — overpowered by morbid thoughts. He was suffering a complete mental breakdown. The Thrales went to his house in Johnson's Court, and were shocked by what they found. Mrs. Thrale said:

...I felt excessively affected with grief, and well remember my husband involuntarily lifted up one hand to shut [Johnson's] mouth, from provocation at hearing a man so wildly proclaim what he could at last persuade no one to believe; and what, if true, would have been so very unfit to reveal.

Mr Thrale went away soon after, leaving me with him, and bidding me prevail on him to quit his close habitation in the court and come with us to Streatham, where I undertook the care of his health, and had the honour and happiness of contributing to its restoration. (*Anecdotes*, pp. 127–128)

Johnson did not give up his house in Johnson's Court nor turn out the miserable inmates, whom he supported. He came back to London on certain days to be with them, and supply a few good meals, but most of the time he lived with the Thrales. They set aside a special room for him in the Southwark house, just above the counting office, and another at Streatham, above the library.

From the end of June 1766 until the first of October Johnson was at Streatham. Mrs. Thrale's first entry in the *Family Book* was made on 17 September.

II. THE *FAMILY BOOK* [1]
1764–1772

*Hester Maria Thrale born on the 17: Sept.*ʳ *1764 at her Father's House,*
Southwark.

This is to serve as a Memorandum of her Corporeal & Mental Powers
*at the Age of two Years, to w*ᶜʰ *She is arriv'd this 17: Sept: 1766.*
She can walk & run alone up & down all smooth Places tho' pretty
steep, & tho' the Backstring [2] *is still kept on it is no longer of Use.*
She is perfectly healthy, of a lax Constitution, & is strong enough to
carry a /Hound/*puppy two Months old quite across the Lawn at*
Streatham. also to carry a Bowl such as are used on bowling Greens
up the Mount to the Tubs. She is neither remarkably big nor tall,
being just 34 Inches high, but eminently pretty. She can speak most
Words & speak them plain enough too, but is no great Talker: She
repeats the Pater Noster, the three Christian Virtues & the Signs of the
Zodiac in Watts's Verses; She likewise knows them on the Globe
perfectly well. She can tell all her Letters great & small & spell lit-
tle Words as D,o,g, Dog, C,a,t, Cat &c. She knows her nine Figures
& the simplest Combinations of 'em as 3, 4, 34; 6, 8, 68; but none be-
yond a hundred: She knows all the heathen Deities by their Attributes
& counts 20 without missing one. Signed — H: L: Thrale.
  *Sponsors to H: M: T. M*ʳˢ *Salusbury, M*ʳˢ *Nesbitt & Sir John Lade.*

All three of Hester Maria's godparents were closely related to her:
her grandmother, Mrs. Salusbury, after whom she was named; her
aunt, Mrs. Arnold Nesbitt (Susanna Thrale), the youngest of her
father's three sisters; and her first cousin, five-year-old Sir John Lade,

---

[1] The text of the *Family Book* is printed here in full, set in *italic* type except for
passages underscored in the original, which are set in roman. Words inserted above
or below the line are enclosed in slashes: /thus/. Words crossed out are enclosed
in pointed brackets. Eccentric spellings (*e.g., persed* for *parsed*) and punctuation
have been reproduced. The cover reads: *The Children's Book or rather Family*
*Book begun 17: Sept*ʳ *1766,* and *The Children's Book* is repeated at the top of the
inside front cover.

[2] A string at the back of a child's pinafore.

son of her father's favorite sister, Ann, who had been a widow since 1759. After four years of marriage her husband had died from the results of a hunting accident, a few months before his heir, Sir John, had been born.

Hester Maria Thrale's christening took place on 24 September 1764 at the Church of St. Saviour's in Southwark (now Southwark Cathedral). James Evans, the rector, officiated.

Frances Thrale was born on the 27: of Sept.ʳ 1765. at Southwark, appeared strong at first — but died on the tenth Day of the watery Gripes[3] *— I had never had a Day's Health during the whole Gestation — the Labour was however particularly short and easy. — Sponsors M.ʳˢ Salusbury M.ʳˢ Plumbe & M.ʳ Nesbitt.*

Frances Thrale was baptized by James Evans at St. Saviour's on 3 October 1765. The pattern of closely related sponsors continued: her first godmother was again her grandmother, Mrs. Salusbury, and her second godmother, her aunt, after whom she was named, Frances Thrale Plumbe, the wife of Samuel Plumbe, a sugar refiner and a City Alderman.

Frances' godfather was Arnold Nesbitt, the other living brother-in-law of Thrale. Nesbitt came from a good Irish family, and was now a prominent merchant in London. He was Member of Parliament for Cricklade, a genial, showy man and a speculator on a large scale. He was involved with Sir George Colebrook in land purchase in Jamaica[4] and Grenada, and with Thrale in other ventures. Seven months after the death of Ralph Thrale, his son Henry had forwarded the marriage of his youngest sister, Susanna, to his close friend Nesbitt.

The terseness of the entry for Frances' birth and death shows that Mrs. Thrale was under great stress. The autumn had not been at all as planned. The Thrales had gone to Brighton (or Brighthelmstone, the earlier form of the name) during the summer, presumably staying at the "cottage" Ralph Thrale had purchased on the east side of

---

[3] Infantile diarrhea presumably caused by an infection.

[4] Nesbitt was also a part owner of ships that plied to the West Indies. In 1774 William Hickey, the diarist, was to visit his office in Bishopsgate Street to arrange passage to Jamaica on his *New Shoreham*; see *Memoirs of William Hickey*, ed. by Alfred Spenser, 4 vols. (London: Hurst and Blackett, 1913–[1925]), I, 332.

West Street.[5] Mrs. Thrale was quietly waiting for her second child to be born, and Johnson had been asked to visit. He was struggling to finish his edition of Shakespeare, but said he hoped to come by the end of August. He did come to Brighton — and was enraged to find that his hosts had departed without letting him know.

They had left suddenly because word reached them that Alexander Hume, one of the members of Parliament for Southwark, had died. This was an opportunity Thrale had been waiting for — to seek election to Parliament. The Thrales hurried to London, and there Thrale saw the Borough electors; he met their requirements, and in short order received their approval. On 23 September, four days before Frances' birth, his candidacy was announced. Thrale had long had an interest in politics. At twenty-six he had stood for Abingdon, and been soundly rejected (1754: *Miscellanies*, I, 292–293, n. 6), but the desire for public life remained, and he particularly wanted to represent the Borough of Southwark because his father had before him. Thrale launched a vigorous campaign.

He was joined by his wife as soon as her health permitted, and though the rough and tumble world of politics was a new experience, she was effective and she enjoyed it. Dr. Johnson also joined the campaign (after they had made up about Brighton) and he too greatly enjoyed the hectic activity. He sponsored Thrale's candidacy with gusto, and was ready at all times to furnish advice and to draft communications. Thrale, Mrs. Thrale, and he were a very effective triumvirate.

On 23 December 1765 Henry Thrale was returned as a Member

[5] On 28 August 1755 Ralph Thrale purchased this "copyhold" property in the old part of Brighton from one John Howell. All copyhold property was governed by the ancient customary laws of the "Manor" in which it was situated — in this case the Manor of Brighthelmstone — and administered by the local Manorial Court.

If a copyholder wished to devise his copyhold property by Will, he was obliged to appear in the Manorial Court and, in effect, make a formal declaration of his intention. This was called "surrender to the use of the Will." Failure to carry out this procedure would result in the property descending, on his death, to the heir according to the custom of the Manor. In the Manor of Brighthelmstone the custom in this respect was exceptional: descent was to the youngest son or, failing sons, to the youngest daughter.

Henry Thrale inherited this property on his father's death and duly surrendered it to the use of his will (Court Rolls, 26 August 1760).

of Parliament for Southwark, an office he was to hold through various elections until 1781.

Henry Salusbury Thrale was born the 15: Feb.ʸ 1767. strong & lively at Southwark — his Sponsors are Mʳ Nesbitt, Mʳ Plumbe and Mʳˢ Salusbury — he appears likely to live thank God.

The Thrales' hopes for an heir were now realized. The boy was named after his father, and called Harry. He was christened, like his two sisters, at St. Saviour's, Southwark, the ceremony taking place on 3 March 1767, James Evans again officiating. Mrs. Salusbury was a godmother for the third time; and the godfathers were Thrale's two brothers-in-law, Arnold Nesbitt (a sponsor for Frances two years before) and Alderman Samuel Plumbe (whose wife was one of Queeney's godmothers).

Hester Maria Thrale   London /17: March 1767./
    Six Months have now elapsed since I wrote down an Accᵗ of what She could do; the following is for a Record of the amazing Improvements made in this last half Year; Her Person has however undergone no visible Change. She cannot read at all, but knows the Compass as perfectly as any Mariner upon the Seas; is mistress of the Solar System can trace the Orbits & tell the arbitrary Marks of the planets as readily as Dʳ Bradley.⁶ The Comets She knows at Sight when represented upon Paper, & all the chief Constellations on the Celestial Globe. the Signs of the Zodiack She is thoroughly acquainted with, as also the difference between the Ecliptick and Equator. She has too by the help of the dissected Maps acquired so nice a knowledge of Geography as to be well able to describe not only the four Quarters of the World, but almost. nay I do think every Nation on the Terrestrial Globe, & all the principal Islands in all parts of the World: these — with the most remarkable Seas, Gulfs, Streights &c. She has so full an Acquaintance with, that She discovers them coloured, or penciled, separate or together in any Scale small or great, Map or Globe. — She can repeat likewise the Names of all the Capital Cities in Europe besides those of Persia and India — China I mean: also the 3 Xtian Virtues in English, the 4 Cardinal ones in Latin, the 1:ˢᵗ Page

---

⁶James Bradley (1693–1762): Astronomer Royal.

of Lilly's Grammar [7] *to the bottom, the seven Days of the Week, the 12 Months of the Year, the twos of the Multiplication Table, the four points of the Compass the four Quarters of the World, The Pater Noster, the Nicene Creed & the Decalogue; the Responses of the Church Catechism to the End of the Duty to our Neighbour, & the Names of the richest wisest, & meekest Man &c. She has also in these last six Months learned to distinguish Colours, & to name them: as also to tell a little Story with some Grace & Emphasis, as the Story of the Fall of Man, of Perseus & Andromeda of the Judgment of Paris & two or three more. These are certainly uncommon performances* [8] *of a Baby 2 Years & 6 Months only; but they are most strictly true. She cannot however read at all.*

In May, though it is not mentioned in Mrs. Thrale's journal, Queeney was inoculated against smallpox by Daniel Sutton. Mrs. Thrale asked Johnson whether, in view of this, he thought Queeney's cold bathing should be stopped. He answered from Oxford that he could not advise her, "having no principles upon which I can reason. Mr Sutton's art is wholly in his own custody, but in observing his directions you have all the security that his success and his interest can give, and I think you must trust him" (*Letters* 189.1).

Daniel Sutton was the acknowledged expert for the prevention of smallpox, having advanced a more successful technique than that introduced by Lady Mary Wortley Montagu in the 1720s (inoculating

[7] "Lilly's Grammar" or the Eton Latin Grammar. The original compilation was made by William Lily (1468?–1522), first high master of St. Paul's School. The book went through many editions and in 1758 was appropriated by Eton College. From Shakespeare, through Johnson, to Lamb, there are references to this Grammar.

[8] They were, and Queeney's accomplishments at two and a half may strike the modern reader as not only uncommon but astounding, for adult expectations of children are much less today than in the eighteenth century.

Earlier and later examples of equal precocity are, however, not hard to find. John Evelyn's eldest son, Richard (1652–1657), at two and a half had Latin and French at his command. James Mill's eldest son, John Stuart (1806–1873), was learning Greek at three.

Similarities include the fact that the child is the eldest (and in these cases the eldest of several children), that a knowing parent is the ever-present tutor, devoting an inordinate amount of time to the child's instruction and recitation. The basic necessity is a remarkable memory — total and accurate recall. Like the others, Queeney had an extraordinary memory. Richard Evelyn was even more advanced, he could *read* English, French, and Latin at two and a half, and Queeney could not read at all.

the skin with material from another human case). With this method one out of every fifty persons treated died, and all those inoculated were capable of spreading the disease. Sutton claimed that he could reduce the danger by preparing the patient with a week or two of purging (which process was neither very dangerous nor very helpful). After this he used the live smallpox inoculation as before, but with his "secret remedy" (antimony, mercury, and calomel). Sutton's results were sufficiently effective to win official medical approval in 1745.

Not until 1796, however, was a dependable method of smallpox inoculation discovered, that of Edward Jenner, who used the vaccinia lymph (cow-pox). His research originated with an observation remembered from his boyhood, that dairy maids who had had cow-pox never had smallpox.

By the time Daniel Sutton visited Queeney, he not only had a celebrated reputation, but he also possessed a substantial fortune.

17: Sept.ʳ 1767. A little blue Cover Book will now best shew the further Acquisitions of Hester M: Thrale who has this Day completed the second [i.e., third] and begun the third [i.e., fourth] Year of Her Life by repeating all the Responses in that book by Heart — this 17: Sept. 1767. at Brighthelmston[e]. She is yet a miserable poor Speller, & can scarce Read a word.

The Thrales were in Brighton again. He enjoyed hunting on the Sussex Downs, and she was convinced that the brisk sea air and cold sea bathing did wonders for health. Beyond this, Brighton offered pleasing gaiety — nightly assemblies and agreeable society. They decided to have something better than Ralph Thrale's cottage, for they hoped to spend a few months at the seaside every year. They acquired an additional property, a substantial house, also on West Street. It was of light-colored stone, three storeys high, with two bay windows on both the ground and first floors, a very pleasing house.

The transaction was handled by Charles Scrase, who had been Ralph Thrale's lawyer, a family friend whom Thrale had known all his life, and whom Mrs. Thrale had come to like very much. He was a single man of sixty (two years Johnson's senior). Brighton[9] was

---

[9] In 1779 Scrase was to build a two-storey red brick house on the Steine. In 1819 ꜱyal York Hotel was built on the site (now municipal offices).

where Scrase now resided, and the Thrales felt comfortable knowing that he was there, looking after their interests.[10]

Early in 1768 Parliament was dissolved, and Thrale was forced to canvass again for his seat. This time the election was unusually violent, with demonstrations and riots in London, and Southwark as well, because John Wilkes was campaigning for a Middlesex seat. This political firebrand was against the King, the Prime Minister, and the establishment — his platform: radical reforms and enfranchisement of the lower orders. Four years earlier Wilkes had been accused of seditious libel by both Houses of Parliament, and he avoided trial by fleeing to France, an outlaw. Now he was back in London, and his "patriots" were swarming in the streets, crying "Wilkes and Liberty!"

Thrale was a steadfast conservative, against Wilkes, his policies, and his "patriots." Thrale fought a steady, vigorous, forthright campaign, and Johnson and his wife were by his side. She was again handicapped by pregnancy, a baby due in April, but despite her queasy condition, nerves, and exhaustion, she carried on to the end. When the polling time came, on 23 March, she expected the worst — and could hardly believe the news that Thrale had been elected for the Borough of Southwark at the head of the poll. (Wilkes was also elected for Middlesex but went to jail on his outlawry charge, rather than to the House of Commons.)

A few days after the election Mrs. Thrale's fourth child was born.

Anna Maria Thrale so named after my Dear Aunt & Friend the first Wife of Sir Tho.ˢ Salusbury my Uncle — was born at Streatham 1.ˢᵗ April 1768. Sponsors — M.ʳˢ Salusbury, M.ʳˢ Smith & M.ʳ Crutcheley [sic]. /a small Child./

The choice of Anna Maria as a name for the baby was an unfortunate move, as far as the Salusbury relationship was concerned. Sir

---

[10] The Thrales should not have felt comfortable, for something had gone wrong. The new property was also a "copyhold." See note 5, page 23 . Charles Scrase duly appeared in the Manorial Court to receive title to it, on Thrale's behalf, from the previous holder, one Josiah Dornford (Court Rolls, 15 October 1767). However, Scrase did not carry out the procedure of surrendering the property to the use of Thrale's will, which was to result in the property descending, on Thrale's death, not in accordance with his will but in accordance with the Custom of the Manor. Scrase must be blamed for this omission, kind friend and respected lawyer though he was.

Thomas had now been happily married to the widow King for almost four years. They had had no children (nor did they ever have). There was still hope that Hester Thrale might inherit from her uncle, and a daughter named Sarah, after the present Lady Salusbury, who "had once profess'd a Friendship" for her niece (*Thraliana*, p. 37), might have been a diplomatic gesture. But the name of Sarah was never considered; Mrs. Thrale's mother continued adamant in her scorn of the second Lady Salusbury, and Hester's attempt to please her uncle while ignoring his wife (a woman of pride and force) only made a bad situation worse. It would have been far better to have chosen a name having no connection with Sir Thomas.

Nor was Johnson pleased with the name of Anna Maria; he had hoped for Elizabeth. As he wrote to Mrs. Thrale on 19 April from Oxford (where he was visiting to spare the household his presence during the period of Mrs. Thrale's confinement), "I design to love little Miss Nanny very well but you must let us have a Bessy some other time" (*Letters* 203). His desire to have a Thrale daughter named after his wife was somewhat unreasonable, as the Thrales had never known Mrs. Johnson, and what they might have heard about "Tetty" from Garrick and others could not have stirred their enthusiasm. Johnson, however, was persistent in his request.

Anna Maria was the first Thrale child to be christened in the country. Her service was held at St. Leonard's, close to Streatham Park, the rector, James Tattersall, officiating. Mrs. Salusbury was again a godmother, and the other was Thrale's aunt Anne, the widow of Richard Smith, who had come with her nephew on his courting visit to Offley Place nearly six years before. Jeremiah Crutchley was Anna's godfather. This young man in his twenties was soon to be a constant visitor to Streatham and to the Southwark house. Mrs. Thrale may just have come to know him, for she misspells his name on this occasion, and does not do so later. In time she began to think that Crutchley was her husband's natural son,[11] but this was the indulgence of fancy on her part, for every legal source sustains Jeremiah's legitimacy. His father, Jeremiah, had been a close friend of Ralph Thrale (the Crutchley family had been dyers in Clink Street,

[11] Jeremiah Crutchley "is supposed by those that knew his Mother & her Connections, to be Mr Thrale's natural Son, & in many Things he resembles him, but not in Person; as he is both ugly & aukward. Mr Thrale certainly believed he was his Son, & once told me as much . . ." (*Thraliana*, p. 497).

Southwark) and Jeremiah, Sr.,[12] carried on this business very successfully, adding to it a brewing trade. When he died at 43 (in 1752) both Ralph Thrale and Henry Thrale received bequests, and both served as executors of his estate (together with Alice Crutchley, his widow, and Thomas Wimbush, his clerk). Jeremiah, Jr., was not yet seven when his father died, and the Thrales acted as guardians, Henry continuing in this protective capacity after Ralph Thrale died. That Henry Thrale should suggest Jeremiah Crutchley for a godparent of the new baby was wholly understandable.

17: Dec: 1768.

Hester Maria Thrale is this Day four Years & a Quarter old; I have made her up a little red Book to which I must appeal for her Progress in Improvements: She went thro' it this Day quite well. the Astronomical part is the hardest. She can now read tolerably, but not at sight, and has a manner of reading that is perfectly agreable free from Tone or Accent. At 3 Years & a half however She wrote some Cards to her Friends with a Print taken from the Picture which Zoffany [13] drew of her at 20 Months old: but as I lay in soon after, the writing was totally forgotten, & is now all to begin again. She has this day repeated her Catechism quite thro', her Latin Grammar to the end of the 5 Declensions, a Fable in Phædrus, an Epigram in Martial, the Revolutions Diameters & Distance of the Planets: She is come vastly forward in Sense & Expression & once more I appeal to her little red Book. With regard to her Person it is accounted exquisitely pretty;

[12] Jeremiah Crutchley, Sr., was married at St. Paul's Cathedral on 4 March 1742 to Alice Jackson, from a good Devon and Cumberland family. Their first child was a daughter, Alice, who was born in June 1744 but lived for only a few days. Jeremiah was born on 20 December 1745 (Henry Thrale at this time was 17); a daughter, Elizabeth, was born in October 1747; a second son, John, was born in October 1749; and another daughter named Alice in July 1751. The Crutchley family Bible at Mappercombe Manor names all the godparents, and Henry Thrale appears, not as Jeremiah's godfather, as has sometimes been said, but as godfather to the younger son, John, who lived only to the age of two and a half, dying in 1752, ten days after his father. In his will Jeremiah, Sr., provided generously for his wife and all his children, and showed his "dear son Jeremiah" the preference due to an elder son and heir.

Jeremiah is buried in the same tomb with his father and his infant brother, John. (Tomb 210, in the cemetery at Lee, a town which is now part of metropolitan London.)

[13] She so astonished Zoffany that he told the King of her odd performance (*Thraliana*, p. 308, n. 3).

*her Hair is sandy, her Eyes of a very dark blue, & their Lustre particu-
larly fine; her Complexion delicate, and her Carriage uncommonly
genteel. Her Temper is not so good; reserved to all, insolent where
She is free, & sullen to those who teach or dress or do anything towards
her. Never in a Passion, but obstinate to that uncommon Degree that
no Punishment except severe Smart* [14] *can prevail on her to beg Pardon if She has offended. 17: Dec: 1768. —*

In the spring of 1769 there was another child.

*Lucy Elizabeth Thrale was born 22: June 1769. large strong and hand-
some likely to live: her Sponsors were M.ʳˢ Salusbury, M.ʳˢ Cotton of
Bath & D.ʳ Samˡ: Johnson who insisted on her being called Elizabeth.* [15]

The baby's first name, Lucy, was after her Welsh great-grand-
mother, Lucy Salusbury of Bach-y-Graig, who had died in 1745, and
Johnson was indulged with Elizabeth for his "Tetty," who had died
in 1752. Johnson himself was honored by being asked to be Lucy
Elizabeth's godfather. He wrote to Mrs. Thrale from Oxford (he
had again absented himself during her lying-in): "I always wished
it might be a Miss . . . Mr. Thrale tells me that my furlough is
shortened, I am always ready to obey orders, I have not yet found
any place from which I shall not willingly depart, to come back to
you" (*Letters* 217). And to Thrale he wrote the same day: "I think
myself very much honoured by the choice that you have been pleased
to make of me to become related to the little Maiden. Let me know
when she will want me, and I will very punctually wait on her" (*Letters* 218).

Lucy's first godmother was, as for the other children, Mrs. Salusbury. Her second was Sidney Arabella Cotton of Bath, the infant's
great-aunt, a maiden sister of Mrs. Salusbury, the one to whom Mrs.
Thrale had written about her engagement. The title of "Mrs." Cotton in the journal is simply an honorific given to a spinster of a certain
age and class.

[14] This means a whipping. The rod lay on the mantel-piece of the nursery, and
was frequently used, for Mrs. Thrale, unlike mothers today, who avoid a show-
down with a child, strongly believed in corporal punishment.

[15] This passage is written in the *Family Book* following the one dated "1: Jan.ʳʸ
— 1770." It is printed here at its proper chronological place.

QUEENEY AT TWENTY MONTHS WITH BELLE
BY ZOFFANY

The Thrales showed courage in naming Johnson as a co-sponsor with Mrs. Salusbury, for though he was honored and loved by the rest of the family, he was heartily disliked by her, a feeling which he reciprocated. From the moment these strong characters met, they were in conflict, each shrewdly aware of the other's eccentricities and shortcomings. She found him rude and tiresome. He scorned her conversation, and upon one occasion was so provoked by her foolish talk about foreign politics (she particularly enjoyed reading and discussing news from the Continent) that he fabricated a story and had it printed in the newspaper — an imaginary battle between the Russians and Turks, then at war.[16] This *jeu d'esprit* was to cure her of credulity, and the deceit succeeded until she recognized Johnson's style — then she vowed she would never forgive him.

Complaints and clashes between the two were constant — and childish; the basic cause was their jealousy over Mrs. Thrale, for each was convinced that the other had improper and too much influence. An example was when Mrs. Thrale spoke of her husband's impersonal behavior and Johnson burst out:

... how for Heaven's Sake Dearest Madam should any Man delight in a Wife that is to him neither Use nor Ornament? He cannot talk to you about his Business, which you do not understand; nor about his Pleasures which you do not partake ... You divide your Time between your Mamma & your Babies, & wonder you do not by that means become agreable to your Husband. This was so plain I could not fail to comprehend it, & gently hinted to my Mother that I had some Curiosity about the Trade, which I would may be one day get Mr Thrale to inform *me* about as well as the *Jacksons* who I observed had all his Confidence: but She saw no need She said for me to care [about the trade] that I had my Children to nurse & to teach, & that She thought that was better Employment than turning into *My Lady Mashtub*. those were her Words ... (*Thraliana*, pp. 309–310)

In the latter part of the summer, after Mrs. Thrale had recovered from her lying-in and the infant Lucy seemed well enough established to be left in the hands of her nurse, the Thrales took Queeney on her first journey — to Brighton.

In a short while Johnson arrived from Lichfield — also his first visit in the West Street house. The party stayed by the sea for five weeks, and while they were away all went well at Streatham, where Mrs. Salusbury remained, in charge of Harry, Anna, and Lucy.

[16] See Clifford, p. 67 and *Miscellanies*, I, 235.

When winter came the Thrales made their accustomed move from Streatham to Southwark, and Mrs. Salusbury, as usual, left Streatham for London.

Henry Salusbury Thrale went into Breeches at the Age of two Years & 3 Months: he was not quite two, when he carried a Bag containing 27:ˢ in Copper from the Compting House to the Breakfast parlour in the Borough: He is remarkably strong made, course & bony: — not handsome at all, but of perfect Proportion; & has a surly look with the honestest & sweetest Temper in the World.
1: Dec: 1769. —

This winter Mrs. Salusbury had brought Anna Maria to live with her in Dean Street, a more salubrious place, "out of the smoke of the city, and yet not in the blaze of the court," as Johnson once put it (*Letters* 285). She wished to give her full attention to the health and needs of her little granddaughter.

1: Jan.ʳʸ — 1770.
Anna Maria Thrale is remarkably small bon'd & delicately framed, but not pretty, as She has no Plumpness in her Face: her Hair is black, her Eyes light blue, with fine Eyebrows & Eyelashes; her Complexion well enough, her Spirit uncommonly high; wonderfully passionate from the very first, & backward in her Tongue tho' forward in general Intelligence: She could kiss her hand at 9 Months old, & understand all one said to her: could walk to perfection, & even with an Air at a Year old, & seems to intend being Queen of us all if She lives which I do not expect She is so very lean — I think she is consumptive — but my Mother says not, & She lives chiefly with her: who seems well inclined to spoyl her, & make her think herself something extraordinary.[17]

Mrs. Thrale and Queency made daily five-hour visits to Dean Street throughout the winter, and though Mrs. Thrale complained to her mother that she was pampering Anna Maria, she appreciated having

[17] This passage is followed in the *Family Book* by the one reporting the birth of Lucy Elizabeth Thrale on 22 June 1769, which is printed at its proper chronological place.

this delicate child taken off her hands; she had enough to cope with herself — Queeney (five), Harry (almost three), and Lucy (six months) — and another baby expected in the summer. Mrs. Thrale, as usual, felt squeamish and ill.

Hester Maria Thrale was four Years and nine Months old when I lay in of Lucy; and then I first began to teach her Grammar shewing her the Difference between a Substantive and an Adjective as I lay in Bed; She has made since then a Progress so considerable, that She this Day 1: Feb: 1770 persed the first Couplet of Pope's Iliad, beginning of her own accord at the Vocative Case; tho this Coupplet [sic] is I think rather uncommonly difficult from the awkward Transposition of the Words — I mean awkward only to a Child.

Anna Maria Thrale died yesterday. She had apparently drooped since last Month begun, and on the second of this threw up her Victuals: my Mother was shocked & amazed; so was not I; I never had much hoped to rear her; when Bromfield was called he purged her very roughly, after having first given a puke to clear as he said the passages. She continued notwithstanding to pine away, fits of languor and screaming succeeding each other by turns; no danger however was apprehended except by myself who had long fancied her in a Decay; till her Fits of Rage sometimes accompanied by inflammatory Symptoms of the most violent kind threw her into a kind of Delirium: on this they blisterd her wch somewhat abated her Fury, & when her Paroxysms of Rage returned they bled her with Leeches till She lay absolutely insensible: in this Stage of the Disorder James was called who pronounced it a Dropsy of the Brain & gave the Emetick Tartar but without effect. The next day Tuesday 13. her D^{rs} left her, finding it impossible to stir up any Sensibility; yet My Mother who never quitted her a moment revived her once again by the Application of a Feather dipped in Wine & had the Satisfaction of seeing her take nourishment, which revived all her hopes; but on the 16th She fell into a violently inflammatory Fever & died Yesterday 20: March 1770. had She lived to the 1.st April next She w^{d}: have been two Years old: it is remarkable that She had never perspired or drivelled like another Child from her Birth, & to that I attribute her last Illness. I am now myself near five Months gone with Child, and I fear the

Shock & Anxiety of this last fortnight has done irreparable Injury to
my little Companion — if so I have lost two Children this Spring —
how dreadful!

Robert Bromfield of Gerard Street, who was called on 2 March, was
the physician who had delivered Anna Maria, as well as her brother
and sisters. A Licentiate of the Royal College of Physicians (with a
medical degree from Aberdeen), he was physician to the British
Lying-In Hospital.

Robert James, who was called for consultation, was also a Licentiate
of the Royal College of Physicians, with a degree from Cambridge,
and he was, incidentally, Dr. Johnson's Lichfield schoolfellow, author
of the *Medicinal Dictionary*. James was an authority on fevers (and
had patented a fever powder); he was also a highly regarded authority
on children's diseases.

Anna Maria presumably died of meningitis and since she suffered
discomfort for some weeks before the acute and final illness, the meningitis might have been of tuberculous origin. The recorded lack of
perspiration could have been due to a congenital absence of sweat
glands, a rare condition which is associated with recurrent fevers.
There is no further supporting evidence for this in the journal, however.

Bromfield and James's treatments of purges, blisters, and bleeding
(leeches were the usual method for bleeding children rather than the
lancet) were wrong for Anna Maria, but correct for the time. Antibiotics would be used today, with expected success.

I passed this last Winter chearfully too, to what I ever did a Winter
since I was married: for I have been at an Oratorio — the first Theatre
I have set foot in, since my eldest Daughter was born; & this Time
She went with me: I never have dined out, nor ever paid a visit where
I did not carry her, unless I left her in bed; for to the Care of Servants
(except asleep) I have never yet left her an hour and this is the 21:
March 1770. She is now five Years & a half old. I have been always
regular in my dutyful Attendance on my Mother, whom I have con-
stantly waited on every day since we parted, and always carried the
Child with me. Poor Anna lived at Dean Street this last Winter, I
fear my Mother will be sadly hurt at her Death, how shall I do to
comfort her?

Mrs. Salusbury was so overwhelmed by the death of her little granddaughter that she fled to Bath, where she stayed for several weeks with her sister, Sidney Arabella Cotton.

Henry Salusbury Thrale was three Years old on the 15: Feb: last 1770. I have been so perplexed about poor Miss Anna, that I forgot to write down the State of my Son's Person or Capacity so must do it now. My Mother is gone to Bath to change the Scene, and I have a little Time to myself: he is still stout, bony, large limbed, & nicely proportioned though not handsome, his Hair is course, so is his Skin, but his Temper is artless and his Nature compassionate. he would give all he had to the poor, and loves his Friends with an honest Fondness. he can repeat his Catechism quite thro' without missing, & the Westmr Grammar [18] *as far as the Distinction between Sing: & Plural which he knows perfectly both in Words & Things. he can say the names & number of the Muses, knows the heathen Gods by their Attributes & tells their Names & Offices; likewise the Names of the three Fates, three Furies, four Infernal Rivers, & is upon the whole well versed in Tooke's Pantheon.* [19] *also the four four [sic] Elements, the four Quarters of the World, the 7 Days of the Week the four Seasons & 12 Months of the Year and can count twenty without missing one.*

3: April 1770.

My Mother returned from Bath the beginning of this Month, but could not bear the Thoughts of going back to Dean Street: She therefore remained at Croydon [20] *where I visited her once every day, and we were preparing to settle at Streatham all together for the Summer — when on the 22: of May 1770 I had been as usuall to pay my Duty at Croydon, and had returned home to the Borough perfectly well: I was sitting with Mr Johnson & Mr Thrale till towards 11 o'Clock*

[18] The *Westminster* (*School*) *Grammar* of Latin and Greek was the rival of Lily's or the *Eton Grammar*. Some said it had the merit of being clear and concise, qualities which the other lacked.

[19] Tooke's Pantheon: *The Pantheon, Representing the Fabulous Histories of the Heathen Gods and Most Illustrious Heroes* was a translation, by Andrew Tooke, master of the Charterhouse School, of Father François Antoine Pomey's *Pantheum Mythicum*; the first edition (1698) was followed by many others during the eighteenth century.

[20] Croydon: Mrs. Salusbury stayed in Thrale's small house there.

*at Night, I felt sudden & violent pains come on; I hasted to bed & by
1 o'clock in the Morning was delivered with very little pain of a small
weakly female Infant, whom we called Susanna Arabella; / The Child
presented wrong but being small it did not signify. / & asked M^rs
Salusbury, Mrs Nesbitt & Mr Brook[e] of Town Malling to stand
her Sponsors, tho' her Life was little to be expected as She was born
two months or more before her full Time, and as She was miserably
lean and feeble indeed, quite a mournful Object.*

*She lives however, & Doctor Johnson comforts me by saying She
will be like other People; of which however if She does live I make
very great doubt. — She sucks well enough at present but is so very
poor a Creature I can scarce bear to look on her; Evans says he never
christen'd so small a Child before, & Bromfield said he never saw but
one born so very little & kept alive to a Year old —*

4: August 1770.

The "mournful Object" was named after Susanna Thrale Nesbitt,
her aunt, and Sidney Arabella Cotton, who was godmother to Lucy
Thrale. Susanna Arabella was christened at St. Saviour's, as all the
babies born in Southwark had been; James Evans, the rector, officiated
as before. Evans was a devoted friend of Thrale (whose support he
greatly appreciated), and Mrs. Thrale liked "little Evans" for his
virtue and knowledge and pleasing behavior.

As always, Mrs. Salusbury was one of the godmothers, and Susanna Nesbitt was the other godmother (she was also a sponsor for
Queeney). Francis Brooke of Townmalling, a retired attorney in his
seventies, who had been a close friend of Ralph Thrale, was the godfather. Henry and Hester had visited Brooke in September 1768,
during a brief tour of Kent, on which they had taken Johnson for the
benefit of his health. (It was at Brooke's house that Johnson passed
his fifty-ninth birthday.)

Susanna Arabella, small and weak, received little admiration from
anyone except Johnson. He was her staunch defender from the start,
declaring that Susy would survive and furthermore that she would
be beautiful one day. Mrs. Thrale had no such hopes.

I saw the Corsican Fairy this Year   sure Susan will not be like her!

The "Corsican Fairy," Maria Teresia (born in the 1740s), was an entertainer, a lovely-looking, perfectly proportioned, alert little person, thirty-four inches high (the height given for Queeney Thrale at two years of age). Polite and beguiling, the Corsican Fairy conversed with ease and danced with elegance.

Shortly before 1770 the Corsican Fairy had made her first appearance in London; she had been admired by a number of fine persons, and indeed had been seen three times by Their Majesties. After a tour in the provinces, the Corsican Fairy made her second London appearance in January 1770. She could be seen in Mr. Zucker's Rooms in the Exeter Exchange from 9 A.M. to 10 P.M. for a shilling. "N.B. Any of the Nobility or Gentry desirous of having her at their own Houses, she will attend them upon their paying three Guineas." [21]

I took Queeney with me to a Play last winter, not a play — it was an Oratorio; & we saw the King [22] *there; when She came home She swaggered poor Harry with telling him the Wonders She had seen. I saw the King said She, do you know what a King is? Yes replies Harry, a Picture of a Man, a Sign of a Man's head —— no, no, cries the Girl impatiently the King that wears the Crown: do you know what a Crown is —— Yes I do, says Harry very well, it is 3:ˢ and 6:ᵈ   This happen'd sometime in April /or March/ but I forgot to write it down till now the 13: of Aug: 1770.* [23]

Mrs. Thrale had already noted the fact (on 21 March) that she had attended the oratorio; she sometimes forgot if she had recorded an event, or where she had recorded it, for she was now writing in four notebooks other than the *Family Book*. One was devoted to the sayings of Johnson, another to the comments of celebrities, also the "blue Cover Book" and the "little red Book" devoted to Queeney's achievements.

[21] Statement in a Huntington Library handbill.

[22] George III, who had become King in 1760, was the "steadiest and kindest patron" of the stage and "for fifty years, a constant attendant on its delights" (Mangin, p. 223).

[23] In the beginning this was simply a coin with a crown imprinted on it; since the sixteenth century it has been a coin with the value of 5 shillings. Harry's comment to Queeney is either a confident but wrong guess typical of a small boy, or it is an inadvertent error on the part of his mother.

Attendance at the oratorio was a memorable event and an amusing though inaccurate account of the evening was given years later to Mrs. Thrale's biographer, Edward Mangin, by a lady who had been present that night at Covent Garden. She remembered seeing Mrs. Thrale, she said, "a new married belle," who looked "lovely, and was adorned with diamonds." When Mangin reported this to Mrs. Thrale (by then Piozzi) she replied that her mother had "disapproved of my going into public so much, that I never did set my foot in a theatre till my eldest child, born in 1764, went with me to an oratorio. No diamonds did I ever possess" (Mangin, p. 178).

17: Sept.ʳ 1770.

Hester Maria Thrale is this Day 6 Years old; her Person & Face have undergone so little change that a Servant of my Mother who left her just five Years ago knew her again & said She was not altered — She is tall enough of her Age, elegantly shaped, and reckoned extremely pretty. Her Temper continues the same too; reserved and shy with a considerable Share of Obstinacy, & I think a Heart void of all Affection for any Person in the World — but Aversion enough to many: — her Discretion is beyond her Years, and She has a solidity of Judgement [which] makes me amazed.   her Powers of Conversation and copiousness of Language are surprising even to me who know her so well, & She yesterday cited me the Story of Cleopatra's dissolving the Pearl as an Instance of Prodigality.[24] She read and

---

[24] Cleopatra and the pearl: As Pliny tells the story, Cleopatra was contemptuous of Anthony's enjoyment of daily, sumptuous banquets — given by others. Niggardly entertainments, she said, and when he asked in surprise what greater magnificence could be contrived, she replied that she would spend 10,000,000 sesterces on a single banquet for him. (A sesterce was worth from four to five cents, therefore, the cost was the equivalent of $400,000 to $500,000.) This he said was impossible. The two made a wager, and next day Cleopatra set a fine banquet before Anthony, but it was exactly like those he was used to. He laughingly told her so, and she thereupon ordered the servants to place in front of her a chalice containing vinegar. She was at the moment wearing in her ears the two largest pearls in all history. She took off one of her priceless earrings, and dropped the pearl into the vinegar and swallowed it. The umpire for the wager quickly placed his hand on the other pearl, which she was planning to destroy in a similar manner; he declared that Anthony had lost the battle. Pliny, *Natural History*, Translated and edited by H. Rackham (Harvard University Press and William Heinemann, 1940), III, 243–245.

Sir Joshua Reynolds (in 1759) painted a fine portrait of Kitty Fisher, the celebrated courtesan, as Cleopatra in the act of dropping the pearl into the chalice of vinegar. The picture is now at Kenwood.

*persed to D.ʳ Goldsmith yesterday & he wonder'd at her Skill — She
has a little Compendium of Greek & Roman History in her Head;
& Johnson says her Cadence, Variety & choice of Tones in reading
Verse are surpassed by nobody not even Garrick himself: it was Pope's
Ode to Musick that She read to ⟨him⟩ Johnson   Goldsmith heard
her read the Messiah. She is now regularly catechised and was this
day so thoroughly and strictly examined as to her Religion that I am
convinced from her unpremeditated Answers that She would now be
thought qualified for Confirmation by most of the best informed Di-
vines.*

17: Sep.ᵗ 1770.

Queeney's intelligence was now a source of wonder. The combination of her Johnsonian memory and her intensive tutoring had turned
the six-year-old child into an even greater prodigy than her mother
had been at that age. Johnson was not sure that this forced precocity
was wise, but Mrs. Thrale had no doubts, and she delighted in having
her daughter examined by distinguished persons.

Queeney was extremely shy because she could not bear to be
laughed at, and beyond this reserve her manner was cold and proud.
She stood before her inquisitors with assurance, answering their questions in a distinct voice, properly and cautiously, with judgment far
beyond her years.

On 16 September, the writer Oliver Goldsmith was Queeney's
examiner. This brilliant little doctor had been introduced to the
Thrales by Johnson a while before; and he was now coming often to
Streatham, where the Thrales received him with great kindness, a
proof of their hospitality and understanding, for his behavior had
been strange when they met:

... the first Time he dined with us, he gravely asked M.ʳ Thrale how much a
Year he got by his Business? Who answered with singular Propriety, we don't
talk of those things much in Company Doctor — but I hope to have the honour
of knowing you so well that I shall wonder less at the Question. (*Thraliana*,
p. 83)

Dr. Goldsmith was a very odd man, ugly, and yet pleased with his
own person; always pausing to admire himself when he passed a look-
ing-glass. He was extravagant in his dress and in all his tastes. And
he was insatiably curious: one day Mrs. Thrale had discovered him

examining everything in her dressing room, "every Box" on the dressing-table, "every Paper upon the Card Rack" (*Thraliana*, p. 81). He had a passion to know everything, and an eagerness to shine in conversation. He was jealous of any competition, argumentative, and ill-tempered. On the other hand, he was guileless, sociable, and affectionate.

As far as the performance of little Queeney was concerned, he certainly must have viewed it without a trace of envy, and hence with pleasure, but he made no memorable comment for Mrs. Thrale to record. What Queeney thought of Goldsmith on this occasion is not told, but a few years later she said she hated him because he was so disagreeable.

Sometime during the summer or autumn of this year, 1770, when the family was at Streatham, Mrs. Thrale made her last visit to Offley Place. News had reached London that Sir Thomas Salusbury was dying, and his niece felt her old affection for him very strongly and her future interest as well. She was determined to go to his bedside. This was the first time:

I had said I *would* do any thing since I came of Age, and now I *would* not be deny'd. My Mother try'd all *her* Power, & when that failed, my Husband's had little Chance; nor did he trouble himself much either to encourage or contradict me, but laugh'd at the project as a wild one, & said Lady Salusbury would shut me out of Doors he suppos'd, and so I should come back. (*Thraliana*, p. 310)

The visit at first went well. Mrs. Thrale found her uncle's condition improved; he was able to walk about the house and grounds without difficulty and he seemed to enjoy her company. He treated her with tenderness, kissing and caressing her, inquiring after her children, and showing many special signs of favor in front of his wife and the servants, calling her "his *Heiress* his *Niece* &c.," while "Lady Salusbury sate like one Thunderstruck — yet swelling with rage."

Sir Thomas escorted his niece to her room that night as in the old days, but the next morning his attentions were restrained, and the mistress of the house never appeared. In parting, however, Sir Thomas again seemed affectionate, and promised repeatedly "to come & see me & my Son & my Daughters" (*Thraliana*, p. 310).

Mrs. Thrale returned to Streatham in high spirits after this independent journey:

I found my Mother & My Master well pleased too, & chearfully resumed my usual Employments and Amusements. I was grown fond of my Poultry my Dairy &c. & had now no other Desire than that of sitting down safely & quietly at Streatham to which of late I had rather begun to attach myself. (*Thraliana*, p. 311)

While everything was going along pleasantly in the country, an accident occurred, which Mrs. Thrale did not record, for she took little account of it at the time. And she did not actually witness the scene, but one afternoon while Mrs. Salusbury was playing with three-year-old Harry in the green parlor, the boy became rough in his play and accidentally his head struck his grandmother a hard blow on her breast. Within a week's time, when Mrs. Thrale was shown a small lump on her mother's breast, she called Bromfield, who gave treatment; later, John Hunter was called, the eminent anatomist and surgeon.

This was the beginning of Mrs. Salusbury's tragic struggle against cancer, the cause of which Mrs. Thrale always believed was Harry's blow. Present medical opinion, however, questions this: a blow may rarely — possibly — cause cancer, but far more frequently it is incorrectly blamed for a palpable lump, which existed prior to the blow. This was very likely true in Mrs. Salusbury's case.

12: Octr 1770.

This Day Lucy & Susan were inoculated by Daniel Sutton who inoculated all the rest — I have no fears but for Susan; She is very weakly — Lucy will do well enough, but it may hurt such a tender Poppet as Susan perhaps — tho' none of them yet ever had more than 20 Pustules, & one would think that could not hurt a Mouse. —

30: Jan.^{ry} 1771.

on the fourteenth of this Month Hester Maria Thrale was examined before a Mr Bright of Abingdon who was astonished at her powers & Skill in persing some Lines of Dryden's Virgil, explaining every difficult word, & even telling the derivation of most. She likewise read Pope's Temple of Fame, & gave a particular Account of every Heroe mentioned in the Poem; his Life[,] Country[,] Adventures, every *thing: She likewise shewed her Knowledge of Geography by naming the Situation, Latitude and Longitude of all the places we could think on, She displayed her Acquaintance with Antiquity in giving an Acc.ᵗ of the old Runic & Gothic Divinities, & in short performed so well that the man acknowledged fairly that had the Examination passed in Latin, She would have been qualified for a Degree in the University of Oxford.*

The Reverend Mr. Henry Bright, head master of the Abingdon Grammar School, found Queeney at six-and-a-half made of very different mettle from her seventeen-year-old cousin, Ralph Plumbe, who was a pupil in his school. Alderman Plumbe had hopes of his son going to Oxford, and Eton had been the preparatory step, but there the boy was not successful. He was consummately ignorant, the "booby" of many Thrale family jokes. In 1770, the year before, when the Streatham circle had examined Ralph's University potential, the interview went thus:

How many feet are there in an Hexameter Verse says Dʳ Johnson — nine — replied the Lad. — You have read Ovid — Oh yes, who was the Goddess of Chastity — Queen Dido cried the Boy. what Prose have you read enquired my Mother — Sallust he replied — Who then was the great Carthaginian General — Pigmalion I think says he — or Agamemnon I forget which. (*Thraliana*, p. 101)

After this, as an act of friendship rather than the furtherance of a just cause, Johnson had written to Henry Bright, urging him to take Ralph for private tutoring at Abingdon (*Letters* 226, 226.2). Bright had accepted Ralph, and now, at the end of holiday time, Bright was at Streatham. His interview with Queeney, recorded in the *Family Book*, was in contrast to the further examination of Ralph. Someone in sport asked the boy:

... how many Weeks there were in the Year; the Pupil however gravely replied he did not know. I warrant says Bright ... grievously mortified, he knows how many Cards there are in a Pack — Yes! cries the Lad I know there are 46 ... (*Thraliana*, p. 102)

Queeney was better prepared for Oxford than her cousin.

This eldest Girl of mine could at the Age of Six Years, look words in the Dictionary with perfect readiness, could tye up a Bow of Ribbon for Breast & Sleeve-Knots as neatly as any Woman in the House;

could do the common Stitch upon Catgut, & has actually worked Doctor Johnson a Purse of it; could be trusted with a little Brother or Sister as safely as any Person of twenty Years old, & had such a Share of Discretion, that three Days ago being somewhat hot & uneasy with a troublesome Cold, & I had recommended Turneps, Apples or Other light vegetables to her rather than more feverish Food, — We happen'd to have some Company at Dinner who officiously help'd her to Plum Pudden   She took it therefore & looked pleas'd keeping it before her till She observ'd her Friend engaged in Talk; & then beckoning a Servt She sent it quietly away — for /said/ She to me afterwards, I knew it was not fit for me to eat, but one could disoblige Mr Such a one by a peremptory *Refusal* — those were her Words. *She is now taking Senna & other offensive Medicines for the Worms, which She does with a Courage & Prudence few grown people possess —*
30: Jan: /1771./ God preserve her precious Life!

Queeney was to be plagued for years to come by attacks of worms. This disagreeable complaint is communicated by eating uncooked foods, such as milk, cheese, fruit, and salads,[25] dirtily handled, contaminated with human or animal excreta. It can also come from too close contact with pets.

The treatment for worms was a vermifuge, such as tin with wormseed and a repeated purge. Senna, a compound of dried leaves from the cassia shrub, served this purpose.

Queeney's worms were the round type (as opposed to thread worms which are not dangerous, only painful in the irritation they cause). But round worms are dangerous if they block the small intestine, appendix, or common bile duct. If this blockage is not effectively cured, round worms can cause death.

15:Feb: 1771.
This Day Henry Salusbury Thrale is four Years old — strong & healthy and very tall of his Age — so amiable besides that even Queeney loves him, who is of no loving Disposition, and /he/ has a

---

[25] Queeney loved "eating unripe cherries [and other unripe fruits] and sucking milk and water through a straw," and she loved "cucumbers, radishes, stumps of cabbages, and other such dainties" right out of the garden (Baretti, pp. ix, 360).

very good Capacity: *He reads the Psalms quite smartly, seldom stopping to spell his Way; can repeat the Grammar to the end of the Genders, & knows a Subs: from an Adjec: in English or Latin perfectly well, also a Noun from a Verb. he can likewise put the Adjective to the Substantive, & the Article to the Noun in Latin taking Care to make them agree, (I mean Nom: Cases only) & in this Exercise it is not easy to puzzle him. he has not yet attempted writing, nor to read a written Paper, nor pretends to any Acquaintance with with [sic] the Globes; but he has his Catechism all by heart, & reads vastly better than his Sister did, knows a deal of the Heathen Mythology, and is manly to a most uncommon Degree, with regard to general power of self Assistance &c. he lies all alone, bare-headed, buttons his own Clothes on, and needs no help either at eating or emptying any more than his Father does. he bids fair with Gods blessing to be a noble Fellow — his Face however is ordinary enough, but he is larger than any Boy of his Age tho' not fat; indeed Harry commenced Man very early, he went into Breeches at two Years & 3 Months old: I asked him to day if he remembered ever wearing Petticoats; and he said no, not the least.*

22. June 1771.

This Day Lucy Elizabeth Thrale is two Years old: She is as handsome as her Sister, & as stout as her Brother: a full Yard high,[26] and very large made; yet not clumsy: wonderfully active with her feet, but so backward with her Tongue, that a few Words, & those imperfectly pronounc'd make up all her perfections. She is however very handsome indeed, & very healthy; if we deduct a strange thing that happen'd to her when She was 6 Months old, & the Effects yet remain. She then caught a Cold which settled in her Head, & produced an Imposthume [an abscess] which Bromfield attended, & Syringed as he thought fit: — however it occasioned a running behind her Ears, and from her Ears, which running has never ceased, yet as She is a prodigious fine Girl with regard to every Thing else we

[26] By present-day predictions, the final height attained by a boy is expected to be slightly more than twice his height at the age of two, that of a girl slightly less. According to this, Lucy could be predicted at maturity to tower over her mother (who was four feet, eleven inches) and to be about four inches taller than Queeney. Lucy's height would, however, be expected to be some four inches less than that of her aunt, Lady Lade, who, without shoes, measured six feet.

must be contented with this ailment   I suppose it never will do her any harm tho' Mr Johnson told yesterday a Story of Miss Fitz-herbert's dying in Consequence of just such a Thing, which shocked me dreadfully tho' I took no Notice but it lay on my Spirits all that Day & Night — & this Morning I can scarce bear to think on't. 22: June 71.

Lucy was suffering from an inflammation of both middle ears and both mastoids, the result of an infection from her cold. Syringing may well have spread the infection further, increasing the danger.

Mrs. Thrale's first conjecture that no harm would come to Lucy was not as valid as her second reaction of fright at hearing the story about little "Miss Fitzherbert," one of the six motherless children who had been under the care of Johnson's remarkable friend, Miss Hill Boothby,[27] almost twenty years before. The "eldest Miss" had been perfectly well, flying about the Tissington fields with the others, until this running of the ears had started. No cure had been found, and the beautiful young girl had died; not a cheerful parting tale to have from Johnson.

He was setting out that day for another "furlough" (Lichfield and Ashbourne), not to be in the way when the next baby arrived at Streatham, an event expected at any moment. Mrs. Thrale was worried about her pregnancy; the illnesses of Lucy and her mother were added anxieties.

Johnson had finally come to appreciate Mrs. Salusbury, as he observed the cheerfulness, courage, and spiritual calm with which she faced death. He now valued her sterling qualities and forgot the silliness; he admired and loved her. He continued to hope that some

---

[27] Johnson most probably had Hill Boothby in mind when he recorded in his diary for 22 April 1753 (the year after Tetty's death) that he proposed "to seek a new wife without any derogation from dear Tetty's memory."

Johnson had been acquainted with Hill Boothby in Derbyshire for many years. She was well-born, sensible, of great piety and strong intellect, wit, and charm — an admirable choice. Time and circumstance, however, conspired against any possibility of marriage for her closest friend, Mrs. Fitzherbert, died in March 1753 (just before Johnson recorded his intentions). Hill Boothby loyally took over the management of the Fitzherbert household and the care of her friend's children. Her own health began to fail soon thereafter, and in 1756 she died. Johnson was so distracted by grief at Hill Boothby's death that his friends had great difficulty controlling the violence of his actions.

remedy might be found for her disease, and he was constantly consulting friends and doctors about possible treatment. Dr. Wall recommended taking the waters at Malvern, and Johnson offered to go there from Lichfield at his own expense to attend the patient, since her daughter was not able to leave home. But Mrs. Salusbury did not wish to try the experiment. (It would not have helped her.) She appreciated Johnson's kindness, nevertheless, in suggesting the trip. She too had revised her opinion of her old enemy, and now regarded Johnson with respect and affection. She was now even grateful for his possessive treatment of Mrs. Thrale, because she knew he would remain her daughter's wise and loving counselor when she herself was dead.

After Johnson said goodbye on 21 June, life went along pleasantly at Streatham for the rest of June and into July. If only the exasperating baby would be born! On 30 June "good natured, friendly" William Henry Lyttelton dropped by on horseback to see how Mrs. Thrale did. This tall, aristocratic friend had been her husband's companion on his Grand Tour of the Continent years before. And since those carefree days Lyttelton had distinguished himself: he had been appointed Governor of the colony of South Carolina in 1755 and, from 1766 to the present, had served as Ambassador to Portugal. Lyttelton was now coming home to live — in Worcestershire, at Little Hagley, which he would have to manage for himself as his wife, Mary Macartney, had died over five years before (they had married two years before the Thrales). But he was making out pretty well, he said, and he invited the Thrales to visit him. Mrs. Thrale "of pale face and monstrous size" replied that someday she hoped they might come. Lyttelton wished her well with the baby, and told her to write to Johnson, who was at Ashbourne, and urge him to come over to visit, for he would soon be home and if Johnson "would but visit him he should be *so* proud of himself and make *so* much of [his guest]" (*Letters* 253A).

The days passed tiresomely at Streatham, for the baby refused to make its appearance. In letters of early July, Johnson kept hoping for an announcement, but by the middle of the month he stopped inquiring and wrote about a general nursery project, which had been discussed before he went away, a chemistry laboratory, to be set up at Streatham. Johnson said he would try to obtain iron and copper

ore on his journey, as well as lead ore so that he and the children might
see how lead could be smelted (*Letters* 259).

Thrale was making extensive renovations at Streatham, and on 24
July Johnson asked if the builders could be told to "leave about a
hundred loose bricks. I can at present think of no better place for
Chimistry in fair weather, than the pump side in the kitchen Garden"
(*Letters* 264).

By the time he wrote this letter, the baby had finally arrived, the
Thrales' seventh child — their sixth girl. She was very large, as is
characteristic of over-due babies; and the labor was difficult, but in
the end all was well with both mother and child. Thrale wrote to
Johnson with relief, "our Mistress . . . gives us good expectations of
her recovery, considering how much more she suffer'd, than usual"
(*Letters* 264.3A).

22 July 1771.[28] *Sophia Thrale born: large & likely to live — Spons.ʳˢ*
My Mother Mˢʳ Nesbitt & Queeney.

Early in August Johnson returned to London and was permitted
to rejoin his family at Streatham. He was pleased by Mrs. Thrale's
good health; and delighted by his introduction to Sophy, who seemed
to be thriving. He found Mrs. Salusbury, though failing, still gallant, active, and cheerful. Johnson was soon engaged in the serious
work of revising his *Dictionary*, but he found time to supervise the
building of his "furnace," and when this was done, experiments were
immediately undertaken. For the rest of the summer "the pump side
in the kitchen Garden" became the center of Streatham activity. As
Mrs. Thrale said:

[We] diverted ourselves with drawing essences and colouring liquors. But the
danger Mr. Thrale found his friend in one day when I was driven to London,
and he had got the children and servants round him to see some experiments
performed, put an end to all our entertainment; so well was the master of the

---

[28] This entry gives Sophia Thrale's birth date as 22 July, and so does the Thrale
Family Bible, but the Register in St. Leonard's Church gives the date as 23 July,
and Mrs. Thrale's later entries in this journal give the date as the 23rd. See the
entry for 23 July 1776.

The 23rd of July was the anniversary day which Sophia was to celebrate throughout her life, so presumably it is correct. She was probably born in the middle of
the night.

house persuaded, that his short sight would have been his destruction in a moment, by bringing him close to a fierce and violent flame. (*Anecdotes*, p. 237)

Geology and the collection of natural curiosities were strongly recommended to take the place of chemistry. And soon Johnson made a present to Queeney of a pretty little cabinet, which he promised to fill with rocks and shells and other interesting specimens. But Johnson could never become as enthusiastic about the cabinet as he had been about the furnace.

15: Feb: 1772.

Harry is now five Years old, & can repeat his five Declensions to the end, can name 'em separate too, & tell the Genders Declensions &c. whatever way you ask him likewise the Verbs Participles & Adverbs in English, the Nom: & Acc: & Voc: Cases of the nouns in English & the Imperative mood among Verbs. I asked him this morning what part of Speech ring was? I don't know now says he whether you mean the Noun or the Verb. He reads English well enough to be pleased with the Scripture History & Pilgrims Progress — & dearly loves a dismal Story in the Newspapers. I set him yesterday however to Nelson's Feasts & Fasts [29] *— this says he little Ma'amey to be sure is a very good Book; all about our Saviour & the Apostles, but it is* monstrous dull Fun. *I saw a little Boy yesterday whose beauty I was admiring — Oh mighty fine says Harry, but if you set him to Decline* Via, *I warrant he'd not do that so prettily. —*

30 May 1772.

Susanna Arabella Thrale is now two years old: small, ugly & lean as ever; her Colour like that of an ill painted Wall grown dirty. The Children call her little Crab, Papa & myself have named /her/ Gilly, from a Gilhouter the Cheshire word signifying an Owl. She seems to have good Parts enough, & could walk on her little crooked Legs as early as any of the others could on their straight ones: — but her Temper is as perverse as very Poyson. She labours under an umbilical Rupture /too,/ and at present Her Belly seems to swell & harden

---

[29] Robert Nelson's *Companion for the Festivals and Fasts of the Church of England, with Collects and Prayers for Each Solemnity*, London, A. & J. Churchill, 1704, and subsequent editions.

strangely; James treated it as a Worm Case, but nothing verminous ever appeared notwithstanding our Searches & Expectations. Pinkstan & Prior have by Turns tried at her Rupture, which would mend under their Care, but for her crying which is incessant —— She speaks very plain but has never been put to learn even her Letters; Bromfield thinks her scorbutick & has purged her accordingly; Lawrence recommended bark & cold bathing & Pinkstan will have her be fumigated — She has gone thro' all the rest, & shall now begin to be smoked. I know not what can be done for her, I will send her to my Mother at Stre[a]tham; perhaps country air may do something — we can but try.

Little Susan's sallow color did not indicate jaundice. She had been two months premature and in consequence suffered from anemia and rickets. Her hernia was due to a weakness of the anterior abdominal wall at the navel; and the eighteenth-century treatment for this was strapping a penny over the part. Susan's incessant crying slowed her recovery.

Susan's rickets were caused by a deficiency of vitamin D, which resulted in both a softening of the bones and a weakness of the muscles. This deficiency would have been corrected by adequate exposure to sunshine, so Mrs. Thrale was right to hope that country air might "do something."

Scurvy was not clearly distinguished from rickets until the end of the nineteenth century, and there is no evidence in Mrs. Thrale's journal to support a diagnosis of scurvy, but in any case, purging, worming, the taking of bark (a powder from the cinchona tree given to reduce fever), cold bathing, and fumigation (a tobacco smoke enema) would not have been effective remedies for it.

James and Bromfield were familiar doctors at the Thrales' house; and this time Fleming Pinkstan, a surgeon closely associated with James, and Prior were called in as consultants. Herbert Lawrence of the York Buildings was an old family friend (distantly connected to Mrs. Thrale through the Cottons). He had met the Salusburys through his brother, Major Charles Lawrence (later General Lawrence, Governor of Nova Scotia). During John Salusbury's long absences there, Herbert Lawrence had taken a kind interest in his family. He had tutored Hester, advised her, even written poems in

QUEENEY'S CABINET
GIVEN HER BY DR. JOHNSON

her praise. It was Lawrence who had been summoned to Dean Street when John Salusbury had had his fatal attack ten years before.

7: June 1772. Sophia Thrale aged 11 Months got a Boil in her Neck wch was obliged to be lanced; I hope it will not injure her Beauty, of which She has a considerable Share. it discharged copiously & there will be a Scar but not a great one.

Sophy's boil cleared up satisfactorily, but there were many other harassments. Thrale was making additions to the house — a library and other rooms — and there were constant difficulties with the builders. Every day Mrs. Salusbury needed more attention. And Mrs. Thrale felt ill herself most of the time, for she was again in her chronic state of pregnancy.

Suddenly, added to all these troubles in June, came the shock that Thrale faced bankruptcy. In the past he had indulged in reckless speculation with his brother-in-law, Arnold Nesbitt (though Mrs. Thrale did not yet know the extent of this involvement), but until the present year he had taken no irresponsible risks in his own business. Now, it appeared that Thrale, in a desire to outbrew his rivals Whitbread and Calvert, had been led into a bizarre project by his crony, the chemist Humphrey Jackson, of whom Mrs. Salusbury and Hester had always been suspicious. Jackson had convinced Thrale that it was possible to brew beer without malt and hops! Under Jackson's guidance, and in opposition to John Perkins, the able chief clerk, and all others at the brewery who knew about this wild scheme, it was undertaken — of course, with ruinous results. And not only was the total output of Jackson's beer worthless, but he had further increased his friend's financial embarrassment by leading him into another experiment, the production of a liquid to "preserve ships' bottoms from the worm" (Hayward, II, 25). Thrale, with the help of some government money, had erected thirty enormous vats in East Smithfield to make this stuff — a second disaster. Thrale could not seem to comprehend what had happened to him.

In a sort of daze, he turned to Johnson and his wife, neither of whom had ever been concerned with the business. They — and Perkins — proceeded to take over the management of the brewery, and the first matter in hand was to find credit for new brewing. This

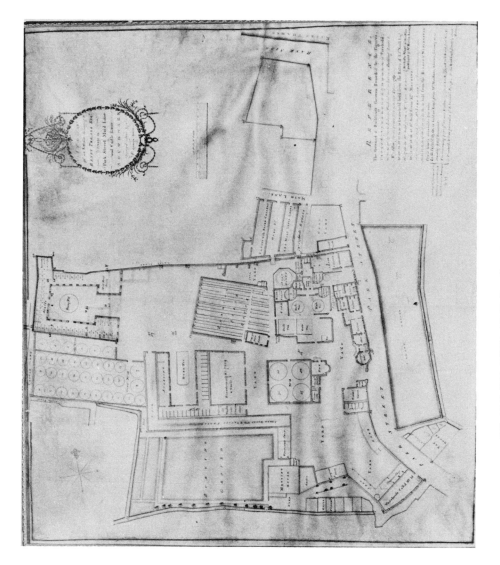

PLAN OF THRALE BREWERY COMPOUND

was not easy even in good times, but now it was virtually impossible, for the failure in June 1772 of the Fordyce banking house [30] in London had created a financial panic, business after business had collapsed, and commerce was presently at a standstill.

The second problem was the near mutiny of the men at the brewery. Johnson insisted that Mrs. Thrale talk authoritatively to all the clerks, who were "resolved to depart." She spoke well, and they responded as Johnson hoped they would. They "declared they would not live *with M*^{*r*} *Thrale*, but they would do *anything* for *me*; only says They Madam get rid of that Fiend! [Jackson] he will entirely ruin your whole Family else. I did so, and we soon began to understand each other. Money was raised, the Beer was mended, our whole Conduct in the management of our Trade was changed . . ." (*Thraliana*, p. 312).

Mrs. Salusbury rose to the occasion and, showing her devotion to her son-in-law, offered all her savings (about £3,000). Thrale was able to borrow £6,000 from Mr. Rush, a friend of his father's; and £5,000 from Lady Lade (Mrs. Thrale could not help here, as she had not spoken to her sister-in-law in over two years — *Letters* 294A). But Mrs. Thrale gained help from another quarter. Though she was now in the sixth month of pregnancy, she drove to Brighton and begged £6,000 from the family friend, Charles Scrase. John Perkins, the chief clerk, admired this action so much that he never stopped repeating Mrs. Thrale's "short letter to our master, which only said, 'I have done my errand, and you soon shall see returned, *whole*, as I hope — your heavy and faithful messenger, H.L.T.'" (Hayward, II, 27). These four loans made it possible to keep the brewery in operation, though there were still debts overhanging of £130,000.[31]

This frightening financial crisis affected Thrale's health and altered his whole personality. He was never again the carefree, high-spirited, light-hearted fellow whom Hester Salusbury had married. He became withdrawn and morose, and began to suffer from that "horrible Stupor which at last quench'd entirely the Spark of Life . . ." (*Thraliana*, p. 805).

---

[30] Alexander Fordyce, head of the bank, had made a fortune by anticipating the rise in India stocks in 1765, but with the dispute between England and Spain over ownership of the Falkland Islands, these stocks fell precipitously and Fordyce used money entrusted to his bank to cover his losses — and broke for £100,000.

[31] "Yet in *nine years* was every shilling paid," HLT in Hayward, II, 27.

In September — amid all the brewery turmoil — Mrs. Thrale was delivered of her eighth child, Penelope. She recorded no specific day in the journal — the baby was born on the 15th, at Streatham.

Sept.ʳ 1772. Penelope Thrale /was/ born — liv'd but 10 hours, looked black & could not breathe freely — poor little Maid! one cannot grieve after her much, and I have just now other things to think of — this has been a sad Lying In: my Mother dying — & every thing going wrong   Well! as old Townsend says God mend all! [32]

Penelope was a blue baby because of her difficulty in breathing, caused perhaps by an obstruction, but more likely by congenital heart disease or malfunction of the lungs.

The baby's chances had been greatly hazarded before its birth, for Mrs. Thrale had hardly recovered from her painful labor with the big baby, Sophy, before she conceived again. She was weak throughout the pregnancy, and under great emotional and physical strain. She did not take proper precautions nor sufficient rest. She drove herself to total exhaustion.

6: Oct.ʳ 1772. Lucy is now three Years & a Quarter old; She begins to read some particular Psalms, & three not very easy Epistles: She says the Catechism to the Sacraments; the 7 days of the Week, 12 Months of the Year, 2ˢ and threes of the Multiplication Table, the Aliquot Parts both of a Pound & a Shilling; & knows the different Coyns at Sight: She tells the four Points of the Compass, the 4 Qu.ʳˢ of the World, & the capital Cities all over Europe, which She knows very well on a Map & Globe. her Ear runs worse & worse.

From this reference to a running in only one ear, one might assume that the infection in the other had subsided. Even if this were so, Lucy's condition continued to be worrisome all summer, and that of Mrs. Salusbury even more disturbing, as her strength lessened and the pain increased. Mrs. Thrale was able to stay with her mother most of the time, but Tuesdays she set aside for business at the brewery.

Thrale was becoming active again, and though this marked an encouraging improvement in his health, it also presented difficulties. Mrs. Thrale and Johnson worked well together, and they respected

[32] Old Townsend was Thrale's chief brewer.

Perkins, who had been in a position of trust at the brewery for over ten years. They found him loyal and sound of judgment — an excellent manager. In turn, Perkins had the highest regard for them both, but he no longer had confidence in his master and made decisions without consulting him. Thrale, annoyed and humiliated by Perkins' insubordination, treated him harshly and began to think of discharging him.

Johnson was the steadying influence upon Thrale, Perkins, and Mrs. Thrale, and each of them sorely regretted his departure from London when the time came to make his promised visits to Lichfield and Ashbourne in October. Mrs. Salusbury was also sorry to see him go, and presented him with something she thought he might cherish, a chair, covered in needle-point "of Mrs Thrale's Work when She was a good little Girl and minded her Book and her Needle" (*Letters* 278.2A).

During October and November, Johnson and Mrs. Thrale were in frequent communication; his letters filled with business comment: "I think you were quite right in your advice about the thousand pounds . . . in great matters you are hardly ever mistaken . . ." (*Letters* 284). He applauded his master's renewed interest in the brewery and hoped he was now a wiser man. He urged Mrs. Thrale to keep up her spirits: "Do not be depressed. Scarce years will not last for ever; there will sometime be good harvests" (*Letters* 289). At the end of his letters he customarily inquired after Mrs. Salusbury, giving an expression of his respect and affection, also a message of spiritual comfort. In his letters to Queeney he continued these inquiries and urged the little girl to help her grandmother and to please her. He also told Queeney that, alas, he had found no natural curiosities for her cabinet. In December, however, Miss Aston gave him some shells and he said he would bring them home if he could contrive a way.

When Mrs. Thrale wrote at the end of November and in the beginning of December she told Johnson how impatient the family was to have him home. His tower room above the counting office was kept aired and his room at Streatham was ready as well.

18: Octr 1772. I ran a Race with Harry but could not beat him, neither could he beat me; Queeney, who could with Ease have dis-

*tanced us both, looked on to see fair Play — Harry is near six Year
old now; & I near 32. but my Lying In is but just over, so I may not
have all my Strength.*[33]

During her lying-in, and the pregnancy before it, Mrs. Thrale had
worried about another problem besides the brewery, and that was
what should be done with her mother's Dean Street house, for Mrs.
Salusbury was no longer capable of running it. Thrale's brother-in-
law, Alderman Plumbe, said he wished to rent the house for his
family, and this seemed a sensible solution. If it were ever possible,
Mrs. Salusbury would be able to take back her house,[34] for it remained in the family so to speak. But Streatham was obviously the
place for her to be now. Mrs. Thrale planned to stay with her mother
in the country most of the time this winter, even though her husband
would be in Southwark.

9. Dec.ʳ 1772.

*Lucy's Ear & Head gets very bad indeed; the Inflammation is very
violent, & even offensive do all we can to keep it sweet & clean. My
Mother says it should be dried up, for it is really an odious thing for
a beautiful Girl /like/ this to be tormented with, & now none of the
Nursery Maids will sleep in the same Bed. — as Lucy says herself —
"We* must *go to Pinkstan." Lucy is very saucy, but wonderfully
amiable; I am indeed accused of a partial Fondness towards her, but
She is so lovely one cannot resist her coaxing — Queeney never would
be fondled, nor delight in any Caresses I could give her, — She has
a Heart wholly impenetrable to Affection as it should seem, & Lucy
is softness & kindness itself. but I have of late fancied Queeney did
love her Brother — I am sure 'tis a Sign nobody can help loving him
if She does.*

The mention of "Lucy's Ear & Head" suggests that both the ear
and the mastoid were now discharging foul-smelling pus, caused by
the invasion of secondary bacteria.

[33] The passage following this in the *Family Book* is dated "15: Feb: 1773." It
is printed in its proper chronological place, following the entry for "9. Dec.ʳ 1772."

[34] Mrs. Salusbury's house was No. 24 Dean Street, standing until 1965, when it
was demolished; see *Survey of London*, XXXIII, *The Parish of St. Anne Soho* (The
Athlone Press, University of London, 1966), pp. 130, 133–134.

Two days after this entry was made, Johnson returned to London. This meant much to the Thrales, for they needed his help and comfort, in business and at home; but ironically, he was not able to give either. The curse of old age and its ailments — gout, cough, and fever — laid him low. Out of kindness, he stayed away from the Thrales, but he tried to be helpful. On 12 December, the day after his return to London, he wrote to Edmund Hector, the surgeon, pressing him to give minute details of the mercury treatment for cancer, which they had discussed during Johnson's recent stay in Birmingham (*Letters* 291). ". . . I therefore entreat, that you will state it very particularly, with the patient's age, the manner of taking mercury, the quantity taken, and all that you told or omitted to tell me. To this request I must add another that you will write as soon as you can."

1773–1774

15: Feb: 1773. this Day H: S: Thrale is six Years old, he is got as far as the Verbs in his Latin Grammar; he must now begin to read construe and perse in that Language — tomorrow we will make our Commencement with the Scrap of Latin at the Head of some Psalm or another. Writing also should now be set solidly to work upon it is high Time to be sure, but I have of late been so much & so anxiously employed both in the Affairs of the Trade & my sweet Mother's Illness that I hope my Negligence is excusable — Yet I am not pleased with myself: Harry might do more I think, & I do all I have done.[1]

It is hard to see how Mrs. Thrale could have done more: she was caring for five children and for her dying mother, and struggling with the management of the brewery.

She was keeping a business memorandum book, one more journal to claim her attention; and she was writing letters about business to Johnson, for though he was still confined to his house, he was actively involved in problems of the trade.

On 20 February she wrote to him about Perkins' report on "the bad Beer" and also how extremely pleased the chief clerk was when Thrale brought him to tea in the drawing room. In the midst of this, she said, Thrale's sister, Lady Lade, had come in (that tall woman, once a beauty, now rather ugly in appearance and stout; but still lively, with an air of dignity and haughtiness, and lovely manners that hid her lack of knowledge). As ever, she was too youthfully and gaily dressed.

. . . you know I have not seen [her] now these two Years and more: She took a great many very rough Words from me so patiently and so prettily, that we kiss'd and friended and promised to quarrel no more: She had been with my Mother first. Then went I to Mrs Nesbitt's Rout . . . (*Letters* 294A)

[1] This passage, here printed in its proper chronological place, is written in the *Family Book* between the one headed "18: Octr 1772." and the one headed "9. Decr 1772."

On 10 March she wrote to Johnson about Thomas Alexander, a chemist, who was threatening a lawsuit for fraud. Mrs. Thrale said she had followed Johnson's directions in handling the man, and "Your Advice was precisely right, upon my talking in a higher & more fearless Tone my friend Alexander was much disconcerted — apparently so . . . [He] profess'd his Confidence in Mr Thrale's honour & Perkins's Honesty, both which he said I had clear'd to him. he then expatiated in praise of my powers of Negotiation . . ." (*Letters* 300C).

Another harassment in March was an old story raked up by the *Westminster Magazine* about Thrale and Polly Hart, the courtesan, ". . . Genius of the Wood and Table; equally sylvan, festive, and gay. She had spirit to lead the Hounds in the Field, and Wit to entertain *them* in the house." Thrale's liaison with Polly Hart had ended before his marriage. The story was pointless now, but mortifying.

Mrs. Thrale's real trial was the increasing illness of her mother. The cancer had spread, and Dr. James saw no hope (*Letters* 300); neither did Pinkstan. All they could think of doing was to purge their patient. Mrs. Salusbury was now "*so* weak She [could] hardly totter down Stairs, but [she would] not keep up [Stairs], tho She fainted yesterday with the Effort" (*Letters* 300A).

On 11 March Mrs. Thrale was so alarmed by her mother's condition that she sent for Dr. Thomas, the clergyman who kept a boys' school in Streatham, to give her mother the Holy Sacrament.

Johnson realized that the end was near and sent Mrs. Thrale letters of tender consolation.

21. March 1773.
My Mother's Illness has lately increased so fast that it has required all my Attention & shall have it — My Children I shall keep My Mother is leaving me, and Filial Duty shall not be cheated of its due. what Gratitude do I not owe her? what Esteem have I not of Her? what Tenderness do I not feel for her? Oh my sweet Mother! I have now past many days & Nights in her room in her Room [sic], while Mr Thrale proceeded with his Affairs in London — they thank God do mend every day, but nobody can guess what a Winter this has been to me, & big with Child too again God help me! This Morning therefore finding myself incapable of attending to every body, & every thing, I fairly resolved to walk up the Common with Harry to Dr Thomas who keeps a Boy's School here; & may at least keep up that Knowledge

he has, & perhaps get more: he will likewise go on with his Writing more commodiously there, while I give to my Mother my undivided Attention; & She seems vastly delighted too that She has lived to see him a School-boy. As for Hetty, She already knows so much of History, Geography, Astronomy & Natural Philosophy; that She begins now to study for her own sake, & does not so much require keeping to Hours as younger Children do; She has besides a sort of every-day-Wit; a degree of Prudence, Discretion and common Sense, that I have seldom seen in a Girl even of twelve or thirteen Years old, which makes her a most comfortable Child; in spite of her bad Temper & cold heart; I really can consult her and often do — She is so very rational. We were reading a strange Story in the papers t'other day of a Murder at Bristol when Queeney objected to the strangeness of some Circumstances, which /says/ She renders the Person's Guilt very disputable — Well done Queeney! exclaimed Dr Johnson, thou shalt be upon the grand Jury.

The judicious little girl was a helpful person to have around the house during these anxious days; she was always quiet, considerate, and polite to her grandmother. But her brother, Harry, though he meant well, was too noisy and exuberant. Mrs. Thrale carried through her idea of sending him to Dr. Thomas' school in Streatham. Johnson's comment on the fact that she had ceased to be her son's teacher was that the boy would "be happier now he goes to school and reads Milton" (*Letters* 304).

At the brewery things were going along satisfactorily. The relationship between Thrale and Perkins had improved somewhat, perhaps because Johnson was active again and could mediate. He wrote to Mrs. Thrale that "Perkins says . . . the Customers are much pleased with their beer. That is good news, and Perkins is always a credible witness" (*Letters* 301.3).

In April an amusing and romantic interlude lightened the gloom of the household, a situation in which everyone at Streatham participated, even Mrs. Salusbury, ill though she was. The drama was taking place in her house in Dean Street, now inhabited by Alderman Plumbe and his family. Fanny Plumbe, his pretty daughter, had fallen in love with a twenty-two-year-old lad, Jack Rice, son of a former High Sheriff of Surrey. This was a suitable match — but Fanny was only fifteen, and Alderman Plumbe was determined she would not be married at such an age.

Fanny and Jack were very much in love, and they were able to win the sympathy of a number of their elders: Rice's father offered support for his son, Mrs. Plumbe pleaded for her daughter's happiness, and the Thrales and Mrs. Salusbury sided with the young ones, as did Dr. Johnson, surprisingly enough. But Alderman Plumbe would listen to no one. He would never give his consent; he would lock his daughter up in a convent. When this was threatened, Jack and Fanny decided to elope, to go to Scotland and be married at Gretna Green. The Thrales, however, persuaded them to go to Holland instead and arranged with the obliging Dr. Thomas to go along and be chaperone. The three departed for Holland, and Jack and Fanny were married there.

On 23 May Thrale wrote to the bridegroom, urging him to stay abroad until the senior Rice had settled his "Independency." And generous Thrale added, "If you should have occasion for more money than you chuse to trouble your Father for, you may draw on me for any sum you please" (Rice, 1). On 15 June Thrale wrote to the newlyweds in Rotterdam, suggesting that "when you have seen Holland & are tired of it, go to the German Spa where you'll meet Mrs. Nesbitt & more of your Friends than you think of at present" (Rice, 2).

Meanwhile Alderman Plumbe, as soon as he was aware of his daughter's flight, turned "his wrath upon [the Thrale] House, where [they] stood a regular Scige" (Rice, 6). Thrale himself stayed in Southwark, but Mrs. Thrale held fast at Streatham. If he knew all, she wrote to Johnson, "I suppose we should not see him for a fortnight . . ." In London Fanny's mother had made herself ill with wild apprehensions. She was "foolish & frantic to a supreme Degree" but "the Children [were] well & happy" (*Letters* 311B) and, as Mrs. Thrale had written to Johnson, "it would be really a choice Thing to see *some*body happy . . ." (*Letters* 308A).

23: May 1773. Susanna Arabella Thrale is this Day 3 Years old: Her general Health is mended, her Rupture almost well; but her Colour still like that of a Clorotic Virgin at 15, instead [of] a Baby; and her Stature very low: her Temper is so peevish & her Person so displeasing, that I do not love to converse with her: I was saying yesterday to my Mother — sure this Child swallowed something in her Infancy, that makes such a Creature of her: — Ay replies my Mother, a Wasp I fancy. She has however good Sense I am sure, and has learned the Cate-chism & Te deum by heart very prettily — We never attempted teach-ing her to read. her Appetite & Digestion begin to mend, and as She has gone thro' so much, I now expect her to live; but She has a stiffness in her Joints, & a Palpitation in Her Bosom that I cannot account for, nor can any of the people we consulted.

So much for little Crab.

Susan's appearance of a "Clorotic Virgin," of someone suffering from green sickness, was probably due to the iron-deficient anaemia of prematurity, which responds very slowly to a diet containing iron. The palpitations were presumably caused by the anaemia, and Susan's joints were stiff because of the weakness of her muscles.

30: May 1773.
Lucy's Ear is got quite well; my Mother & Pinkstan agreed to dress it with the Ex: Saturni of Goulard — this was in January — it healed with a quickness & cleanliness that amazed me, but a large Swelling soon began to appear in that Side of the Throat so as to alarm us all: It was as big as a Hen's Egg I am sure, and the Child was sadly dis-tressed by it — this remained more or less I think till about a Week ago; when after strict Diet, very severe Purging, & Sarsaparilla Tea, it dispersed, and there is now no Sign left on 't; but the poor Girl is cruelly reduced by all this Discipline.

The Saturni of Goulard with which Mrs. Salusbury and Pinkstan treated Lucy's ear was a mixture of sub-acetate lead, a lotion named after its original maker, the French doctor, Thomas Goulard. A "gou-lard," as it was called, was commonly used to combat inflammation or infection. In Lucy's case the ear improved. The large swelling on the side of her throat was probably due to an inflammation of the tonsil-lar glands, and this in time subsided.

Purging was believed to be helpful for Lucy, and sarsaparilla tea was given to purify the blood and to increase perspiration and the flow of urine. None of these treatments had any effect upon the basic problem of mastoid infection.

Lucy's illness caused Mrs. Thrale much anxiety, and her mother's condition even greater concern; she was giving all her time and strength to caring for them. It was no time for Johnson to come home, particularly since he was again ill himself — a severe inflammation in his seeing eye. But with little feeling for her problems, he wrote on 29 May, begging to come to Streatham. He wanted to talk to the "dear Lady," Mrs. Salusbury; he longed to be in his own room again, and he told Mrs. Thrale that he hoped "at least to give [her] some little solace or amusement" (*Letters* 311.1).

Mrs. Thrale dreaded having three invalids on her hands, but she unwisely took pity on Johnson and sent her coach for him on Wednesday, 2 June. What Johnson found at Streatham was not the solace for which he longed. He was saddened by the state of his godchild and his moments with Mrs. Salusbury were melancholy. Mrs. Thrale cared for his eye, but she had no time to entertain him. She was either with Lucy or her mother during the day, and she was up half the night comforting the latter, for Mrs. Salusbury was no longer able to lie down. She could breathe only when propped up in a chair, and wanted all the windows wide open for air. This had given her a cold and a bad cough. She had trouble eating, and her limbs were becoming numb.

And here was Johnson, thundering about the house, or sitting alone in his room, thinking about death, which he dreaded, watching its awful approach just beyond his door. Thrale was not at home to stop his morbid fancies (he absented himself in Southwark whenever Streatham was unpleasant). Mrs. Thrale could be caught only in glimpses. The children were kept out of the way, and just occasionally did a friend come to the house.

From Mrs. Thrale's point of view the gloomy, complaining, demanding presence of Johnson was unbearable. Last summer he had been her greatest strength, but now he was a burden. He was always in the way, under foot, irritating, and distracting. He realized this himself, only too well, and from his room sent a note in French. She must tell him what was permitted and what forbidden; whether he might wander freely or if he should stay within prescribed bounds. She could even lock him in his room if she wished (*Letters* 307.1). Mrs. Thrale, beside herself and with a hundred worries, wrote back that she was sorry he was "obliged to be so much alone; I foresaw some ill Consequences of your being here while my Mother was dying thus; yet could not resist the temptation of having you near me" (*Letters* 311.1A). Obviously it had been a mistake. There was no need for him to be tortured by the agonizing scene at Streatham. There was nothing he could do to help. If he stayed, she told him, he must keep to himself, except when company came. But what he should really do was to go away and be cheerfully occupied. His eye was better, he was well enough now, so why did he not make the journey he had often talked about, a tour to the Hebrides, with the young barrister, his Scottish friend, James Boswell?

Johnson did not feel well enough for a Highland ramble yet, and he was well aware of the fact that Boswell could not leave Edinburgh until after the court recess in late August. Johnson knew he was unwanted at Streatham and he was miserable there, but he could not bear to leave.

18: June 1773.

On this fatal & ever memorable as miserable day did I lose my dear Mother; & in her, my Companion, my Friend, my Confident; my Correspondent: whose Kindness softened all my Sorrows, & whose generous Fondness was contented to partake of all my Cares. to whom now shall I tell the little Foibles of my heart, the Tendernesses of my Husband, or the reparties of my Children? to whom shall I now recount the Conversations of the day? & from whom hope Applause for the Labors of Education? to whom shall I carry my Criticism of a Book, secure of Approbation if the Remark be a good one, & certain of Secresy if detected in being absurd? with whom shall I talk over Events long past, Characters known only by ourselves, and Accidents we have together been sharers in? On this day She died, & left me destitute of every real *every* natural *Friend: for Sir Thoˢ Salusbury has long ago cast me off, & Mʳ Thrale & Mʳ Johnson are the mere Acquisitions of Chance; which chance, or change of Behaviour, or Intervention of new Objects or twenty Things besides Death can rob me of. One solid Good I had & that is gone — my Mother!*

Her Illness was a Cancer in the Breast, occasioned originally by a Blow of my little Harry's head two Years & nine Months ago, as She was playing with him in the green Parlour at Streatham after dinner, I was not by, but in a Weeks Time, observing her frequently to unbutton her Jesuit,[2] and handle the part: I insisted on knowing what had happened, and found a very small Lump which gradually & in despite of Medicine & Surgery increased in Size & Pain till today /when/ it ended in Death. it never broke at all tho' sometimes it would bleed;

[2] Jesuit: a dress which buttoned up to the neck, a kind of indoor morning gown.

but the Swelling was enormous, & the blackness quite horrible. Hunter & Bromfield for the 1:st Year, James & Pinkstan for the last 21 Months had the Care of her health, but nothing could have saved her. She felt her Dissolution approaching very hastily from the 12: of this Month, & guessed nearly the very time when She was to leave us: her Voice fail'd her first I think on that day, but so little that we were disputing with each other concerning the Truth of the Symptom, till M:r Murphy who dined here the 13:th & had not seen her for 3 Weeks, confirm'd my Fears and said She was otherwise much alter'd — He said "You have already kept your Mother too long, dear Madam, — you must now part very soon, and I confess I wish the Crisis over for your sake." I liked Baretti's [3] *Speech better — it was "God bless you dear Mad:m & give you patience & her Patience, and as long a Continuance as both may be able to bear." She however preserved her dear Intellects entire when her Voice was gone, & even kept her powers of delighting by her humour to the last.*

She saw me one day the 15: I think lamenting over her & on my enquiring how She did — She replied in allusion to the old Story of the Irishman — "not dead but speechless." She had long ordered what Mourning the Children should wear for her, & who should carry her to Streatham Church; & on the Thursday Night her Voice returning we spoke together quite freely — I helped her off her Knees when She had done Devotion — & said May Heaven hear your Prayers — She answered gravely, I have had Time given me; I hope I have used it. I mentioned the vigorous beating of her pulse as a happy Symptom, but spoke of the dismal Alteration in her face; & added that She looked as if She had nothing now to do but lie down & die: why what said She can I have else to do? — See my Master! so we always call'd M:r Thrale, & She repeated again — See my Master. Shall I send for him said I? not tonight She made Answer — I shall live till tomorrow, he will then come to Dinner won't he? The Conversation changed, & we talked of the new Library & of the Workmen: I mentioned a Macaroni Plaisterer, She pointed to her Maid Sally, & smiling expressed that the

---

[3] Giuseppe Baretti was a scholar and writer, then living in London. He was author of *The Italian Library* (lives and works of Italian authors), 1757; *A Dictionary of the English and Italian Languages* (with a dedication by Johnson), 1760; *A Grammar of the Italian Language*, 1762; and *A Journey from London to Genoa*, 1770 (the subject suggested by Johnson).

Johnson had introduced Baretti to the Thrales, and he was now a frequent guest at Streatham.

HESTER MARIA COTTON SALUSBURY, JOHN SALUSBURY,
AND BELLE
BY ZOFFANY

*Fellow sh:^d court her — No Madam replies the Girl he is a married
Man. She made me handle her Breast that Night, touched it roughly
herself & shewed us that all soreness & Pain was gone. Her Legs were
swelled vastly, but quite easy — like Sally's Face said She after a Fit of
the Toothach. She slept very easy in the night, but had as usual all the
Windows open, the Morn^g however shewed a Still more visible Alter-
ration [sic] in her Countenance & at 7 o'clock her Utterance was quite
gone. She try'd to take her Coffee but there was no passage   Harry
had the Toast as he always had, & after Prayers the Children read the
Lessons to her as usual — She heard & understood us all perfectly well:
however I Saw we must send for Mr Thrale as Life ebbed apace, &
dispatched a Messenger accordingly: I then called up Mr Johnson who
when he felt her Pulse wonder'd at its Vigor but when he observed the
dimness of her Eyes and universal languor, he leaned on the bed, kissed
her Cheek, & said in his emphatical Way — May God bless you Dear
Madam for Jesus Christ's Sake. at these Words She looked up and
smiled w:^th a sweet Intelligence that express'd Hope, Friendship &
Farewell — all at once. Mr Thrale by this Time was arrived: he found
her up, endeavouring to evacuate the Bladder which She accomplished,
and he helped her other Attendants to replace her in Bed — She made
Signs for more Air, & when we had set open doors & Windows,
& She seemed somewhat refreshed I told her Mr Seward [4] was returned
from Italy, where he had been for his Health — She pointed to her
head, as enquiring whether his Headach was removed — Oh Yes
reply'd I he is got quite well — & enquires much after you — She
smiled & looked pleased: She pressed my Master's Hand and acknowledged She knew him tho' all power of Utterance was wholly lost: after
this which might be about 1 or 2 o'clock She never stirred nor changed
her Posture but the Pulse kept beating regularly till 6 in the Afternoon
when It fluttered awhile — and then stopt — & stopped forever. She*

---

[4] William Seward: This young man of twenty-six was becoming a favorite at
Streatham. He was the only son of a brewing rival of Thrale's (Calvert and Seward). He had been at Oxford, Oriel College, from June 1764 until December
1766. After this he had traveled upon the Continent, spending much of the time in
Italy. He returned to London a confirmed lover of literature and the fine arts and,
to the dismay of his father, announced that he had no desire to continue in the
family business.

Young Seward was an odd character, frigid and humorless, extremely critical,
and somewhat affected, yet amiable and very intelligent, of high moral character
and capable of great kindness. He enjoyed perpetual ill health.

had dressed her head & worn her Chintz Gown every day till the last, and had been led or carried to the Dressing Room when unable to move without help. on the Monday preceding her Death — (She died on Fryday) Mr Thrale had carried her with the Assistance of her Servant to see the new Rooms that were building, — & She with no small difficulty because of her Voice, had given her Opinion of each. She is now in Heaven rejoicing doubtless at her Deliverance from a Life of Trouble Sickness and Sorrow; and has not left behind her an Equal in every valuable & pleasing Quality. I have now known her as I may say 20 Years, & seen her in the Characters of Daughter, Sister, Wife[,] Mother, & Mistress of Servants, performing absolutely to perfection: & "Finis coronat [5] *— Oh let me die the Death of the Righteous, and let my last end be like hers!* ——

Mrs. Salusbury was sixty-six when she died. She had been a remarkable woman, strong-minded, strong-principled, and deeply religious, and over the years she had not lost her charm, elegance, and wit. If circumstances had been different, she would have shone in society; but, without money, she had no choice but a simple life and she accepted this with dignity and cheerfulness. She had devoted herself for over twenty years to her husband and her daughter, and for the last ten to this daughter and her family. She loved her grandchildren and was always happy to assume responsibility for their care and to help with their tutoring. She had been godmother to all except Penelope (who had no godparents — there had barely been time for a christening in her ten hours of life).

Mrs. Salusbury's attitude toward the Thrale family was what one might expect. As an aristocrat, she never forgot that the Thrales were in trade, and neither did her daughter. Mrs. Salusbury held Hester back from forming any intimacy with Thrale's sisters, but Hester also instinctively held back. Neither she nor her mother, however, was lacking in respect; they assumed all the usual family responsibilities and fulfilled the expected duties.

Mrs. Salusbury's special affection for Henry Thrale, and his for her, was a rare relationship, which spoke well for the characters of both. A mother-in-law's constant presence traditionally causes trouble, but there was never any friction between these two. Thrale continued to

[5] Finis coronat: the end crowns all.

treat Mrs. Salusbury with the same consideration and deference that he had shown when he first met her at Offley Place over ten years before; and Mrs. Salusbury's admiration for him never flagged. In the last months of her life she expressed the wish to be buried not in Wales with her husband, but in the Thrale vault at St. Leonard's, and her son-in-law promised that this would be done. She worried at the last that Hester might become a "teizing Wife," and told her daughter that, "if *She* had had *such* a Husband, She would have never cross'd him in any thing" (*Letters* 307A).

Mrs. Salusbury's feeling for her daughter was the most remarkable relationship of all; as close as a mother and daughter could possibly be — a domination which began when John Salusbury was absent on his missions in Nova Scotia. As the only parent, she had molded her daughter's character and mind, trained and disciplined her, controlled every action. Before Hester's marriage to Thrale, she and her mother "had never been twelve *hours* apart from each other" and after marriage, they were never "more than twelve *Days* apart" (*Thraliana*, p. 55). Mrs. Thrale could never have become an independent person so long as her mother lived. From childhood to the time of her mother's death, she followed Mrs. Salusbury's every command and direction, and loved her more than any living person. "For true Love of one's Mother & real preference of her to all human Kind, I believe I am a singular Example. Johnson says it was not right though!" (*Thraliana*, p. 355).

Mrs. Thrale was never to have a child who had any such attachment for her.

22: June 1773.
Lucy Eliz: Thrale is four Years old today; She is a lovely Girl but somewhat chop-fallen [dejected] from the Discipline She has undergone on account of that humour in her Head — it is however all over, & the Hair is grown again. She has lost some Time for improvement of late, for want of attention; because of poor Grandmama's Illness — but we must now go to Work in earnest & make up past Neglects.

Lucy was enjoying a remission in the progress of her disease, and this Mrs. Thrale mistook for improvement in her condition. July offered some consolation to her.

THE NEW ROOMS AT STREATHAM
CEILING PAINTING BY FELIX KELLY

As for her husband, July was a memorable time for an event which occurred then — he received an honorary degree from Oxford. Lord North had been installed as Chancellor the past October, two years after becoming Prime Minister. It was, and still is, the custom for the new Chancellor to designate the degree recipients at his first Encaenia (the annual commemoration of the University's founders and benefactors). This was a three-day occasion in 1773, taking place on the 7th, 8th, and 9th of July. A degree of Doctor of Divinity was conferred upon Frederick Cornwallis, Archbishop of Canterbury, twenty honorary M.A.'s were granted, and sixty-eight honorary degrees of Doctor of Civil Law — a very long list.

While visiting Oxford, Thrale stayed with Robert Chambers, Principal of New Inn Hall, and Vinerian Professor of Law. He was a good friend of Thrale's, introduced a while before by Johnson (who had helped Chambers write his law lectures). Chambers, now thirty-six, had recently been appointed to the Supreme Court of Bengal, a post he planned to assume early in the next year.

Mrs. Thrale, in deep mourning for her mother, was not present at Encaenia and neither was Johnson. He was nursing his health; the inflamed eye was gradually growing stronger — "I can now write without trouble, and can read large prints" (*Letters* 313). He was making preparations to join Boswell. Their tour to the Hebrides was finally materializing.

In Oxford, Thrale talked to Robert Chambers about the possibility of conducting Johnson on his way north as far as Newcastle, Chambers' native town, where he wished to go for a farewell visit with his relations before leaving England. Chambers agreed to the plan, for which his guest was grateful. Thrale enjoyed his stay at New Inn Hall very much, also the visits to his old college, University. On Thursday, 8 July 1773, he received his DCL, and on the following day his friends, Sir Joshua Reynolds, the painter, and Dr. James Beattie, the Scottish poet and philosopher, were granted the same degree. Encaenia was a pleasant interlude.

26: July 1773.
Mͬ Thrale took Queeney & I a little Excursion up the River to Richmond &c. and when we returned at night I found Harry very feverish & some Spots appearing as he lay in Bed — they were all well in the Morning —

The excursion up the Thames was to dine with Sir Joshua Reynolds, at his pretty house on Richmond Hill. Reynolds had become a friend through Johnson some while ago; Thrale had liked him immediately, but Mrs. Thrale had had reservations. Reynolds was not her idea of a knowledgeable, cultivated gentlemen, not a university man. He was self-made, not that she was against that, but she disliked his bland-ness and pointless vanity. She also disliked the way he treated his sister, Frances, who acted as his housekeeper and hostess. He suffered her presence with obvious discomfort. Mrs. Thrale wondered if Sir Joshua's rude behavior might be the result of jealousy, for Miss Rey-nolds had artistic and literary talents in her own right.

The true reason lay more in Frances herself. She was not an attrac-tive person, not good-looking nor pleasing in manner, and she was always irritating. She was never able to make up her mind about any-thing. She was perpetually fearful and miserable; she knew that she was unlovable. The tensions between the Reynoldses notwithstanding, the Thrales had a fine, carefree day at Richmond Hill, but they returned home to find something very disagreeable.

27: July 1773. It is the Measles, I find Dr Thomas has it in his School &
now all the Girls must catch it too — God send us happily through!

Mrs. Thrale wrote to Johnson the same day, 27 July. He was ex-pected at Streatham on the 28th, and earlier she had promised a warm welcome. His new room, she had hoped, would be ready. (It was in the addition to the house, the room with a bow window, above the library. His old room was "pulled to pieces.") But if Johnson had not had measles, she now warned him, he "must sleep away" (*Letters* 313A).

10: Aug: 1773.
I think the Measles are done with though they have left the Children
enough affected too. Queeney has lost her Appetite, and continues to
cough; Lucy looks peking, tho' She had it much the lightest, owing
I guess to her being well emptied afore: Sophy was quite blind with
them, yet She recovered most quickly — indeed Susan seemed to be
no worse with them than She is without — it was only an Excuse for
her to cry without ceasing & disturb the others.

I sent for no D^{rs} nor 'Pothecaries, but kept diluting all I could with cooling Liquors varied so as to avoid Disgust. I have had all the Symptoms of the Disorder myself — the Truth is I am near 8 Months gone with Child, so perhaps my Baby has catched them too. I had them long ago in good Earnest. ———

Mrs. Thrale's treatment of the children was standard for the time. The "cooling Liquors" were valuable in preventing dehydration and imaginative in their variation. They were not, however, effective in attacking the basic infection.

It is unlikely that Mrs. Thrale now had measles herself for a second time. She had had an attack which put her "in some Danger" when she was eleven (*Thraliana*, p. 801). But even if she had contracted measles at this time, her pregnancy was too far advanced to injure the baby she carried. The child was expected at the end of October or in the early part of November.

On 13 August, after the measles siege was over, the Thrales gave a dinner party at Streatham. Sir Joshua Reynolds and his sister, Frances, came, bringing James Beattie with them; and also present were Goldsmith, Baretti, and Sir Thomas Mills [6] (Clifford, p. 121, n. 2). The Thrales had first met Beattie in 1771, and the next year Mrs. Thrale jokingly told Johnson that if she ever took another husband it would be Beattie, he was so amiable, kind, and courteous (*Life*, II, 148). Though happily married, Beattie himself had found Mrs. Thrale's "vivacity, learning, affability, and beauty" exceedingly attractive; he thought her "indeed one of the most agreeable women [he] ever saw . . ." (*Thraliana*, p. 1083, n. 2).

Johnson was not present at the Thrales' party for his journey to the Hebrides had begun; he had left Chambers in Newcastle and was on his way to Edinburgh, where he was to meet Boswell the next day, 14 August. His birthday this year was spent with the MacLeods at Dunvegan Castle on the Isle of Skye. Queeney, his frequent fellow-celebrant, spent hers at Streatham.

---

[6] Sir Thomas Mills, knighted in 1772, was generally supposed to be the natural son of Lord Mansfield (Lord Chief Justice). In her *Thraliana* character-ratings, Mills is credited (out of a possible 20) with the following scores: morality 18, scholarship 0, general knowledge 10, voice and person 9, manner 9, wit 0, humor 1, and good humor 19. Only Lord Sandys, a friend of Thrale's at Oxford, Dr. Burney, and Boswell equalled Sir Thomas Mills in good humor.

17: Sept.ʳ 1773

H: M: Thrale is 9 Years old today; still very handsome in her Face &
elegant in her Air, no Dancing Master has as yet been try'd. her
Knowledge of English Literature is clear & compendious & I am per-
fectly Satisfied with it — but it is time to begin some new Language.
She writes well enough too but no extraordinary hand. her Temper
continues the same, and her Health is good in general, only from Time
to Time She has a Touch of the Worms.

During the autumn Mrs. Thrale was greatly concerned about her
uncle, Sir Thomas Salusbury — his health and his actions. An agent
of his had gone to Bach-y-Graig, and come to Streatham as well, at-
tempting to gain possession of the legal papers concerning her father's
mortgage on the Welsh property, now hers since her mother's death.
Sir Thomas had paid the £6,000 mortgage for her father in 1755, but
she was sure that this money was never meant to be repaid. She saw
Lady Salusbury's hand in the hiring of the agent. Fortunately this man
got nowhere, because the papers were safely held by the Thrales' attorney, Bateman Robson. However, the Salusburys had made their
intention clear.

In October Mrs. Thrale learned that her uncle was very ill, and
that he might be taken to Bath to try the waters. She wrote to Johnson,
asking whether or not she should go to see him. Johnson answered from
Auchinleck, where he and Boswell were visiting the latter's father, "If
Sir Thomas goes to Bath, it may deserve consideration whether you
should not follow him. If you go, take two Footmen, and dress in such
a manner as he may be proud to see" (*Letters* 337). Johnson's letter
was written on 3 November and by this time all was over — Sir
Thomas had died on 28 October and Offley Place,[7] with his entire es-

---

[7]Offley Place belonged to Lady Salusbury until her death (1804), when it passed
to Sir Robert Salusbury of Denbigh. It continued to be owned by various Salusbury
descendants until sold in 1928 to a Colonel Acland. In 1943 Colonel Acland sold it
to the Froebel Institute of Education. Since 1962 Offley Place has been under the
control of the Hertfordshire County Council, a residential center for short study
courses.

The handsome house is still surrounded by a large park with fine trees. Offley
Church is across the meadow from the house, and in the chancel of the church are
Penrice memorials, including those of Sir Henry Penrice and his daughter, Anna
Maria, the first wife of Sir Thomas Salusbury.

Facing Sir Harry is a marble monument by Nollekens, to the memory of Sir
Thomas and his second wife, Sarah. Their life-size figures, in classical dress, stand

tate, was left to his widow. The possibility of his niece inheriting anything was totally extinguished, and the mortgage on Bach-y-Graig was
now a debt she owed to Lady Salusbury.

Johnson wrote to Mrs. Thrale from Edinburgh on 12 November:

I never had much hope of a will in your favour, but was willing to believe that
no will would have been made. The event is now irrevocable, it remains only
to bear it . . . Be alone as little as you can; when you are alone, do not suffer
your thoughts to dwell on what you might have done, to prevent this disappointment . . . Remit yourself solemnly into the hands of God, and then turn
your mind upon the business and amusements which lie before you. (*Letters*
338)

17: Oct. *1773.*
*This Day my eldest daughter H: M: Thrale begun to study Italian
under the instructions of M.* *Baretti whose Skill in modern Languages
is unrivalled I suppose; his Expectations of Credit from her are high
and will not I hope be disappointed.*

Mrs. Thrale had liked the idea of having this distinguished scholar
teach Italian to Queeney, and she made Johnson urge Baretti to undertake the assignment. Johnson did so, "assuring me," Baretti later said,
"that, after a few years attendance in that occupation, a rich man like
Mr. Thrale would make me easy with an annuity for the remainder of
my days" (*European Magazine*, June 1788, p. 398).

In this way Baretti came to Streatham, as part guest — part tutor.
Every day except Sunday he worked in the library with Queeney,
an hour in the morning, an hour in the afternoon. At first he gave her
vocabulary lists: nouns, verbs, adjectives, articles, and prepositions; and
after she was familiar with these, he began instruction according to his
ingenious method of "dialogues."

Queeney would choose a subject and Baretti would dash off an
illustrative conversation: Italian for several speeches, then an English
translation. Fine "bubbles full of air," he called his dialogues; "empty
bladders all," the formidable child declared (Baretti, p. 37). They were
imaginative and entertaining talks about the Streatham nursery and
barnyard, brilliant nonsense to hold Queeney's attention and to make
her laugh, for she loved nonsense even more than jumping over settees

under an oak tree, where, as the story goes, their engagement was finally made,
after having been broken.

MONUMENT TO SIR THOMAS AND
LADY SARAH SALUSBURY
BY NOLLEKENS

OFFLEY PLACE

FROM AN ENGRAVING BY VARRALL AFTER NEALE

or bouncing on chairs or tumbling on the grass with Harry, or gnawing her gloves. (It must be remembered that Queeney was not yet ten.)

She was exceedingly bright but hard to control and Baretti soon discovered that even if he could make her sit still she often became sullen, and then he could accomplish nothing at all. In time a "Covenant" was drawn up, witnessed by her mother and Johnson, in which Queeney solemnly promised to come promptly to her "Taskmaster" at the appointed hour and to be good natured, polite, and attentive throughout her lesson. After this was over, she promised to read the most recent dialogue several times by herself, and then copy it into her little red book. She was responsible at all times for the contents of this book.

Soon it contained a great number of dialogues between "Maestro" and his pupil, and these are extremely interesting for the details — personal and domestic — which they give: "Maestro's" forgetfulness (almost coming to breakfast without his shoes), his shortsightedness, clumsiness — and his pointless and expensive habit of taking snuff; "Esteruccia" (as he called her) continuing to jump about like an idiot, her bashfulness and fear of being laughed at, her passion for eating, and her torment from worms (*tortorelle*, "little doves," they called them).

There were dialogues between Streatham birds and animals: Macaroni Cock and his wife Cottager, white as snow; between a peacock and his hens who discussed shocking world tragedies reported in the newspapers as well as Miss Hetty's being scratched by a cat; a conversation between the latter and a dog, who accused the cat of loving liberty as much as the Americans; confidences of the two coach horses, Poppet and Ramper, who complained of the time the coach was so full of children it was ready to burst. In a dialogue between Esteruccia and Old Nurse, this steady drinker of brandy insisted she was forty-two; it was only the rude livery fellows who said she was sixty. And in an exchange between Esteruccia and Bet, the chambermaid said she took no delight in learning except what she knew, and asked Miss Hetty if Italy was truly as large and fine a town as London. (Bet also had a passing slur for Maestro, that he was not a Christian but "a papish.")

Little Harry Thrale was mentioned in a number of dialogues: when he and Queeney had had a fight because he would not let her see the five kittens born the day before; when Harry had pulled the tail of a cow, and thrown a quid (firecracker) at Old Nan, a maid. Harry was basically a good boy but, as the dialogue of the rod recorded, he was whipped at least two or three times a week just for jumping ditches and climbing trees. There was not a tree in the neighborhood he had not climbed. Harry found no pleasure unless some danger was involved. Harry was only six but he was a handful.

Harry, however, was not Baretti's responsibility — only Queeney was a constant pupil, and her mother was an infrequent one. Baretti had promised to read and explain the Italian poets to Mrs. Thrale but, he complained, the chatelaine of Streatham spent so much time with her chickens and turkeys and geese and ducks and peafowls that there was little left for Dante.

Baretti got along better with the master of the house, courteous, easy-going Thrale, and he loved all the children. He encouraged their spirits and freedom and saw no reason for strict discipline. Here, obviously, was an immediate cause of friction between the teacher and Mrs. Thrale, for she insisted upon complete obedience from her children. She carried an ivory whistle in her pocket to call them if provoked (and they came on the run). Her treatment was hot and cold, as she herself admitted, she kissed them if they pleased her and boxed their ears if they did not — with "blows of her Salusbury-fist," which Baretti said "she herself called her beautiful hand . . . of such a stoutness and size, as would not disgrace . . . a coalheaver of the Thames . . . " (*European Magazine*, June 1788, p. 395).

One day, early in Baretti's residence at Streatham, he asked the little girls to come across the "Ha-ha! drawbridge" and walk with him in the great field — not aware of the fact that their mother had forbidden them to cross the drawbridge. As the children were delightedly tumbling about in the field, Mrs. Thrale came out of the house and spied them. According to Baretti, the sight "kindled" her rage. She stormed at the girls and at him — for there was a pond in the field, and "What do children know . . . of the difference between land and water?" Baretti soon after asked Sophy this question and she replied "I [would] rather be whipped than go cross the pond . . . I should be drowned like a rat if I did; and, [to] be sure, whipping is not so bad as drowning!" (*European Magazine*, June 1788, p. 394).

According to Baretti, Mrs. Thrale was not only ignorant of the little girls' "distinct ideas about solids and fluids," but also about taste, for not long after this incident she said to him, when they were alone at the table, "It is not the taste of fruit . . . but the pretty appearance of

GIUSEPPE BARETTI

THE STREATHAM PORTRAIT BY REYNOLDS

it, that strikes children's fancies, as their palate does not at all distinguish the difference between an apple and an onion; and this I know by long and repeated experience." Sophy (again Baretti's little *"cheval de bataille"*) was summoned and her confident mother cut and put in her mouth a large slice of onion, and told her to eat it. Sophy did so with "astonishing intrepidity." When Baretti, however, asked if she would not rather have an apple, Sophy said indeed, but she had eaten the onion because "when Mamma bids me do a thing, I must do it, and quick, or she gives me a good box on the ear; but, to be sure, I would rather eat an apple than an onion at any time, as I love apples very much, and onions not at all" (*European Magazine*, June 1788, p. 395).

Baretti, a haughty and emotional man, held a difficult position in the Thrale household as these examples of disciplinary contretemps show. He was, Mrs. Thrale once said, "for ever in the State of a Stream dam'd up" (*Thraliana*, p. 43). He not only violently disagreed with her methods of discipline, but also with her insistence upon doctoring. She was constantly dosing the children with her own remedies when they were ill.[8] Like Johnson, she was an amateur doctor, but he in the main was content doctoring himself, while she wanted to treat everyone within range.

24: Nov: 1773.
*on the 15: of Aug: having gone thro a most miserable Summer between my Mother's Death, the Children's Measles, & every thing; M*r* Thrale took Queeney & I to Windsor to visit Lady Lade, shew the Child the Palace, & drown my Anxiety — We left the little ones therefore with Old Nurse & Sally, & Harry goes to School all day — coming home at Night & Meal Times. The Journey quite restored Queeney's Appetite & Complexion, which this late Illness had in no small Measure affected, but after ten Days absence I found Lucy very dull and drooping in her Spirits I know not how: I concluded these odious Measles had left a Foulness which wanted Purging, & as She complained of the head-ach I gave her a gentle Puke. She mended on this, & the other Children laughing at my Uneasiness protested that Lucy was as saucy as ever; the maids said so too, but I did not heed them The Child herself once told me a blind Story of a Blow Harry had given her /but/ I believe it meant nothing. however in a few Days the foetid Smell of her Ear*

---

[8] She always, incidentally, put a bit of spirits in the glass, so that liquor would have the association for them of evil taste.

*returning I purged her again, & the Symptom disappeared: She was
now very languid & her Appetite failing.*

Lucy's talk of a blow that Harry had given her (Mrs. Thrale was
still haunted by her mother's story) had no bearing upon her present
condition; the attack of measles did. It lowered her resistance to infection and the fetid smell marked the return of secondary infection to
her ear.

On 12 November Johnson had written to Mrs. Thrale from Edinburgh. He worried about his goddaughter, "Surely my dear Lucy will
recover; I wish I could do her good. I love her very much; and should
love another godchild, if I might have the honour of standing to the
next baby." And he had a message for Queeney:

I have been able to collect very little for [her] cabinet; but she will not
want toys now, she is so well employed [learning Italian from Baretti]. I wish
her success; and am not without some thought of becoming her school-fellow.
I have got an Italian Rasselas. (*Letters* 338)

Mrs. Thrale now sought medical help for Lucy.

*/I/ applied to Pinkstan who ordered the Sarsaparilla Tea & bid me do
nothing else. Lucy however [was] fading away very fast, though every
body in the house persisted She was well, I took her to Herbert Lawrence, who said it was the original humour repelled by Pinkstan, which
was fastening on her Brain but that he would try to restore it. a Blister
was accordingly laid on behind the Ear, & a very small running recom-
menced but would not continue: in the mean Time the Child was going,
& oh what were my Feelings for my Lucy? my Dear, my favourite
Girl!*

The sarsaparilla tea which Pinkstan ordered induced perspiration
and discharge of urine, but was a useless treatment. Its futility was apparent to Mrs. Thrale when she carried Lucy to London to be examined
by Herbert Lawrence. He said that Pinkstan's treatment in January,
the goulard, which had healed the running ear, had only succeeded in
producing the swelling on the throat, and he now thought there was
water on the brain. He placed a patch behind the ear to raise a blister to
draw out the inflammation. This was of no benefit.

While the family was watching Lucy with anguish, Mrs. Thrale's new baby was born — a boy at last — but she did not make a separate entry for this important event, just a phrase in passing. She was too distraught about Lucy.

Bromfield, who was on the 8: of Nov: called to deliver me of my second Boy — Ralph Thrale — was quite of Lawrence's Opinion as to Lucy, said the old Humour was repelled upon the Brain & advised me to call in James. I did so, and he like the rest inveighed loudly against Pinkstan — yet hoping foul Bowels might still be the Cause, he would have her once more roughly Purged which She was; & all the Maids were enraged, as they thought evacuation the sole Cause of her Complaints. A large Blister on the Head had however the best Effect of any thing; the Child however growing worse & her Fever increasing even to Delirium, they bled her with Leeches w:^{ch} rouzed her once /more/ & She even eat with an Appetite Our Spirits were then raised; fresh Blisters were applied, & the Camphor Julep administered: this threw her into a copious Perspiration and I think kept her alive till the 22:^d of November, when She expired, being on that Day four Years & 5: Months old. — 24: Nov: 1773.[9]

Queeney behaved with the greatest propriety both on this Occasion, & the late melancholy one of my Mother's death, but Harry shewed only a small Share of Sensibility for his Grandmama, and none at all for poor Lucy.

Susan's Health improves surprizingly, She has mended ever since the Measles. The Rupture is well, & She gets more Strength and Spirits. 30: Nov: 1773.

On 5 December, Ralph, the Thrales' ninth child, was christened at St. Leonard's. Thrale's pride in having a second son can be seen by the name chosen for the boy, Ralph, in honor of his father whom he so greatly revered. Johnson's hint that he would like to be a sponsor was ignored; aristocrats were chosen instead: two of Thrale's Worcestershire friends, Lord Sandys of Ombersley Court (a loyal New Col-

---

[9] Lucy's mastoid abscess led to an abscess on the brain which caused her death. Antibiotics, with possible surgery, are now given for mastoiditis as soon as it is diagnosed. And today there is every hope for a quick and complete restoration of health.

lege, Oxford man) and William Henry Lyttelton of Little Hagley (who would soon be Lord Westcote). Mrs. Thrale's friend, Miss Burgoyne, daughter of Sir Roger and Lady Frances Burgoyne (a sister of Lord Halifax), was the godmother. These sponsors are noted in the *Family Book*, but not until May 1775.

31: Dec.ʳ 1773.
I am now come to the End of the Year 1773. during the last six Months of which, I have suffered the Loss of a Parent, a Child, & the almost certain Hopes of an ample Fortune, in the full expectation of which I had been bred up from twelve Years old. In the midst of this Distress I have brought a Baby, which seems to be in some measure affected by my Vexations; he is heavy stupid & drowsy, though very large; & what those who do not observe him as I do — call a fine Boy — but I see no Wit sparkle in his Eyes like the Mother in Gay's Fables. What is most singular is my own recovery from a Scene of Sorrow & Trouble scarcely to be equalled; from the Loss of the finest Girl I almost ever saw, & the cutting Mortification of seeing my Estate snatched from me in a manner most base & vile by wretches whom I despise. My Uncle too, upon whose Lap I lived for 20 Years — (the happiest I have known;) is now wholly lost to me, & injuriously as he has treated me I half regret him: I had depended upon ending my Days at dear Offley, where they first began to be agreeable, & had relied upon enjoying the Society of my new Friends, where I had once been merry with my old ones. I had indulged the Vanity of thinking how I should enrich my Family, how my Husband would double his Attention, my Children their Duty, & my Acquaintance their Flattery.

How I should manage when possessed of the Hertfordshire Estate, was the chief enquiry of my solitary Hours; & many a delightful Moment /has been spent/ in recalling the beloved Places to my View where I once was happy in the favour of all my Relations Friends & Admirers. Whose Disappointment then can surpass mine? and grievous & heavy I confess it is for to bear! but I hope it has kindled no bad Passions in my Breast — I have not neglected my duties because my Heart was full; nor appeared less chearful before those who have no business to partake my Concerns: I have never failed to hear the same stated Lessons I ever heard, nor suffered the Children to be neglected because I was miserable: As I have now no soothing Friend to tell my Grief to, it will perhaps sink the sooner into Insensibility;

D.ʳ Johnson is very kind as can be, & I ought to be thankful that M.ʳ Thrale does not, as most Husbands would — aggravate by Insult and Anger the Sorrows of my Mind. It however happily for me — operates upon him quite another way: he would rather be without the Estate I I [sic] believe, than hold it of a Wife: He therefore bids me keep up my Spirits, for that we do not want it, & that He would never have lived at Offley if we had had it &c. ——

So Farewell to all I formerly loved — to my Mother, my House in Hertfordshire, my lovely Lucy — and to this accursed Year 1773.

3: March 1774.
Susanna Arabella Thrale on this Day first went to my Friend M.ʳˢ Cumyns; who having passed thro' various Shades of Life now keeps a high-prized Boarding School at Kensington. a Situation considerably below her Abilities, but her Life has been unfortunate. Under her Care I expect our Susan will improve much more than at home, where She is not exceedingly admired, and where She will not learn, because She must not be fretted. Her long Series of ill health has given her a Habit of self-Indulgence, which I do not chuse to undertake the breaking through, as I am not partial to her Person, & might be too rough with her perhaps — so She goes a Carte blanche to M.ʳˢ Cumyns, who will make a point of doing her [best] by the Girl, as we have shewn her no little Friendship.

Mrs. Cumyns (Betsy Thornton) had been one of Mrs. Thrale's earliest friends. The Thornton family lived near East Hyde, her grandmother Cotton's house, and during Hester's visits there the little girls played together and became inseparable friends. The two were exact contemporaries, born on the same day of the same year.

Time passed and Betsy married a "M.ʳ Cumyns who was a shocking Scoundrel." He took all her money and reduced her "to the necessity of keeping a School in Kensington Square" (*Thraliana*, p. 291). Mrs. Cumyns, though no longer attractive in appearance, was a fine, good-hearted woman, with a great deal of useful knowledge and more than a little ornamental knowledge. Her school was well thought of, and Mrs. Thrale felt safe in entrusting Susan to her friend's care, though the child was not yet four. Dr. Johnson gave his Susy a Bible and Prayer Book as a going-away present.

9: May 1774.

When Queeney was about 8 Years old, She one Day was diverting herself by enumerating all the Misfortunes She could think of, and saying how they should all happen to me. Papa sayd She shall die, so shall Gmama; Mͬ Johnson shall be affronted & never come here again, Harry shall go to Sea and be cast away, and I shall die — poor Lucy must die too, & you shall have nothing left at all but Susan for your Child, & Kit (that was a poor wretch of a Fellow) for your Man.

I think I am hastening to that State for my Part — My Mother & Lucy are gone — Thank God the rest are all well however and Sophy bids fair to be a very fine Girl — of the same kind as Lucy, but far inferior — She is nevertheless a pleasing Child & quite healthy & stout thank God.—

The Thrales had been considering the possibility of making a trip, not simply an excursion of a few days, but a journey lasting two months or so, like Johnson's very successful excursion to the Hebrides. (He had returned at the end of November, full of his adventures, and eager to set out for more with the Thrales.) The plan was for a classical ramble through Italy.

The spring seemed an ideal time: Perkins was managing well at the brewery, the children were in good health, and Mrs. Thrale for once was not pregnant. Johnson was fired with enthusiasm for Italy. Thrale was wholly amenable, and Baretti had agreed to be courier for the party.

Queeney (not yet ten) wished very much to go. In his dialogues, Baretti had been preparing her for the trip, perfecting her language and explaining the manners and customs of the country. "How happy I shall be," said Esteruccia, "when I see half a dozen of cardinals!" Why? asked Maestro. Because, she said, they "dress very fine, and ride about in coaches, like so many English ladies" (Baretti, p. 70). One evening there was so much talk of the "future journey to Rome" at supper that Queeney "dreamt of nothing else the whole night long" (Baretti, p. 93). Next morning in her dialogue with Baretti, they "flew" over the whole route — delicious enchantment — until Mrs. Thrale's whistle "destroyed at once the whole charm of [their] flying" (Baretti, p. 108).

Mrs. Thrale naturally wanted to see Italy and its classical treasures, but not at this particular time. There were too many problems with her mother's Welsh estate (now hers) that ought to be settled first.

Johnson said her mind should be on higher things, and was so sure of the Italian journey that he reported the plan to Boswell. When the latter wrote on 13 May 1774, he was fearful that the party might be going abroad before he could come to London to see Johnson.

In this letter Boswell told the Thrales how shocked he was to hear of the sudden death of Oliver Goldsmith, who had died on 4 April of a fever which Johnson claimed was made "more violent by uneasiness of mind. His debts began to be heavy, and all his resources were exhausted" (*Letters* 357). The Streatham circle was saddened by the loss of Goldsmith and Mrs. Thrale fretted over the report that in his fatal fever Goldsmith had doctored himself with James's fever powder, a remedy she often used in the Thrale nursery.

To return to the Italian trip, the project was abandoned in the end because of Mrs. Thrale's worries about her Welsh property. She had put little Harry's "life into lease" for it, as the expression went, so it would be his one day. She wished to inspect the property and meet with the old agent, Edward Bridge. It was important to discuss general problems of management with him, and the particular problem of the mortgage payment, which Lady Salusbury now claimed was owed to her. Thrale and Johnson were sympathetic and, though they were not stirred by the thought of a trip to Wales, they agreed to go for Mrs. Thrale's sake.

So the Italian excursion was postponed and Johnson turned his mind to an examination of Salusbury papers pertaining to Wales: deeds, legal documents, correspondence from Bridge, and letters from various members of the family. Johnson found the task so absorbing that he looked at other papers in the mass of material, even though they did not bear on the issue, such as John Salusbury's Nova Scotian diaries and Mrs. Thrale's letters from her tutor, Dr. Collier. (Her early mentor, two years older than Johnson, was still alive, but she had lost all touch with him.)

*[A]s my Father's Estate is now become mine, I think it very fit — so does M*ʳ *Thrale, that we should go down thither & shew ourselves: we therefore propose to take our Queeney & to leave both the/little/Girls under the Care of M*ʳˢ *Cumyns where they will be safer than with Ser-*

vants, & Sophy will be learning some thing: besides — I see Susan improve every Day, and begin to have good hopes of her myself.

5: July 1774.
Tomorrow we set forward on our Journey to Wales; Yesterday, — no! this very Morning I set Sophy safe at Kensington with her Sister, who is so altered for the better it quite charms me; I never saw any thing like the Improvement only from March to July — 'tis incredible. yet I am very lowspirited at leaving them, — the two Boys too — what will become of them? Ralph is just eight Months old, a fine Boy to look at, but strangely backward somehow in his Understanding — however if he lives & thrives — that will come; Old Nurse doats upon him, & will I am sure be careful; my sweet Harry! I have ordered him to board at Thomas's School during our Absence, and come home only to bed; — for I thought he might take Liberties of chusing his own Dinners if he tabled here, and not only eat too much perhaps, & of improper Things — but turn his Mind too much towards his Belly the only Fault I think he naturally has.

I can do no better for them all, yet somehow I am not satisfied with myself: had my Mother been living perhaps I had done better; perhaps I have lost my Virtue with my Parent: She would not have approved my leaving them, & then I should not have gone. I shall now perhaps neglect them more & more — Oh God forbid! and grant us if it be thy blessed will, a a [sic] happy meeting at my return from Wales. I cannot write for crying tonight, I am so very low spirited: I shall perhaps be better in the Morning. Adieu to my Dear Children then! — Adieu indeed, for to God's care do I commit them — late at night
5: July 1774.

The journey to Wales took place from 5 July to 30 September 1774, and both Mrs. Thrale and Johnson kept diaries. Though the main purpose of the trip was to inspect Mrs. Thrale's property, the usual travelers' sightseeing was undertaken as well, and social visits along the way added pleasure. A few acquaintances were renewed, and Johnson and the Thrales introduced each other to their various friends and relations.

The Thrales, Queeney, and Johnson set forth from Streatham and after dropping Baretti in London they went to Barnet, where they stopped briefly at the Mitre (managed by a former employee of Lady

Lade). On to St. Albans, where they had a good dinner with Thrale's first cousin, Ralph Smith of Kingsbury, and his wife, Mary. The Smiths' hospitality was warm and Thrale had much trouble getting his party away to visit the widow of his other first cousin, Henry Smith of New House, St. Michaels, and her eighteen-year-old son, Henry. This young man made an excellent impression upon Thrale — and he was not to forget him.

Finally, the party drove on toward Dunstable. As they came close to Offley, many memories were revived for Mrs. Thrale. The countryside was little changed: she remembered where she had walked and fished with her father, where her uncle's first wife, Anna Maria Salusbury, had fainted in the coach, where her uncle had hunted and she had watched him, hill-topping in the postchaise — and the place where she had written "foolish verses which were praised by [her] foolisher Friends" (Broadley, p. 159).

The party spent the night at Dunstable, and the next morning headed for Lichfield. Johnson had proposed rising at six to make the heavy day's journey (eighty-three miles) before dark. All were up at that time except Johnson, and he appeared around ten, with the result that it was midnight by the time the party reached the Swan in Lichfield. And Queeney had caught cold.

The visit to Lichfield meant a great deal to Johnson. His friends there had heard about the Thrales and he was eager that they should make a good impression. When Mrs. Thrale joined him next day in a "morning night gown and close cap" Johnson sent her back to change into something "more gay and splendid" (Broadley, p. 160). This accomplished, they all set out, first to Mr. Green's Museum, a "curious collection of all natural and artificial rarities" (Broadley, p. 161), which must have interested Queeney but discouraged her when she compared it with her own sparse collection in the cabinet Johnson had given her. Next they visited the Cathedral, and then went to the house where Johnson had been born. (Mrs. Thrale lingered there, deeply moved.) After seeing the birthplace, they paid a call on Lucy Porter, Johnson's step-daughter. Miss Porter — or "Mrs." according to her courtesy title — was now almost sixty. She was found at cards with friends, but she immediately abandoned the game and gave her full attention to the Thrales, showing them about her fine house and pointing out the portraits of herself and her mother, Johnson's Tetty. In the evening the Thrales and Johnson visited Elizabeth Aston at Stow

Hill. This maiden lady, a year older than Johnson, showed them great courtesy, and it was clear to everyone that she had a particular regard for Johnson and that it was reciprocated. Mrs. Thrale found "some dignity and much oddity both in the mansion and the possessor," but she admitted that Elizabeth Aston was "a high-bred woman, quite the remains of an old beauty, lofty and civil at once" (Broadley, p. 162).

Johnson noted Anna Seward in his journal, simply giving her name. Mrs. Thrale's comment (not in her diary) was that "Dr. Johnson would not suffer me to speak to Miss Seward" (*Life*, V, 429, n.1). This self-satisfied celebrity took a condescending view of Johnson; in return he thought little of either her verse or herself. But Mrs. Thrale was disappointed not to meet the "Swan of Lichfield," a year her junior.

Apart from this omission, all the great of Lichfield met and were charmed by the Thrales: this included Dr. Erasmus Darwin (grandfather of Charles) and Peter Garrick (eldest brother of David). There was something around Peter Garrick's eyes that reminded Mrs. Thrale of her mother; Queeney saw the resemblance too, and so did Sam and the other servants with them. (These did not include a maid for Mrs. Thrale. She was such a novice at traveling, she recorded, that she had not thought to bring a maid — a fact she regretted throughout the trip.)

After Lichfield the party went to Ashbourne, where Queeney's cold became complicated with a cough and an attack of worms. From 9 to 20 July the Thrales enjoyed the liberal hospitality of Dr. John Taylor, Johnson's early friend at the Lichfield Grammar School as well as at Oxford. Taylor, a substantial divine who enjoyed good living, had a fine house in Ashbourne, handsomely furnished. Everything around him was "both elegant and splendid": beautiful pictures, "a glorious Harpsichord," a lawn, a lake, and a waterfall, "deer in his paddock, pheasants in his menagerie, the finest coach horses in the County, the largest horned cattle" in England, and "a Bull of an enormous size" (Broadley, p. 164). His table was bountiful and the wines excellent.

Nothing was too much trouble for the Thrales' obliging host: there were dinners at Okeover, excursions to see the gardens at Ilam, to see Chatsworth, the great Devonshire House (and library), to see the crags of Dovedale, and to see Kedleston, a house newly built for Lord Scarsdale — also to see Mr. Meynell's kennel of fine fox hounds.

Thrale's own pack had been sold (Fellowes, p. 25). Taylor's kindness was overpowering, and when the party left Ashbourne on 20 July, Mrs. Thrale worried that her relations would not stand up to Johnson's friends.

There is a fleeting romantic note that should be mentioned. During their stay in Derbyshire, Taylor's friend, Edward Okeover, introduced the Thrales to an accomplished youth of seventeen, William Gilpin, in his first year at Queen's College, Oxford. William was traveling about England with a Christ College, Cambridge friend, John Parker of Browsholme, Clitheroe; both were seeking pleasure and improvement during the long summer holiday. Gilpin was captivated by nine-year-old Hester Maria Thrale (despite her cold) and he declared that he would speak to his father about her upon his return home.

After leaving Ashbourne, the travelers set out for Cheshire, passing through Buxton, where Mrs. Thrale bathed in the delightful waters. They went on to Macclesfield for the night, and next day came to Combermere Abbey, where, as a little girl, Mrs. Thrale had spent many happy days with her uncle, Sir Robert Cotton. This spacious place (once belonging to the Benedictines) had, at various times, had additions of different materials: timber, stone, brick, plaster — "the best house that ever I saw of that kind," Dr. Johnson commented (Broadley, p. 228). It was situated on a large mere, or lake, on which was a small island with a summer house, and great shade trees. The property consisted of several thousand acres — planted fields, rolling pasture, and woodland.

Combermere Abbey, for the last twenty-six years, had belonged to Sir Robert Cotton's brother, Sir Lynch. He and his wife were now close to seventy and not very well nor very active, but they showed their niece and her party every civility during their stay (21 to 26 July). Mrs. Thrale was self-conscious about her uncle and aunt; Sir Lynch was absurdly rustic in his odd ways and his sense of humor was embarrassing (Johnson called him "gross").

Mrs. Thrale found Lady Cotton as empty as ever. (Johnson called her "weak and ignorant.") The greatest amusement encountered during the stay at Combermere was the runaway marriage of the youngest daughter of the house, Hetty Cotton, who had visited the Thrales early in their marriage. Hetty, now in her mid-twenties, was five years older than her bridegroom, Corbet D'Avenant of Adderley Hall. He was a son of Colonel Thomas D'Avenant, whose present (second)

COMBERMERE ABBEY

LLEWENNY HALL

FROM A DRAWING BY BIRA, ENGRAVED BY ANGUS

wife was Hetty's eldest sister, Elizabeth. Quite a family situation. Mrs. Thrale records:

Mr. Thrale and Dr. Johnson lent their assistance to pacify the Parents [of Miss Hetty] and smooth the objections, but . . . great wrath is expected from the young gentleman's Father and Mother . . . (Broadley, p. 178)

On 26 July the party left Combermere Abbey and proceeded to Chester, where they saw the Cathedral and Johnson and Queeney walked the city wall, which, he recorded in his diary, contained "one mile three quarters, and one hundred and one yards" (a fact Mrs. Thrale said he could have learned "from any one"). She was very angry with Johnson for keeping Queeney up beyond her bedtime, walking the wall in the dark, where some accident could easily have befallen her — and him as well (*Life*, V, 585). What remained of the night was spent at their inn, and the next morning the party proceeded to North Wales, to the Vale of Clwyd in Flintshire, where they visited Sir Lynch's eldest son, Robert Cotton, and his wife at Llewenny Hall.

This enormous house had also belonged to Sir Robert Cotton, and was another place where Mrs. Thrale had made lengthy visits as a child. Llewenny had a great deal of superfluous space, a vast hall and a gallery that was "75 of my steps" (Broadley, p. 182). Combermere was far more livable; Sir Robert had chosen this in the end, and it was Sir Lynch's choice now. His eldest son, Robert, had Llewenny — plenty of room for a growing family.

Mrs. Thrale had known "Bobby" from childhood. He was two and a half years her senior, and uncle Robert had teased her by saying she should marry her cousin. Hester had replied that she liked "Coz Rowley" better (the next of many brothers) but, with her usual tact as a visitor, had quickly added "but I like you best of all, & will marry who ever you please for I'm sure you know best" (*Thraliana*, p. 284, n. 4).

She had seen a good deal of Bobby Cotton when he was a Westminster boy; he had spent every weekend and holiday with Mrs. Salusbury and Hester, though the lodging they then had in Charles Street was very cramped for space, "a two Pair of Stairs Room for our Bed Chamber, and the Use of a Parlour — Boarding included — for 40ᶠ a year" (*Thraliana*, p. 290). They placed a little bureau bed beside their own for Bobby.

He had grown into a fine man, upright, capable, generous, and charming. And seven years earlier (1767) he had married Frances Stapleton of Bodryddan, a Flintshire heiress, pretty, efficient, modest, and sweet-tempered. The atmosphere at Llewenny was very different from Combermere. The younger Cottons were not provincial, they were cultivated and gracious, their hospitality was open-handed and their company delightful except for the fact, Johnson complained, that Fanny was "the poorest talker . . . that ever opened lips" (Hayward, II, 323).

The Cottons had five children by the time of the Thrale visit, and Stapleton Cotton, "little Rapid," the baby born the year before, much admired by the Thrales and Johnson, was one day to become a Field-Marshal.[10] All the children adored their mother — and watching them made Mrs. Thrale feel badly about having left her own babies.

She was particularly concerned when a letter arrived from Baretti (in charge at Streatham) informing her that Harry had a black eye and Ralph was cutting teeth with pain. These distant worries soon bothered her less, however, than an immediate one: Queeney had a pain in her head (a frightening thing, remembering Lucy), and she recorded in her travel journal, "I have nobody to tell how it vexes me. Mr. Thrale will not be conversed with by *me* on any subject, as a friend, or comforter, or adviser. Every day more and more do I feel the loss of my Mother. My present Companions have too much philosophy for me. One cannot disburthen one's mind . . ." (Broadley, pp. 193–194).

While at Llewenny (28 July to 17 August) the Cottons, Thrales, and Johnson saw the ruins of Denbigh Castle, attended services at St. Asaph Cathedral, and tried to see the library, but the key was lost. They visited Tremeirchion Church, where Mrs. Thrale's father, John

[10] The Field-Marshal, Sir Stapleton Cotton, 6th Bt. (1809) and 1st Viscount Combermere (1827), made Combermere Abbey his main residence. This property passed to his son, Wellington Henry Cotton. The 2nd Viscount let Combermere Abbey to Elizabeth, Empress of Austria, for two seasons of hunting (1881–1882); and from the end of the nineteenth century, for twenty years, he let the property to Katherine, Duchess of Westminster, widow of the first Duke.

In 1918 Combermere Abbey was sold by the 4th Viscount to Sir Kenneth Crossley, Bt., and upon his death in 1957 (his son and grandson having predeceased him), it passed to his granddaughter, now Viscountess Garnock. The property is being farmed at present by the Garnocks, who are in the process of restoring the house to its eighteenth-century size, removing later additions and the Gothicized stucco facing of 1820.

Salusbury, was buried, and she was distressed by the condition of this small building: the "seats all tumbling about," "the Altar rail falling," "the cloth upon the table in a thousand holes, and the floor strewed with rushes" (Broadley, p. 186).

Throughout the visit, Mrs. Thrale, assisted by her husband and by Johnson, worked with the agent Bridge on the problems of her Welsh estate. They made several visits from Llewenny Hall to Bach-y-Graig, which was less than two miles away. Bach-y-Graig had been built in the sixteenth century by Sir Richard Clough, the second husband of Catherine of Berayne, Mrs. Thrale's ancestress.[11] It was a red brick structure, in the Flemish style, six storeys high. With its curious pyramid shape and its private observatory on the roof, the house was the wonder of the whole Vale of Clwyd when it was built. Now it was in a dilapidated state. Thrale, nevertheless, found his wife's "poor old house" better than he expected; Johnson and Mrs. Thrale found it worse. The floors had been stolen, the windows stopped; the trees were decayed, or lopped, or too young to have value.

Bridge was a scoundrel, Mrs. Thrale soon discovered. Her mother had thought him "the worthiest of Mankind, [but he has] plundered us for 20 Years most grossly . . ." (*Thraliana*, p. 315). "Mr. Thrale persecutes Bridge every day for this odious account, but cannot get it" (Broadley, p. 206). Finally the account came and, after it was reviewed, Mrs. Thrale dismissed Bridge and arranged with her Bach-y-Graig tenant to pay rent to her cousin, Robert Cotton.

Mrs. Thrale left Llewenny Hall regretfully, for a close family friendship had been renewed. Everyone had enjoyed the visit — she pressed the Cottons to come to London soon and they promised that they would.

From Llewenny the travelers proceeded to Conway and to Bangor (where they visited the Cathedral and its library). On to Caernarvon, and from there, Mrs. Thrale led them to Bodvel Hall,[12] the house where she had been born. "I picked up an old woman who was at my chris-

[11] Catherine of Berayne, Mrs. Thrale claimed, was a granddaughter of Richard Velville of Berayne, an illegitimate son of Henry VII.

Catherine's marital career was remarkable. She was first the wife of Sir John Salusbury (who built Llewenny), then the wife of Richard Clough, then of Maurice Wynn, and finally of Edward Thelwall. She had so many distinguished descendants that she was known as the "Mother of Wales."

[12] Bodvel Hall and some 350 acres surrounding now belong to Mr. & Mrs. G. E. Morris, who farm the property.

tening, and she told me many things of my poor dear Mother, what she suffered at my birth" (Broadley, p. 201). Johnson wrote that she "remembered the rooms [of the house], and wandred over them, with recollection of her childhood. This species of pleasure is always melancholy. The walk was cut down, and the pond was dry. Nothing was better" (*Life*, V, 450).

On the return from Caernarvon to Bangor, as they passed through the lovely hills and valleys near Mount Snowdon, Queeney counted goats; her father promised her a penny for each seen, and short-sighted Dr. Johnson kept the account: "[Queeney's] goats, one hundred and forty-nine, I think" (*Life*, V, 451, n. 2).

From Bangor the party went to visit at Gwaynynog, the fine house of John Myddleton, an Oxford man and contemporary of Thrale. From 29 August to 7 September Myddleton provided splendid entertainment, and despite her business worries and another Streatham report from Baretti, this time giving news that Harry had made himself sick by eating too many cherries, Mrs. Thrale enjoyed herself greatly. "Here we are loved, esteemed, and honoured, and here I daresay we might spend the whole Winter if we would" (Broadley, p. 206). Myddleton was so flattered to have entertained Johnson that a few years later he erected an urn in his park to commemorate the great moralist's visit.[13]

On 7 September the Thrales and Johnson left Gwaynynog and "set out in search of fresh adventures" (Broadley, p. 207). They passed through Wrexham, saw Chirk Castle, traveled through Oswestry, Llanrhaiadr, and on into Shropshire, through Wenlock and Bridgnorth, to Ombersley Court in Worcestershire. Here, from 14 to 16 September, they visited little Ralph Thrale's godfather, good-natured Lord Sandys, an enormously big, soft-spoken, scholarly man. He had been married since 1769 to a rich widow. Lady Sandys had physical disabilities and was not intellectual nor handsome, but her good humor and kindness made up for all deficiencies. "I liked her the first day," Mrs. Thrale wrote, "and loved her the last" (Broadley, p. 210).

At Ombersley the party was entertained with a liberality of friendship which could not have been surpassed, and it was here that John-

---

[13] This gracious act was not pleasing to Johnson, who wrote to Mrs. Thrale on 18 September 1777 that it "looks like an intention to bury me alive" (*Letters* 548).

The beautiful urn is still at Gwaynynog, which property is at present (1975) owned by Captain Oliver Burton.

BACH-Y-GRAIG HOUSE

FROM A DRAWING BY HOOPER

CATHERINE OF BERAYNE

son ate all the peaches he wanted (only twice in his life, at Ombersley and once at Streatham, did he have his fill of the fruit — *Thraliana* p. 186). "Lady Sandys's care of me was tender . . . "[14] (Broadley, p. 210).

The next stay (16 to 19 September) was with Ralph Thrale's other godfather, William Henry Lyttelton. Something went wrong at Little Hagley, for it was not the happy time promised three years earlier, when their host had said he would make "so much" of a visit. The usually good-humored Lyttelton seemed distracted; his pretty wife was indifferent and, like Fanny Cotton, a poor conversationalist. Lyttelton, after being a widower for almost ten years, had taken a second wife in February, Caroline Bristow, daughter of a late sub-Governor of the South Sea Company, and he may well have been more interested in his bride than his guests, anxious about her reactions to the domineering Doctor and to his friend of bachelor days, with talkative wife and precocious child. Or perhaps as joint hosts the Lytteltons had not yet formed an easy pattern of hospitality; at any rate, the hostess forced Mrs. Thrale to play cards against her will (though she won three shillings), and as Johnson sat to read a while and then walked about "Mr. Lyttelton advertised if he did not use his candle to put it out" (Broadley, p. 211).

Queeney spent most of her birthday (17 September) playing in the grounds of Hagley Park,[15] the beautiful great house nearby, owned at the time by their host's nephew, Thomas Lyttelton. Johnson's birthday, Sunday, 18 September, was spent at Little Hagley — there were no birthday celebrations.

On 19 September, in cold and heavy rain the Thrales and Johnson "made haste away from a place where all were offended" (*Life*, V, 457). On their way to Birmingham, they stopped, and despite the disagreeable weather made a visit to The Leasowes, which had belonged to William Shenstone, the poet (a Pembroke College man). With painstaking care Shenstone had created this ravishing house and property but, ironically, had not lived to enjoy it. The Leasowes charmed Mrs. Thrale.

[14] Ombersley Court still belongs to the Sandys family; its present owner (1975) is the 7th Baron Sandys.

[15] Hagley Park is still a Lyttelton property, the seat of the 10th Viscount Cobham, Governor-General of New Zealand 1957–1962, and since 1963 Lord Lieutenant of Worcestershire. Unlike his ancestor, he is unfailingly hospitable.

In Birmingham the Thrales met Johnson's early friend, Edmund Hector, and his widowed sister, Mrs. Careless. Breakfast the following morning was cooked by Mrs. Careless, and Johnson told them later that he had once been in love with her. As Mrs. Thrale recollected the old lady's figure, she "thought she had the remains of a beauty" (Broadley, p. 214), and was disappointed that she had not observed her more closely. She was even more disappointed not to have asked Edmund Hector for some juvenile anecdotes about Johnson, but by the time the party reached Birmingham, Mrs. Thrale, who had not been well since they left Llewenny, was feeling too wretched to ask Hector any questions about Johnson's childhood.

From Birmingham the travelers set out for Oxford, and along the way met their friend, William Seward, who joined the party. They stopped at Blenheim, seat of the Duke of Marlborough, inspected the park and the library, and then continued on to Oxford. Here they visited several of the colleges, in particular Oriel, where Seward had been, and University, Thrale's college. They dined at the latter and drank "tea in the Common Room [and had] a World of talk" (Broadley, p. 216). During their stay they also went to New Inn Hall, where Thrale had been fourteen months earlier at the time he was given his honorary degree. Robert Chambers, though still nominal Principal, was now in Bengal. In March he had married Jane Wilton, whom Johnson described as "a girl of sixteen, exquisitely beautiful." Chambers, "with his lawyer's tongue, persuaded [her] to take her chance with him in the East" (*Letters* 348). Less than a month after their marriage, Chambers, his wife, and his mother sailed on a ship for Bengal in the company of three other Supreme Court judges.

On 28 September, Mrs. Thrale recorded in her travel journal that, on the way from Oxford to Beaconsfield to visit Edmund Burke and his family, the party paused in the delightful countryside near Benson to inspect Crowmarsh Battle Farm,[16] Thrale's Oxfordshire property

---

[16] Crowmarsh Battle Farm: The word "Battle" comes from the fact that the farm was one of the lands William the Conqueror gave to Battle Abbey at Hastings, as part of its endowment. When this property was taken over by Henry VIII, it was farmed by various tenants. In the latter part of the seventeenth century London speculators bought Crowmarsh Battle Farm, and in 1696 it was sold to Thomas Cowslad of Newbury for £5,300.

In 1742, on the bankruptcy of Cowslad's son, Crowmarsh Battle Farm was sold to Ralph and Henry Thrale (the latter only fourteen at the time) for £1,997.

CROWMARSH BATTLE FARM

of some 400 acres. (From Crowmarsh, according to her marriage settlement, Mrs. Thrale received an annual income of £200, Thrale receiving the remainder.)

Thrale's tenant, Robert Lovegrove, seemed to have everything "neat
and bright" about the place, though Mrs. Lovegrove was not helpful
— she was a drunkard (Broadley, p. 217). Mrs. Thrale gave no indication in her diary of Queeney's first impressions of Crowmarsh, a
place she was to own one day, though this was little guessed at the
moment. Johnson's diary gave no mention whatever of the visit.

It was late at night when the Thrales and Johnson arrived at the
Burkes', but they were greeted with open arms. Everyone anticipated
an enjoyable and leisurely visit, but unfortunately their pleasure was
terminated after a single day. As Mrs. Thrale recorded in her travel
journal, on the morning of 30 September:

When I rose Mr. Thrale informed me that the Parliament was suddenly dissolved and that all the World was to bustle, that we were to go to Southwark,
not to Streatham, and canvass away. (Broadley, p. 219)

It was a bitter disappointment for Mrs. Thrale to have to settle in
Deadman's Place before she had had any time to be in the country:

I thought to have lived at Streatham in quiet and comfort, have kissed my
children and cuffed them by turns, and had a place always for them to play
in, and here I must be shut up in that odious dungeon, where nobody will
come near me, the children are to be sick for want of air, and I am never to
see a face but Mr. Johnson's. Oh, what a life that is! and how truly do I ab-
hor it! (Broadley, p. 219)

Back to Southwark the travelers went.

In thinking over the Welsh journey, Mrs. Thrale realized that a
good deal had been accomplished in the way of her estate business,
and also in the matter of maintaining family ties. But she was sadly
disappointed that none of her companions had appreciated the beauties
of Wales. Johnson preferred to read a book rather than to enjoy
a prospect. Thrale was uncommunicative; Queeney more burdensome
than a two-year-old, for she had to be dressed, mended, combed, and
packed — and her cold, cough, headaches, and worms had been troublesome. Mrs. Thrale herself, from the time of their departure from
Llewenny, had felt ill all the time, and had hated traveling over the
rough roads — she was pregnant again.

Her record continues in the *Family Book*.

30: Sept.ʳ 1774.

*I returned safe home from my long Tour; bro.ᵗ Queeney safe back,
called on my Girls at Kensington, whom I found quite well; (I had
no Time to examine mental Improvements.) and got in good Time
to Streatham where Harry met & rejoyced over us very kindly: he is
wonderfully grown & seems in perfect health tho' having lost a few
Teeth gives him an odd Look, but he appears happy & chearful, and
full of Spirits. Little Ralph is more visibly improved than any of 'em,
except Susan; who now commences both Wit and Beauty forsooth;
She is in no respect the same Child She was two or three Years /ago:/
so that if She did not grow very like Harry, I tell Mʳˢ Cumyns I should
think She had changed her.   Every thing however happens to per-
plex me, & now that I hoped to come home & be quiet examine my Children & see what deficiencies could be supplied, and enjoy a little Quiet
after the hurrying Life I have been leading of late — here is the General Election broke out, duce take it! —— and my Attendance is
wanted in the Borough.*

2: Oct.ʳ 1774.

*Before I launch into this new Confusion let me mention a Word of my
little ones; Queeney kept her Birthday running about Hagley Park.
She was pretty well all the Journey, except a severe Cold & cough
whilst we were at Ashburne, & now & then a Slight Touch of the
Worms. but nothing really formidable. upon the whole She has been
active, intrepid and observing: & tho' we may have lost some Italian,
we have I think gained some Images which will make more than amends.
Nothing escapes this Girl's penetration, nothing intimidates her Courage, nothing flutters her Fancy. — Mean Inns, or splendid Apartments
— for we have experienced both, find her Mind always prepared to
enjoy the one & to defy the other. Mʳ Johnson tells how She wished
to see a Storm when we cross'd over to Anglesey, & how She rode 15
Miles once on a Single hard Trotting in the Night among the Moun-
tains of Snowdon. These are certainly noble Qualities and great performances for a Girl scarce ten Years old, yet is Queeney no very desirable Companion —*

*Sullen, malicious & perverse; desirous of tormenting me even by
hurting herself, & resolute to utter nothing in my hearing, that might
give Credit to either of us. She often tells me what She thought on
such an Occasion what She could have said &c. when we are alone,*

but has an affectation of playing the Agnes [17] when we are in Company together. However when my Back is turned, & She sees no Danger of giving me any Delight, her Tongue is voluble enough I find, & her Manner so particularly pleasing, that a Young Fellow who saw her in Derbyshire half a Dozen times persuaded his foolish Father at his Return to propose him to marry her; protesting he would rather wait seven Years for Miss Thrale, than have any other Girl he ever saw in his Life. — an early Conquest I must confess! so much for Hetty, or Queeney or Niggey as we called Her.

Queeney's suitor was William Gilpin, the Oxford student, who had met the travelers in Derbyshire and vowed that upon his return he would speak to his father.

This gentleman, the Reverend Mr. William Gilpin, was far from "foolish"; he was a distinguished scholar, artist, and headmaster of the Cheam School, which was about ten miles from Streatham. After meeting Queeney, it is likely he agreed with his son that the young lady had unusual possibilities, and it would be wise to take time by the forelock.

During the past summer, at the same time that young William Gilpin had been acquainting himself with the beauties of Derbyshire, Lancashire, and Yorkshire, headmaster Gilpin had been making a sketching tour through Hampshire, Sussex, and Kent. Life in the Gilpin family would not be dull.

Ralph is most exceedingly come on; grown vastly handsome, & much more intelligent; has a healthy Colour in his Cheeks, & promises mighty well indeed — he makes no Effort to talk however, but Nurse is beginning to set him on his Feet. She is not a little proud of him.

Harry is the very best Boy in the World, has minded his Business as If I had been watching him, I shall make Mr Jones [18] a Present — I see there has been great pains taken on both Sides, and no Faults found on either — that is sweet.

The Girls do very well as to health, and Mrs Cumyns writes me wonderful Acc.^{ts} of Susan's prowess in the literary Way, so wonderful

---

[17] Thrale-Johnson family talk: they called a creeping, clinging-vine kind of woman after Molière's Agnes in *L'École des Femmes*.

[18] John Jones was a cousin who lived at nearby Mitcham. The Thrales had asked him to keep an eye on Harry during their absence in Wales.

indeed that I do not believe them; but when this odious Election is over — I shall see. The Truth is Susan is so changed in her Face & Figure that if every thing else keeps Pace — all She says may be true. I used to joke with my poor Mother & say — Susan would be come the pillar of the Family perhaps — as every thing happens contrary to one's Expectations — little thinking it however — but as Goneril says in King Lear

Jesters do oft prove Prophets! — [19]

Now for this filthy Election! I must leave Queeney to the Care of M. Baretti I believe, or him to hers; & She must keep House here at Streatham, while I go fight the Opposition in the Borough: Oh my sweet Mother! how every thing makes your Loss more heavy! 2: Oct: 1774.*

The campaign of 1774 was a bitter contest. Thrale, representing the Ministry, faced four other candidates in Southwark, and feelings ran high in the Borough. As before, there was rioting in the streets, and again the mob was led by Wilkes's "Patriots." The choice of this name for Wilkes's rabble infuriated Johnson, it was an outrageous deception. He took the word as a title for his pamphlet, *The Patriot*, in support of Thrale. Thrale was the *true* "patriot," devoted to his country and its welfare, without self-interest. Thrale sought the counsel of the strong and the wise, not the idle, ignorant, and dissolute. Thrale did not make empty promises, sound alarms without foundation, deny the government due praise, insult the King, deceive the credulous, disseminate discontent, and instigate rage.

Look at Wilkes: "No man can reasonably be thought a lover of his country, for roasting an ox, or burning a boot, or attending the meeting at Mile-end, or registering his name in the Lumber-troop. He may, among the drunkards, be a *hearty fellow*, and among sober handicraftsmen, a *free spoken gentleman*; but he must have some better distinction, before he is a *Patriot*." It was candidate Thrale who had the rights of the citizens at heart, who was the "Patriot." An elector who voted for him, voting "honestly for known merit, may be certain that he has not voted in vain." [20]

[19] *King Lear*, V.iii.71.
[20] *The Patriot, Addressed to the Electors of Great Britain* (London: T. Cadell, 1774), pp. 15, 32.

Mrs. Thrale took an active part in the campaign, though handicapped, as before, by pregnancy and business worries. She canvassed hard, never sparing herself, exerting all her power of argument and charm. "We lead a wild Life," she told Johnson on 4 October, "I write surrounded by people making a noise & scarce know what I say . . ." (*Letters* 360A).

The voting was close, but on 18 October Thrale was returned for Southwark, second in the polls.

31: Oct.̣ 1774.

Well we have won the Race by a Length or so & that is all. M.̣ Thrale is once more elected for Southwark, & his best Friends say he may thank his Wife for his Seat — the Truth is I have been indefatigable, and our Endeavours have been crown'd with Success.

12: Nov.̣ 1774.

About a Week ago, when the Election was over & every thing quiet; I took a Ride to see my Girls at Kensington, intending to fetch them home the following Day: as I had now rested myself from the cruel fatigues I had undergone of getting Votes all day, & settling Books with the Clerks all Night; but in Hogmore Lane down fell my Horse, down of course fell I — we were on a smart Gallop — the Pommel struck my Side with great Violence, & my Lip was cut almost through: add to this the two black Eyes I had gained, and an immense Swelling at my Jaw, which tho' not broke was greatly injured: as soon as I recovered my Senses, I insisted on being carried to M.̣s Cumyns's, where I took as I concluded a last leave of my poor Girls, & begged her to be kind to them, telling her that M.̣ Thrale would probably send Queeney thither too if I should die, as was most to be expected, being four months gone with Child & so monstrously bruised. I then drove home, where I immediately fainted, & have kept my Chamber ever since & perhaps must wear a Mask for the remainder of my Life long or short.

Although Mrs. Thrale was in a state of shock after the accident, badly bruised and bleeding, she was not seriously injured. There was no necessity of a mask, though the cut on her lip from the horse's hoof was to leave a slight deformity on the right side of her mouth for the rest of her life.

Mr Thrale appeared more concerned than I had any Notion of, and behaved with more Tenderness than I Supposed to have been in his nature: but I had lately been useful to him, and tho' he did not love me much the better for that when I was well, he pitied me the more for it when I was sick. Queeney's whole Care was to keep out of my Sight; She was shocked at the Spectacle extremely, but not I believe at all more grieved than She would have been to see a Stranger in the same mangled Condition. Poor Harry cried as loud & as long as if he had been whipt to death, & the Children at Kensington hung about me & whimpered terribly.

20: Novr 1774.
Mr Thrale had a mind to inoculate Ralph before we went to town, & I tho't him much in the right. So Dan: Sutton who inoculated the others has performed the Operation — He is a fine boy & will do well I doubt not — God knows it is a mighty slight Business, none of 'em yet had ever 50 Pustules — it is in fact nothing at all — but a mere Farce.

On the morning when Daniel Sutton came to inoculate Ralph, Johnson was present and, discoursing on money, he observed that it resembled poison ". . . a small Quantity would often produce fatal Effects; but given in large Doses though it might . . . leave the Patient well." Sutton, according to Mrs. Thrale, was a fellow of very quick parts but "as ignorant as dirt both with regard to Books and the World." He listened and grinned and gaped and finally said ". . . half out of Breath I never kept such Company before and cannot tell how to set about leaving it now" (*Thraliana*, p. 168). This compliment pleased Johnson greatly.

On the last day of November, an important event occurred, connected with the brewery: Thrale's chief clerk, John Perkins, took a second wife. (The first Mrs. Perkins, a Polhill of the tobacconist family, had died childless some five years before.) The new wife was Amelia Mosely Bevan, in her late twenties, a widow, pretty, talented, charming — and rich. She had been attracted to Perkins (seventeen years her senior) as someone able and ambitious and also handsome and virile.

With his marriage Perkins gained strength and independence. The future brightened for him; not so for the Thrales.

[2]8: Nov.ʳ 1774.

*Here I am well paid for my Presumption The Child [Ralph] is
vastly ill indeed — dying I think — the Confluent Sort, Sutton never
Saw any thing so bad himself: Oh Lord Oh Lord! What shall I do?
Johnson & Baretti try to comfort me, they only plague me — Up every
Night and all Night long again! — well if this don't kill me & the
Child I carry, sure we are made of Iron.*

Sutton's smallpox inoculation of material from another human case
had given the baby the disease itself, the virulent, confluent sort, where
the pustules enlarge until they touch.

Mrs. Thrale's fear that Ralph's smallpox might endanger the child
she carried was probably unfounded. Her pregnancy was too far
advanced for damaging structural change or severe toxemia (blood
poisoning).

19: Dec.

*Ralph is recover'd, but so altered one could not know him, had one
not seen the Progress of the Disorder. so languid too — he will now
[be] thrown backward with a witness* [21] *— he seems all relaxed I think,
& has no Strength left to battle with his Teeth which are coming every
Day. Tomorrow we go to London — this house smells like a Hospital
— I must have the Nursery all new papered, before I come back to
lye in, or the new comer will catch the Infection.*

*God give us a quiet Winter! My Mother's Death, no; the Uproar
in the Trade & the Story in the Newspapers 1772 — was the beginning of my Miseries; then came my Mother's death; then came Lucy's,
then Sʳ Thoˢ Salusbury's, then the Election, then the Fall, then Ralph's
Smallpox; Oh when, when, shall I ever know peace & Happiness again.
I will come home hither on the 20: of next April if I can — I expect to
lye in the first Week in May, but these distractions during Pregnancy
ruin my Children.*

Something which certainly made Mrs. Thrale a little more cheerful at Christmas time was Johnson's present, an advance copy of the
book he had written about his tour with Boswell to the Hebrides. The
expedition had been an enormous success and his account of it was
eagerly awaited. He wrote her that "Mr. Strahan does not publish [A

---

[21] An archaic expression, meaning "with a vengence."

Journey to the Western Islands of Scotland] till after the Holidays, and insists that only the King and you shall have it sooner, and that you shall be engaged not to lend it abroad." Johnson added that there "are errata in it which I wish you to mark. I do not forget Carter" (*Letters* 365.2).

Charles Carter was Mrs. Thrale's riding master (a son of the late Captain Carter), a nice young man, who had exerted all his power to serve Mr. Thrale at the late election. He was very decent, courteous, conservative — and extremely hard up — he had a wife and fourteen children. Mrs. Thrale, by way of helping him, had been taking lessons (Mrs. Salusbury would never have allowed this, but she was independent now) and was "learning to ride in the Borough" (*Thraliana*, p. 116). She did not give up lessons with Carter after her bad fall.

Johnson liked the man and was also trying to help. He felt that there might be a chance of establishing a riding academy at Oxford, with Carter as its head, because profits from the sale of the *Life of Clarendon* had been willed to the University for the teaching of riding, fencing, and dancing, needed reforms the Earl of Clarendon had thought, but none of these improvements had yet been undertaken. Johnson promised to stir up his Oxford friends to see if anything could be done for riding.

Meanwhile Mrs. Thrale was trying to educate the young Carters; all were exceedingly handsome children but their only proficiency was handling horses. She was trying to enter the eldest Carter boy in a good school, Christ's Hospital, and she was trying to find a place for Laura, the eldest of the twelve girls. She soon discovered that Laura could "neither read, nor write, nor work, nor wash," so she took her into the Thrale nursery, where she taught her to read and taught her her prayers and her catechism (*Thraliana*, p. 117).

20: Jan: 1775.

was the 1:ˢᵗ day I could get Time to have my Girls home, and this is the 25:ᵗʰ I have examined Susan closely, & find all M.ʳˢ Cumyns said was true: Her Improvements more than equal my hopes, my Wishes, nay my very Fancies. She reads even elegantly & with an Emphasis. says her Catechism both in French & English: is got into Joyn hand ¹ with her pen, & works at her Needle so neatly, that She has made her Sister a Shift ² all herself. She knows the Map of Europe as well as I do, with the Capital Cities, Forms of Gov:ᵗ &c. the Lines Circles & general Geography of the Globe She is Mistress of; & has a Knowledge of the Parts of Speech that She cannot be ensnared by any Question. her Person too is so improved it is wonderful, People now reckon her rather pretty, & having learned early to dance, gives her a mighty graceful Carriage, which will carry off greater defects, than I hope She will ever have. When I have new Clothed her She shall return to School; the putting her there was the /most/ fortunate Fancy I Ever took in my head.

Sophy is tall, large-made, handsome & good humoured, knows little enough to be sure, but her Letters & some of Watts's Hymns: yet She is very amiable; I will keep her at home, Queeney & I can tutor her mighty well, & it will be an amusement.

A better or finer, a wiser or kinder Boy than Harry cannot be found: he goes to Jennings's free School ³ here in Southwark, & is half adored by Master and Scholars, by Parents & Servants — by all the Clerks —

¹ Joyn hand: cursive writing.
² Shift: a chemise of linen or cotton.
³ Jennings's free School: possibly the free grammar school for the parishioners of St. Saviour's, Southwark.

by all his Friends and Acquaintance. he has Charity, Piety, Benevolence; he has a desire of Knowledge far above his Years, and is perpetually passing by Boys of ten Years old at the same School: he always does his Exercise at a Night in my Dressing room, and we always part after that is over pleased with each other — he is so rational, so attentive, so good; nobody can help being pleased with him.

Queeney begun to learn to dance this Week of Mr Abingdon who studied under my old Master Mr Leviez: I used to say I would teach this Science to my own Family but these frequent Pregnancies disable me.
                                                          25: Jan: 1775.

Mr. Abingdon's efforts were not successful. He "used to come at vexatious hours" (*Thraliana*, p. 50), and it soon appeared the art of dancing was something Queeney did not choose to conquer, perhaps because it was the one thing she did badly.

Among the many things she did well was her Italian. And Baretti became so pleased with his method of teaching a language that he interested Robinson and Cadell, the publishers, in bringing out a full volume of his dialogues, so that other young ladies might learn Italian. With this large audience in view, he directed his talks with Queeney away from the Thrale nursery and barnyard to more intellectual subjects: personalities in the Streatham circle — Reynolds, Garrick, Sheridan — and particularly Johnson, whose "country will for ever be as proud of him as old Greece was of her Plato" (Baretti, p. 266).

When master and pupil discussed Johnson's *Journey to the Western Islands of Scotland* and his rough letter to James Macpherson, the impostor (translator of Ossian, an ancient poet who never existed), Queeney said, "Old Nurse has the story at her finger's end . . . and there is not a footman in the house that has not heard of it" (Baretti, p. 258). There are innumerable references to life at Streatham. In addition, the published volume has a preface by Johnson and a dedication to Queeney, an early honor but highly appropriate since she was the inspiration of the book itself. This ten-year-old was fast becoming "Miss Polyglot" for Baretti was employing his special method to teach her Spanish and French as well as Italian.

Mrs. Thrale had no such record of achievement. Her preoccupation with family and business constantly increased, as did her social obligations. There was no end to the friends who had to be seen.

Among these were the young Rices, Jack and Fanny, whose elopement two years before had caused so much excitement. They were
now happily settled in London, and the Thrales saw a great deal of
them.

28: Jan: 1775.
Susan returned to Mrs Cumyns Yesterday, I keep Sophy at home: Ralph
fades away visibly, I knew he would never recover the Smallpox be-
sides he cuts Teeth every day, & that helps keep him back.

Throughout February Mrs. Thrale was concerned and unhappy
about Ralph's condition, but one event occurred during this month
which briefly made her forget her worries: Sir Joshua Reynolds invited
the Thrales to dine at his house to meet his friend, Elizabeth Montagu,
the celebrated bluestocking (sometimes called "the Duchess of Distinction"). At the time of the invitation, Mrs. Montagu's husband,
a son of the first Earl of Sandwich, was very ill (he was to die in May);
Mrs. Montagu did not often go out these days, but Reynolds assured her
that the dinner would be a needed diversion and that only a small company would be present.

So, on Wednesday, 8 February, the two met, Mrs. Thrale thirty-four
and Mrs. Montagu fifty-five, brilliant in diamonds and conversation.
She was enchanted with the lively, pretty, well-informed younger
woman and showed in no uncertain terms that she was eager for her
friendship. Mrs. Thrale was highly complimented.

15: March: 1774 [sic, for 1775].
Queeney is ill now; Good Lord have mercy on me; the Loss or Pres-
ervation of my Reason depends I doubt it not on that dear Girl's Life —
What has this World left to make me amends for my Queeney?

On the first of April, Johnson wrote a letter to Mrs. Thrale from
Johnson's Court, giving two pieces of Oxford news, one good and one
bad: the bad was that there were unfortunate complications in the
riding-school project for Carter; the good, that "they have sent me a
degree of Doctor of Laws, with such praises in the diploma, as, perhaps, ought to make me ashamed; they are very like your praises. I
wonder whether I shall ever show them to you" (*Letters* 386).

Johnson was staying at this time in the city, rather than in the country with the Thrales, another "furlough," for the arrival of Mrs. Thrale's tenth baby was imminent. Her "well days" were over for a while.

10: Ap.l Hetty's Ailments were all verminous; I ought not to [have] been frighted so: a little Tin and Wormseed with a bitter Purge or two carried 'em all off. this filthy Disorder takes a thousand forms: — sometimes a Fever, sometime[s] the Piles — sometimes a train of nervous Symptoms in quick Succession — and yet always Worms!

Though Queeney was now cured of her present attack of worms, the eldest Carter boy (whom Mrs. Thrale was trying to get into school) was not so fortunate. He became very ill in March, and Johnson and Mrs. Thrale "supported the weight of his Expences jointly." When the cause of illness was discovered to be worms, Mrs. Thrale took the boy to a Dr. Evans in Knightsbridge, famous for his treatment of worm cases, "but too late, the Creatures had eat into the Intestines and the Boy died" (*Thraliana*, p. 118).

14: Ap.l 1775. M.r Thrale had something of a Polypus in his Nose & sent for Pott the great Surgeon to extract it: he would afterw.ds make me produce poor Ralph who is in a miserably declining State & shew him him [sic] to Pott. I was very unwilling, he was sick, he was asleep /I said/ or any thing to keep him out of Sight; but come down he must, so I fetched him: ["]What d'ye talk of Sickness & Teething["] cries out the Man immediately! "This Boy is in a State of Fatuity, either by Accident, or more probably from his birth, you may see he labours under some nervous Complaint that has affected his Intellects; for his Eyes have not the Look of another Child sick or well." Oh how this dreadful Sentence did fill me with Horror! & how dismal are now the thoughts of all future Connection with this unhappy Child! a Thing to hide & be ashamed of whilst we live: Johnson gives me what Comfort he can, and laments he can give no more. This is to be sure /one/ of the great Evils Life has in it, and one had no business to prepare for a Sorrow so uncommon — I shall therefore bear it the worse perhaps. Oh Lord give me patience to bear this heaviest of all my Afflictions!

The dreadful sentence of Pott could not be questioned, for Percivall Pott [4] of St. Bartholomew's Hospital, Fellow of the Royal Society, had every reason to know. He was a man of authority and wide experience, a remarkable diagnostician and the outstanding surgeon of the day. He would have known if surgery offered any hope, but his reaction was immediate, emphatic, and negative. As Mrs. Thrale had many times suspected, Ralph had not been right from birth.

Pott was blunt with the Thrales, and as a man of common sense, one noted for sympathy and gentleness of heart, this could only mean that he thought the kindest thing was to make them face reality — make them hope the little boy would die.

Hester Thrale reacted to the cruel truth one way, Henry Thrale another.

16: Ap^l 1775.
Mr Thrale is a happy man! he likes Ralph in his Sight as well as e'er a Child he has, and wonders /at/ me for fretting that he is to be an Ideot. The Truth is I never thought the Boy quite like other people, but I was so afraid of turning my Thoughts that way, that I am now as much shocked as if I had never suspected it. Bromfield told me to day he was always *apprehensive about his Intellects, /&/ that he said so to Old Nurse while I was in Wales last Summer I proposed the Cold Bath; "any thing Dear Mad^m["] replied he ["]that may contribute to quiet y^r Mind, but while you are trying every Means to preserve the Life of little Master I fear your* truest *Friends will scarce be able to wish You Success.["]*
Melancholy Conversation!

21: Ap^l 1775.
Here I am, returned to Streatham with my little Flock, & here if it please God I shall in a fortnights Time add to them another Child. The Situa-

---

[4] All medical men remember the name of Pott from the term "Pott's fracture."

In January 1757, while riding in Southwark, Pott had been thrown from his horse and suffered a compound fracture, the bone coming through the skin. He knew the danger he was in if anyone moved him without extreme care, so, as he lay in great pain on the freezing cobblestones, he purchased a door from a house and hired two chairmen to lift him on to it according to his directions, and to carry him gently across London Bridge to his house near St. Paul's, where he could send for a doctor he trusted. In this way Pott saved his leg from amputation.

During his convalescence Pott took up writing, and began his *Treatise on Ruptures.*

*tion of the youngest Boy pierces my very Soul, & I could bear it better
if the Nurses & Children were not perpetually raising hopes of his
doing well, which tho' never confirmed — are yet never to be relin-
quish'd. Thus one cries Ralph takes notice of* this — *another Ralph
admired* that *& ev'ry Detection brings me new Distress — The rest
are well, & I ought to be thankful: I shall perhaps have only this one
Misfortune. ——may that expiate my criminal pride in my own & my
eldest Daughter's Superiority of understanding!*

Thurs : 4: May — 75. Frances Anna Thrale born;

This little girl was the second Thrale daughter to be called Frances.
The first Frances, who had been born in September 1765 and named
after Thrale's sister, Mrs. Plumbe, had lived only a few days. The
present Fanny was named after Mrs. Plumbe's daughter, Frances
Plumbe Rice (who was now a mother herself at seventeen),[5] and also
after Frances Stapleton Cotton, a favorite of Mrs. Thrale since her visit
to Llewenny the past summer.

Five days after the child's birth, Mrs. Thrale sent a note to her niece,
"I write from my Pillow to claim Dear Mrs Rice's Promise of giving
her Name to my little Girl who promises to be a *pretty* Fanny as well
as herself" (Rice, 14).

The baby's godfather was Thrale's trusted friend and exact contemporary, John Cator,[6] M.P. for Wallingford. Cator was a rich timber
merchant who had his lumberyard near the brewery in Southwark,
and, like Thrale, he also owned a fine house in the country, Beckenham
Place, in Kent. Cator and his wife had had an only child, Maria, born
in the year the Thrales were married (1763), but the little girl had
died at three.

The christening of Frances Anna Thrale took place at St. Leonard's
in Streatham, James Tattersall, as usual, officiating.

While recording Fanny's birth and noting her sponsors, Mrs. Thrale
was distracted by thoughts of Ralph, and made a muddle of the entry,
giving his sponsors of two years before (see pp. 326–327) along with

---

[5] Fanny Rice was to have thirteen children, and in 1790, a few weeks after the
birth of the last, was to die at the age of thirty-two.

[6] Though another birth date has often been ascribed, the Quaker Register from
the Friends House, Euston, gives 21 January 1728 as Cator's birth date. He married
Mary Collinson at Devonshire House on 30 August 1753.

Fanny's sponsors, and describing the new baby's appearance in the same entry with a mention that Ralph was to be sent to Brighton, where she hoped that cold sea bathing might benefit him.

D.ʳ Bromfield who attends me has some hopes of the Sea for poor Ralph — he shall go down to Brighton when my Month is up. Ralph's Sponsors were L.ᵈ Sandys and M.ʳ Littleton [sic] & Miss Burgoyne; those of Frances Anna are M.ʳˢ Cotton of Llewenney, M.ʳˢ Rice, and J.ⁿ Cator Esq.ʳ of Beckenham. She is a small delicate Child, but bears no visible Marks of my many Troubles during Gestation.

13: May 1775.

Johnson tried to be light and cheerful about Ralph's trip when he wrote from London to Streatham on 20 May, saying, "Ralph like other young Gentlemen will travel for improvement" (*Letters* 393). This was the phrase Mrs. Thrale had used in describing the young bloods, William Gilpin and John Parker, on their ramble in Derbyshire.

Mrs. Thrale wrote to Johnson on the same day, saying that she had a cold and was in a fretful mood, still confined to the house, for her month of lying-in was not up until the fourth of June. She complained that "my Master never [comes] near me but on those Days that he would come" anyway, "Saturday Sunday & Monday." And she took Johnson to task about the promised epitaph for her mother. Two years had gone by since Mrs. Salusbury's death, and still no epitaph "for that Dear Lady whose Remembrance gives me more delight than many a pretended Lover feels from that of his Mistress" (*Letters* 393A).

Johnson had not forgotten his promise to write the epitaph, but he had yet to get around to it, and now he was about to set out on the round of visits which had become an annual custom. This time he expected to be gone until September — Oxford, Lichfield, Ashbourne.

In Oxford he finally bestirred himself and on 1 June sent a letter to Mrs. Thrale, enclosing the epitaph,[7] which he said he had written

---

[7] In lapidary inscriptions, Johnson said, and possibly with this epitaph in mind, a man is not upon oath. A translation of the text is as follows:

Hard by is buried Hester Maria, daughter of Thomas Cotton of Combermere, Baronet of the County of Cheshire, wife of John Salusbury, Gentleman of the County of Flint.

In person charming, charming too in mind, agreeable to all at large, to her own circle very, very loving, so highly cultivated in language and the fine arts that her talk never lacked brilliancy of expression, ornateness of sentiment, sound wisdom

Iuxta sepulta est Hestera Maria
Thomæ Cotton de Combermere Baroneti Cestriensis Filia,
Ioannis Salusbury, Armigeri Flintiensis, Uxor;
Forma felix, felix Ingenio,
omnibus jucunda, suorum amantissima;
Linguis Artibusque ita exculta
ut loquenti nunquam deessent
Sermonis nitor, Sententiarum flosculi,
Sapientiæ gravitas, leporum gratia;
modum servandi adeo perita
ut domestica inter Negotia Literis oblectaretur,
Literarum inter Delicias rem familiarem sedulo curaret.
multis illi multos Annos precantibus,
diri Carcinomatis veneno contabuit,
nexibusque Vitæ paulatim resolutis,
é terris, meliora sperans, emigravit.
Nata 1707, Nupta 1739, Obiit 1773.

MRS. SALUSBURY'S MOURNING TABLET

COMPOSED BY DR. JOHNSON, CUT BY WILTON

"last night." The epitaph was of course in Latin, some sixteen lines, twice too long, he said, and she must tell him what to delete. Toward the end of the letter he asked that Harry be paid the penny owed for calling him the morning he set out from Streatham (*Letters* 399).

On 6 June, when Johnson wrote to Mrs. Thrale, he told her that he had dined with Dr. Bright, the Abingdon headmaster, "who enquired after Harry and Queeney, to whom I likewise desire to be remembered." He hoped that the latter would write him a long letter, and he asked Mrs. Thrale to assure the young Miss that "if I can find any thing for her cabinet, I shall be glad to bring it" (*Letters* 401).

From Lichfield he wrote on 10 June that he was pleased to hear Ralph had gone to Brighton, and "I hope little Miss [Fanny] promises well" (*Letters* 404). Everyone in Lichfield remembered the Thrales, he assured her, "You left a good impression behind you." He then returned to the subject of the epitaph, which "must be short-ened," and she must tell him what part could best be spared (*Letters* 405).

Mrs. Thrale did not wish to spare anything in the inscription, any one of the 547 letters and 23 stops, and neither did her husband, "he will not have your Writing or my Mother's Praises curtailed" (*Letters* 406A). But Johnson was not to worry; their friend, Joseph Wilton,[8] the distinguished sculptor, had promised to cut very small letters, and so the problem was solved. Mrs. Thrale was in good spirits when she wrote Johnson this, and on the same day she recorded in the *Family Book:*

16: June 1775.
*I fetched Susan home & once more examin'd & found her Improve-ments truly surprizing; her Knowledge of Geography is amazing, & Baretti praises her pronunciation of the French. M*rs* Cumyns's Letter* [9] *which I keep in this Book does not exaggerate, but rather falls short —*

---

and graceful wit. So skilled at holding the happy mean that amid household cares she found diversion in literature, and among the delights of literature diligently at-tended to her house affairs. Though many prayed for length of days for her, she wasted away under a dread cancer-poison, and as the bands of life were gently loosed, passed away from this earth in full hope of a better land.
    Born 1707. Married 1739. Died 1773.
    [8] Joseph Wilton was one of the founders of the Royal Academy. His only daughter, Jane, was now the wife of Robert Chambers, the Bengal judge.
    [9] The letter is no longer in the *Family Book;* its whereabouts is not known.

Susan was making a fine record at Mrs. Cumyns' school, but it was a different story with the eldest daughter of the riding master, Laura Carter, whom Mrs. Thrale had sent there also. Laura was impossible, saucy, sly, and unruly. "She was so insolent Mrs Cumyns huffed her well & say'd She would tell Mrs Thrale. what care I says Laura? — what care *you* when all the Clothes on your Back are of her bestowing! — why so are *yours* I have a Notion replied Miss Laura again — so there we are *even*. This could not be borne, & Mrs Cumyns turned her going — & I would see her no more"[10] (*Thraliana*, p. 118).

When Mrs. Thrale told Johnson of Laura's rudeness to Mrs. Cumyns, he could not understand the girl's strange behavior (*Letters* 395). He was also sorry to have her report that Carter's payments at the Southwark stable were in arrears. The owner was now demanding possession of his two best horses, Prince and Lizard. Lizard was the old stallion, the celebrated war-horse that had carried the Duke of Cumberland over the plains of Culloden, where he crushed the hopes of Charles Edward, the Young Pretender. Lizard was "inestimable as a Pillar Horse, and the most useful Creature living for Learners"; he was old and not fit for common work. The stable owner would probably sell him at auction, and he would bring only "a Trifle." Mrs. Thrale was tempted to buy Lizard herself "if I knew any good Body that would give him his keep when I had done. This is what I have half a hope of from Dr Taylor" (*Letters* 411A). On the first of July, Johnson responded that Dr. Taylor's only adequate stall had recently been given to Shakespeare, an old race horse he had bought for a stallion.[11]

In his letter Dr. Johnson said that he imagined Mrs. Thrale was now at Brighton, "where I hope you will find every thing either well [with Ralph], or mending. You never told me whether you took Queeney with you; nor ever so much as told me the name of the little one" (*Letters* 413).

This was Frances Anna, born two months ago. There had been no

[10] Twelve years after this (1787) "a fine Lady & very rich" was to accost Mrs. Thrale (by then Piozzi) and she could not guess who the person was. It was Laura (Lady Beaumaris Rush of Roydon), "the finest of the fine at every Publick Show" (*Thraliana*, p. 682).

[11] Gallant old Lizard lived to be forty, and then Carter was obliged to kill him for he could not afford having mashes made, and Lizard's chewing days were wholly over (*Commonplace Book*; under "Old Age").

time to think of this poor baby. Ralph was the child who filled her mind.

Who knows at last what Ralph may come to? when She [Susan] was as young we had as little hope of her, but then she never was stupid, her Ailments were never in her Head. well I shall see him soon, he was sent to Brighthelmstone the 4.ᵗʰ of this Month [June], I will visit him when I think there can have been any Change wrought: — my Letters from Nurse are very encouraging upon the whole — but one is afraid even of hoping in such Cases, tho' all /yᵉ/ D.ʳˢ think the Sea likely to be of Service, & even Johnson hopes something from Change of Air.

As a wholly incidental note, the day after Mrs. Thrale made this entry in the *Family Book*, the battle of Bunker Hill took place, 17 June 1775. When the news reached Johnson about six weeks later, he wrote to Mrs. Thrale, "America now fills every mouth . . . "(*Letters* 427).

4: July 1775.
I went to see my little boy at Brighton, and found him rather worse than better: more heavy more lethargick & insensible than ever I had known him at home: Old Nurse talked of Teeth again, but I soon saw yᵗ: Teeth had a small share in his Complaint & apply'd to Kipping the Apothecary of the Place, who immediately said his Brain was oppress'd, & beg'd me to consult D.ʳ Pepys.

Henry Kipping, a surgeon and apothecary, lived at 28 West Street, a short distance from the Thrales' house. He was a respected practitioner, good-humored and sympathetic. He recognized Ralph's symptoms at once for he had "lost one Child by this Disorder and [had] one alive who [was] an Ideot" (*Letters* 417A).

Lucas Pepys, whom Kipping called for consultation, was an able young physician who practiced in London during the winter and in Brighton during the summer. Pepys had been educated at Eton and Christ Church, Oxford, and trained for medicine at Edinburgh and Oxford. He had received his Oxford M.D. the year before this. Pepys's professional manner was authoritative and firm; his social manner gentle and ingratiating. In 1772 he had married the Countess of Rothes (whose stepmother, the dowager Countess of Rothes, in 1770 had married Bennet Langton, a friend of Johnson and the Thrales).

Lucas Pepys was a rising doctor; in September of this year he was to be elected a Fellow of the Royal College of Physicians, and in 1804 he would become President of this august body.

From him [Pepys] I heard the same dreadful Sentence, & Blisters & Stimulatives of all kinds were applied. Some Matter one Day ooz'd from his [Ralph's] Ear like Lucy's, but soon Stopt, producing no Effect.

She wrote to Johnson in anguish. Ralph was having:

. . . fits of Rage — proceeding from Pain I guess — just as Lucy & Miss Anna had — Kipping says the Brain is oppressed of which I have no doubt. What shall I do? What can I do? has the flattery of my Friends made me too proud of my own Brains? & must these poor Children suffer for my Crime? I can neither go on with this Subject nor quit it . . . I opened the Ball last Night — tonight I go to the Play: Oh that there was a Play or a Ball for every hour of the four & twenty. (*Letters* 415A)

his [Ralph's] Muscular Flesh however seemed rather to increase than diminish, & as Reason appeared to be in greater Danger than Life I left him on the 8:th under the Care of Kipping[,] Pepys & old Nurse & returned to Streatham with my Master, Hetty, & Harry who had accompany'd me on this Disagreable Errand.

While Mrs. Thrale was in Brighton, Johnson had written anxiously from Ashbourne about Ralph, "I hope occasional bathing, and keeping him about two minutes with his body immersed, may promote the discharge from his head, and set his little brain at liberty." Dr. Taylor, Johnson said, would "be very glad to see you all here again" for a visit, but "I told him that he must not expect you this summer, and ⟨he⟩ wants to know — why?" (*Letters* 415).

Mrs. Thrale was back in Streatham when she received Johnson's next letter, written three days later, on 9 July. He was "sorry that my poor little friend Ralph goes on no better. We must see what time will do for him." He hoped that Harry was well, and that Queeney would be "kind to my Hen and her ten chickens, and mind her Book" (*Letters* 416). Earlier, he had said that Queeney seemed to be revenging her long tasks upon Mr. Baretti's hen, "who must sit on Duck eggs a week longer than on her own" (*Letters* 408). His questions to Mrs. Thrale — would they all be together again in September? and would it be in Brighton? — she could not answer.

Johnson's thoughts turned to travel and in his letter of 11 July he played with the notion of spending money: Taylor would buy property and make a fine garden, but Johnson wondered:

If I had money enough, what would I do? Perhaps if you and master did not hold me, I might go to Cairo, and down the Red Sea to Bengal, and take a ramble in India. (*Letters* 417)

This meant a visit to the Chamberses no doubt; Mrs. Thrale answered with spirit:

Mʳ Thrale say'd when we read [your letter] together, that you should not travel alone if he could once see this dear little Boy quite well . . .

My great delight like yours would be to see how Life is carried on in other Countries . . . when *we* go to *Cairo* one shall take one Department, another shall take another, and so a pretty Book may be made out amongst us . . . Well! now all this is Nonsense and Fancy and Flight you know, for my Master has his great Casks to mind, and I have my little Children, but he has really half a mind to cross the Water for half a Year's Frisk to Italy or France . . . (*Letters* 419A)

Shortly after this letter was written, Mrs. Thrale recorded in the *Family Book*:

I was however soon summoned back to Sussex, the Child had a Convulsion Fit or two, & a Seton [12] *was tho't adviseable which however did no good & when I went down on the 13:ᵗʰ I found him dead. on Inspection the Brain was found almost dissolved in Water, & something amiss too in the original Conformation of the Head — so that Reason & Life both might, had we known all been despair'd of from the very first.*

God preserve my other five! This poor Child is much better dead than alive

written the 20: July 1775.

Mrs. Thrale makes no mention of any enlargement of Ralph's head, nor does she quote any observation of the post-mortem appearance of the brain and skull suggestive of it. Congenital hydrocephalus (an in-

---

[12] Seton: a thread or tape drawn through a fold of the skin to maintain an opening for discharge.

creased amount of fluid in the ventricles of the brain), even in a moderate degree, causes an enlargement of the skull which is apparent to a lay observer.

The description of the brain as "almost dissolved in Water" and of an abnormality in the "original Conformation of the Head" suggests the possibility of a different congenital disorder — hydrancephaly. This is a congenital abnormality in which the development of both the brain and the skull is distorted by a bag of clear fluid which forms between the mal-developed brain and the skull. Mrs. Thrale's account is not sufficiently detailed for the diagnosis between hydrocephalus and hydrancephaly to be made with certainty.

Whichever the cause, there had been no hope for Ralph from the start.

When Johnson heard the news in Ashbourne he wrote with tenderness about the little boy:

Poor Ralph! he is gone; and nothing remains but that you comfort yourself with having done your best. The first wish was, that he might live long to be happy and useful; the next, that he might not suffer long pain. The second wish has been granted. Think now only on those which are left you. (*Letters* 422)

22: July 1775.
While I was at Brighthelmston this last Time I had a long Talk with Scrase concerning the Settlement of my Welsh Estate, which M.r Thrale has given me leave to dispose of my own Way: I have accordingly agreed on this Method — It is 1.st to be entailed on my eldest Son of course, & on his Issue Male or Female; if he dies without Issue, then to any & every Son I may still have by M.r Thrale; then to my eldest Daughter & her Sons: in default of such Sons to the Sons of my second Daughter, & if She has no Issue, or only Females — then to the Sons of my next Daughter — if none of them bring Sons, then to the Daughters of my eldest Daughter, & so on: If all dye without Children then to M.r Thrale & to his Heirs for ever: the further & compleat History of this Transaction I have left in a separate Bundle, & marked accordingly. —

When Mrs. Thrale made her lonely trip back to Brighton on 13 July, Kipping and Scrase gave what consolation they could, and the latter made the burial arrangements. In St. Nicholas's Church, at the west end of the nave, is the gravestone for the infant Ralph Thrale.

Mrs. Thrale stayed on in Brighton. The sea bathing helped her nerves and Scrase's company was consoling, the very sight of him raised her spirits as he rode by "with his little Dogs about him . . . fresh and comfortable & active & kind" (*Letters* 585.1A). He was sympathetic and understanding and, as she recorded in her journal, he was extremely helpful in discussing the disposition of her Welsh estate, cautioning her to consider all future possibilities. For instance, Harry (or other sons yet unborn) might die without issue. All her daughters might die without issue. Thrale might marry again, and might have children by a second wife. This touched a sensitive nerve, and Mrs. Thrale hotly protested that in such a case, she would have her estate go to her cousin, Robert Cotton. But Scrase was able to argue her out of this position, as being unfair in view of the fact that it had been Thrale who "had delivered up [her] Welch Estate to [her] to settle & dispose of as [she] pleased" (*Thraliana*, p. 317). She finally agreed that in default of all her children and issue, the property should go to her husband and his issue "for ever" (*Thraliana*, p. 318).

Scrase then made Mrs. Thrale consider the opposite possibility: what if Thrale should die, and she should marry again? If such a situation occurred, would she not be sorry to see the daughters of her first marriage inherit her estate, to the prejudice of a son or sons by the second husband? Such an unthinkable supposition shocked Mrs. Thrale; she refused to consider it.

But Scrase, with her interest at heart, did not let the matter rest. On 30 July, after she had returned to Streatham, he wrote to Thrale, urging that no entail be set up, that the settlement be so arranged that during the Thrales' joint lives it might at any time be revoked or altered. Thrale thought this was a wise precaution, and a draft was drawn up for discussion with Johnson when he returned to London.

Mrs. Thrale had left Brighton on 17 July, and was grateful, when she returned to Streatham, to find the five children well. Baretti had "been very good, and taken care of my little ones like a Nurse while I was away, & has not failed writing me &c. & I am sorry I was so peevish with him" (*Letters* 421A). On her annoyance with Baretti, Johnson had said:

Poor B⟨arett⟩i! do not quarrel with him, to neglect him a little will be sufficient. He means only to be frank, and manly, and independent, and perhaps, as you say, a little wise. To be frank he thinks is to be cynical, and to be independent, is to be rude. Forgive him, dearest Lady, the rather, because of his misbehaviour, I am afraid, he learned part of me. I hope to set him hereafter a better example. (*Letters* 420)

23: July 1775.
Sophia is this Day four Years old: She is a fine healthy, sprightly sensible Child — remarkably stout-made, and handsome enough, though not eminent for Beauty. She can say a World of things by heart; & Baretti has taught her some Italian Words for his & her Diversion; She reads only four Psalms that She has studied, but her Repetition of the Pence Table, the two's 3ˢ & 4ˢ of the Multiplication Table, the Catechism & a heap of other Things — among the rest — Pope's Universal Prayer & Addison's Morning Hymn with two long ones of Dʳ Watts's, take a deal of Time to hear them over; She likewise works neatly at her Needle, has a good Disposition & very competent Capacity. ——

The day after this entry was written there was celebration at the brewery, for a baby was born to Amelia Perkins — a boy. He was named John, after his father, and Mrs. Thrale was asked to be the child's godmother. The Perkinses doubtless wished to show their sympathy for the loss of Ralph and hoped to give the Thrales a little compensating pleasure through their own boy. A gesture of this sort is kind, but at a point so close to sorrow, it is extremely painful to receive. However, Mrs. Thrale did not wince; she accepted the honor graciously, and possibly at this time presented to the new parents a blank journal like the Thrale *Family Book* (to become a Perkins' heirloom), "the Family Ocasional Book (the Green Book)."

At the end of July Sir Lynch Cotton died, and Mrs. Thrale's cousins at Llewenny became Sir Robert and Lady Cotton. Poor, eccentric Sir Lynch had not been much loved by his family. "I am sorry for him," Johnson wrote to Mrs. Thrale. "It is sad to give a family of children no pleasure but by dying" (*Letters* 427).

In Johnson's next letter to Mrs. Thrale he asked if she kept his letters. They might one day have the power to relieve sadness with the memory of more cheerful times. They would always be, he said, "the records of a pure and blameless friendship" (*Letters* 428). This day Mrs. Thrale wrote in her journal:

2 Aug: 1775.
Sophy has terrified me into Agonies; She came down this Morning

drooping & dismal & complaining of her Head — I concluded Sentence was already past, & that She was about /to follow/ her Brother & Sisters, so I fairly sate me down to cry — but it ended in nothing, She eat a good Dinner, & when the Dancing Master came was as alert as usual: She said just now to me "I believe Ma'amey that Headach of mine was only a Mad Dream." — it was a dreadful Dream to me I know.

By 17 August Johnson was home with the Thrales again. He studied the Welsh property settlement, suggested a few minor changes, and agreed with Scrase and Thrale that it was wise not to set up an entail. Scrase's draft was sent to Bateman Robson, Thrale's London solicitor, with instructions to draw up the formal document. (Robson had worked under Scrase at Lincoln's Inn, before the latter's retirement.)

27: of Aug: 1775.
We talk of going to France for a Couple of months & taking Queeney; I think She will pick up some French in the Country, & as Baretti is to be of the party will lose no Italian: A little Voyage too may be of Service in ridding her of these odious Worms — little Doves as She calls them — they are the very plague of her Life & I dare not use Mercury.[13] *— I think the Mercury Ralph took in the Small-Pox injured his Intellects: Tin and Wormseed*[14] *are safer, if not so efficacious   We shall carry plenty with us.*

2: Sept.ʳ 1775.
I went today to survey the famous School for Boys at Loughboro' house:[15] *M.ʳ Thrale fancies Harry will be safer there than at D.ʳ Thomas's, where he does to be sure take strange Liberties as to ranging about, climbing Trees &c. but I am afraid knowledge will not be im-*

[13] Mercury: very dangerous. In Ralph's case, however, the brain was damaged before mercury was given.

[14] Wormseed: a name for various bitter plants such as swine fennel and sulphurwort, effective in destroying worms.

[15] Loughborough House School: an academy for young noblemen and gentlemen, located in Loughborough Lane (now Evandale Road in the SW 9 district of Brixton). The school was approximately two and a half miles from Streatham, and in the days when schoolboys used to walk, it would have taken Harry something over an hour for the journey. Loughborough house was pulled down in the 1850s.

proved much at Loughborough House: there is more Attention paid to
Convenience & Security there than to the Acquisition of Learning
I believe, but when they see how forward my Son is, I think they
will push him too: however Safety is doubtless the first Thing, & as
Johnson says Robert Perreau [16] *cannot be safer than he will be at this*
School. My Fanny must be safe in Old Nurse's Arms I think — &
I took Sophy to her Sister at Kensington Yesterday: nothing in the
World ails her — it was all a Mad Dream *as She said. I have charged*
Mrs Cumyns & Perney's People & Nurse, to send for Bromfield Jebb
or Pinkstan if anything happened to the Children in my Absence, I
likewise begged Bromfield to call from Time [to time] & see them.
he thinks the Journey a charming thing for Queeney so indeed does
every body.

Richard Jebb, a new name among Mrs. Thrale's doctors, was an
eminent practitioner, a physician at St. George's Hospital, and a Fellow
of the Royal College of Physicians. Jebb had attended Oxford, but
being a non-juror (not a member of the Church of England) he could
not receive a degree, nor pursue his medical training there. Thus, he
went to Aberdeen. Jebb was both skilful and charming, and was soon
to be physician to various members of the royal family. Mrs. Thrale
felt an immediate confidence in Jebb, and was assured that if anything
went seriously wrong with the children, he would find a way to reach
her.

As for her personal business, the important thing to do before departure was to sign her Welsh property settlement. Johnson and John
Cator, little Fanny's godfather, were to be the trustees. Cator had
been chosen because both her husband and Johnson esteemed him for
his loyalty and shrewdness, and she agreed, though she was not fond
of Cator socially — a pompous, purse-proud tradesman with a loud
voice, vulgar speech, rough manners, and a curious fondness for gazing
at himself in a mirror, the way Goldsmith used to do. From a business
point of view, however, she respected Cator, for though poorly educated, he had intelligence and good judgment, was "skilful in Trade, and
solid in Property" (*Thraliana*, p. 418). And he had a special attribute;
as a timber merchant, he appreciated the value of the trees Mrs. Thrale

[16] Footnote in the manuscript: *Robt. Perreau was a condemn'd Prisoner in New-*
gate — no not condemned *neither when this was wrote.* (Robert Perreau, charged
and later convicted of forgery, was hanged at Tyburn on 17 January 1776.)

wanted to preserve, "fifteen Thousand Oak Trees" at Bach-y-Graig, all "number'd and marked" (*Thraliana*, p. 320, n. 6).

The Welsh property settlement was signed on 5 September, and technically, from that day on, Johnson and Cator were in control, though Mrs. Thrale retained discretionary power, the provision which Johnson and Scrase had pressed, and for which she would be extremely grateful in years to come.

With her business done, Mrs. Thrale turned her attention to the actual preparations for the journey. She was pleased by the prospect, ready for a "frisk," even if it were not to Cairo. New sights and fresh adventures would soothe the memory of the agonizing months she had spent watching over Ralph and having all her hopes for the boy come to nothing. And, fortunately, she felt well at the moment — she was not pregnant.

She directed her packing and Queeney's with care, remembering the mistakes she had made on her journey to Wales. And one of these she took pains to remedy: on this trip, not only would Mr. Thrale have Sam, but she would have Molly, to take care of her clothes and to help with Queeney.

Last year Baretti had been left in charge at Streatham, but now he was to be the courier for the party, a post which he much preferred and for which he was admirably qualified. This expedition to France was, in a way, considered a trial run for the more elaborate excursion, planned for next spring, to Italy.

By the night of 14 September, Mrs. Thrale was packed and ready — and in her luggage was a fresh leather-bound travel journal. Again she was going to keep a diary of the trip, and Johnson promised to keep one as well.

14: Septr 1775.
Tomorrow Morning we set out for France, & this may be my last writing in this Book! let me conclude with a Prayer for my pretty ones.
Oh thou most adorable Creator, Redeemer & Comforter of Man — most holy Trinity preserve my Children! grant them the valuable Gifts of Health, Virtue & sound Understanding! which are only in thy Power to bestow, & if it be thy gracious Will to hear the Supplications of thy humble Servant, grant them I beseech thee such a Measure of thy Grace, as will enable them at all Times & on all Occasions

*to prefer the hope of future happiness thro' the merits of their dear
Redeemer, to any Temptations however specious of temporal Felicity,
too often purchas'd with Guilt,*
Thou who takest account of even the Sparrow's *Young ones — have
mercy upon mine; thou who gavest Power to Elijah to restore the Son
of the Shunamite have mercy upon mine. Thou who gavest the
Syrophœnician Woman's Daughter to her Mother's prayers preferr'd
in* Faith *— have Mercy upon mine; for thou only art the Lord, thou
only, oh only adorable Trinity, art to be worship'd, and prayed unto;
thro' his Name who purchas'd by his precious Blood our costly but
complete Redemption —— Amen blessed Jesus Amen.*

On Friday morning, 15 September 1775, the Thrales, Queeney,
and Johnson, with Sam and Molly, set out in carriages for Canterbury.
Baretti was to meet them at Dover.

On the way, the party visited the cathedral in Rochester, "the first
thing new to me," Mrs. Thrale recorded in her travel journal. She was
not greatly impressed; "it was below Worcester or Lichfield"
(*Journals*, p. 69).

At Canterbury, however, she had never been "so struck with the
sight of any Cathedral before — it is truly grand & majestick" (*Journals*, p. 69). The night was spent in Canterbury, and next morning
the party loitered there so long that, when they arrived at Dover, they
met a furious Baretti. The packet had just sailed on a fine tide; and
they were forced to wait at Dover until the following morning.

This was 17 September, Queeney's birthday. She was eleven, and
she celebrated the day by crossing to France:

The Weather was lovely — the Ship all our own, the Sea smooth & all our
Society well but Queeney, whose Sickness oppressed her beyond Conception.
Sam and Molly too were cruel sick, but Queeney worst of all . . . (*Journals*,
p. 70)

The ship on which the party sailed was a neat sloop, commanded by
Captain Baxter, who had once been a Southwark school-fellow of
Thrale.

Once in France, Mrs. Thrale's enthusiastic cathedral viewing continued. She was much struck by the great church in Calais, and next
day she was astonished by the cathedral of St. Omer, a stupendous
and noble edifice: "let us never more talk of English Churches"

(*Journals*, p. 73). She thought the cathedral of Arras at "the first Coup D'Oeil exceeds them all" (*Journals*, p. 73). Few superlatives remained.

As for Johnson, he was more interested in libraries, and he inspected all those he could. In Calais a handsome Capuchin friar took the party to see his monastery chapel and refectory. He also tried to show the library, but this was locked. Mrs. Thrale commented in her travel diary that, "I was not sorry, for Mr Johnson would never have come out of it" (*Journals*, p. 71).

On the Doctor's birthday, 18 September, the party visited the great church in Calais, then Baretti took Mrs. Thrale to a convent of Dominican nuns. In St. Omer the party inspected the Jesuits' college and schools. The theatre there was much finer, she thought, than that at Brighton and is "kept in order purely for the use of the Boys" (*Journals*, p. 72). In Arras, they looked at the Benedictine library, which resembled "All Souls exceedingly in Size and Disposition" (*Journals*, p. 73).

Baretti's plan for the travelers was to rise early in order to arrive in good time at their night's destination, which admitted running about the town in the afternoon to see everything of interest. Johnson struggled with the hardship of early rising.

As they made their way south to Paris, the weather was sunny and warm. The high road was a source of wonder; trees lined both sides, like an avenue on a nobleman's property. The great road was paved and continued so to Arras. There, they turned off on to poor roads, deeply rutted, where there was always the danger of overturning. The country they drove through was fertile, and all of it cultivated. The cattle, however, were miserable, poor and lean — but how could they be anything else without pasture? Mrs. Thrale commented on the fact that they saw more pigs than sheep. And the poultry were "extremely beautiful both at the Barn Door & the Table" (*Journals*, p. 77). She would endeavor to get some chickens for Streatham. The post horses supplied were wretched and their tack so bad it could be ridiculed in a farce, but the horses they saw along the road, which belonged to people of quality, were handsome.

There were no stately homes in the countryside, like those of the English *grands seigneurs*. Aristocratic gentlemen in France, it seemed, did not live in the country. They "flocked" to nearby towns, with the exception of the richest and grandest, who had residences in Paris (*Journals*, p. 74). There was no evidence of fox-hunting, no sportsmen visible, nor sporting dogs "tho' the Country is more inviting to the pursuit of Game by Hunting, Coursing & Setting than any I ever saw in England, & for a far greater Extent of Ground" (*Journals*, p. 75). Game was "constantly moving on each Side" of the carriage, "Hares, Pheasants, Partridges . . . feeding fearlessly by the Roadside" (*Journals*, p. 129).

Mrs. Thrale remarked that the gardens they saw were in the style of those in England fifty years before, "High Walls, straight Lines, & Trees tortured into ugly and unmeaning Forms" (*Journals*, p. 87). The appearance of the people was curious: the women wore long, black, ugly cloaks, down to their heels, and the men were whiskered or mustachioed. One thing which Mrs. Thrale found charming was the national characteristic of politeness, " . . . if you meet a French Gentleman on the Road he always pulls off his Hat to you, & the very Custom House Officers behave with a respectful Civility" (*Journals*, p. 75).

On 22 September, as the travelers approached Rouen, Mrs. Thrale thought the countryside resembled Bath. They drove into the old town and established themselves at an inn, not so fine as the ones at Calais and St. Omer, but better than one would find at Shrewsbury, Lichfield, or Birmingham (*Journals*, p. 78). While they were dining, they were joined, as pre-arranged, by Mrs. Strickland. Cecilia Towneley Strickland was six months Mrs. Thrale's junior, an even earlier friend than Mrs. Cumyns. This intimacy went back to the days when Hester had stayed at the house of her uncle, Sir Robert Cotton, in Albemarle Street, and had played with the nearby Towneley and Halifax and Burgoyne children, also with young Master North (now Prime Minister). He had pinched her and pulled her hair till she squealed (*Thraliana*, p. 286).

Cecilia Towneley came from an aristocratic Roman Catholic family, her great-grandfather on her mother's side being Henry, 6th Duke of Norfolk. Cecilia had been educated at the convent of Notre Dame de Sion in Paris and, the year before Hester's wedding, had married Charles Strickland of Sizergh Castle, Westmorland. Within the next few years the couple had had three boys and a girl — a very happy marriage, abruptly ended by Charles Strickland's death in 1770. His widow was now in Rouen, seeing the daughter, Mary Cecilia, a graceful little girl of nine, who was attending the convent school of the Poor Clares.

Mrs. Thrale was delighted to see her old friend, and the rest of the party liked Mrs. Strickland at first sight. She was a tall, elegant woman, full of spirit and drive. She had plans for the party and presented Mrs. Thrale the same evening to Mme. du Perron, widow of a Rouen official and sister of the celebrated author and anglophile, Mme. du Boccage, who had come to London in 1750. Mrs. Montagu and Lord Chesterfield had both made much of her, the latter wittily declaring that he preferred her translations of Milton to the original (*Life*, IV, 331, n. 1.). Mme. du Boccage was someone they hoped to meet in Paris, and an introduction was immediately promised by Mme. du Perron. Meanwhile, Mrs. Thrale was reading Mme. du Boccage's *Letters on the English Nation* and finding the book hard going.

Mrs. Strickland took general charge of the party in Rouen, and since she was a great lady (as well as an efficient one) Baretti was not offended by her action, in fact he was delighted. "Stricky," as Johnson called her, arranged for the sightseeing, attendance at plays and other entertainments, also introductions. She escorted the ladies to convents and introduced Johnson to various priests, including l'Abbé Roffette, with whom the Doctor was able to carry on a vehement conversation in Latin. This was a joy for Johnson — as well as a vindication, for though he read French and wrote it with considerable ease, he was too proud to blunder in speaking. He felt safer in Latin.

In the matter of language, Mrs. Thrale had no trouble. She conversed fluently, if not grammatically, and was her usual bright and lively self. Queeney was improving daily (one of the purposes of bringing her to France). If only she would not be so bashful! As for Thrale, his French was very limited, only what he remembered from his Grand Tour of long ago; but he was never at a loss, for Baretti, "with his extensive power over every modern language" (Hayward, I, 93) was always at hand.

On 26 September the party started for Paris. Mrs. Strickland came along, so there were now six in the group, plus Sam and Molly. On the morning of departure Baretti felt ill, and Mrs. Thrale tried to give him some medicine, but he refused. He had a fear of all medicines, and he was particularly suspicious of Mrs. Thrale's "doctoring."

CECILIA TOWNELEY STRICKLAND
BY ROMNEY

The day's journey proved to be a pleasant one. It was the first time that they had seen French vineyards and though the white supporting sticks were ugly and the short, ragged vines were "not half so pretty to the Eye as a Hop Garden," they were still a fine sight. And it was delightful "to pluck ripe Grapes" as they drove along the high road (*Journals*, p. 87). For a while in the afternoon the party sat on a bridge over the Seine and enjoyed the beautiful view of the fertile fields. Cherries, apples, grapes, asparagus, lentils, and French beans were in large plantings all around. The valley, Mrs. Thrale thought, as they again rode along, was in "some Respects superior to that seen from Richmond Hill and Wood alone is wanting" (*Journals*, p. 87).

These reflections were interrupted by a frightening accident in the carriage which carried Thrale, Baretti, and Queeney — on the edge of a precipice between Vernon and St. Denis:

[the] Postillion fell off his Horse on a strong Descent, the Traces were broken, one of the Horses run over and the Chaise carried forwards with a most danger-ous Rapidity, which Mr Thrale not being able to endure till somebody came up — jumped out with intent to stop the Horses for Baretti & Queeney — how-ever he only hurt himself & they went on till Sam came up, who had been miserably embarrassed with a vicious Horse which had retarded him so long, and afterwards flung him. (*Journals*, p. 88)

When Thrale leapt from the coach he landed in a chalk pit, and when he was lifted out, he was as white as a ghost. He was in a state of shock, but able to stand and, with help, could walk. The party pro-ceeded slowly to St. Germain, and there a surgeon was procured. He declared that Thrale had broken no bones, and advised him to go at once to Paris, be bled and rest. It was decided that Baretti should accompany him, to give "Assistance, & get us some Habitation to re-ceive us at Paris" (*Journals*, p. 88). The others stayed at St. Germain for the night.

As the carriage veered dangerously toward the precipice, John-son had shown no concern at all. Perhaps his near-sighted eyes did not fully reveal the terrifying scene, or perhaps, as Baretti thought, fear was a sensation to which Johnson was an utter stranger. Baretti praised his calm and said it was "true Philosophy," but Mrs. Strickland "did not give it so kind a Name" and soon Mrs. Thrale saw Stricky's "Indigna-tion towards him prevailing over her Friendship for me" (*Journals*, pp. 88–89).

Next day Dr. Johnson and the three ladies continued their short journey to Paris. Queeney was slightly bruised from yesterday's accident but it was nothing serious. Mrs. Thrale fussed about her and was deeply concerned about her husband's condition, but despite her anxieties she enjoyed the approach to Paris. The cleanness of the air so near a great metropolis surprised her: "no Sea Coal being Burned, the Atmosphere of the narrowest part of Paris is more transparent & nitid than that of Hampstead hill" (*Journals*, p. 95).

Baretti had found a house in the rue Jacob, not only convenient but elegant. And when the party arrived, Mrs. Thrale discovered, to her relief, that her husband was greatly improved. The Paris surgeon said she should "thank the *Virgin Mary* for the miraculous Escape" (*Journals*, p. 90). Thrale would be well in short order. This good news, together with a reassuring health report on the children at home, put Mrs. Thrale in excellent spirits. And the next morning, Johnson explained his behavior of the day before to Mrs. Strickland. It was anger at Mrs. Thrale that made "him sullenly forbear Enquiry, when he found [her] unwilling (as he thought it) to give him a ready or rational Answer." They were friends again (*Journals*, p. 90).

Things began very well in Paris. Baretti was at his best, displaying all his useful powers, "he bustled for us, he catered for us, he took care of the child, he secured an apartment for the maid, he provided for our safety, our amusement, our repose . . ." (Hayward, I, 94). One thing Baretti could not control, and which Mrs. Thrale regretted greatly, was the change in the weather; the warm, sunny days were gone. On 6 October she wrote that the ". . . Weather is now Broken up & the rainy Season begun; but we must bear the Cold if we can" (*Journals*, p. 104). Another thing she did not like was the noise and clamor in the rue Jacob. The streets in Paris were noisier than those in London, "being narrower one hears every carriage on both sides the way, & there being no Terrace for Footpassengers, they come up close to one's door. The Houses too are so very high that they make an Echo, & every Sound is so reiterated that it stuns one" (*Journals*, p. 94). From her window looking on to the narrow rue Jacob, she saw continuous quarrels, over-turns, and confusion. Yet, when she made any inquiry, there was remarkable courtesy; as she had remarked before "you are sure to meet no Insults from the Populace of Paris, where every Man thinks himself the Protector of every Woman" (*Journals*, p. 95).

The important moment for meeting Mme. du Boccage was set for

Saturday, 30 September, and in the morning the party waited upon this distinguished bluestocking of sixty-five, a year younger than Johnson. She greeted her visitors with superfluous civility, so it seemed to Mrs. Thrale, praising wit, beauty and so on, and her manner of asking them to dine was curious: they were to come next Thursday if she had any "pudden" to give them. Mrs. Thrale's immediate reaction to Mme. du Boccage was disappointment. She determined, however, not to form an opinion until after they had met again.

On Thursday, 5 October, the little "society" returned to the fine house of Mme. du Boccage. On entering, they were led through a sort of hall, where the footmen were playing cards. For dinner, they were served hare, "not tainted but putrified," a leg of mutton "put on the Spit the moment the Sheep was killed & garnish'd with old Beans, there was one Dish with three Sausages only & one with nothing but Sugar plumbs" (*Journals*, p. 103). This and an English pudding. There was no withdrawing of the ladies from the gentlemen after the meal; all together the company went into the drawing room. Here:

. . . stood the Busts of Shakespear, Milton, Pope & Dryden; the Lady sate on a Sopha with a fine Red Velvet Cushion fringed with Gold under her feet, & just over her Head a Cobweb of uncommon Size, & I am sure great Antiquity. A pot to spit in, either of Pewter, or Silver, quite as black & ill coloured, was on her Table; and when the Servant carried Coffee about he put in Sugar with his Fingers. (*Journals*, p. 102)

The most agreeable thing which happened this day, so far as Mrs. Thrale was concerned, was meeting one of the dinner guests, an Italian nobleman, who hailed Baretti, and then gave his full attention to the Thrales — Count Manucci, a charming young Florentine. He soon became the Thrales' constant companion in Paris; as did his friend, the Hungarian, Count Bathiani, "an amiable Boy indeed," "Johnson is quite in Love with little Bathyan," and she wrote in her travel diary that she hoped her son Harry would be like him one day (*Journals*, p. 107).

It did not take the Thrales long to become the center of a small, congenial group. Besides the two Counts, there was the charming M. Le Roy, an architect; the gracious Abbé François; and the Benedictine Father Wilkes and his prior, the learned and helpful Father Cowley (all introduced by Mrs. Strickland). Also there were various young English travelers of rank who discovered the Thrales. Mrs. Strickland had plenty of beaux, which pleased her (*Journals*, p. 143). And despite the daunting start, pleasant relations were established with Mme. du Boccage. She and her nephew-in-law and pretty niece, Count and Countess Blanchetti, were included in the "grand dinner" the Thrales gave on 11 October to celebrate their twelfth wedding anniversary (*Journals*, p. 110).

The Thrales' days in Paris were filled with running about churches and libraries (the King's Library and the Library of the Sorbonne profoundly impressed Johnson), museums, palaces, great houses, theatres, operas, fairs, pleasure gardens, shopping, and visits to the Gobelin tapestry factory and the Sèvres porcelain works. There were excursions to Versailles to see the royal apartments, the Grand Trianon, the Petit Trianon, the theatre, and the menagerie: also the gardens, where Mrs. Strickland gathered a great many horse-chestnuts to bring home to Sizergh Castle [17] (*Journals*, p. 60), and Johnson ran a race in the rain with Baretti, and won (*Letters* 437). There were visits to Choisy, the hunting lodge, so elegant and serenely situated; to Belle Vue, once the house of Mme. de Pompadour; to Meudon and to St. Cloud. There, Mrs. Thrale found the pictures superb; but better still she liked those of the Duc d'Orléans in the Palais Royale. One "View of one Room in this House is worth crossing the Seas for" (*Journals*, p. 147). She half cried over some of the paintings and she recorded in her travel journal, 6 October, that this excursion, with a delightful British traveler, Domenick Mead, added to our "Society," "has been my happiest Day hitherto; I have spent it with English Men and among Italian Pictures" (*Journals*, p. 104).

One of the special events which the party attended was a horse-race, at which Marie Antoinette was present. Mrs. Thrale was struck by the beauty of this young woman, who had been Queen for a little over a

[17] Over twenty years later, Mrs. Thrale (by then Piozzi) recorded in *Thraliana* that Mrs. Strickland had been a great nuisance at Versailles, doing nothing but picking up horse-chestnuts fallen from the trees. "We were all very angry at her" but the guide said to let the lady alone, "it was Louis le Grand who planted these Trees . . ." Later, Mrs. Strickland "plagued us all again by guarding this Bag of Marons as She called 'em, with a ridiculous Attention . . . from our Custom house Officers at Dover.—Well! . . . my sweet Old Friend [has sent] me a *Hundred* Horse Chesnuts in a Bag . . ."

These were from the trees at Sizergh, now grown high. Mrs. Strickland's hundred horse-chestnuts were planted on the grounds of Brynbella and, by May 1796, "98 out of the Hundred young Princes of Bourbon are *come up*" (*Thraliana*, p. 959).

year. (She was not yet twenty — only nine years older than Queeney Thrale.)

As for the race, it was far less interesting than the sight of Marie Antoinette. It was, in fact, ridiculous: the heaviest weights were placed on the weakest horses, and all the jockeys wore green, and thus became indistinguishable and invisible (*Journals*, p. 99).

Count Manucci arranged for the Thrales to make a two-day visit to Fontainebleau. The countryside, as they approached, was lovely and reminded Mrs. Thrale of Tunbridge Wells, though more rocky. The royal apartments, she thought, "exceeded in Richness and Splendour all we had yet seen" (*Journals*, p. 127). The stables and kennels, however, they all agreed, were wretched — filthy.

The French court was for the moment residing at Fontainebleau, and the party watched the public dining of the King and Queen. Again Mrs. Thrale commented on Marie Antoinette's beauty. She was by far the prettiest woman at her court. Of the near-sighted, twenty-one-year-old Louis XVI, she said, ". . . the King is well enough — like another Frenchman." This public dining was a curious thing. On the table there was a damask cloth, but not fine. The plates were silver, but "not clean and bright like Silver in England." The dinner consisted of "five Dishes at a Course." The King and Queen sat like straw figures, "they did not speak at all to each other . . . but both sometimes turned & talked to the Lord in waiting . . . " The Queen was very inquisitive about Queeney. "She would have our Names written down, & was indeed very [condescending but] troublesome with her Enquiries" (*Journals*, p. 125).

Back in Paris, one day, while Mrs. Thrale and Queeney were visiting the Blue Nuns with Mrs. Strickland, Thrale and Johnson went to see Antoine Joseph Santerre, the brewer (who would command troops around the scaffold at the execution of Louis XVI). Santerre "brews with about as much malt as Mr. T., and sells his beer at the same price though he pays no duty for malt, and little more than half as much for beer," Johnson wrote in his diary. "Beer is sold retail at 6p. a bottle. He brews 4000 barrels a year [Mrs. Thrale and Johnson were endeavoring to restrain Thrale's brewing to 80,000 barrels]. There are seventeen brewers in Paris [of] whom none is supposed to brew more than [Santerre] — reckoning them at 3000 each they make 51000 a year" (*Journals*, p. 180). This meant that Thrale outbrewed all of Paris by 29,000 barrels.

The travelers, including Queeney, were kept busy. She was often given a run in the Luxembourg Gardens, and she was taking dancing lessons from a teacher recommended by M. Leviez, Mrs. Thrale's old instructor. Mrs. Thrale had called upon Leviez her first day in Paris, with the hope that he might teach Queeney, but she had found the old man sadly broken, no longer able to give dancing lessons.

As for Mrs. Thrale's diversions, besides sightseeing and shopping and attending public events and going to the opera and to plays (the French actors were excellent), she reserved time to keep up her travel journal and to write letters, also to enjoy reading over those she had received from England. These included a note from Harry on 14 October, sending his love and duty and Mr. and Mrs. Perney's respects. "Mr Perkins calld on me last Sunday and said he could send you a Letter from me," he wrote. "I hope you have all had an agreeable Journey and are all very well. I should be glad to know how you like Paris, and when you will return? I am very well." On 21 October Harry wrote that "Lady Lad [sic] was so kind as to call on me last Thursday: She would have me go to her House in the Holidays; but Mr Perny [sic] said I must not go without your consent . . . She said Sr John Lad's [sic] Tutor might give me some Lessons." [18]

On 1 November, the Thrales left Paris, where, she recorded, they had spent a month of "extreme expense." Johnson had made some jottings in his diary: the rue Jacob house cost a guinea a day. "Coach 3 guineas a week" (and Thrale kept two). "Valet de place, 3L. a day . . . Ordinary diner 6L. a head. Our ordinary seems to be about five guineas a day. Our extraordinary expences, as diversions, gratuities, cloaths; I cannot reckon. Our travelling is ten guineas a day" (*Journals*, p. 184). Baretti, the treasurer-general, kept the official account and according to this the expedition of fifty-nine days cost Thrale eight hundred and twenty-two louis d'or [19] (a louis d'or being the equivalent of a guinea). [20]

Certainly Thrale had spared no expense, and Baretti no trouble, and Mrs. Thrale had had "a prodigious fine Journey of it" (*Journals*, p.

[18] Harry's letters are owned by Mr. Eric Sexton of Camden, Maine.

[19] Twenty-four livres made up a louis d'or. This continued to be true until the French Revolution. It was Napoleon who changed the currency to francs.

Among the itemized expenses were these: at St. Germain the physician for Mr. Thrale, 48 livres; his Paris surgeon, 144 livres; the dancing master, 90 livres; tailor's bill for Mr. Thrale, 2568 livres; couturière's bill for Mrs. Thrale, 679 livres.

[20] Baretti's account and Mrs. Thrale's bill for gowns are in the possession of Professor James L. Clifford (1975).

143). With regret, she parted from Mrs. Strickland and Manucci; the former was returning to Rouen, and the latter to Florence, where he urged them to come and visit next spring. In turn they pressed him to come to England before they set out, and he promised that he would. Baretti had grown tired of Manucci, perhaps jealous. He granted that the Count was "a good and most pleasing man," but he told Mrs. Thrale that he was surprised she had such high regard for someone who "read very little in his language and next to nothing in any other" (*Journals*, p. 64). Mrs. Thrale paid no attention to Baretti's opinion. She was charmed by Manucci and longed to entertain him at Streatham.

As the Thrales made their way north to Calais, they varied their route, passing through Chantilly, Noyonne, Cambrai, Douai, and Lisle. Their stops in Cambrai and Douai were made pleasant by introductions from Father Cowley to a number of Benedictine priests. In the prior's letter, along with the introductions, was the assurance to Johnson that his overnight stay with the Benedictines in Paris would never be forgotten and that his cell would always be reserved for him. Father Cowley hoped to come to England, perhaps next year or the year after. In Dunkirk, their final stop in France, the travelers were entertained by Captain Andrew Fraser and his agreeable young wife (whose parents were neighbors of the Thrales in Streatham).

At Calais the party again boarded Captain Baxter's packet and so to Dover. On the crossing Queeney and Molly were as seasick as they had been before; Sam, Mrs. Thrale noted in the margin of her journal, "was too ill to be Seasick" (*Journals*, p. 165). On the subject of health, Queeney had maintained a better record than she had the year before in Wales: some worms, bruises from the accident, a sprained toe, a cold and a cough, caught from her mother, who had suffered a bad cold. Baretti had been ill once and Thrale had been hurt in the accident. Johnson was the man made of iron.

Mrs. Thrale's final dread was the Custom House officers at Dover, but all went well: no fuss was made about the Sèvres, the presents, or the toys, nor about her three Paris gowns. Thrale had offered her "any Silk at any Price" (*Journals*, p. 139) and one of her gowns had been made of "plain White Silk . . . peculiarly elegant — trimmed with pale Purple & Silver by the fine Madame Beauvais & in the newest and highest Fashion" (*Letters* 519.1A). This beautiful dress caused no trouble; neither did Johnson's Paris wig.

The last record of Mrs. Thrale's journal of her French tour, Saturday, 11 November, at Dover, is typical of an English traveler returned safely home: "I see now that [England] is better than France" (*Journals*, p. 165).

Two days later, Mrs. Thrale resumed recording in the *Family Book*:

on the 15: of Sept. 1775. *We set out for France, & after a Month spent at Paris & another in travelling from place to place we return'd to Streatham this 13th of Nov.* 1775. *Queeny behaved sweetly all the way; learnt French faster than I hoped for, & made no Small Improvement in Dancing — She was vastly sick at Sea, & has not recovered her Looks yet, but the Serv.ts all say She is grown. — We picked up Harry on our Road home; he looks wonderfully well in health, but says he is not happy; the Boys are childish and despicable Companions, & the Confinement such as he has never been used to: he is the the [sic] eighth Boy from the Top, now he is 8 Years & a half old — construes Ovid very smartly — & does his Tasks with a degree of Intelligence that Dr Johnson says is not common even at 12 Years old: all this about Harry was written on the 17:th after we had examined things a little, he was prodigiously happy to see us returned.*

20: Nov.

I have seen my sweet little Girls — Susan will really be a lovely Lass after all: I never found fault with Sophy. Harry's Schoolmaster complains that he says naughty words — has called some young Lord or Duke an Impudent Dog perhaps, — no worse Crime I dare say. All the World praises his Parts & his Scholarship.

Harry says the Boys at this Loughboro' House are just like Babies, & treated as such by the Master; who daddles [21] *after them with a Rod as he expresses it, all about the Room: — Harry it seems has been treated with more Severity for laughing at this curious Operation.*

25: Nov: 1775.
I have heard of my Son's naughtiness: it consisted in telling his Schoolfellows a staring Story about what was done at a Bawdy house, for w:ch Conversation Old Perny very wisely flogg'd him well & I hope we shall hear no more of it. The Truth is Harry is but too forward

---

[21] Daddle: to walk unsteadily.

in some *things; he told me Yesterday he wondered Baretti was not ashamed of belonging to a Country where they cut the Men, as we cut the Horses — & all to make them* sing *forsooth.*[22] *I bid him never talk to his Sisters on such Subjects, & got rid of it myself as I could, /but/ Harry makes reading so much his Amusement that he must know every thing that Books contain: The other Day Bob Cotton [a linen draper in Parliament Street] was saying how he had saved some Lady on Horseback from great Danger — Oh ho cries Harry I'll warrant you'll marry her at last as Tom Jones did Miss Sophy Western: Lord Child say'd I didst thou ever read Tom Jones? — Yes to be sure replies Harry one* must *read Tom Jones, & Joseph Andrews.*

29: Nov:
Queeney is quite beautiful since her French Expedition, grows plump & blooming, & more more [sic] full of Tongue, tho' always too shy; and Harry has not a Complaint except of his Fellow Students that they are such Darlings as he calls them. he begs hard to go to Westmʳ & shall, when we return from Italy: it is for that Reason Mʳ Thrale chuses to set out next Spring, because Harry will be safe at this place till our Return, & then he shall break his Chains poor Fellow.

The expedition to France had clearly been a success, for the Thrales, barely home, were already making preparations for the more ambitious journey — to Italy. Baretti readily agreed to be courier again (though he had had much trouble in France as "the chief mover of too large a caravan, most members of which had a good proportion of wants and whims" (*European Magazine*, August 1788, p. 91).

For Italy, Baretti thought in terms of a year's absence, with a winter in Tuscany, and a return through Switzerland. Thrale and Johnson had no objection to this, but Mrs. Thrale wanted a trip of six months only, April to October, so that they might be home when Harry entered Westminster, that distinguished school re-founded by Queen Elizabeth I (it had been a Benedictine monastery school). At Westminster Harry would be following in the footsteps of his cousin, Sir Robert Cotton, past worthies such as Ben Jonson, John Locke, and John Dryden, and current celebrities such as Edward Gibbon, William Cowper, General Burgoyne, and Warren Hastings.

The headmaster, Samuel Smith, maintained the high academic stan-

[22] Castrati: male singers in Italy, castrated so they would retain soprano voices.

dards for which the school was known, though he was not the strict disciplinarian that Richard Busby had been in the past. This was just as well, for Harry, though basically obedient, required a certain amount of freedom. He was already looking forward to frequent attendance at the theatre, an interest stimulated by his friend, Arthur Murphy, and he hoped this would be made easy by another family friend, the playwright, George Colman, a Westminster "old boy," who it was said extended a hearty welcome at Covent Garden to all present boys. George Colman, the younger, was now attending the school.

The future appeared to be well arranged for Harry; and Susan and Sophy were thriving. All the children seemed healthier than when Mrs. Thrale had left for France — except for the baby, whose condition was disturbing.

Here is little Fanny very ill & of her head too — it will turn my Head at last; Old Nurse is gone to Town to consult Dr Lawrence — Good News if it please God! never happy long together!

At first Mrs. Thrale thought that Fanny had only a bad head cold; her wet-nurse [23] had one, and others in the household also had heavy colds. They had got over them, but Fanny did not improve, and Old Nurse wanted to consult Herbert Lawrence, for of all the children's doctors, he was the one in whom she put the most trust. Old Nurse carried Fanny to London, where Lawrence told her the child had influenza — there was an epidemic.

Lawrence attended Fanny, but her condition grew steadily worse.

This 11:th of Dec: 1775.
I buried my poor little Fanny; She was 1:st seized with the Influenza w:ch affected every body, among the rest her [wet-]Nurse, & herself so violently we could not remove it Dr [Thomas] Lawrence of Essex Street, says that killed her, not a Dropsy of the Brain as I first apprehended; & this ought to Comfort me a little: the other four are healthy active & vigorous as possible; I hope I may be permitted to keep them so —— but be it as it may: I must endeavour not to provoke Gods Judgments on my Family — & then, like poor old Patriarch Jacob — if /I/ be bereaved of my Children I be bereaved.

[23] Many years later the fact was recognized that wet-nurses (with their own outside domestic contacts) were frequently carriers of infection to the babies they suckled.

Mrs. Thrale's acceptance of little Fanny's death was philosophic — as it had been for others of her babies — the inevitable consequence of the terribly high mortality among infants. With birth — death was always half-expected.

Fanny's [Wet] Nurse is dead of the Influenza, follow'd her poor little Mistress very soon.[24]

Sat: Jan: 20: [1776] Susan returned to School after the Holy days — She improves prodigiously in all respects, and is very much admired for a fine Girl Body & Mind, home & School. ——

During January and February Baretti was in feverish correspondence with his brothers and with friends in Italy, urging their cooperation in the proposed journey. The party would consist as before of the Thrales and Queeney, Johnson, and himself, "the leader of the march." Two four-wheeled chaises would be required for those mentioned, and a third chaise as well, to carry Molly, Sam, and the luggage. Another man with them would ride as postillion. Other servants would be hired when they stayed in a place for any length of time. They wished to travel in comfort.

Baretti planned to retrace some of the route of the past autumn, crossing the channel from Dover to Calais, and going on to Paris, after this south to Lyons, and across the Alps to Turin. From here, he was making arrangements to take the party to visit his family, near Valenza (between Turin and Milan); and for this stay he pressed his brothers to borrow or hire what was necessary — furniture, bedding, plate — whatever was needed to make the accommodations suitable. There should be a Bible for Mrs. Thrale. She is "gay and joyful if she is not shocked by any disregard of religion or morals, even the slightest, being a great biblist . . ."[25] There should be other books about, old rather than modern, in Italian, Latin, and Greek. An agreeable priest to speak Latin to Johnson should be provided if possible.

After this visit the party would go on to Genoa, Milan, Parma, Bologna, Rimini, San Marino — and finally Rome. The trip was to be an education for the Thrales and a triumph for Baretti.

[24] This sentence is written in the *Family Book* at the foot of the next page, following the entry headed "15: Feb."

[25] E. S. De Beer, "Johnson's Italian Tour" in *Johnson, Boswell, and Their Circle* (Oxford: Clarendon Press, 1965), p. 160.

15: Feb: Harry's Birthday
He is happy healthy wise & good: has begged Money for the Men to
make merry, & invited his own Company for the parlour. his Selection
was Murphy, Perkins & Tom Cotton, to whom I added a friendly
Att:ʸ here in the Borough, & Count Mannucci [sic] who we knew at
Paris came in by Chance. he landed Yesterday. Old Perney & little
Blake from Loughboro' House filled up our heterogeneous Mass of
Company, & Johnson was here of Course; he does love little Harry!.
——— I measured My Son Yesterday with his foster Bro:ʳ [son of Patsy
Burnet] who is the same Age of Course; but he was big enough to eat
the Boy, & taller by a head /indeed/ — he neither looks nor talks like
a Child of 9 Years old only. ———

Harry Thrale's ninth anniversary was a joyous occasion. He begged
money, as was the birthday custom, for the clerks at the brewhouse to
celebrate. He was a favorite with them and, to his father's pride and
pleasure, wholly in his element at the brewery, much happier than at
the Loughborough House School. His father hoped that someday
Harry would outbrew Whitbread and Calvert.

Harry's own birthday party took place in the Thrales' parlor. The
guests he asked, with the exception of young Blake, his schoolfellow,
were all adults: Johnson; John Perkins; Harry's cousin, Tom Cotton,
the fourth son of Sir Lynch, who worked in London as an auditor for
North Wales; old Mr. Perney, Harry's master at school, and his idol,
Arthur Murphy, the playwright.

Manucci's appearance was a surprise, and added excitement, for
Harry had heard much of the Italian friend, whom his parents had met
abroad. And the Thrales were delighted that the Count had been able
to arrive before their departure for Italy — now scheduled for 9 April.
Manucci had many travel suggestions to make, and he assured them that
by the time they reached Florence he would be home again to receive
them.

Early in the next month, Mrs. Thrale recorded in the *Family Book*:

6: March 1776.
I saw Susan at School, nothing can do better than She does; when Sir
Robᵗ Cotton comes to Town I shall fetch her home to shew him that
he ought to send his Girls [Frances and Sophia] to Mʳˢ Cumyns's, if he
has a mind to see them accomplished.

Sophy is very good & lives with me & Queeney who tutor her by turns; She reads prettily now, & says long Strings of Stuff by heart, which nobody but her Sister & I will give the hearing to. The Catechism of course.

In early March there was suddenly good news about Johnson's and Mrs. Thrale's private charity — Mr. Carter. Johnson was advised that Oxford's Vice-Chancellor and the Proctors had given their consent for the erection of a riding house and for the appointment of Carter as riding master. This was wonderful, and Johnson wrote at once to his friend John Douglas, Bishop of Salisbury, who controlled the Clarendon account, requesting that the royalty money be forwarded to the proper authorities.

Within a few days the astonishing answer came: there were not sufficient funds to carry out any such ambitious scheme. It seems strange that Johnson had not ascertained the financial situation at the outset, but nonetheless this was a sad end to the two years' striving of Johnson and Mrs. Thrale. "Our Assiduity thus defeated, our Kindness slackened, and we left the poor Creature to sink at last after all our unavailing Efforts to support him" (*Thraliana*, p. 119).[26]

In contrast to their disappointment about the outcome of the Carter project was their excitement about the plans for the Grand Tour of Italy. Baretti was making constant changes in the itinerary, enlarging it to include Sicily and adding stops in small towns between Turin and Genoa in such number that Johnson became concerned. The party must not be cheated out of proper stays in the great cities — Rome, Florence, Naples, and Venice — even if Baretti could not accompany them to the last (he was still subject to arrest in Venice for his daring political writings). Johnson insisted that the itinerary be properly proportioned.

He was busily making himself ready, and he wrote to Boswell on 5 March that if his friend had any intention of seeing him before he set out for Italy, he must come quickly and accompany him to Oxford and Lichfield for his farewell visits. Boswell rose to the occasion and was in London by 16 March, where he found to his surprise that Johnson had given up residence at Johnson's Court, in prospect of the long trip abroad.

[26] The profits of the *Life of Clarendon*, such as they were, continued to accumulate, and with better management there was enough money available in 1868 to build the Clarendon Laboratory.

On 19 March the two friends set out from London to Oxford by coach, Johnson carrying with him a volume of romances, *Palmerin of England*, in Italian translation, to improve his knowledge of the language. The next day, while Johnson and Boswell were calling on their friends at various colleges, Mrs. Thrale recorded in the *Family Book*:

on Wednesday the 20: of March 1776. I quarrelled slightly with Queeney in the Morning but we made it up & went out together in search of a Ticket for her to go at Night to Bach & Abel's Concert, but could not get one. I had fetched Harry home yesterday to shew him, /to/ Scrase, Golding & Gregory three old Intimates of his Father who were to dine with us today. They did so, & I left Niggey to make Tea for them in the Evening, & when I returned all were well & fast asleep, & Queeney had done me the Story of Atalanta from a French & Latin Ovid mighty well:

Mrs. Thrale was sorry to miss an evening with Scrase — next to Johnson she loved him best as a family friend (*Thraliana*, p. 372). But the two other old cronies of her husband she was happy to quit, especially Gregory, who was a heavy drinker and a medical quack.

The concert to which she went was given by Karl Friedrich Abel and Johann Christian Bach, the son of Johann Sebastian. These two artists, Bach playing the harpsichord and Abel the viola da gamba, had been giving pleasure to audiences in London for several years.

Mrs. Thrale knew that "Niggey," as she sometimes called Queeney, could be trusted to be a good hostess and that everything would be well managed during her absence. So it seemed to be.

on Thursday the 21.ˢᵗ they all [Queeney, Harry, and Sophy] rose well & lively; & Queeney went with me to fetch her Sister [Susan] from School for a Week — She [Queeney] seemed sullen all the way there & back but not sick, so I huffed her & we got home in good Time to dress for dinner, when we expected Sir Rob.ᵗ Cotton & the Davenants. Harry however had seen a play [27] of his Friend Murphy's advertised, & teized me so to let him see it that I could not resist his Importunity, and treated one of our principal Clerks to go with him: he came home at 12 o'Clock half mad with delight, and in such Spirits Health & Happiness that nothing ever exceeded: Queeney however drooped all Afternoon; complained of the Headach & M.ʳ Thrale was

[27] Arthur Murphy's *The Way to Keep Him*, at Drury Lane.

so cross at my giving Harry leave to go to the play, instead of shewing him to Sir Robert; that I passed an uneasy Time of it, and could not enjoy the praises given to Susan, I was /so/ fretted about the two eldest. when Harry came home so happy however, all was forgotten, & he went to rest in perfect Tranquillity — Queeney however felt hot, & I was not at all pleased with her, but on Fryday Morning [22 March] the boy rose quite chearful & did our little Business with great Alacrity. Count Mannucci [sic] came to Breakfast by Appointment, we were all to go shew him the Tower [of London] forsooth, so Queeney made light of her Illness & pressed me to take her too. There was one of the Ships [on fire] bound for Boston now in the River with our Beer a'board — Harry ran to see the blaze in the Morning, & coming back to the Compting house — I see says he to our 1.ˢᵗ Clerk — I see Your Porter is good Mr. Perkins; for it burns *special well. Well by this Time we set out for the Tower, Papa & Mannucci, & the Children & I: Queeney was not half well, but Harry continued in high Spirits both among the Lyons & the Arms: repeating Passages from the English History, examining the Artillery & getting into every Mortar till he was as black as the Ground.*[28] *Count Mannucci [sic] observ'd his Pranks, & said he must be a Soldier /with him;/ but Harry would not fight for the Grand Duke of Tuscany because he was a Papist, & look here said he shewing the Instruments of Torture to the Count, what those Spanish Papists intended for* us. *From this Place we drove to Moore's Carpet Manufactory,*[29] *where the Boy was still active, attentive & lively: but as Queeney's looks betray'd the Sickness She would fain have concealed, we drove homewards; taking in our way Brooke's Menagerie,*[30] *where I just stopped to speak about my Peafowl: Here Harry was happy again with a Lyon intended for a Show who was remarkably tame, & a monkey so beautiful & gentle, that I was as much pleased with him as the Children: here we met a Mr. Hervey who took notice of the Boy how* well *he look'd. Yes said /I/ if the dirt were scraped off him: It was now Time to get home, & Harry after saying*

---

[28] The Tower of London was a favorite place to take visitors, for it offered a dramatic survey of English history—and one was proud to show it, for this was a fortress which had never been conquered.

The "Lyons" were live, part of the menagerie which was comprised of leopards, bears, wolves, hyenas, and many other animals—always lions, for they were a prime symbol of British royalty.

The "Arms" were cannon, captured from Armada ships.

[29] Moore's Carpet Manufactory was at 63 Chiswell Street.

[30] Brooke's Original Menagerie for Birds, Animals, &c was at 242 Piccadilly.

*how hungry he was — instantly pounced as [he] called it [on] a piece
of Cold Mutton & spent the Afternoon among us all recounting the
pleasures of the Day. he went to Bed that night as perfectly well as ever
I saw Man Woman or Child in my Life. Queeney however took some
Rhubarb, & went on drooping & felt feverish. I looked at her two or
three Times in the Night too, & found her hot & feverish, but her dear
Brother slept as cool & comfortable as possible, & on the Morning
of the next fatal day Saturday 23.ᵈ of March 1776. he rose in perfect
health, went to the Baker for his Roll and watched the drawing it out
of the Oven, carried it to* Batchelors' Hall *as he called it where the
young Clerks live down the Brewhouse Yard; there he got Butter, &
cooked a merry Breakfast among them. After this he returned with
two peny Cakes he had bought for the little Girls, & distributed them
between them in his pleasant Manner for Minuets that he made them
dance: I was all this while waiting on Queeney, who seem'd far from
well; & /I/ was once very Impatient at the Noise the maids & Children
made in the Nursery, by laughing excessively at his Antick Tricks.
By this Time I came down to my Dressing Room to tutor Sophy till the
Clock struck ten which is my regular Breakfast hour — I had scarce
made the Tea when Moll came to tell me Queeney was better, &
Harry making a Figure of 5:10* [31] *so we always called his manner of
twisting about when a/n/ything ailed him: when I got to the Nursery,
there was Harry crying as if he had /been/ whipt instead of ill, so I
reproved /him/ for making such a bustle ab:ᵗ nothing, & said see how
differently your Sister behaves, who tho' in earnest far from well, had
beg'd to make breakfast for Papa & Mᵣ Baretti, while I was employed
above. The next Thing I did was to send for ⟨old Nurse⟩ Mᵣ Lawrence
of York Buildings, to whom Nurse was always partial: my Note expressed to him that both the eldest Children were ill, but Hetty worst:
presently however finding the boy inclined to vomit, I administer'd a
large Wine-Glass of Emetic Wine which however did nothing* any
*way; tho' he drank small Liquids with avidity: and now seeing his Sick-
ness increase, & his Countenance begin to alter, I sent out Sam: with
orders not to come back without some Physician — Jebb, Bromfield,
Pinkstan or Lawrence of Essex Street,* [32] *whichever he could find: in
the mean time I plunged Harry into Water as hot as could easily be*

---

[31] This is the knee-chest position, which one is apt to assume instinctively, to be able to vomit and still breathe, not strangle on one's own vomit.

[32] Thomas Lawrence of Essex Street, friend and physician to Dr. Johnson (as distinct from Herbert Lawrence of the York Buildings).

borne, up to his Middle, & had just taken him out of the Tub, & laid him in a warm bed, when Jebb came, & gave him 1.ˢᵗ hot Wine, then Usquebaugh, then Daffy's Elixir,³³ so fast that it alarmed me; tho' I had no Notion of Death having seen him so perfectly well at 9 o'clock. he then had Pultices made with Mustard put to his feet, & strong Broth & Wine Clysters injected,³⁴ but we could get no Evacuation any way: & the Inclination to vomit still continuing Jebb gave him 5 Grains of Ipecacuanha³⁵ & then drove away to call Heberden's³⁶ help. The Child all this while spoke well & brisk; sate upright to talk with the D.ʳˢ; said he had no Pain now but his Breath was short: this I attributed to the hot things He had taken, & thought Jebb in my Heart far more officious than wise. I was however all confusion distress & perplexity, & M.ʳ Thrale bid me not cry so, for I should look like a Hag when I went to Court next Day — he often saw Harry in the Course of the Morn.ᵍ: and apprehended no danger at all — no more did Baretti, who said he should be whipt for frighting his Mother for nothing. — Queeney had for some Time been laid down on her own Bed, & got up fancying herself better; but soon a universal Shriek called us all together to Harry's Bedside, where he struggled a Moment — thrusting his Finger down his Throat to excite Vomiting, & then — turning to Nurse said very distinctly — dont Scream so — I know I must die.
    This however I did not hear.

Manucci, who was with the Thrales, sent his servant to fetch Baretti, for he had returned to London. Baretti sped back to Southwark, and described the scene he witnessed:

Mr. Thrale, both his hands in his waistcoat pocket[s], sat on an arm-chair in a corner of the room with his body so stiffly erect, and with such a ghastly smile on his face, as was quite horrid to behold. Count Manucci and a female servant, both as pale as ashes, and as if panting for breath, were evidently spent with keeping Madam from going frantic (and well she might) every time she recovered from her fainting-fits, that followed each other in a very quick succession. (*European Magazine*, May 1788, p. 314)

    ³³ Daffy's Elixir: tincture of senna, a laxative.
    ³⁴ Wine Clysters: enemas of wine.
    ³⁵ Ipecacuanha or ipecac: an emetic made from the roots of a South American creeping plant.
    ³⁶ William Heberden was Cambridge-trained and a Fellow of the Royal College of Physicians, an authority on many diseases, and at the time considered the most eminent physician in London. (It was Heberden who had freed medicine from the belief that "humors" were the basis of all disease.)

Mrs. Thrale's journal continues the account of the day, though the entire entry was written more than two weeks later:

Lady Lade who I believe had been here half the Morn^g: watching the Event asked me kindly what She should do for me — I replied Oh take me these two little Girls away — they distract me: She accordingly then carried them [Susan and Sophy] off & set 'em safe at Kensington, where they are still. This most dreadful of all our Misfortunes, w:^{ch} they say happened about 3 o'Clock, or 4, on the 23^d day of March 1776. had such an Effect on poor Queeney that I expected her to follow him: Jebb however did something for her, & advising speedy Change of Scene; I rose in the Morning of the 30:th after a sleepless Night, & in a Sort of Desperation drove away with her to Bath, which little Journey did her infinite Service: Baretti kindly offered to go with me, so he conducted the Troop, & diverted Queeney's Melancholy with all the Tricks he could think on: She is now tho' not recovered, yet I hope out of Danger (as the Phrase is:) I saw the little Girls at Kensington Yesterday as I came home. this is the 9:th of April 1776.

Henry Salusbury Thrale, aged nine years and one month, was buried at St. Leonard's in Streatham on Thursday, 28 March.

The cause of his sudden death was mystifying to all concerned, and it is hard for a present-day medical authority, with only Mrs. Thrale's journal for testimony, to give a diagnosis. Death from a ruptured appendix, which has previously been suggested, seems unlikely, for it would take two or three days for peritonitis (inflammation of the membrane which lines the abdominal cavity) to cause death, and the duration of Harry's illness was only six or seven hours. Death from a fulminating septicaemia (a sudden and virulent infection) or meningitis seem the most probable causes of his sudden and tragic death. Such a diagnosis is strongly supported by the account of Queeney's feverishness before Harry's seizure, and her continued illness after his death. It is not unreasonable to suppose that she suffered from the same infection that killed Harry, but in a milder form. Before the days of antibiotics, a child often died within a few hours of an overwhelmingly acute infection.

Mrs. Thrale's treatment of Harry, as she awaited the arrival of a doctor (giving a large glass of emetic wine, putting him into hot water and then a warm bed) was reasonable, according to the practice of the time, and when Dr. Jebb came he continued the treatment of heat, together with emetics and purges. He came quickly, and though he failed, he did all that any eighteenth-century doctor could have been expected to do. Today's antibiotics would probably have saved Harry's life.

Herbert Lawrence, the old family doctor and friend, did not respond to Mrs. Thrale's urgent call for help, and she vowed she would never have anything further to do with him (*Thraliana*, p. 130). The doctor she turned to now was Jebb.

And following his advice, she and Queeney, accompanied by Baretti, set out for Bath on Saturday, 30 March. As they were about to step into the coach, Johnson appeared.

News of the tragedy had reached him at Lichfield on Monday, 25 March, as he and Boswell were having breakfast at Lucy Porter's house. A letter from Perkins described the terrible event and concluded, "I need not say how much they wish to see you in London" (*Letters* 465, n. 1).

Johnson immediately wrote to Mrs. Thrale:

. . . in a distress which can be so little relieved, nothing remains for a friend but to come and partake it.

Poor dear sweet little Boy . . . When you have obtained by Prayer such tranquillity as nature will admit, force your attention, as you can, upon your accustomed duties, and accustomed entertainments. You can do no more for our dear Boy, but you must not therefore think less on those whom your attention may make fitter for the place to which he is gone. (*Letters* 465)

Stopping only briefly in Ashbourne, Johnson and Boswell returned to London and Johnson at once hurried to Southwark, arriving at the moment Mrs. Thrale and Queeney were departing for Bath, Mrs. Thrale nervous, grief-stricken, and Queeney still unwell. "I expected at that moment," Baretti said, "that he would spare me the jaunt, and go himself to Bath with her; but he made no motion to that effect; therefore, after the sad exchange of a few mournful periods . . . we got into the coach and were soon out of sight" (*European Magazine*, May 1788, p. 315).

Johnson lingered at the house, trying to give comfort to Thrale, but was sent away. He returned the next day and was told by a servant that when he was wanted he would be sent for (*Letters* 467). Boswell was offended that his friend's presence was so unappreciated, but the old man held no resentment. In bereavement, he said, one accepted the actions of those one loved, no matter what they might be.

Mrs. Thrale wrote to Johnson from Bath. She assured him that his friendship

has long been the best Cordial to my Heart, it is now almost the only one. I cold bathe here, & endeavour all I can to excite Appetite, & force Attention; I owe every Thing to Mr Thrale's indulgent Tenderness, and will bring him home the best Wife I can: how has it happened that every body has been so kind? (*Letters* 467A)

Johnson replied, urging her to stay in Bath so long as "the novelty of the place does any good either to you or Queeney . . . What gratification can be extracted from so sad an event, I derive from observing that Mr Thrale's behaviour has united you to him by additional endearments . . . May your love of each other always encrease" (*Letters* 468). This was 4 April, and Thrale had still not asked for Johnson to come to him.

In Bath, the day after arrival, according to Baretti, a letter came from Dr. Jebb, earnestly entreating Mrs. Thrale not to give Queeney any more tin pills, for though it might be true that she had worms, the remedy might well be worse than the disease; it could tear the child's bowels to pieces.

Baretti said that Mrs. Thrale showed him the letter and at the same time determined to give Queeney a dose of tin pills. Baretti was enraged, and told her in no uncertain terms that

she would soon send the daughter to keep company with the son, if she gave her any more of her damn'd pills: and not satisfied with this, I informed the daughter of the horrid quality of the physic that her good mamma administered her against the positive order of Dr. Jebb . . . assuring her that [the pills] would soon destroy her. (*European Magazine*, May 1788, p. 315)

Mrs. Thrale turned on Baretti with fury, and he met her with equal fury, a battle of violent accusation ensued (the only dignity shown was on the part of Queeney who remained aloof from the conflict).[37] In the end, a truce of sorts was agreed upon by Mrs. Thrale and Baretti for the rest of the stay in Bath, but neither one of them ever forgot or forgave. They were enemies for the rest of their lives.

Meanwhile in London, Thrale had gained control of his grief, and

[37] According to present medical opinion the tin pills would have been dangerous only if given in excess.

on 5 April (Good Friday) he came himself to Johnson's house, and spent most of the day there. At seven he went to evening prayers at St. Clement Danes with Johnson. Boswell was with them and thought Thrale manly and composed.

Queeney's health had improved at Bath and she and her mother and Baretti returned to London in time for Easter. The Thrales attended the service at St. Paul's that day, and Boswell, who was also there, observed that Mrs. Thrale was "in tender grief."

On Tuesday, 9 April, she recorded the long entry on Harry's death in the *Family Book*, and the same day she wrote to Johnson (at 8 Bolt Court, where he was establishing a new residence) to say that she had shown Thrale his letter from Lichfield and her husband had ". . . shed Tears over the reading it — they are the first he has shed. — I can say no more" (*Letters* 470A).

So ends my Pride, my hopes; my possession of present, & expectation of future Delight. Mr Thrale & I have agreed to let Italy alone; we had no other Reason for going this Year, but because Harry could have spared us worse when he was at Westm.^r and now what should we go hazarding poor Queeney's Life for? have we /not/ had Sorrow sufficient?

Baretti is very angry we do not go.

On this same day (9 April), when Mrs. Thrale drove out to Streatham for a few hours, she left her husband and Baretti arguing about the trip to Italy; the latter insisting that it would be the best possible distraction for the Thrales, that Johnson's disappointment would be great, and that in the eyes of the world they would look ridiculous not to go. His waiting friends and relations in Italy would be much put out — and some of the luggage was already in Calais — the trip must not be abandoned. Thrale said the trip was not abandoned, simply postponed. For how long, Baretti asked heatedly. He was almost sixty and he would not be fit to manage strenuous travel many years more. They must go now. Thrale held firm. The trip at present was out of the question (soon he was to give Baretti £100 for the trouble he had taken; poor amends, in the Italian's opinion).

Johnson had been told of the cancellation of the trip on Easter Day, and his reaction was very different. "Mr Thrale's alteration of purpose," he wrote to Mrs. Thrale, "is not weakness of resolution; it is a wise man's compliance with the change of things":

Whenever I can contribute to tranquillity, I shall readily attend, and hope never to add to the evils that may oppress you. I will go with you to Bath, or stay with you at home.

I am very little disappointed. I was glad to go, to places of so much celebrity, but had promised to myself no raptures, nor much improvement. Nor is there anything to be expected worth such a sacrifice as you might make. (*Letters* 470)

Baretti was enraged at Johnson's philosophic acceptance.

On 15 April Johnson wrote to Frances Reynolds, to stop a rumor:

Pray tell Sir Joshua, that I have examined Mr Thrale's Man, and find no foundation for the Story of the Alehouse and mulled Beer. [Harry] was at the Play two nights before, with one of the chief men in the Brewhouse, and came home at the regular time. (*Letters* 474)

Two days after writing this letter, on 17 April, Johnson joined Mrs. Thrale and Queeney on a return trip to Bath; Thrale was with them this time. The plan was to take lodgings and to stay for several weeks. The Thrales tried to keep busy and entertained, and Johnson tried to be cheerful. It was hard for them all, even though friends were exceedingly kind. Mrs. Montagu did everything in her power to raise the Thrales' spirits, and her sympathy was deeply felt, for years ago she too had lost her son, an only child. Another bluestocking, Mrs. Macaulay, the historian, a widow of forty-five, was also attentive. (Johnson admired Catharine Macaulay's writing and detested her democratic principles.)

The person who gave Mrs. Thrale the most comfort was Miss Owen, whom she had not seen in many years, but now met again in Bath. Margaret Owen from Wales (Montgomeryshire) had been a childhood playmate, and was a distant cousin, two years younger than Mrs. Thrale. Though Johnson found Peggy tiresome, she was attractive looking, good humored, and warm hearted, easy company for Mrs. Thrale. She was deficient in knowledge, either useful or ornamental, Johnson claimed, and even Thrale joked at her lack of powers to converse. She was the butt of many family jests. And when Boswell came to Bath and was with the family for a few days, Johnson would not let him praise Peggy Owen, saying that she "does not gain upon me, Sir; I think her empty-headed" (*Life*, III, 48).

Early in May Johnson went to London; his friend Dr. Taylor needed his advice on a legal matter, a dispute with a neighbor over some land. He promised to return to Bath as soon as possible.

Mrs. Thrale hoped that Johnson would bring Count Manucci with him when he returned. The Count would be a "Goose Cap" not to wait for Johnson to accompany him. She went on to say in this letter of 8 May that she had received word from Mrs. Cumyns that Susan and Sophy had chicken-pox, "a trifling Thing in any other Family" but "for ought I know [it might] prove fatal in my ill fated House" (*Letters* 476A).

As soon as Johnson received this letter, he went to Kensington to visit "the two Babies." He found them a little spotted, but "brisk and gay." He had brought them a "paper of sweetmeats":

They took great delight to show their governess the various animals that were made of sugar, and when they had eaten as much as was fit the rest was laid up for tomorrow.

Johnson said that he was accompanied on the visit by Dr. Taylor, who liked the children very much. Mr. Evans, the Southwark rector, joined them after a while, and all listened to Susy saying her Creed in French. Both little girls sent love and duty to their parents and to Queeney. As for returning to Bath, Taylor's business still detained him, but he hoped that it would not be long before he could bring Manucci back with him (*Letters* 477). The settlement of Taylor's legal business was delayed and on 14 May Johnson wrote to Mrs. Thrale that Manucci would have to make his way to Bath alone after all (*Letters* 478).

On 18 May Johnson wrote that he had seen Seward upon his return from Bath, and that he gave a good account of the Thrales. Johnson reported that he had been to call on John Perkins in the counting house; he "crows, and triumphs; as We go on, we shall double our business . . . Dr Taylor's business stagnates . . ." (*Letters* 482).

On 22 May he told Mrs. Thrale that, as he was writing his letter to her, Father Wilkes, the Benedictine, had called upon him, bringing good news of Father Cowley, the prior, and of Mrs. Strickland, who was at present in Paris.

Taylor failed in his lawsuits, but by this time the Thrales were ready to return to Streatham. It was a return without pleasure for they knew there would be painful memories of Harry at every turn; also the house needed to be put in running order, and a new staff was required, for when the Thrales had planned to go to Italy most of the servants had been dismissed. Mrs. Thrale wrote from Southampton on 30 May, begging Johnson not to come to Streatham too soon:

If you have any pity for me do not come home till I have got my house a little to rights, & if you can hear of a *Butler* or a *Footman* or a *Maid*, or almost anything do send them to me. (*Letters* 484A)

There was little chance of Johnson's coming home at the moment. He was confined to his own house, suffering from a bad attack of gout, "I creep about and hang by both hands" (*Letters* 485).

26: June   Streatham.
Here am I once more settled for the Summer, with three Children instead of six.

On the 17:ᵗʰ of last April as the Italian Journey was given up we resolved to go all of us to Bath, which had done so much good to our Queeney: we went therefore, & staid till last week; when we came home by Stonehenge Southampton & Portsmouth: seeing all we could find to amuse our Sorrows & heal our half broken hearts: Hetty is quite recovered, looks once more plump & blooming; & when I fix my Eyes on her, I am still foolish enough to hope for some Felicity. when She was at worst, do not said She grieve for my Illness of all things; it's the luckiest Circumstance that could have happened to you, by forcing your Mind from the great Misfortune of all. Susan & Sophy had the Chickenpox while I was away it seems; Jebb attended them by Mʳˢ Cumyns's Directions, & said they wanted a Cook more than a Doctor: every body agreed not to plague me with Accᵗˢ: which would once more have put my Spirits in Agitation so they prudently suffered me to mend at my Leisure. — it is the only Method. Susan's birthday falling out while I was at Bath, my Aunt [38] — who has been mighty kind to me, would have me keep it at her House, & treated me with Cake & Wine &c. in honour of it.

Re-establishing Streatham was a difficult chore, the more so because Mrs. Thrale was again experiencing the difficulties of early pregnancy. (The baby was expected at the end of January or beginning of February.) Johnson wrote to her on 4 June, very glad to hear "that in your present state of mind you are going to be immediately a mother" (*Letters* 486). And Mrs. Thrale replied that the "Birth of another

[38] Miss Sidney Arabella Cotton. See p. 154.

Son" was the "only Event that [could] give present Consolation, or future hope of Happiness in *this Life*" (*Letters* 488A). As for Johnson's wish to come to Streatham, Thrale was away taking up his "restes" (making the annual round of alehouse keepers, to see what stock was left), and she had been ill and was "weak as a Cat," so he must not come unless he was "pretty well: what should we do together if both should want nursing?" (*Letters* 488B).

1: July Streatham.
I have been dangerously ill since I came home — of a Cholera Morbus [39] *the Physicians call it. Oh Lord who hast restored me to Life, give me I beseech thee something to live for! — preserve my Daughters! particularly the eldest! & let me not, Oh let me not I most earnestly beseech thee follow any more of my Offspring to the Grave.*

1 July 1776:
My three little Girls are all with me, the thin remains of my ruined Family; I find myself with Child again however, & perhaps if God Almighty spares me any very great Troubles during Gestation, I may see another Son to live: I shall not remain here long enough to rear him — but no matter, may I but stay till I have seen my Husband without one Debt in the World; my Daughter grown up to Woman's fix'd Estate, a fortune in the Funds ready to portion her — & a Son of my own to inherit my own Estate; I shall contentedly leave him, her, and this troublesome World, & go to my dear Mother since whose Death all Evil has befallen me, /&/ enjoy her Company, and that of my heart's dear Harry to all Eternity. I will write down a Saying or two of his before I resolve to mention him no more. One day last Summer Baretti had given my eldest Daughter a long Task out of Don Quixote in the Spanish: She was fretting over it — So Miss cries Harry are you got in a Quickset Hedge? & cannot get out.

[39] Cholera Morbus was the name given to an acute and severe gastroenteritis, the symptoms of which were diarrhea, vomiting, and muscular cramps. Epidemics were frequent and carried a high mortality.

The London physician, John Snow (1813–1858), in a famous experiment, was to prove that the disease was due to a water-borne cause. During a severe epidemic in the City of London he persuaded the authorities to remove the handle of the Broad Street communal pump, and the spread of the disease was promptly controlled.

Ironically, Mrs. Thrale had just returned from taking the waters at Bath, but she records nothing in her journal to suggest that she contracted the disease there.

Another day when somebody among the Serv:ts was sick, I bid Harry fetch me Buchan's [40] *domestick Med'cine to consult, or rather says I — calling him back — fetch me* Tissot [41] *'tis the better Book — Tis so replied Harry archly.*

I hate Dr Goldsmith says Harry one Day to his Sister, because he does not love Mr Murphy — I hate him too says She he is so disagreeable; let us however, while we talk of hating so freely, have a Care of Dr Beat'ye [Beattie]

One day last Winter at the Boro house Harry asked me to buy him the Devil upon two Sticks, [42] *& asked me if it was as he had heard — full of good things: really Love replied I, I remember but one Thing in it that struck me, but I'll tell you that. The Devil seeing how gayly the the [sic] Grand Inquisitor lived, how delicately he fed, what favour he was in with the Ladies &c. — said — now if I were not the Devil, I should wish to be the grand Inquisitor. Dear me cries Harry and how like that is to the Speech Alexander made the Philosopher in the Tub! that if he was not Alexander, he would wish to be Diogenes.*

On a more serious occasion — we had been reading; it was the 22:d Chapter of Saint Luke; & were speaking of Peter's denying Christ with so much Confidence. — Harry condemning him without mercy — Yet says I you must remember that this very Peter suffer'd Death for our

[40] *Domestic Medicine; or the Family Physician*, by William Buchan, was a doctoring aid for the reader. The book appeared in 1769, the first such English treatise. Its success was immediate—nineteen editions were issued during the author's lifetime.

[41] Tissot was professor of medicine at Lausanne, and author of *Avis au Peuple sur sa Santé*, Lausanne, 1761. This popular book, also a doctoring aid, was translated into seven languages.

[42] The 1774 edition of *The Devil upon Two Sticks* (though there were several earlier editions) was probably what Harry requested—*The Devil upon Two Sticks. Translated from the Diable Boiteux of M. Le Sage. To which are prefixed, Asmodeus's Crutches, A Critical Letter upon the Work, and Dialogues between Two Chimnies of Madrid*. London: John Bell, 1774.

The passage recalled by Mrs. Thrale is in chapter VI; on page 107 of the 1774 edition it reads: "Bless me! cried Don Cleofas, what happy mortals are these inquisitors! Indeed they are, replied Asmodeus; I myself almost envy their happiness; and, as Alexander once said, That, were he not Alexander, he could wish to be Diogenes; so I might well say, That, were I not a devil, I would be an inquisitor."

Saviour's Doctrine, & that most willingly —— I know he did replies Harry, but that was after he had receiv'd the Holy Ghost.

Another clever saying was recorded by Baretti. One day Harry was asked by his father, what his mother and Johnson were arguing about; Thrale had entered the room and found the two in excited conversation. "They are disputing, replied Harry; but Mamma has just such a chance against Dr Johnson, as Presto [a little dog] would have, if he were to fight Dash" (*European Magazine*, June 1788, p. 397).

Now is not this a Child to grieve after? is not this a Loss irreparable? Virtue, Health, Genius, Knowledge & perfect Bodily Proportions. —— & now — all carried to the Vault all cold in the Grave & I left to begin the World anew —
Childless with all her Children — wants an heir? [43]

At the end of June, Thrale avoided the problems at home and went fishing with James Evans. The rector of St. Leonard's was a great favorite with the Thrales.

Streatham was still not properly staffed — no butler — and guests were expected, Lady Cotton (Fanny) and "a whole Troop" from Wickham. Thrale would be back for the weekend; meanwhile his wife was inspired to write a verse about the domestic tumult — rather than to do much about it. She and Queeney had gone to the Nesbitts in Wickham:

> Mrs Nesbitt was just driven out at the Door
> But had left Master Arney, the Dogs & Miss Moor [44] . . .
> They offer'd us Cherries, Tea, Coffee and Cake . . .

Upon inquiring about their butler, she learned that they would "discard him with Pleasure," but she saw no reason "why we should receive" "a Man half a Miss, a perfum'd Macaroni . . ."

---

[43] Alexander Pope, *Moral Essays*, Epistle ii, line 148.

[44] "Little Arney" was Arnold Nesbitt's natural son. He had another natural son, Colebrook, a full brother to little Arnold; and Elizabeth Moore was his natural daughter. Nesbitt never had any issue by Susanna Thrale, and at his death (1779) he was to make bequests to Arnold, Colebrook, and Elizabeth.

Nesbitt was ailing at the time of this visit—he had not been a well man for three years.

Back at Streatham there was no time for rest —

> Our Pea Chickens droop, and our Pheasants don't lay,
> And the Weather's uncertain for cutting the hay;
> . . . Oh my sweet Love! — what a sad World is this . . .
>
> (*Thraliana*, pp. 265–267)

Streatham was indeed in a topsy-turvy state, and no creature there was more unhappy than Baretti. Miserable and humiliated since the trip to Italy had been abandoned, he was becoming more and more sullen. Queeney kept telling her mother that he had "grown very odd and very Cross [and] would not look at her Exercises," complaining that the house "was no better than Pandæmonium," what with few servants and an onslaught of guests (*Thraliana*, p. 45).

On 6 July, Baretti later wrote:

> . . . Madam took it into her head to give herself airs, and treat me with some coldness and superciliousness, [and] I did not hesitate to set down at breakfast my dish of tea not half drank, go for my hat and stick that lay in the corner of the room, turn my back to the house *insalutato hospite*, and walk away to London without uttering a syllable, fully resolved never to see her again . . .
>
> (*European Magazine*, June 1788, p. 398)

23: July 1776.
Sophia Thrale is five Years old today; She Has read three Epistles &
three Gospels: I do not make her get much by heart: The Thing is —
I have really listened to Babies Learning till I am half stupefied — &
all my pains have answered so poorly — I have no heart to battle with
Sophy: She would probably learn very well, if I had the Spirit of teach-
ing I once had, as She is docile & stout; able to bear buffeting & Con-
finement, & has withal reasonable good parts & a great Desire to please.
but I will not make her Life miserable as I suppose it will be short —
not for want of Health indeed, for no Girl can have better, but Harry
& Lucy are dead, & why Should Sophy live? The Instructions I
labor'd to give them — what did they end in? The Grave — & every
recollection brings only new Regret. Sophy shall read well, & learn
her Prayers; & take her Chance for more, when I can get it for her.
at Present I can not begin battling with Babies — I have already spent
my whole Youth at it & lost my Reward at last. ———

Sophy was not like Queeney, cold, retiring, and stand-offish; Sophy was sociable, and warm and pleasure-loving. When asked this year what she would do if she had fifty thousand pounds, she immediately replied that she "would have a vast many Friends, and entertain them with Feasts *as grand*" (*Thraliana*, p. 147).

Queeney was more selective. She enjoyed only high society and, even in this milieu, a person had to be an intellectual as well as an aristocrat to please her.

Somebody at Bath asked my eldest Daughter one Evening what She thought of The Rooms the Company &c. & if She had ever seen *such; it was this Spring May 1776. and Hetty was but eleven Years old & a half —— Yes Sir said She — I think the Room very like the* South Seahouse; [45] *& the Company —— very like* the Clerks.

*Another After-Noon at a Ball I shewed her M*ʳˢ *Macaulay; and now said She I have seen the two great Literary Ladies — M*ʳˢ *Montagu & M*ʳˢ *Macaulay; and I have seen —— that one wears* Black Wool *in Her Ears; and that the other —— wears* White. [46] *this was at Bath last April or May 1776.*

*We lodged at Bath upon the North parade this Spring — the Corner House. M*ʳ *Thrale slept on the 1*ˢᵗ *Floor next the Dining room, Johnson slept on the 2*ᵈ *Floor, so did Queeney, so of course did I: and there were some dirty Irish people lodged ⟨at⟩ in the Parlours. I think says Hetty our House is like the Tree in Sophy's Fable Book. The* Eagles *inhabit the top, the* Fox *possesses the Middle, & the* pigs *wallow at the bottom.* [47]

April or May 1776.

*These three Bons Mots of Queeney's were written down on the 1*ˢᵗ *of September 1776.* [48] *if God should spare her Life till the 17*ᵗʰ *of this Month, She will be 12 Years old. She is very handsome, and has a stouter look than I ever expected her to have, for She was for many*

---

[45] The South Sea Trading Company. This remark is a good example of what Baretti called Queeney's "laconism."

[46] Padding the ears was thought to prevent deafness. Whether the wool was black or white was simply a matter of preference, perhaps in time becoming a personal distinction. The Ladies of Llangollen placed wads of brown paper lightly in the orifices of their ears, to protect their hearing.

[47] Hetty probably had Fable LXXX in mind, which deals with an eagle, cat, and fox; a later edition perhaps of *Fables of Æsop and Others. Newly done into English* (London: J. Tonson and J. Watts, 1722), pp. 140–141.

[48] They were also written down in *Thraliana* in May 1777.

Years rather slight and delicate & inclined to leanness: She begins now to spread however, & her Breast grows apace; She is neither eminently tall nor short of her Age but vastly well; & near my own Height [49] *when we change Shoes as we did to day for sport. She has a very competent Knowledge of the three great modern Languages, French, Spanish & Italian: writes a moderately good Hand, but will I fear never make a capital Dancer. She has a Love for Needle work of all kinds, but is capricious, & desirous to range from one Thing to another without ever finishing any: We have never tried her at Musick or Drawing; but in Pictures She is at least* half *a Conoscente, and is seldom mistaken when She guesses at a Painter's hand, or describes his Power — The Truth is, She has a general Knowledge of every thing which is perfectly astonishing, & I overheard her last Winter telling her poor dear Brother who is since dead, & was wondering how Cleopatra could like to drink Vinegar tho' She had dissolved a Pearl in it — The Vinegar says Queeney was not sower after the Dissolution of the Pearl: — the Acid of the Liquor imbibed the Alkaline Qualities of the Pearl, & made her a* neutral *Draught.* [50] *It is /in/ this general Knowledge more than in particular Performances that this Girl's Superiority of Understanding appears: She has indeed a Mind very uncommonly stored, I have never yet seen her Fellow at five & twenty; and I am not partial to her, Why Should I? She loves me not. and in Truth now her Brother is gone She has I think no great Kindness for any body. Baretti endeavoured by flattery, Caresses, & even by inciting her on all occasions to Oppose my Will, & shake off my Authority, to obtain her Friendship: — but in vain! When he was gone She could not suppress her Joy, & I believe She did endeavour to undermine him while he staid, but I had not observed it. She has a heart however quite empty of Tenderness or Gratitude.*

No peace saith my God for the wicked! no quiet Gestation for me! on Sunday Night the 3.ᵈ of Sept.ʳ Mʳ Thrale told me he had an Ailment, & shewed me a Testicle swelled to an immense Size: I had no Notion

---

[49] Mrs. Thrale's height was four feet eleven inches.

[50] Queeney's chemical analysis is precocious nonsense. No vinegar exists which would dissolve a pearl. (See the story on p. 39 .) As Pliny's editor says, "Cleopatra no doubt swallowed the pearl in vinegar knowing that it could be recovered later on." Pliny, *Natural History*, Translated and edited by H. Rackham (Harvard University Press and William Heinemann, 1940), III, 244, footnote.

but of a Cancer — *Poor Fool! & press'd him to have the best help that
could be got — no he would have only* Gregory [51] — *a drunken crazy
Fellow that his Father had known: however when I pressed him with
an /honest/ earnestness and kind Voice to have* Hawkins,[52] Potts [53]
*or some eminent hand — he said it was nothing dangerous with a Smile;
but that since I had an Aversion to M.ʳ Gregory he would send for one
Osborne; a sort of half Quack, whose Name I have sometimes read
in the papers as possessing the Receipts of a M: Daran [54] a famous
Practitioner in the* Venereal *Way: I now began to understand where I
was, and to perceive that my poor Father's Prophecy was verified
who said If you marry that Scoundrel he will catch the Pox, /&/ for
your Amusement set you to make his Pultices. This is now literally
made out; & I am preparing Pultices as he said, and Fomenting this
elegant Ailment every Night & Morning for an Hour together on my
Knees, & receiving for my Reward such Impatient Expressions as disagreable Confinement happens to dictate. however tis well tis no
worse — he has I am pretty sure not given it me, and I am now pregnant & may bring a healthy Boy who knows? All my Concern is lest it
should after all prove a Schirrus [55] — my Master denies it's being the
other Thing very resolutely, & says he has felt it ever since he jumped
from the Chaise between Rouen & Paris exactly this Time Twelve-
month: [56] if this should be true we are all undone, undone indeed! for
it can end in nothing but a Cancer, & I know but too well the Dreadful
Consequence of that most fatal Disease — Yet I will* hope *it may be
only a Venereal Complaint, if so there is no Danger to be sure & this
Osborne may manage it rightly.*

My poor Heart which is ever beating for some Family Cause, is now

---

[51] Gregory had dined with the Thrales three days before Harry's death.

[52] Caesar Hawkins was a doctor long connected with St. George's Hospital, now a surgeon to the King. Hawkins was to be knighted in 1778.

[53] The distinguished surgeon, Percivall Pott, had extracted Thrale's nose polyp and diagnosed little Ralph's condition in April 1775

[54] Jacques Daran, after wide travel and practice abroad, in Germany, Austria, and Italy, had settled in Paris, a specialist in venereal diseases. His *Disorders of the Urethra* and *Treatise on Gonorrhea* were well-known books, and he had emissaries in England, Spain, Portugal, the West Indies, and other places, ready, for a shared fee, to provide his secret remedies, both internal and external, for the treatment of venereal complaints.

[55] Schirrus [*i.e., scirrhus*]: a hardened swelling or tumor, a cancer.

[56] 27 September 1775.

more than ever oppressed: if he dies — the Band is burst, and we are all turned a Drift — but I will hope better things, & I saw the Surgeon smile yesterday, & charge him to live remarkably low — abstaining from Wine Spice &c. denials in such Cases are never to be regarded — I do think it is only a Consequence of Folly & Vice, no real & dangerous Disease.

7: Sep.ᵗ 76.

I suppose now we shall hardly go to Brighthelmstone! M.ʳ Thrale's having been infected about seven Years ago when he put himself under Daran's [agent's] Care to whom he gave fifty Guineas for curing him of a Venereal Complaint in the Urethra, makes me so unwilling to believe him now when he talks of a hurt: — the more so as he never mentioned any such hurt till now: be this as it will M.ʳ Thrale's Confidence & Kindness are absolutely unattainable by me — as well as his eldest daughter's: I thought I had so behaved on that last Occasion, setting him down myself at Daran's ⁵⁷ door, and keeping his Secret inviolable even from my Mother, as that he needed not have neglected any Ailment he might contract for fear of my Suspicions or Resentment; and now this Osborne tells me he did consult him two Months ago about this tumefied Testicle, that he advised him Vomits which he never took, & that he has been neglecting himself all this while les.ᵗ I /sh.ᵈ/ think he might be tainted forsooth: as if I cared for any thing in Competition with a Life so precious to his whole Family.

Thrale's complaint kept the family at Streatham for most of September, but they still hoped to go to Brighton later, and Johnson promised to join them when his attack of gout abated.

On 15 September the convalescent Thrale showed that, though he had been petulant, disagreeable, and complaining, he did appreciate his wife's care and understanding, for he gave her a delightful present, an ingenious one, showing special thought and recognition of her talents — six calf-bound blank books, each with a label on the cover, "Thraliana," stamped in gold.

⁵⁷ Not "Daran's door"; Daran did not leave Paris, his treatments were provided elsewhere by his agents. Since the man who treated Thrale about 1769 was not Osborne, it may have been the surgeon, Thomas Tomkyns, who studied under Daran in France, and became his assistant for a while. Tomkyns translated the *Observations on the Disorders of the Urethra* (London: A. Millar, 1750), and proclaimed that he was the only person in the city who could supply Daran's secret remedies.

When they were in Paris the year before, Mrs. Thrale had been captivated by French "anas" (compilations of clever sayings, anecdotes, and observations), and she was forming a collection of as many of these little books as she could find — ones which were printed. William Seward was helping her, for he shared the same enthusiasm for anecdote and "ana." She had talked about keeping an "ana" book of her own.

And for years Johnson had been urging her "to get a little Book" to record anecdotes and observations and verse, "ev'ry thing which struck [her] at the Time" (*Thraliana*, p. 1).

It took Thrale to set the project in motion, and he did it handsomely. Showing his confidence in his wife's persistence to fill every page, he gave her not "a little Book," as Johnson had advised, but *six* little books. The present was an inspiration on his part — far more than anyone then realized.

The family was still at Streatham for Queeney's birthday three days later, and for Johnson's the day following.

17: Sept.̲ 1776.
On this day is my dearly beloved Queeney twelve Years old — I wished poor old Nurse Joy this Moment, & gave her a Guinea & we both cried. We are going to London to put this sweet Girl's Life into a Lease,[58] *may She hold it as her Great Grandmother Lucy Salusbury did for 76 Years. I ought to be thankful that I have seen her arrived within Sight of Woman's Estate; and so perfect a Creature too in Mind and Person! May God bless her! & continue her on earth many happy Years as an Example of Virtue & Wisdom adorn'd by Learning & Beauty! and may I never see Death or distress befall her*
most fervently prays ——— H:L:T.

Toward the end of September the Thrales, Queeney, and Johnson went to Sussex. Their trips this year, to Bath and to Brighton, were poor substitutes for the pleasures Baretti had planned in Italy — no widening of horizons, increasing of knowledge, no excitement of new sights, new friends, and new adventures — only the same restricted life, in the familiar little towns, the same old friends, and the same routine. At Brighton, one sea-bathed in the morning and went to an assembly in the evening.

[58] For Mrs. Thrale's Welsh property; Queeney was to replace Harry as her heir.

Johnson, as usual, found Brighton a sad place, devoid of any intellectual stimulation; and Queeney agreed. Thrale, however, whose health was the most important concern, seemed perfectly happy to be with his old cronies. He saw a good deal of Scrase and of Sir John Shelley of Michelgrove, retired Keeper of the Tower of London Records, Privy Counsellor, and Treasurer of the King's household. The "silly and civil" Shelleys is how Mrs. Thrale thought of them, but she found Lady Shelley's company agreeable, and Queeney had a playmate in the eldest daughter (*Letters* 554A).

One pleasant event was celebrated during the stay, the Thrales' thirteenth wedding anniversary on 11 October. A charming poem in their honor was delivered this day by William Weller Pepys, a brother of Lucas, the physician. Though both Pepyses lived in London, they were much at home in Brighton, for their mother had been a daughter of a well-known doctor there. The elder brother, William Weller Pepys, had the honor of being one of the eleven Masters of Chancery. He was a distinguished, upright man, with a show of learning and elegance — very socially correct. He was a favorite of Mrs. Montagu (one wit called him her "Prime Minister"). Mrs. Thrale found Pepys delightful. Johnson did not — said he was artificial — to which Mrs. Thrale retorted that to be sure he talked "pompously of some Things that you despise, as Gardening for example" (*Thraliana*, p. 174).

On the Thrales' anniversary, however, Johnson felt well disposed toward William Weller, for his complimentary verse was splendid, a compliment to Thrale upon his choice, and a compliment to his lady, beautiful and brilliant — possessing all perfections of head and heart. Might the Thrales have many more years of happy marriage (*Thraliana*, pp. 53–54).

October passed, and soon the season was over. "The place was very dull," Johnson wrote Boswell, "and I was not well" (*Letters* 502).

30: Oct.
We are returned from Brighthelmstone where we have spent five Weeks: for the first fortnight I continued the fomentation to My Master's Ailment night & Morning, but no Alteration appear'd: I then wrote to Osborne asking Leave for him to bathe in /the/ Sea as he seemed to be so inclined, & received permission: he accordingly took fourteen Dips & I cannot help fancying the Tumour abated in this

last fortnight; however I long earnestly that the Man may see it and say so too. Be this as it may, I have wronged my poor husband grossly with my wicked Suspicions: it was undoubtedly the leaping from the Chaise in France so long ago that produced the Tumor at first — for he often feels pain I find in the great Muscle of the Thigh which he strain'd at that same fatal Time, & this Disorder in the Scrotum has been coming ever since tho' he never would speak on't. perhaps he was afraid of my being frighted, perhaps of my suspecting his being tainted with the bad Distemper — he says he felt it very plain when his heart was griev'd at the death of his Son, and I dare say if it is a Schirrus — that Grief increased the Obstruction, but Osborne rather supposes it a Hydrocele,[59] *& wished before we left Stretham [sic] that Hawkins might be shew'd it, — I will make my Master shew it now. ——*

30: Oct.ʳ 1776.
My sweet Queeney is come home from Brighthelmstone healthy plump & blooming & grows apace: She was half the Head taller than Shelley's eldest Daughter who is older, & looked so elegant among the Dowdies I have seen, that I restrain my Vanity with the utmost Difficulty. at every Ball however She exposed herself; it is amazing that She should dance so vilely with such a Figure & so good Instructions; but whether it is /from/ bashfulness or naughtiness I know not, or a Mixture of both — but She does dance most incomparably ill to be sure.

Somebody was speaking at Brighthelmstone of a Woman who went about for a Show — writing with her Toes; what does She write says another? at least interrupts Queeney — She does not *write* Manuscripts.

Johnson was repeating Sir Harry's [sic] Wotton's[60] *Sonnet beginning Ye meaner Beauties of the Night I knew Queeney had never heard it — whose Verses are those d'ye think said I to her, Cowley's*[61] *quoth She I doubt not, though I can't remember them. Bravo my Dearest cries Johnson, now that* was *well guessed: — they are not Cowley's, but they are exactly in his Style.*

[59] Hydrocele: a soft, watery benign tumor, as opposed to the hard cancerous tumor or scirrhus.

[60] Sir Henry Wotton (1568–1639), diplomat and poet.

[61] Abraham Cowley (1618–1667), poet.

We had a strong Iron Chest brought hither before we went last away, as there has been so much Housebreaking of late — I was saying to Queeney I think this Chest will keep the Plate very safe — as it was putting up: Yes replies the Girl but it will do still more — it will keep the Thieves away for these Fellows here (meaning the Workmen) will tell their Companions how they set up a strong Box at Squire Thrale's this Morning & so the Housebreakers who probably drink at the same Alehouses — will hear of it, and not think it worth their while to come hither. ——

Another day we were reading the News Paper & I was struck with a Story of a Murder which I read aloud; — Queeney however listening laid hold of some minute Circumstances from which She gathered that the Person suspected could not be guilty; Well done Queeney says M Johnson thou shoudst be on the Grand Jury. This happened some Time ago, & I fancy I have written it down before.[62]*

30: Oct. *1776.*

I have not seen my two little Girls yet since I came home but Mrs Cumyns says they are well. ——* [63]

13: Dec. *1776: Streatham.*
We have been to London for a Week and are returned. M Thrale has consulted Hawkins about his Ailment, which turns out a mere Hydrocele, occasioned by the Accident of jumping from the Chaise between Vernon & Paris: Hawkins has let off the Water once, but it is filling again: and he must have it radically cured by the Seton & Caustic* [64] *after the next Tapping the Surgeons tell him. upon the whole 'tis a bad Thing, but better than I thought for every way. While he went to Town on this Errand, Miss Owen & Queeney & I took a Lodging at Bob Cotton the Linen-draper's in Parl.* *Street, & diverted our selves with going to Plays, Operas, & other Amusements. Queeney grows*

[62] Yes, 21 March 1773
[63] On 4 December 1776 John and Amelia Perkins had a second son, and again with insensitive kindness, they touched an open wound: they named their boy Henry, after the Thrales' lost heir.
[64] Caustic: a substance which burns and destroys living tissue, such as nitrate of silver.

*handsomer & taller & fatter, and is much admired: She stood her
Week's Raking* [65] *very well & Yesterday — the first Day since we
came home to settle — She begun studying Musick under D[r] Burney,
who is justly supposed at present the first Man in Europe, & whose Instructions I have long been endeavoring to obtain for her. Says Miss
Owen this Burney's Name is MacBurney by rights His Family is Irish
& they were all MacBurneys till of late — Hibernias perhaps then
quoth Queeney.* [66] ——

*Have I not reason to rejoyce in this dear Girl? & likewise to be happy
about my Master & his Ailment! — I shall fetch the Girls home on
Monday; — I have seen them two or three Times & they are as blythe
as Birds: we shall e/n/quire into their Improvements when we have got
them at home: I long to see poor Popy [Sophy], but thought it was
invidious to take her away & leave her Sister, but after Xmas Susan
shall return by herself & leave little Sophy for me to play with, I shall
expect her to read quite readily.   Streatham the American Fastday* [67] — *13 Dec: 1776.* ——

Mrs. Thrale's purpose in coming to London was to have a little diversion and "bustle" before the birth of a new baby. She prayed for a
boy. The child was expected in late January or early February.

During the long last weeks of waiting she found Peggy Owen's company agreeable, "a vast Comfort to have a Lady about one —
and I have had none so long" (*Letters* 505.3A). Miss Owen was delighted to be needed and promised to stay through the lying-in, indeed
through the whole winter if her friend desired it.

While they were in London the Thrales and Peggy Owen saw a good
deal of William Seward and of the celebrated Dr. Charles Burney,
musician and author, to whom he had introduced them earlier this
year. Thrale and Johnson liked Burney, and Mrs. Thrale thought he

[65] Raking: the dissipation of society.

[66] A version of this story is told in *Thraliana*, p. 50.

[67] American Fastday: George III proclaimed 13 December a day of general fast
and prayer for the safety of the military forces in America, for the protection of the
loyalists, and the reformation of the rebels. The Archbishops and Bishops of England
were directed to compose a suitable prayer for the Fastday. Beilby Porteus, Bishop
of Chester, preached before Their Majesties.

was an enchanting person, so talented, knowledgeable, and high-principled, and his manners, she said, were as sweet as his music.

For his part, Dr. Burney was charmed by the Thrales, and it took
very little persuading to make him agree to give music lessons to the
remarkable Miss Queeney. It was arranged that Dr. Burney would
come to Streatham once a week, give the lesson, and then stay to
dinner, allowing all present to enjoy his company and conversation.
Mrs. Thrale noted the occasion of Queeney's first lesson in the *Family
Book*.

On the same day that she wrote this entry Johnson sent a letter to
Boswell, in which he said:

Mrs. Thrale is big, and fancies that she carries a boy; if it were very reasonable
to wish much about it, I should wish her not to be disappointed. The desire
of male heirs is not appendant only to feudal tenures. A son is almost necessary
to the continuance of Thrale's fortune; for what can misses do with a brewhouse? Lands are fitter for daughters than trades. (*Letters* 505)

Sat: 21: Dec: 76.
*I have got my Girls at home, Susan has a Black Eye & Sophy a Cough:
it will not however prove the hooping Cough so I am content. Susan's
Temper is not good, She denies her Knowledge to avoid exhibiting;
Mʳ Johnson says She is therein the wiser — I do not suspect her Wisdom, I suspect her for having no natural Compliance in her Disposition,
& I fear I am but too right. There is something strangely perverse in
Queeney's Temper, full of Bitterness and Aversion to all who instruct
her — I expect She will like Burney however, his Manner is so elegantly soft & gentle, I fancy if She hates that Man, She will be the
first to hate him. Susan has somewhat of the same sullen moroseness
in her Composition; Mʳˢ Cumyns complains that She is not to be moved
to Compliance when She resolves to be perverse. Sophy is more like
other people's Children, of a soft gay Disposition — thanks one for a
Cake & cries if She gets a Cuff; the others put me in Mind of what my
Father said of a Wench that lived with us in old Times — 'Tis all one
to this Girl if She is kiss'd or ⟨cuff'd⟩ /kick't/ She can but hate one and
She does that naturally.*

*Sophy has learn'd to read very prettily, and Susan writes with tol-
erable facility   they can both work, & are I think quite well done by
on the whole. —*

Mr Thrale's Complaint was *venereal at last --- What need of so many Lyes about it!* [68] *--- I'm sure I care not, so he recovers to hold us all together.*

---

[68] The journal gives no conclusive evidence to support Mrs. Thrale's certitude, and none has been found elsewhere. The hydrocele could have resulted from the injury in the accident or from a venereal infection, or from a number of other causes.

7: Jan: 1777.

I have now begun a new Year in my Children's Book; may it prove a fortunate one to them or it cannot be so to me: all is well with them at present, and I go on myself as usual in my Pregnancy, but with more attention to every Sensation as I consider it of unusual Importance. The Truth is I did pray earnestly for a Son and I am strangely prepossessed with a Notion that God has heard my Prayers; but perhaps like poor Rachel I may pay my own Life for it — Well no matter! I shall leave a Son of my own to inherit my paternal Estate & for the rest Mr Thrale may provide himself with Children & chuse a Wife where he will: it is not his Principle to lament much for the Dead, so my Loss will not break his Heart; & as for Queeney I defy him to find her a Mother She will appear to like less than her own. Miss Owen is very likely to be my Successor; we often joke about it — & such Jests have always some earnest in them: She would not wrong my Girls I dare say; and if I have a Boy I should leave him a certain Provision: Mr Thrale would probably be partial to her Children in point of personal Fondness ——— but that is a very small Affair, and I doubt not his equitable Proceeding to them all in the main Business of Life. My Master has not yet set about ridding himself of his Hydrocele for good & all; however it is almost inclined to go away of itself, and will be cured with great ease in a Constitution so perfect as his. Poor Mr Johnson would have the greatest Loss of me, and he would be the most sensible of his Loss: he would willingly write my Epitaph I am sure if my Husband would treat me with a Monument; which I do believe he would too, if any body would press him to it before the first Year was out — after that he would be married again, & his second Lady would perhaps make Objections. ——— so if I do die this Time Then

Farewell Light and Life, and thou blest Sun serene! [1]

---

[1] This quotation has not been identified.

Mrs. Thrale was in a morbid state. Peggy Owen, once a solace, was now a threat and of little help. Cecilia Strickland, in London at the moment and on constant call, was not much better. No one could make Mrs. Thrale comfortable during the day, and she was unable to sleep at night — so many burdens.

And on 15 January, the ultimate — a letter from Johnson begging to come and be nursed! He was suffering from terrible breathlessness (emphysema with an acute attack of bronchitis). At night he could gain only fitful sleep by sitting up in a chair. His doctor, Thomas Lawrence, had had him bled of twelve ounces of blood, but that same night he could not sleep at all — and in desperation, with the help of his servant, Frank Barber, he had bled himself of about ten ounces more. He begged to have Mrs. Thrale's coach fetch him to Streatham: "I do not know but clearer air may do me good; but whether the air be clear or dark, let me come to You" (*Letters* 506).

Mrs. Thrale replied:

Oh sad! Oh sad! indeed I am very sorry; and I unable to nurse You — for Goodness Sake do as Dr Lawrence would have you & be well before you come home — and pray don't be bleeding yourself & doing yourself harm. My Master is very angry already. (*Letters* 506A)

On Saturday, 8 February, the Thrale's eleventh child was born — a girl — Cecilia Margaretta.

26: Feb: 1777: Here am I once again in my Dressing room as well & almost as strong as ever — except my Eyes which are very weak indeed. The Labour was rough & tight, but no Boy nor no Death ensued; I was odly prepossess'd that both was intended to happen. I have now however my four Daughters together again — I never had but four living at once,[2] *& perhaps in his own good Time God may be pleased to add two Sons to them. The Young Child is large stout, fat, & big boned like Lucy & seems disposed to be fair hair'd like her — She is baptized by the Name of Cæcelia* [sic] *Margaretta, in compliance with Mrs Strickland's Fancy, & Miss Owen's, who each bespoke a Name: Stricky could not stand Godmother because of her being a Roman Catholick, so M^{rs} D'Avenant* [Hetty Cotton] *& Miss Owen & Mr Seward are the Sponsors: — it is a lovely Child sure enough — God grant it but Life & Grace.*

[2] From May to December 1775, the Thrales had five living children: Queeney, Harry, Susan, Sophy, and Fanny.

Cecilia Margaretta was duly christened by James Tattersall at St. Leonard's Church in Streatham on Monday, 17 February 1777.

Thursday 6: March 1777. Another Agony! Queeney was taken strangely ill yesterday Morning — She went to bed y^e: Night before in perfect Health, but Yesterday Morning a Fever seemed coming on with Nausea at the Stomach & Pain in the Head — I durst do nothing of my own Accord, so bad has been my Success; but I drove away with her to Jebb, who gave her an Emetick at Night & a rough Mercurial Purge today — I think it will cure her   if it does not I am more undone than ever — I think however hers would be a Loss I could not outlive: but She does mend I see, The D^r has promised to come down here to Stretham [sic] on Sat:^y Evening to visit her.

Sunday 9: March.
The D^r [Jebb] came last Night as he said, & found his dear Patient well and playing at Whist. Today I have been to Church to return Thanks for my little Ciceley, & indeed for my restored Queeney who is worth Millions to me —
God is very gracious to me & yet I have a Trick of complaining. Let me suffer for it Oh Lord if it be thy blessed Will — but let not my punishment be the ill Health or Death of my Children!

Sunday 9: March
Streatham 1777.

Now that Mrs. Thrale's month of lying-in was over, she, Miss Owen, and Queency came again to London and enjoyed a fortnight of gaiety. Johnson wrote to Mrs. Thrale:

Did you stay all night at Sir Joshua's? and keep Miss up again? Miss Owen had a sight — all the Burkes — the Harris's — Miss Reynolds — what has she to see more? . . .

You are all young and gay and easy. But I have miserable nights, and know not how to make them better; but I shift pretty well a-days, and so have at you all at Dr. Burney's to morrow. (*Letters* 512)

"To morrow," 20 March, Johnson, Mrs. Thrale, Queeney, Miss Owen, and Seward called on the Burneys at their house in St. Martin's Street (which had once belonged to Isaac Newton). It was here that Mrs. Thrale first met Dr. Burney's twenty-four-year-old daughter, Fanny. The pretty, shy young woman made no impression on Mrs.

Thrale; it was Fanny who recorded a vivid impression of Mrs. Thrale in her diary.

Thrale was not with the callers at the Burneys, he was in Brighton, taking care of his health, and giving directions for the "dressing up" of the house "against the Season." He urged his wife to bring Miss Owen and Queeney down, and Mrs. Thrale thought that the sea air and bathing, and the pre-season quiet, would be refreshing for them all after their social rigors, so the three ladies left the smoke of London and went to Brighton for a few days (*Letters* 512A).

They found Thrale in excellent form, riding and enjoying himself with Shelley, Tom Cotton, and Seward. It was a poor April fool's joke which reported Thrale's "death" in the paper, a shocking jest to frighten "a Man's Friends so foolishly," Mrs. Thrale said, and she felt especially sorry for Lady Lade because her son, Sir John (now eighteen), was ill with consumption; her spirits should not be further disturbed. Thrale himself was not in the least fazed by the report, he was "as live as a Lark notwithstanding all this Nonsense" (*Letters* 512A). On 5 April the *Public Advertiser* assured its readers "that the Paragraph concerning the Death of Henry Thrale Esq; has no Foundation in Truth" (*Letters* 513, n. 1).

By Tuesday, 8 April, the Thrales were home again at Streatham, and Johnson came there on the 10th, bringing **Dr. Taylor.** The latter stayed only for the day, but Johnson settled down with his family for several weeks.

Hetty has enjoy'd her Health since then [i.e., since March] without remission, and on the 5.ᵗʰ of May I had the Satisfaction of seeing her confirmed at Sᵗ Saviour's Southwark by Porteus Bp [Bishop] of Chester,³ and of being perfectly convinced that even his Lordship did not better understand the Nature End & Use of that Sacred Office than She did: — I saw Susan too Yestermorning at Kensington, & took away as a Specimen of her Needle Work a Map Sampler very cleverly done; after hearing her performance on the Globe, & finding it quite capital in its Way. — how happy ought I to be!   *13: May 1777*

29: May 1777. I have all my four little Daughters about me, and think

³ Beilby Porteus: This pleasing man of ability and strong views had been born in the colony of Virginia. He held a degree from Christ's College, Cambridge, had been appointed Rector of Lambeth in 1767, and Chaplain to the King in 1769. He was made Bishop of Chester in 1776.

*well of them all in the main: They are each eminently tall of their Age,
Susan is really surprizing when one recollects her beginning; & She is
exceedingly clever as can be, translates French into English readily &
writes /a/ very smart hand; her Map Sampler completed between the
Years of six & seven is a good Specimen both of her Work & Geography, but She is special ill Tempered to be sure, tho' I think her Health
can hardly be mended.*

*Sophy is a fine open Countenanced well proportioned Girl, of a good
disposition and as the old Phrase was of a towardly Wit: Cecilia is lively
& forward of her Months, and bids fair to be a bit of a Beauty like her
eldest Sister. Hetty was always inclinable to be sandy and so is She,
but Hetty has been always exceedingly admired — I wish poor Ciceley
may have half her Share.*

*This moment my little favourite Terrier Presto having hurt himself to
an Agony bit my Face as I stooped to kiss him: —— Sure he was not
mad with his pain Sure he was not — That would be an horrible End
indeed! a horrible closing of the Books — Lord bless me!*

29: May 1777.

I am ashamed of my own Folly   the Dog is not mad; only I am absurd.

————

Presto recovered and all was well. The little terrier had originally
belonged to Harry and, because of this, held a special place in everyone's affection — even Queeney's, who thought little dogs made people
act in a ridiculous way. She liked Triton, one of the big dogs, best.

The next winter (1778), Presto was to be in trouble again, "sick and
like to dye," and Queeney begged an epitaph from her mother. Mrs.
Thrale complied with a verse, which Queeney said she would place
over Presto's grave. She planned to dig this under a little apple tree
that Harry had planted.

Presto, however, surprised everybody. He recovered and lived on
for many years more, dying finally at Brighton, sometime after 1784
(*Thraliana*, p. 226 and n. 2).

Apart from the problems of children and dogs, this May and June
(1777) were filled with gaiety for Mrs. Thrale: another brief trip to
Brighton, much entertaining at Streatham, and gadding about with
friends in town and country. Lady Lade was very kind and David

Garrick and his wife conferred many favors, among these, places for Sheridan's new play *The School for Scandal*, "which is a *Thing* it seems" (*Letters* 519.1A).

One day Mrs. Thrale and Queeney promenaded at Ranelagh,[4] and she made a great effort to secure a ticket through Dr. Taylor — a second for her daughter, if possible — for a fête at Devonshire House. The fête in the end was postponed (although Taylor had been able to provide one ticket) and Mrs. Thrale was not able on this day to wear her elegant Paris gown of white silk, trimmed with pale purple and silver, but she continued to show it off at other important occasions. She put it to particularly good use by wearing it when she posed for Reynolds' double portrait of herself and Queeney, painted for the Streatham library.

After the library had been filled with books (Johnson had been given £100 to fill any deficiencies on the shelves), Thrale had the inspiration of commissioning Reynolds to paint portraits of the stars of the Streatham circle, "the persons he most loved to contemplate, from amongst his friends and favourites" (*Memoirs*, II, 80). By the time the Thrales met Dr. Burney there was space left for only one more frame and this distinguished man of music was selected to fill the "last chasm in the chain of Streatham worthies."

Reynolds "much delighted in . . . his Streatham gallery" (*Memoirs*, II, 81). Fourteen of his portraits finally lined the walls. They were above the bookcases in this order: Lord Sandys, Lord Westcote (William Henry Lyttelton), the double picture of Mrs. Thrale and Queeney over the mantel, Arthur Murphy, Goldsmith, Reynolds himself, Robert Chambers (to be knighted in 1778), David Garrick, Thrale (over the door), Baretti, Burney, Burke, and Johnson.

In time (1780), as might be expected, Mrs. Thrale wrote a character verse for each portrait.

July 12. Hester has got an inflam'd Eye & Jebb is gone to Italy [5] *what*

---

⁴ Ranelagh: a place of public entertainment, on the site of the gardens and villa of the Earl of Ranelagh, built from the designs of William Jones in 1742. The principal room was the Rotunda, finely painted, gilded, and illuminated. The room was 150 feet in diameter, with an orchestra in the center, tiers of boxes all around, and balconies filled with little ale houses. The chief amusement was promenading in an eternal circle. Ranelagh was the great rival of Vauxhall, and had the advantage in inclement weather of being under cover.

⁵ Jebb was attending the Duke of Gloucester on his journey.

DR. JOHNSON
THE STREATHAM PORTRAIT BY REYNOLDS

shall I do? — Bromfield prescribes Leeches, starving & purging — &
then Goulard [6] *— always something to harrass one.*

17: The Eye mends — is well indeed — but the other seems inclined
to be bad too; Oh unlucky — and Susan was to have been fetched home
& carried with her Sister Sophy to see Vauxhall [7] *on Saturday.*

Here is Sophy's Birthday! She is six Years old this Day, and has begged
Money for the Serv^{ts} to make merry. God bless her She is a sweet Girl;
of an angelic Temper, fine proportion'd Person, clean Skin & strong
Health: Abingdon says She will be the finest Dancer in England — She
has quite an Appetite & Genius for it; if She was his Child he says She
should make his Fortune by her Success on the Stage: as to Reading She
does very well, can read Gulliver by herself to divert herself, and I
think that's very fair — She has had but little Teaching — her Lan-
guage however in Talk is strangely copious, elegant & correct — and
She has a sweetness of Disposition which no Child of mine ever had
but my lovely Lucy, whom Sophy resembles in Character, but is not
half as handsome — Sophy's Face has a bald Look for want of Eye-
brows, — & her Hair is course & vulgar, — her Shape however is ex-
quisitely turned, and there is a vast deal of Strength too.   24 July 77.

Queeney's Eyes are got well: nothing wanting now but a Son — no
hopes of that at present however, but God may — & I hope will be
gracious. ——

8: August 1777.
Something has happened now however to cure Hester's Eyes and all
her other Ailments if She had any: God be praised that this Change of
Constitution *has come on without pain Sickness or Sorrow, except*
the inflammation which I suppose belonged to this Affair — the Blood
which could not readily find its proper *Place of Evacuation, filled the*
Vessels of the Eye. [8] *how thankful ought I to be that no worse Dis-*
orders befel her at so critical a Period of a Life so precious; I hardly

---

[6] Goulard: see p. 63

[7] Vauxhall: public pleasure gardens on the Surrey side of the Thames, a fashionable resort since the time of Charles II. Vauxhall was celebrated for its walks lit with
thousands of lamps, its concerts and entertainments, its suppers and fireworks.

[8] At puberty the sweat ducts proliferate and may become blocked with secretion,
and infected. This condition perhaps caused sties.

thought it would have happened so early, but tis a Sign She has strong Fibres I hope — I was a forward Minx myself, & very strong always.

In August the Thrales were given astonishing news by their favorite, James Evans, rector of St. Saviour's (and recently of St. Olave's, Southwark, as well).[9] Evans told them that he had been married since 1771! He had kept the fact secret, he said, until the death of his uncle, as this gentleman greatly opposed his marrying. For six years, Evans explained to the Thrales, he had maintained a platonic relationship with his wife, not even a tête-à-tête "for fear of Temptations he could not have resisted" (*Thraliana*, p. 109).

Mrs. Thrale soon met Mrs. Evans. She was a pretty woman, of good family, someone who had had other matrimonial prospects. That she should have accepted such a relationship with a man — one who lacked rank, fortune, and good looks — was inconceivable. Evans had greatly pleased Mrs. Thrale over the years, his nice manners, his sharp mind, and his virtue and helpfulness. "I did love little Evans," she recorded, "but when he married, I lost all Comfort of *him*" (*Thraliana*, p. 372). Thrale, however, thought no less of married Evans and remained his staunch supporter.

The Thrales paid Mr. Cator a visit in August. Beckenham Place in Kent was not far from Streatham; it had extensive grounds and fine planting. (Mrs. Cator was a daughter of Peter Collinson, the naturalist, and she had inherited her father's taste and skill.) Mrs. Thrale reported the excursion to Johnson, who was in Oxford and soon going to Lichfield; he had started on his annual round of visits at the end of July. Cator's house, she said, was "splendid & his Countenance gay, but he does not like the additional Land Tax."

She went on to say that she supposed in Lichfield Johnson would be seeing Miss Aston, whom "I don't value." At Streatham, Miss Sidney Arabella Cotton was expected in about a fortnight. Mr. Thrale "does not rejoyce much" at the thought of this visit, but she herself rather looked forward to reminiscing with her aunt (*Letters* 532A).

In a few days Johnson replied; he was now in Lichfield. Lucy Porter, his stepdaughter, he was glad to say, was much better than last year,

[9] On 29 March 1777 Lord North humbly recommended "Mr Evans for the vacant living of St Olave in Southwark at the request of Mrs Thrale . . ." *The Correspondence of King George the Third from 1760 to 1783*, ed. Sir John Fortescue, III (London, 1928), 435.

but Elizabeth Aston was very ill; implying a reprimand to Mrs. Thrale for her low opinion of his friend, he added, "If she dies I have a great loss" (*Letters* 535). Later in the month he wrote about the improvements at Streatham, hoping they were proceeding in good order, and that he would be able to "perambulate" his master's new walk when he came home. Very little was happening in Lichfield. He imagined that Streatham was the center of activity.

It was. A great many interesting visitors came to stay this summer: among them, Lord Westcote (Lyttelton, who was agreeable again), the William Weller Pepyses, and Dr. Burney. They and everyone else enjoyed the routine. Guests were independent during the day, reading, writing letters, or busying themselves with a project (Dr. Burney was working on his next book). They were free to walk about the park or meditate in the summer house (as Johnson often had), or to inspect the walled gardens, the orchard, the hothouses, the stables, the dairy, and the poultry houses — and they could view Thrale's new lake and island,[10] or do what Johnson wished to do, take the perambulating two-mile walk around the property. Streatham Park was liberty hall, and only at meal times were guests obliged to meet and join in the "flash" of conversation and debate.

One of the missing "regulars" this summer was William Seward; he was traveling through Scotland and Wales and, as might be expected, he was complaining of his health all the way. Nevertheless, he was enjoying Scottish hospitality and Welsh castles very much. To please Mrs. Thrale he had made a visit to the Vale of Clwyd and inspected her old family house, Bach-y-Graig. He did not please her, however, by writing that "some few of [her] Trees had been felled." She was reading the letter aloud to Thrale, Burney, and William Weller Pepys, and when she came to this passage she said in passion that she "had rather [her] right hand suffered mutilation than those Woods . . . The two Men stared, & my Master was silent & sullen; but no matter, the more

---

[10] Thrale was never happier than when he was building something. In another year Johnson had asked Mrs. Thrale about "my Master's summer projects. Is he towering into the air . . . Is he excavating the earth, or covering its surface with edifices? Something he certainly is doing and something he is spending. A Genius never can be quite still" (*Letters* 421).

In one of the parlor games the family played (where everybody was like an animal) Thrale was put down as a "Beaver," "he has such a Turn for Building" (*Thraliana*, p. 414). In the same animal kingdom Mrs. Thrale was a "Rattlesnake," Johnson an "Elephant," Baretti a "Bear," Seward a "Porcupine," and Hetty D'Avenant a "Squirrel."

People know that 'tis against my Will they are cut, the less danger they will be in of falling. Make no Answer to this part of my Letter I beg of you," she told Johnson (*Letters* 539B).

Besides entertaining, the Thrales made a number of excursions. One of these was to Joshua Reynolds at Richmond Hill on 13 August. The Garricks were among the guests, and the William Weller Pepyses, and Bennet Langton and his wife, the Dowager Countess of Rothes. The Langtons brought along, uninvited, "their two pretty Babies" (George, five, and Mary, four). The children were unbearable with their prattle, every word of which their father repeated and explained. Their mother had no control, no "Salusbury fist." George and Mary were finally sent for a walk with a maid. Garrick had been sick, and desired a table by himself for dinner, near an open window. Back came the children, right up to Garrick. "I actually saw him change Colour at their approach, however," said Mrs. Thrale, "he was civiller to them than anybody there except myself. Pepys . . . whispered me that he wished them all at the Rope-Walk — & added can one ever come to this oneself? I really never had such difficulty to forbear laughing" (*Letters* 537A).

Another excursion the Thrales made in August was a visit to the old attorney, Francis Brooke of Townmalling in Kent. Johnson had been with them on their earlier stay in 1768 and he remembered Brooke's house as a favorite place. Mrs. Thrale wrote to him now:

. . . here is news of Town-malling — the quiet old-fashioned place in Kent, that you liked so because it was agreeable to your own notions of a rural life; I believe we were the first people, except the master of it, who had for many years taken delight in the old coach without springs, the two roasted ducks in one dish, the fortified flower garden, and fir trees cut in figures. — A spirit of innovation has however reached even these at last. — The roads are mended; no more narrow shaded lanes, but clear open turnpike trotting. A yew hedge . . . newly cut down too by his nephew's [sic] desire. Ah those nephews! And a wall pulled away, which bore incomparable fruit — *to call in the country* — is the phrase. Mr. Thrale is wicked enough to urge on these rough reformers; how it will end I know not. For your comfort, the square canals still drop into one another; and the chocolate is still made in the room by a maid, who curtsies as she presents every cup. Dear old Daddy Brooke looks well and even handsome at eighty-one years old; while I saw his sister, who is ninety-four years old, and calls him *Frankey*, eat more venison at a sitting than Mr. Thrale. (*Letters* 1788, I, 376–377)

Queeney wrote Johnson her own rather stiff report. Townmalling

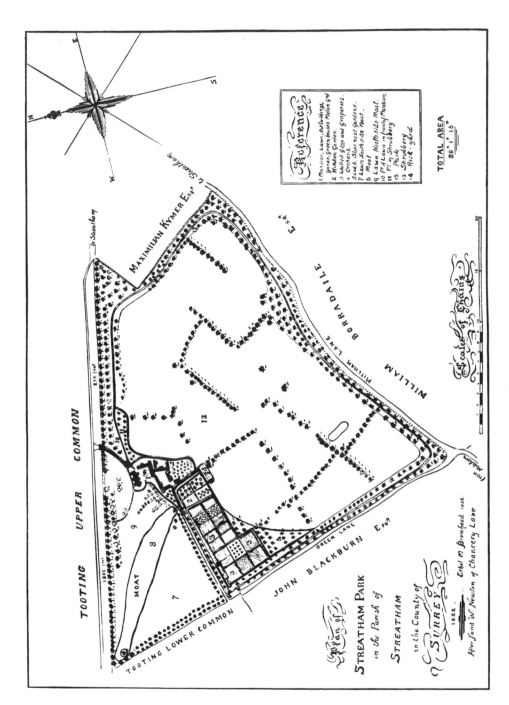

PLAN OF STREATHAM PARK

DRAWN BY ETHEL BROMHEAD

DR. JOHNSON'S SUMMERHOUSE AT STREATHAM PARK
AFTER A WATERCOLOR BY STANFIELD

she found "a very pretty odd old fashioned Place." The cascades were "quite charming, and M͡r Brooke was vastly civil and gave Mama some fine old China, and sent some to Susan who is his Godaughter. I liked it all much upon the whole, but it seems there have been Alterations made by which my Mother thinks it not mended" (*Letters* 539A).

Sep.͡ 5: We dined in London yesterday with a friend, & Hester brought home a sore Throat which alarms me, as I think there is Some Degree of Fever; if She's no better tomorrow Bromfield must be consulted; I have only ventured to give 2 Drams of Salts just to procure one Motion /a Day/ which with forbearance from Meat or Wine will perhaps do all that's wanted.

Ciceley has run a horrible Chance today 9: Sept.͡ there were Beggars on the Common Sitting under the Trees where Nurse takes her — *all full out of the Smallpox: — God send She took no Infection from them, but it makes my heart beat —— Oh what will make that poor heart cease to beat? no Experience of Misery 'tis Plain: I suppose it would beat in an Air Pump* [11] *like that of a Frog!*

10:͡th of September I saw my Susan yesterday; She is very well and grows prodigiously tall & thin: Her French, her Work, her Geography & Grammatical Knowledge go on to my Wish, but She no more than Hester will ever be a dancer: M͡rs Cumyns has a Notion She has some Weakness in her Loyns, which is very possible; as her Infancy was so uncommonly feeble: I therefore ordered her the Cold Bath this Summer & I think it agrees very well. ——

17: Sept.͡ my Eldest Daughter's Birthday: She wished to spend it with her friends the Pitcheses, [12] *so as they could not come to us we went to Them. Hester is taller than one of their Daughters who is 17 Years old, & a bit of a Beauty — Hester is not so handsome as She has been: She grows long & thin & gangling, & her Colour is not so high as it was during mere Childhood; her extream shyness is also no friend to her*

[11] Air Pump: a machine for exhausting the air by means of the strokes of a piston. As the frog asphyxiated, its heart beat more forcibly. Wright of Derby painted "An Experiment with an Air-Pump" (and bird). This picture was exhibited at the Society of Artists in 1768, and now hangs in the Tate Gallery, London.

[12] Sir Abraham and Lady Pitches, who were near neighbors of the Thrales, had five children, all daughters. Peggy, the daughter who was seventeen, was Queeney's particular friend.

Figure, though I think her Carriage will be that of a Woman of Fashion in spite of her, & I even expect her to be very eminently handsome when her Person is formed — many think her exquisitely pretty now — She is exactly my own height without Cap or Shoes. Her Temper never was good — sullen, capricious & perverse; Her Understanding /however is/ solid, her Penetration keen, and her Wit sarcastick — Her Health delicate but not bad, and her Knowledge great & uncommon. She has a general Taste too for Arts, for Dress, for everything — a contempt for Vulgarity — a discriminating Eye, & a Tongue /but/ too acute to catch at /& expose/ the Ridiculous.

If her Shyness does not prevent both She will surely bid fair to be both a Wit and a Beauty —   *17: Sept.ʳ 1777.—*

Besides spending time with the Pitcheses on her birthday, Queeney had a dinner given in her honor at Streatham. Thirteen sat down to table, which made Mrs. Thrale extremely nervous. She could not forget the superstition that this number was bad luck, nor the other superstition that if one escaped safe on one's birthday, the rest of the year would be less dangerous. Murphy called attention to Queeney's flushed cheeks (he thought from excitement), but Mrs. Thrale worried that this might be the first sign of consumption; her cousin, Sir John Lade, was now thought to be dying of this disease. Something dreadful always happened, Mrs. Thrale lamented, when Johnson was away.

She need not have worried; the only thing which went wrong at Queeney's party was at the dance, to which Mrs. Thrale treated the servants. "Dignan the Cook . . . got drunk too soon, tumbled down Stairs and broke a Rib; but he will do very well again and dance next Year" (*Letters* 548A).

19: Sept.ʳ this last Birthday of our eldest Daughter's — the 17ᵗʰ last past — is made remarkable by her being put to her allowance: her Father now pays her 40 Guineas a Year commencing at this Quarter — We shall see how She manages it.

20: Sept.ʳ I think myself once again pregnant, and am astonished ay & disgusted too to find M.ʳ Thrale not at all rejoyced at it: I confess I am as glad as possible, & I thought he would have wished for a Son but no,

*he seems rather offended than delighted, so indeed he is commonly
with all I do; he would have been offended enough, and reasonably
enough had I not bred I suppose. —— I care not however, tis a Security to me of my own Estate not going out of my own Family at
least, if I have Children to inherit it myself. I have prayed hard for a
Son I am sure, and I hope God has heard my Prayers.*

M. *Thrale's Affairs are now so very prosperous, that he thinks of
nothing but to plan future Expences: and rejects Counsel as Insult, and
Restraint as Injury —— long may his Affairs be prosperous! though
while they are so, he never plainly will lay up a Shilling, or admit the
possibility of a cloudy Day: — when his profusion has incur'd Distress
— tis my Duty to assist, it is now my Duty to look on only, & throw in
a gentle Warning when it will be accepted,* & *that is seldom. neither
am I likely to try very often God knows, tho' I approve not of these
Ponds, Hothouses &c. Surely less ado might serve! Sophy has now
lived with me ever since last Christmas, but while I go to Brighton, She
must go to School;*

It was now 20 September, Miss Cotton had been expected from Bath
for over a month but had still not appeared, an awkward situation, for
Thrale was impatient to be off for Brighton, and he told his wife that
even if her "Uncle was coming from the Grave," he would stick to his
word and "go . . . on the 30ᵗʰ" (*Letters* 547A). Johnson answered
from Ashbourne, that if "Aunt comes now she can do but little harm,
for she will hardly go with you to [Brighton], and she cannot long
trouble you at Streatham" (*Letters* 550). But before this letter arrived:

*Oh here comes my Aunt I vow, & I must send for Susan to see her &
shew herself.*

*Well! My Aunt never saw such an Improvement as that of Susan
in her Life; but Sophy is grown ugly She says, that is course: She thinks
Susan quite a Beauty & a Wit. She may well wonder at her indeed;
for She does repeat Poetry so sweetly, & exhibit her Geography so
finely, does translate French so so [sic] well, & work & write so cleverly that She may well wonder & admire too. Sophy shall pack up with
her & go to Kensington home with Mʳˢ Cumyns who brought Sue
hither till we return from Brighthelmston. I shall take Cecilia there to
dip her in the Sea, She looks pale & that will freshen her: thank God*

QUEENEY THRALE
BY REYNOLDS

the four Girls are all well now & I am breeding again — what would I
have!
   This is Michaelmas Day 29: Sep.ᵗ 1777.

Johnson was delighted to hear that Aunt Cotton "liked my Susey
[sic], I was always a Susey [sic], when nobody else was a Susy" (*Letters* 554). But what, he asked, did Mrs. Thrale do with her aunt — for
the family had gone to Brighton at the time Thrale vowed they would.
A week later Johnson was still curious, "How did you and your Aunt
part? Did you turn her out of doors to begin your journey, or did she
leave you by her usual shortness of visits. I love to know how you go
on" (*Letters* 555).

   Johnson wrote from Ashbourne, where he expected to stay some
while, but he promised not to forget Brighton. He still had to spend
time with Boswell, whom he had agreed to see this autumn. Earlier on,
Johnson had suggested a Baltic expedition, but his friend had shrunk
from this. "I am sorry you have already been in Wales," wrote Boswell,
"for I wish to see it" (*Letters* 545, n. 2). In the end, Boswell, who was
short of money this year, joined Johnson at hospitable Dr. Taylor's
house, and they were there now, having a comfortable, if not stimulating, time.

   Mrs. Thrale wrote to Johnson, reminding him about Brighton.
Peggy Owen was with them, and Dr. Burney, and many old friends
wondered where he was. The Earl of Lucan had inquired, and Hamilton, the parliamentarian, asked for him daily. She added the news
that Miss Burgoyne (who had been a sponsor for Ralph) was much in
evidence, and the Shelleys, of course, were frequent companions, as
well as the Pepyses, both the Lucases and the William Wellers. Dear
old Mr. Scrase had been ill but was well again; his attachment to a
sprightly widow in her fifties was, according to Mrs. Thrale, the cause
of his cure and rejuvenation.

   The Nesbitts were in Brighton; Thrale's brother-in-law was little
seen — he was a dying man — but his wife was often at West Street,
good-natured, vapid, and naive as ever. Thrale had twitted her for surf
bathing at the end of the Brighton beach where gentlemen bathed (by
custom in the buff). "Lord Brother," she said ". . . God knows I
would not give *this* now, — snapping her Fingers — to see all the Men
in Brighthelmstone naked" (*Thraliana*, p. 272). She was not Mrs.
Thrale's idea of a gentlewoman.

"Nezzy," as Johnson called her, had once been a remarkably handsome woman, and she still retained traces of beauty, still the clear, steady eyes of darkest blue, which Queeney's exactly resembled (*Thraliana*, p. 271). But recently "Nezzy" had grown fat. She had palpitations of the heart [13] and was on a strict milk diet. Attacks came every fortnight or so but in between she was spirited enough.

In contrast to the ailing Nesbitts, there was good news from the Lade quarter. As Mrs. Thrale had written to Johnson, Sir John was better, "the Physician has frighted him into more Care they say, & it is to be hop'd He may go on to one & Twenty" (*Letters* 549A). Johnson replied that he was relieved to hear about Sir John, and on the subject of the Lades, he hoped that Thrale would pay off the loan he had made in 1772 — if he had not already done so. The brewery profits last year, he reminded Mrs. Thrale, had been £14,000 (*Letters* 560).

During this stay in Brighton a new friend came into the Thrale circle, who was to become important in their lives. One day by chance Mrs. Thrale met Sophia Streatfeild (twenty-three years old to Mrs. Thrale's thirty-six), a beauty with elegance, learning, and very sweet manners. Miss Streatfeild was a brilliant Greek scholar, and Mrs. Thrale soon discovered that Sophia had been tutored by Dr. Collier. Sophia had been his last pupil, in fact he had died at her house in May of this year, and been buried at her expense. Discovering their mutual connection with Dr. Collier was an emotional experience for Mrs. Thrale, and she soon formed a close friendship with Sophia.

Mrs. Thrale confided that she had treated Collier very badly, for which her mother had been responsible. But even after her mother's death, she had to confess, she had not dared to renew her friendship because she was sure that the irritating way Dr. Collier talked about politics and metaphysics (which had driven guests from her uncle's table at Offley Place) would never be tolerated by Johnson. He would have manhandled the poor man and driven him away — and she could not bear to hurt him a second time (*Thraliana*, p. 17).

Sophia, or "S.S." as her intimates called her, said that she understood perfectly, and Mrs. Thrale appreciated this; she became more and more fond of "S.S." Queeney admired her Greek, and Mrs. Thrale thought, as all men did, that she was beautiful. And everyone was intrigued by

[13] Mrs. Nesbitt's palpitations were probably due to recurrent attacks of rapid heart action, and there is no reason to believe that her milk diet was an effective treatment, though it undoubtedly contributed to her growing fat.

the way she could make herself weep at will, pearly tears brimming at her eyelids, making her face even more lovely as they coursed down her cheeks — very entertaining.

On 12 October Dr. Burney departed for London and Arthur Murphy, another favorite, took his place. Activities continued as before, inviting "Company to Dinner & [daudling] in the Rooms at Night, yet my Master & Miss Owen call that Pleasure, & I like it better now I play at Cards." Mrs. Thrale also told Johnson that "Queeney will not dance, and the People twit me that I will not let her, because I dance myself — even Miss Owen who lives with us believes that to be the Case from Queeney's Manner & management" (*Letters* 556A).

Murphy, in his bathing machine, read plays to the roaring sea, and ashore helped to make things lively. He introduced the Thrales to his friend, Topham Beauclerk, a member of Johnson's Literary Club and something of a rake. And one morning the infamous John Wilkes "came hither to wait on Murphy . . . [Wilkes] professed himself a Lyar and an Infidel . . . [and] gave me nothing but Offence . . ." (*Letters* 556A). Wilkes, in short order, asked Thrale "to a Dinner of Rakes — Beauclerck, Lord Kelly & the Men of *Worth & honour* that are here, & here are plenty too: says Murphy looking at me — *he dares not go*" (*Letters* 556B). Mrs. Thrale besought her husband with all her power not to go (one of the rare occasions when she tried her will against his), but Thrale attended the dinner.

Mrs. Thrale now began to complain to Johnson of the utter frivolity of the life they were living. She was trying to write diligently in *Thraliana*, as he had advised (*Letters* 542), but there was little worth recording . He answered:

> . . . do not play Agnes, [again Molière's "creeping wife"] and do not grow old before your time nor suffer yourself to be too soon driven from the stage. You can yet give pleasure by your appearance, show yourself therefore, and be pleased by pleasing. It is not now too soon to be wise, nor is it yet too late to be gay. (*Letters* 558)

Johnson, in a letter to her a fortnight later, was delighted to hear that Mr. Thrale had made her pull off her wig and dress her own hair. She had written him, "my Master . . . begins innocently to wonder why he ever let me wear a Wig. I remember well however the why, the when, & the where. My Mother thought it a good Scheme to keep young married Women at home . . ." Mrs. Thrale finished her letter by saying ". . . I did think to have burnt it for Joy of the great News from America but there comes no Confirmation of it they say" [14] (*Letters* 561A). Johnson replied, "Every body was an enemy to that Wig. — We will burn it, and get drunk, for what is joy without drink" (*Letters* 562).

It was now November and Mrs. Thrale was still urging Johnson to come to Brighton — at least for a weekend — "the fourteenth of this Month [Friday], dine with us on the Saturday, with Beauclerck on Sunday, Hamilton on Monday, & return with us to Streatham on the Tuesday the eighteenth which is the Day we have fixed upon to leave this Place" (*Letters* 561A).

Johnson had returned to London from Lichfield only a few days before and he had less desire than ever to come to Brighton. He knew it would be a hard, cold, wintry journey, and he dreaded the discom-

[14] She was referring to General Burgoyne's campaign. At the request of Lord North, Burgoyne had drawn up a plan of action for 1777. The strategy was, in essence, to cut off the Continental New England forces from those in New York. Burgoyne proposed that his army (12,000 regulars were promised, and to these he wished to add 2,000 Canadians and 1,000 Indians) should advance from Canada, take Fort Ticonderoga, and then march on Albany, where General Howe would join him from New York. With their combined forces (a pincer movement) they would meet the Americans.

In July 1777 Burgoyne's campaign began, though his force was little more than half the promised strength. After a six-day siege, however, Burgoyne's army captured Fort Ticonderoga.

The news reached Whitehall on the afternoon of 23 August and was greeted with exultation. The King was so delighted "that he rushed in unannounced upon the Queen when she had on nothing but her chemise, and waving the dispatch before her scandalized ladies-in-waiting exclaimed, 'I have beat them! I have beat all the Americans!' — as if he had done the whole thing with his own royal hands . . . the King thought of nothing but how to reward Burgoyne" (Hoffman Nickerson, *The Turning Point of the Revolution* [New York, 1967], pp. 161–162).

The King wished to give him the order of the Bath, and when Lord Derby refused this honor in his brother-in-law's name, the King promoted Burgoyne to Lieutenant General. The Thrales were jubilant about all this. Their close friend, Miss Burgoyne, was a cousin of the General's.

But no "Confirmation" of "the great News from America" ever arrived. General Howe did not come from New York. In mid-September Burgoyne, with only 5,000 men, met the Continental General, Horatio Gates, with his 20,000 men. On 17 October, at Saratoga, Burgoyne and his whole army surrendered. The report of this disaster reached London on 2 December 1777.

If Burgoyne had been victorious at Saratoga, this might have led to final British victory, but his failure encouraged the French, and later the Spaniards and the Dutch, to enter the War on the side of the Americans. At the battle of Saratoga the tide turned irrevocably.

fort, "yet to shew my Master an example of compliance, and to let you know how much I long to see you, and to boast how little I give way to disease, my purpose is to be with you on Friday" (*Letters* 562). And so he made his promised visit, though it was only for three days, and he was far from well. He had great difficulty breathing and despite Mrs. Thrale's disapproval was taking opium for relief.

At the time of Johnson's arrival Miss Owen was about to depart for Wales. She cried at the thought of parting after her "long Range among the Gay Folks of the Town" (she had been the Thrales' guest for the greater part of a year). Johnson teased her by saying that she should think how her "Conversation will illuminate the Montgomerians! — and besides there are some fine young Fellows grown up since your Departure from amongst them" (*Thraliana*, p. 175).

When the Thrales returned to Streatham after their seven weeks' absence they were relieved to find that all was well at home. Johnson reported this to Boswell, and he gave the good news that Mrs. Thrale was once more "in hopes of a young brewer" (*Letters* 565).

Cæcilia did bathe at Brighton, but it did not agree with her; She was cutting her Teeth & the cold Water teized her, but She does very well upon the whole as to Person & Health; and with regard to Sense blessed be God She is reckoned eminently forward — sweet tempered and sagacious: Hester likewise is returned from her Sea bathing very much grown, and perfectly well in Health — & I have seen my two Girls at Kensington, who come on to my Wishes both in body & Mind. — if I could once feel the Child I carry move as if alive, I should be compleatly happy; but here are 14 Weeks now, and I am not yet quick, — odd enough! — considering I have never had a complaint since I begun breeding/this Time/ & I have bathed & done every thing in order to gain Strength & keep my Kid. —⸺ this Stuff is written 1: Dec: 1777. but we came home on the 4:th[15] *from Sussex; I never was very sick with this breeding Bout.*

16: Dec: I fetched home my little Girls from Mrs Cumyns's and this is the 20: the whole four are with me now, healthy, lively, lovely, unobjectible, except that Susan will have a little, a very little, almost un-

[15] This is incorrect. The Thrales and Johnson returned home on 18 November, as the latter told Lucy Porter in his letter from London on 20 November (*Letters* 564).

perceivable defect in her Shape I think, the Consequence of original Weakness no doubt.[16] *Her Temper is sullen too, but her Understanding excellent, and her Knowledge extremely copious and uncommon. She is likewise what every body must acknowledge to be a very pretty Girl, her Hair black, but exquisitely fine; her Colour very good, & her Complexion such as will come wonderfully clear I take it — in about seven Years more. add to this that her second Teeth seem disposed to be fine ones & her Eyebrows are as if drawn with a Pencil.*

M.ͬ Johnson is surprized at her Power over French, & as for Geography & Grammar She is Mistress of them. It is almost ridiculous to say that She has a Taste for Poetry, yet it is true; She gets Verses by heart to please herself, and delights in repeating particular Passages as much as I do; Grongar hill[17] *is a favourite with her — and if Gay's Fables as She says — was not a Book for Children, She should like some parts of it vastly. So much for Susanna Arabella Thrale.*

Sophia Thrale is well formed, beautifully proportion'd, large Limbed *& yet graceful to amaze one: her Head & Neck are not surpassed by any thing in Statuary; and her Face would be handsome too if She had any Eyebrows, which is the only deficiency I know in her Person. They are both tallish of their Years, but Sophy looks two Years younger than Sue; and is so indeed with regard to mental Pow'rs: She has however an Angelick Sweetness of Temper & if She will not be able*

> —— *to draw down*
> *The Pale Moon from the frighted Sky*
> *She'll draw Endymion from the Moon.*[18]

She is Elegant and /yet/ Active, Chearful & yet Gentle, sweet yet not insipid — She can read common English Prose of the Narratory Sort perfectly well, without Tone or Drawl; & understand what She reads so as to make pleasure out of it; She works well at her Needle, and dances better than ever little Maiden did dance who was not bred to the Stage. Her Hair is black & her Face white, but there is a Gayety in the Countenance that many prefer to the Intelligence visible in her Sister's.
—— I will say nothing of Cæcilia till She is a Year old — She is at present all one can wish.

[16] This muscular weakness was the last sequel to Susan's rickets.
[17] *Grongar Hill*: a poem describing the scenery of the River Towy. It is by John Dyer (1699–1758), a Welshman, and was first published in 1726.
[18] This quotation has not been identified.

With regard to myself I am now four Months gone with Child; but I feel none of the usual Motion of the Fœtus, which I fear never was endued with Life nor now ever will be. just before I conceived I dream'd I was deliver'd of a Boy — all bathed in blood, and last Night I dreamt there was a Mourning Coach at the Door to carry my dead Son to the Grave. — I have nobody to tell my Uneasinesses to, no Mother, no Female Friend — no nothing: so I must eat up my own Heart & be quiet — and wait the Event, & perhaps be reproach'd when it happens — would the mourning Coach might carry me off before I see more of my Offspring devoted to Death, would it might!
20: Dec: 1777. —

Sat 17: Jan: 1778
Susan & Sophy are gone back to School healthy handsome & wise if I can judge & in the way of further Improvement; Hester is going to Town with me in high Health & Beauty too; my Child within me is alive & the Pregnancy proceeds well — my little Cæcilia is fair & forward & fresh — Might not anyone say to me —

> *A Pack of Blessings light upon thy Back;*
> *Happiness courts thee in her best Array,*
> *But like a misbehav'd & sullen Wench*
> *Thou pout'st upon thy Fortune & thy Love.*
> *Take heed! Take heed! for such die miserable.*[19]

My Master has given me a fine Gown too, & I am going to Court on Monday next with Mrs Montagu in little & great things now all goes well. —

We did go to Town, Hester & I for a fortnights Pleasure, & we staid seven Weeks; during w:^{ch} Time She never was an hour sick, nor ever did I hear ought of my three little ones excepting good. We are now returned to Streatham, & I hope to Lye in the latter End of May: my present Companion is I thank God brisk & lively & the Pregnancy proceeds just as it ought to do; my little Cæcilia comes on too to my Wishes, & all goes well in the Year 1778. so far as this
7:th day of March — Streatham

Mrs. Thrale's London "frolicks" before lying-in were becoming a regular custom, and this year, from the last part of January until the

---

[19] Shakespeare, *Romeo and Juliet*, III.iii.141–145.

first week in March, she and Queeney (and Thrale to a minor degree) filled their days with social pleasure. The Thrales' circle of acquaintance was becoming larger all the time for they were liked: he was generous and she was entertaining, and their daughter was pretty and accomplished — a very eligible young lady. Mrs. Thrale was proud of Queeney in her new role, but Johnson found it tiresome. "Miss has a mind to be womanly," he complained to Lucy Porter, "and her womanhood does not sit well upon her" (*Letters* 564).

The Burneys were among the friends who gave Mrs. Thrale the most pleasure; and one way she showed her appreciation was to buy a new harpsichord for Dr. Burney's use in instructing Queeney. Mrs. Montagu was another friend whose attention was flattering. And the ultimate was having the King say to Mrs. Thrale, when she went to Court in February, that she did not spend enough time in London. "Was not that fine . . . ?" she asked Johnson (*Letters* 572A).

There was another encounter, not on such an exalted level, but of greater future importance. One cold winter night in late 1777 or early 1778 Dr. Burney gave an evening party for his distinguished friends, the Grevilles, who wished to meet Johnson and the Thrales. Fulke Greville had been Dr. Burney's early patron; now in his sixties, he was "the finest gentleman about town," according to Fanny Burney. His emaciated and imposing wife, Fanny's godmother, was celebrated for her *Prayer for Indifference*, and for being Mrs. Montagu's most serious bluestocking rival. The Grevilles had brought their daughter, pretty, clever Mrs. Crewe ("Baby Crewe," Mrs. Montagu called her). Queeney was at the party and, besides the senior Burneys, four Burney daughters, young Charles Burney, Seward, and the D'Avenants.

Dr. Burney looked forward to an evening of scintillating conversation, but being a little nervous about a first encounter between the aristocratic Grevilles and tradesman Thrale and Johnson (who could be irascible), he thought he would insure harmony by adding a little music. He arranged to have an Italian performer, whom he admired, start things off by playing on the harpsichord and keep things going by singing at intervals.

The evening was not a success. None of the important guests appreciated music, it only impeded conversation. And the party needed different direction. Johnson had to be challenged, he did not initiate talk — something Dr. Burney did not seem to appreciate. Greville was too proud to lead off; he planted himself "immovable as a noble statue, upon the hearth" (*Memoirs*, II, 107), cutting off all heat to the room. Suddenly Johnson bellowed, "If it were not for depriving the ladies of the fire, — I should like to stand upon the hearth myself!" (*Memoirs*, II, 112). Mrs. Thrale, in an effort to divert the company, mimicked the musician behind his back, and was severely reprimanded by Dr. Burney.[20]

This was the first meeting of Mrs. Thrale and Gabriel Piozzi.

Queeney was much admired in London too, & I have gained some new Friends & lost no old ones —

once more let me give God thanks for all his Mercies through Jesus Christ our Lord.

7: March 1778.

This 13.:th day of March 1778. is remarkable for my having intercepted a clandestine Letter, from my eldest Daughter to a Girl in the Neighbourhood; — one of my Friend Pitches's Misses, a Wench I do not much like, but how should Hester & I like the same Wench? This is the first attempt I have observed towards clandestine Correspondence, & should suppose my Miss was rather a forward Miss as to Affairs of that Nature. She had from Infancy a Spirit of keeping Secrets, & Baretti long ago told her She was old enough to write her own Letters & have her own Friendships without the Interference of her Mother, in whom She has no Confidence, nor ever had — She is now thirteen Years old & a half — rather early I sh.:d think, but these are forward Times God knows.

Peggy Pitches was the correspondent, and one of Queeney's coded letters to her survives. It is not the letter referred to in Mrs. Thrale's journal, but one written at a time when Queeney and her mother were visiting Lady Lade for a fortnight. Deciphered, it says in part, "MY DEAR, — My Mother has scolded me so to-day and been in such a passion you can't think . . . I have just been having such a lecture from Lady Lade as would make you stare. Just such stuff as my Mother

---

[20] For descriptions of this party see: *Early Diary of Frances Burney*, ed. by Annie Raine Ellis (London: George Bell, 1889), II, 284–287; *Memoirs*, II, 101–114; and the delightful latter-day account in *The Second Common Reader*, by Virginia Woolf (London: Hogarth Press, 1932), pp. 108–125.

talks, about dignity . . . I begin to wish I was at home, I long so to see you, and to be away from all these lectures." [21]

1. April 1778.

Tis observable that I never bought any Baby things or Dresses for my-self at Lying-In since the first Time till now; & this is the twelfth. I have now got myself a new Bed, new Sheets, new Bedgowns, Half Shifts &c besides Robes &c for the Kid — and now if I should dye! — Why if I should die! what does it signify? Let me but leave a Son, I shall die happy enough: & as for one's Family having a Loss of one that is a Jest; I see People every Day doing just as well without any Mother, or with a Mother in Law [i.e., a stepmother].

M. *Thrale would begin the World anew; & as for the Girls they could but be at School, & there they would be bred like other people which M.* *Johnson says is so good a Thing: Queeney he says is made singular by my Education of her: it is not true however, for She is not singular at all. I was myself a very particular Girl; but my Daughter whatever faults She has, has not my faults, of Confidence Loquacity & foolish Sensibility. —*

*Here is a new Agony — My Master dispirited & almost in Despair about pecuniary Matters looks like Death, & if any Disorder would seize/him/ is likely to dye himself instead of me, whose Spirits always rise on an Exigence whereas his sink: I have been to Brighton for Counsel & Money of that Dear Creature Scrase whose Liberality of Sentiment & Behaviour charms and astonishes me. The Journey did me no harm I think, tho' in the 8.*ᵗʰ* Month of the 12.*ᵗʰ* Pregnancy and if Money or kindness could quiet the mind of M.* *Thrale I should still have a happy Lying In; for nothing of real Consequence has happened to dis-tress him, and Perplexities every one must bear some times — I'm sure he may say —— Graviora tuli* [22] *— & so may I when I recollect the Year 1772. How differently does one feel when one is wanted & when one is not. I used to say nothing should make me cut my Trees down in Wales & now I offered them Yesterday to pacify My Masters Uneasi-ness: but he or his Daughter would at any Time rather suffer Misery in a slight degree than receive Consolation or Kindness from me, which I*

[21] *Notes and Queries*, 11th ser., XI (1915), 298–299.
[22] Graviora tuli: I have borne worse things.

have long known, but cannot help. The worst is I do grudge myself my new Bed &c. when I ordered it I did not think we were in a Way to want Money or I would not have increased my sweet Master's perplexities: conscious that every Man when he begins to wish to save Money, always wishes to save it out of his Wife's Expenses, & when he wishes to spend it, wishes to spend it on his own. However why should it not be so? —

Après tout (as Voltaire says) la Nature est comme la Nature! ——
20: April 1778.

Last year, 1777, had been a time of plenty and Thrale had lost his head. He had made lavish improvements at Streatham and had not been able to resist speculation; he had overbrewed during the winter, so that now there was little capital left to carry on the business, and since money was tight in the city, it had to be raised elsewhere. Mrs. Thrale made a begging trip to Scrase, as she had in 1772. She even offered to sacrifice her woods at Bach-y-Graig — only the past summer the thought of cutting any timber there had aroused her to passion. Thrale scorned this great generosity. As she wrote to Johnson, he was very hard to live with: he "grudges my new Bed so that it makes him half mad, & [the new harpsichord] will be twice the Money of my poor Bed. — Oh Dear me! but he is woeful cross; & glad at heart shall I be to have you with us — for we *grind* sadly else" (*Letters* 575A).

Johnson did what he could to ease the tension, and Sophia Streatfeild was helpful. She was one of the few persons who knew of the existence of *Thraliana*, and on 19 May of this year Mrs. Thrale allowed her the special privilege of writing the title for volume III. Sophy did this in a fine Gothic script.

Thrale was always in better spirits when the lovely "S.S." was at Streatham. He liked her company, her gentle voice and affectionate manner. For Johnson's part, he found her a great improvement over Peggy Owen, though he said, "taking away [Sophy's] Greek, she was as ignorant as a butterfly" (Hayward, I, 118). Mrs. Thrale again imagined that she would die having her baby and this time supposed that her successor would be "S.S." instead of Peggy Owen.

[11 June 1778]
My Master's Depression at any ill Fortune or ill Management of his own — for no other Mishap has he had — will if he takes no Care be as

fatal as his Elevation when Matters go grand; and he will not listen to Advice. Indeed he will no more receive Consolation on a cloudy day than he will Admonition on a bright one — unhappy Turn! All his Ailments must cure themselves — he will submit to no Chirurgeon, at least not to me.

Little Cæcilia comes on charmingly. She is a fine Maiden indeed, healthy sensible & active: eats & sleeps and begins to feel her Feet & use her Tongue quite prettily — She is a sweet Child sure enough. Susan & Sophy are come home for Whitsun Holydays: they grow tall, and improve considerably in their Intellects; I think Mrs Cumyns neglects the Exterior, they have a wild Look, but are healthy & handsome enough — they please me mighty well: My Master is not much in a humour to be pleased, — he has not yet conquered his Panick: here is the 11:^th of June however, & I still undelivered, much to my own astonishment; I expected this Baby the latter End of last Month, but 'twill be a Boy at last I hope to make amends for /so/ long waiting. Sophy has got a swelled Face, but Sue is sprightly & knowing & reads Verse & Prose, French & English like an Angel with a perfect Knowledge of Grammar & Geography beside She has worked a fine Map Sampler to send my Aunt [Sydney Arabella Cotton] at Bath all in shades, very elegant indeed — I warrant it will be enough admired.

On 20 June Mrs. Thrale sent Johnson a letter, "written during Labour":

Do huff my Master & comfort him by Turns according to your own Dear Discretion: he has consulted you now, & given you a Right to talk with Him about his ill Tim'd Melancholy and do keep your Influence over him for all our Sakes. God be praised I have nothing to fear at present for my own Life or my Child's: all is regular & natural but very lingering & tedious . . . (*Letters* 577A)

3: July.
My Baby is come at last — a Girl it is however [23] *but a very large one; the largest Child we ever had the D^r & the Maids say but I think Sophy was as big. The Labour was long & the Birth difficult from the uncommon Size of the Child,* [24] *but the Lying In is delightful; I never was so*

[23] Johnson wrote to Boswell on the same day this entry was made: "Mrs. Thrale, poor thing, has a daughter" (*Letters* 578).

[24] This was due to the very long time the child was carried. The fetus continues to grow *in utero* beyond the term.

well at three Weeks end almost as I am this Time on the thirteenth Day. My Master is content, *and nothing just now* could *have made him* happy: *Mrs Montagu and Miss Streatfeild & Tom Cotton are the Sponsors, and the Name is to be Henrietta-Sophia   Mrs Montagu offered herself as Godmother & said — to comfort us — that She would not have stood for a Boy; all our/other/Friends fret that it was not a Son — but my Master is in his* Aphelion [25] *yet, and cares for nothing — when he warms up to fresh Hope & fresh Extravagance he will be sorry too. The Affairs of the Nation however are at present in such a Situation that the Mercantile Folks will be easily held down I fear; and if so perhaps poor Mr Thrale's last* Perihelion [26] *was in August 1777. — this is 3:^d July 1778.*

N:B: I am sure *I went 10 complete Months with Harriett — I conceived the 24:^th of August, quicken'd 25: Dec:^r & was delivered the 21: June 1778.*

odd Enough! —

/8 July 78./ Poor Lady Lade shed Tears to day at the visible Alteration in her Brother's Countenance & Manner; I had something to do to forbear telling her the whole Truth — yet what had I to do to tell it her? She is nearer related to Mr Thrale than me, & if he chose not to make her his Confident, what right had I to make /her/ mine? —

Mr Thrale is I find brooding in Silence over Schemes of Ruin; he desires to part w:^th Perkins who sets his faults before him some what too strongly indeed for policy, but not for Friendship: & to get himself a chief Clerk who will more Complaisantly see him undo himself, & say nothing. Such a Measure w:^d I verily think finish the Family, & yet the Baseness of hating one's Friends merely because they will not flatter one's Follies, shocks me still more than the Prospect of Perplexity in which such a Step w:^d involve us. besides if he is to hate Perkins for telling him Truth, he will of Consequence hate Johnson, & me most of all I suppose, as I shall be most injured, — & he'll think every Look a Reproach.

17: July 1778.
This Day I walked quite round our new Walk which is very near two

---

[25] Aphelion: The point of a planet's orbit, or a comet's orbit most distant from the sun (dark, melancholy spirits).

[26] Perihelion: The opposite; the point nearest the sun (light, high spirits).

*Miles in circumference though my Month will not be up till the 21ˢᵗ —
pretty good Share of Strength I may say for the 12:ᵗʰ Pregnancy. How
much have I yet to be thankful for? since tho' neither our Fortune nor
our Family are settled, I may even yet entertain hopes of making both
before I dye; though turned of 36: Late in Life however, considering
I have been married 15 Years, & had a Son the /3:ᵈ/ year of my Marriage to a Man who was said to be a rich one. here is however neither
Money nor Son now Life is so far advanced. —*

> *What then is to be done? be wise with Speed,
> A Fool at forty, is a Fool indeed. —*[27]

18: July 1778.

*Well! last night Mʳ Johnson having looked over my Master's Reste-
Book,*[28] *resolved I suppose to talk to him about his Affairs; for as I came in
from walking I found them already entered on the Subject. Mʳ Johnson
observed that there was no need to be low spirited tho we had been Im-
prudent, that such was our Capital we might still be rich, might pay all
our Debts, & lay up five Thousand a Year, while we lived at the Rate
of five Thousand more, if Mʳ Thrale would but promise never to brew
more than fourscore Thousand Barrels of Beer in a Winter. He represented to him that setting his Profits at the low Rate of half a Crown a
Barrel, 80,000 Barrels wᵈ bring him ten Thousand Pounds a Year of
wᶜʰ says he I will allow you to spend three thousand rationally, & two
Thousand foolishly — in building Digging Planting or what you will
— only lay up the other five Thousand for your Children, who really
have a Claim to it; & for yourself in Case of any Emergence that we
may not /be/ found as now totally unprovided with Money, insomuch
that we have been forced on the disgraceful Expe[sic] Expedient of
borrowing from our own Servants — nor can our utter Deficiency of
Cash be long concealed. People will see & hear & conjecture that we
live beyond our Income — or brew our Money /away/ & so have none
— and these Conjectures will ruin our Credit by w:ᶜʰ alone we were
this Year saved from Destruction: for remember Sir said he you had
hanged yourself; only that Mʳ Scrase was contented to cut you down.
besides why should you wish said I to brew more than eighty Thousand
Barrels? is not 10,000£ a Year enough for any Man — why then for*

[27] Edward Young, *Love of Fame*, Satire II, lines 281–282.
[28] The brewer's book of accounts with his victuallers and ale-house keepers.
See p. 460.

*Gods Sake such mad Rapacity? Rapacity so dangerous that it will cer-
tainly be punish'd, as the Avarice of Gamesters always is — by the failure of their own Schemes. The Man who will perpetually play double
or Quits, must lose at last, & that Loss must be Ruin: & if you thus per-
sist in pouring the profits of the Trade back upon the Trade; that Trade
will swell indeed like a Bubble, but like a Bubble it will be sure to burst.
To this I added that Mr Thrale was the most unfit Man in the World to
get into Dificulties, as nobody was so much depressed by 'em, that he
had so lost Flesh Spirits & Appearance by this last Perplexity, that I
thought few Things worth the Anxiety he had suffered since April;
that it was very ridiculous to hazard his Health and Fortune nay his
Life for the sake of a paltry Superiority to Whitbred [sic] & Calvert,*[29]
*Men whose Acquaintance he was ashamed of, & whose Persons he
shrunk from if he met 'em in a Publick Place. I further protested (which
is strictly true) that was my Ruin alone endangered — I w:^d not put*
myself *to the pain of disputation to prevent it; nor put* him *to the pain
of being contradicted in his Pleasures, be they as absurd as they* would:
*but that we had five Girls who had a Claim to my Care, & that it was
for* their *Sakes & his Sake y^t: I spoke so freely as I did: that I knew if
ever he did again bring us into Distress, the very Recollection of this
Conversation would greatly affect him, & that I earnestly begg'd his
promise to brew but 80,000 Barrels of Beer — Mr Johnson seconded me
by earnest and pathetic Entreaties & we at length extorted from him a
Promise that he would brew no more than 80,000 Barrels a Year — for
five Years to come.*[30] —

*Cæcilia Margaret cuts her Teeth in a manner quite different from any
of my Children: has no Fever, Sleeplessness or Loss of Appetite, yet
fades & pines away in her Person losing Flesh & Colour without any
apparent Cause — yet I think She'll get over it too; for after every*

---

[29] Thrale's greatest rivals in the brewing trade were Samuel Whitbread and
Felix Calvert. And Baretti had had the poor taste, while he lived with the family,
to say that if Mrs. Thrale ever "died in a Lying In . . . that he hoped Mr Thrale
would marry Miss Whitbred, who would be a pretty Companion for Hester, and
not tyrannical and overbearing like [her mother]" (*Thraliana*, p. 44). Baretti
presumably referred to the eldest of Whitbread's three daughters, Harriot (1758–
1832). Harriot was to marry James Gordon, Jr., of Moor Park, Hertfordshire,
in 1789.

[30] ". . . & so Johnson bade me write it down in the Thraliana; and so the
Wings of *Speculation* are clipped a little; very fain would I have pinioned her, but
I had not strength to perform the Operation" (*Thraliana*, p. 333).

pining Fit there comes a Tooth or two, & She picks up again till more Teeth breed in the Gum. She is exquisitely fair, has very light brown hair, very light Grey Eyes, and is pretty when in good Case which of late however does not often happen. She walks alone quite well, wants no Backstring & says some little Words as Papa Mama &c. ——

18: July 1778.

Here is a fine Confusion indeed! Sally Bean [31] who always nurses me in Lying In — put her little Boy to lodge wth my Coachman's Wife here up at Streatham & there he has catched the Itch,[32] & doubtless given it to us all; for we were all fond of the Child, & I like an Ideot let him come & sleep here two or three Nights because they said he fretted so at being from his Mother, so I suppose we are all to begin & scratch speedily, but my Comfort is y^t he has been now gone home a fort-night and all's safe yet.

28: July.

My Master looks dismally still, I fear he will never get the better of this Summer's Agitation & Terror.

On a happier note, the Thrales had enjoyed a pleasant visit from Dr. Burney and his wife in July. During their visit there was a great deal of talk about a fascinating novel, which had been published in January — the sensation of the day. *Evelina*, it was called, and the author was anonymous, generally thought to be a man.

Lady Westcote liked the book, Johnson gave it high praise. Sir Joshua Reynolds had to be fed while reading it (since he refused to quit the table). Edmund Burke sat up a whole night to finish the three volumes. Mrs. Thrale and Queeney loved the book and, when Dr. and Mrs. Burney came to Streatham, Queeney quoted whole passages, and her mother offered to lend a copy. Mrs. Burney had to be careful with her reply — for none other than shy Fanny Burney, her step-daughter, was the author of *Evelina*. But Fanny wished no one to know, and the Burneys were sworn to secrecy. (They had known the truth only since June, and had been astounded when they found out.)

[31] Sally Bean: Mrs. Thrale's maid, formerly her mother's maid.

[32] The "Itch" was almost certainly scabies. This is caused by a mite which burrows in the skin, and is conveyed from one host to another by close physical contact. It is highly communicable. Today the complaint would probably be treated by rubbing benzyl benzoate into the skin.

The Burneys guarded their secret, but within a short time Mrs. Thrale discovered the identity of the author on her own. Her first reaction was astonishment, her second, a desire to bring Fanny to visit at Streatham. She had hardly noticed Fanny upon their first meeting, now she longed to know her.

At the beginning of August Dr. Burney brought his daughter to the Thrales for a short visit, and on the 23rd Fanny came for a much longer stay — alone. She found Mrs. Thrale:

so entertaining, so gay, so enlivening, when she is in spirits, and so intelligent and instructive when she is otherwise, that I almost as much wish to record all she says, as all Dr. Johnson says. (Burney, I, 90–91)

When Fanny had first met Mrs. Thrale at St. Martin's Street she had thought her "a pretty woman still," except for a defect of her mouth (the scar of her fall from the horse), "but her nose is very handsome, her complexion very fair; she has the *embonpoint charmant*, and her eyes are blue and lustrous" (*Memoirs*, II, 87).

She had thought that Queeney was handsome, fair, round, firm, "cherubimical," her chief charm lying exactly where her mother failed — "namely, in the mouth" (*Memoirs*, II, 88). Queeney had been reserved and shy at the first meeting, never uttering a syllable. She was still silent, but Fanny appreciated other qualities and began to like her. Queeney's father she was meeting for the first time at Streatham. Thrale was gracious and polite but as withdrawn as his daughter. He did not seem well nor in good spirits. "Indeed, he [seemed] not to be a happy man" (Burney, I, 72).

Dr. Johnson, on the other hand, was in high spirits at Streatham and full of talk. Fanny was now over the shock of his appearance, which had disturbed her at the first meeting. She was able to talk to him, and he responded with gusto. He was extremely attentive. He even admired the way she dressed, and Fanny added in her account, "it seems he always speaks his mind concerning the dress of ladies, and all ladies who are here obey his injunctions implicitly" (Burney, I, 85).

On 27 August, when Johnson had not spoken to her since his return to Streatham from an absence in town, and she was self-consciously withdrawing with other guests to walk in the garden, he stopped her and asked how she did. "I was afraid, sir . . . you did not intend to know me again." He took both Fanny's hands and pleaded near-sightedness as the cause of his neglect, "Then drawing me very unexpectedly towards him, he actually kissed me!" — at which Mrs. Thrale laughed heartily. He then drew a chair for Fanny, close to his own, and they had a tête-à-tête for the rest of the evening. Seward and the others, when they returned from outside, did not presume to intrude (Burney, I, 143–144).

Of all the young ladies Mrs. Thrale had brought into the family circle, the graceful, clever, reticent, admiring "little Burney," it was soon apparent, was Johnson's favorite. Miss Streatfeild, however, remained Thrale's favorite.

25: Sept. 1778.
My eldest Daughter Hester Maria was measured, & found of a pleasing and sufficient height: She was this last Birthday 17: Sep. 1778. fourteen Years old; She is very pretty still, but is of a pale Complexion: her Person Mind and Temper have never indeed suffered any considerable Changes: her Face & Figure are very lovely, her Mind very highly cultivated, & her Temper haughty & contemptuous. She is blue Eyed, fair haired, has a good Set of Teeth, good Shape, & the Carriage of a Girl of Fashion. Books are her Delight, & She chuses her own Studies now for me, who do not interfere much nor would She suffer me. ——— She is my Misstress [sic] completely, but has I think no great Influence over her Papa. We kept her Birthday merrily, gave old Nurse Money, & She treated the Servants with a Dance. If my Master's mad Management does not bereave us all of all our Property — She stands foremost now to inherit our Possessions, and mine thank God are entailed;[33] *little as they are, & greatly as Mr. Thrale despises them they may become our best Friends, and he will take the swiftest Methods to make them so, by feeding the Brew house with its own Flesh till it perishes with a sudden & dreadful Ruin.*

With the precarious state of affairs at the brewery and Thrale's deep depression, there could be no thought of an ambitious trip this autumn; a stay in Brighton seemed the most sensible plan. Johnson, who was not well, was left behind — as he wrote to Mrs. Thrale teasingly, "left at home unregarded and unpitied" (*Letters* 583). To her he seemed to be having plenty of attention, seeing the Burneys and having a fourth portrait painted by Reynolds.

On their way to Brighton, the Thrales stopped at an army camp to

---

[33] This is not correct. See pp. 128

see Sir Robert Cotton, a colonel in the Guards. Cotton took his military duties seriously, as did all good Englishmen, for the battle news from America was alarming, and so were reports from the Continent.

Johnson was interested in the Thrales' visit to the camp, and he hoped it had diverted Thrale. "Is my Master come to himself?" he inquired when he wrote to Mrs. Thrale:

> Does he talk and walk and look about him, as if there were yet something in the world for which it is worth while to live? or does he yet sit and say nothing? He was mending before he went, and surely has not relapsed. (*Letters* 583)

Johnson requested an account of the camp from Queeney, for this, he told her, is "perhaps the most important scene of human existence, the real scene of heroick life" (*Letters* 585.1). Queeney had no such reaction; she thought the camp a very dismal, uncomfortable place, and she felt sorry for her cousin. Johnson replied with some heat:

> Sir Robert Cotton, whose degradation seems to touch you, is not the greatest man that has inhabited a tent. He is not considered out of Cheshire, nor perhaps in it, as standing on even ground with Alexander and Darius; Cæsar and Pompey; Tamerlane and Bajazet [Bayezid I]; Charles, Peter, and Augustus. These and many more like these, have lived in a camp like Sir Robert Cotton.
>
> In a camp you [see] what is the lowest and most portable accommodation with which Life can be contented . . . and it gives ladies the particular pleasure of seeing evils which they are not to share. (*Letters* 585.1)

After their visit to Sir Robert, the Thrales proceeded to Brighton, where they settled themselves in the comfortable West Street house, and were once more surrounded by the Shelleys, and by Hamilton, Beauclerk, and Scrase. Mrs. Montagu was in residence, and her company gave a great deal of pleasure to Mrs. Thrale, as did that of Mrs. Byron, a new friend, widow of Admiral "Foul Weather Jack" (and grandmother of the poet who was to be born in 1788). Sophia Streatfeild was also in Brighton.

"I hope you will let Miss Stratfield know how safe you keep her book," Johnson wrote of a volume he had returned, "It was too fine for a Scholar's talons. I hope she gets books that she may handle with more freedom, and understand with less difficulty. Do not let her forget me" (*Letters* 583).

Mrs. Thrale replied that:

Miss Streatfield does not forget you, we talk of you often, and we went today together to see Ruins and wished for your Company.

My Master mends but it is gradually: he is not yet a good Tête a Tête but he behaves tolerably in Company — every body however says he is *strangely broke* . . . (*Letters* 583A)

In time, "S.S." went home to Tunbridge Wells, where she lived with her widowed mother — but not before she had made the Thrales promise to come for a visit. In mid-October they drove to Kent, where they were graciously received by Sophy and her mother and much entertained. From conversation with Sophy, Mrs. Thrale had not thought she would get on with Mrs. Streatfeild but, as she wrote to Johnson, she liked her "vastly better than I thought I should" (*Letters* 585.1A). Mrs. Streatfeild was thin, delicate, and perfectly formed. She was lively and entertaining; and though extremely genteel had an actress's talent for mimicking her friends and family. She was "continually frisking, flaunting, and playing tricks, like a young coquet" (Burney, I, 261). She adored her daughter, but Sophia, it was obvious, could not bear her mother.

While visiting the Streatfeilds, the Thrales saw something of the Burneys' friends, the Grevilles, and Johnson was told that the lofty Mrs. Greville "downs every body" with her commanding manner and loud voice, which, it was said, was formed upon *his* manner (*Letters* 585.1A). This was a charge which Johnson emphatically denied, "if she makes any thing like a copy, her powers of imitation are very great, for I do not remember that she ever saw me but once" — the famous evening at St. Martin's Street (*Letters* 586). The Grevilles' daughter, "Baby Crewe," and her coldly civil husband were part of the set of talkers at Tunbridge, Mrs. Byron was there, and Mrs. Montagu herself was present, which heightened the drama of every conversation. Watching her and Mrs. Greville in verbal combat was highly stimulating. Even Queeney thought so, and she did not play "Agnes" for once. She was charming, and her precociousness astonished everyone.

In reporting some of the literary gossip to Johnson Mrs. Thrale wrote that:

Mrs Montagu cannot bear Evelina — let not that be published — her Silver-Smiths are Pewterers She says, & her Captains Boatswains. The Attorney General [Wedderburne] says you must all have commended it out of a Joke . . .

As for business, Mrs. Thrale wrote that she had heard:

All goes on well at the Brewhouse . . . & the Money that was borrowed when the Leaves were coming out will be paid — or may be — before they are fallen: neither must this be published. (*Letters* 584A)

Johnson was delighted with the good news about money, and replied that:

I think it very probably in your power to lay up eight thousand pounds a year for every year to come, encreasing all the time, what needs not be encreased, the splendor of all external appearance. And surely such a state is not to be put into yearly hazard, for the pleasure of *keeping the house full*, or the ambition of *outbrewing Whitbread*. Stop now and you are safe, stop a few years and you may go safely on hereafter . . .

In this letter his comment on Mrs. Montagu's criticism of *Evelina* was that vanity "always oversets a Lady's Judgement." As for Wedderburne, "we never could make any thing of the Lawyer, when we had him among us." He added, "If Streatfield has a little kindness for me, I am glad. I call now and then on the Burneys, where you are at the top of mortality. — When will you come home?" (*Letters* 585).

Thrale had no desire to return to London, and after the delightful stay in Tunbridge he took his family back to Brighton. It was the familiar routine once more, satisfactory for Thrale but dull for his wife and for Queeney. At the end of October she did have one pleasant social conquest to report to Johnson — the flattering attention of the Duchess of Devonshire. This enchanting and beautiful young woman suffered even more than Mrs. Thrale from the lack of a son.

As for business, Mrs. Thrale said that her husband "means to make [Scrase] an Offer of his Money back. Please God we may yet be happy even on *my* Terms which are very Insolent too. Every Debt discharged, 20,000£ laid up, and a Son — added to my five Wenches which must be always healthy." Of the Burneys, she said that they "are a sweet Family, I love them all, we have a Centre of Unity indeed for we all worship you alike . . ." (*Letters* 585.1A).

Johnson answered that he had told Fanny Burney "how you took to them all, but I told her likewise how You took to Miss S[treatfeild]. All poysons have their antidotes . . . I wish you would come back again to us all . . ." (*Letters* 586).

On 9 November Johnson had hopes that the bad weather would drive his family home. A week later he was even more impatient, though he was willing to forgive their long absence if Thrale had left the black dog of melancholy behind him. "Pray make my compliments to Mr Scrase," he said. "He has many things which I wish to have, his knowledge of Business, and of law," and then playfully, "He has likewise a great chair. Such an one my Master talked of getting . . ." In this letter he also had a message about *Evelina*, that his black servant, "*Francis* wants to read it" (*Letters* 591).

On 21 November Johnson wrote that the season in Brighton must now surely be over:

You are by this time left alone to wander over the Steene, and listen to the waves. This is but a dull life, come away and be busy and count your poultry, and look into your dairy, and at leisure hours learn what revolutions have happened at Streatham. (*Letters* 592)

Finally on 26 November the family came home. Thrale's spirits were considerably revived.

27: November 1778.
*We are returned from a Drive to Tunbridge & Brighthelmstone, where my Daughter was happy in keeping high Company, which is her first Pleasure; & where I tryed to think but little of our Affairs because I cannot think to please myself: M**r Thrale however is recover'd from his Anxiety & Depression and resolves to enjoy himself & his Friends as usual. Oh if we are to ruin a Fortune which might make many happy! let my dear Hester get out of the house at least before it falls upon our heads.*

We have however a noble Income, & we ought not to take thought for tomorrow — I will try to be chearful if I can.

9: December 1778.
Henrietta Sophia my last little Daughter was measured against the Son [34] *of my friend M**r Pepys, whose Lady lay in six weeks before myself: She is the same Height & larger in every Limb; only he has the bigger Head, which is no recommendatory Circumstance: he is however a lovely Boy, & She a charming Girl: Harriett is Pepys's favourite Name for a Woman, & M**rs Montagu is Godmother to both, so we always say they shall be married as soon as the* Lady *is of Age.*

[34] This was little William Weller Pepys, named after his father. He was born 4 May 1778 and died in 1845, unmarried.

The other Side shall say how Susan & Sophy come home from School this Xmas, & then I will close my first Volume of Family History. —— *Hester's* Friends, *the Daughters of my Neighbour Pitches have disgraced themselves about a strange Equivocal Thing that lives near 'em called par Excellence — The It.*[35] *Hester is among the first to be ashamed of them.* —

This is the last Day of the Year 1778. My Children are all about me & my house is full of Friends. Susan and I read two Acts of Molière's Bourgeois[36] *today She understands it to a Miracle, and translates with some Idea even of giving an English Turn to the Idiom, or an English Idiom to the Phrase. Sophy reads English Narrative to amuse herself perfectly well without any Tone or Drawl; they both work well, & write very prettily, spelling as exactly as myself. Sue can do /Sums in the/ the three first Rules of Arithmetick — Pounds Shillings & Pence quite readily, & pretends to tinkle the Harpsichord but I think She has for that Affair neither Ear nor Fingers. Susan's Geographical & Grammatical Knowledge amazes even me, but She never will dance I think; when Sophy gets a good Master She will be eminent in that Art — Hester is well — & beautiful, Susan is a pretty Girl as need be; Cecilia is much liked, & Harriett quite a Cherubim. Sophy is much the plainest as to Countenance but her Form is most complete and her Temper enchanting. Hester & Susan are touchy, moody, & capricious.*

*M*ʳ *Thrale is once more happy in his Mind, & at leisure to be so in Love with S:S: that it is comical. She is a charming young Creature every body must love her. We have her, & F: Brown[e] & Murphy*

---

[35] In January of the next year (1779) an entry in *Thraliana* reads: "Peggy Pitches is fallen in Love with a Creature called by People in Contempt The It — as his figure & Dress are so Equivocal many Folks take him for a Woman. What will not a Wench fall in Love with!" (*Thraliana*, p. 356).

Peggy had a long attachment to the "It," and this was followed, when she was twenty-three, by a happy though unusual marriage to a blind man, Viscount Deerhurst, two years her senior. She became his second wife on 10 January 1783. Deerhurst was a delightfully agreeable man — social, cheerful, and clever (with a special talent for making extemporaneous Latin verse). After his father's death in 1809 Deerhurst became the 7th Earl of Coventry, the "Blind Earl" for whom the beautiful Worcester porcelains were made, with roses and leaves in relief, so he could have the pleasure of "feeling" the design.

[36] Molière's *Bourgeois Gentilhomme*: During the Christmas holidays Susan and her mother were reading this play, and Susan's amusement was "to make Sophy & sometimes Hester help her to act the two or three 1ˢᵗ Scenes" (*Thraliana*, p. 361).

SOPHIA STREATFEILD
MINIATURE

that Lot — Hester is well & beautiful, Susan is a pretty Girl as need be; Cecilia is much liked, & Harriet quite a Cherubim. Sophy is much the plainest as to Countenance but her Form is most complete and her Temper enchanting. Hester & Susan are touchy, moody, & capricious.

Mr Thrale is once more happy in his Mind, & at leisure to be so in Love with S:S: that it is comical.. She is a charming young Creature every body must love her. We have her & Fs Brown & Murphy Seward & the D'Avenants & Johnson here, besides Tom Cotton & occasio-nal Comers in. I think I am again Pregnant, I think I am; then let as con-clude the Old Year with humble Thanks to Almighty God for all his Mercies thro' Jesus Christ our Lord, & most of all for the Health of my dear Children, & for the Boon I hope I have obtained by my Prayers & Tears — That I shall never follow any more of my Offspring to the Grave Amen Lord Jesus! Amen!

it so.. — I will not fret about this Rival this S.S. no I won

THE FAMILY BOOK

LAST PAGE

& Seward & the D'Avenants & Johnson here, besides Tom Cotton & occasional Comers in.

Christmas at Streatham this year was full of gaiety, "a charming Collection of Company in our House . . . for Wit, Beauty, Literature, & the polite Arts I think few could match it" (*Thraliana*, p. 356). Attorney-General Wedderburne and his wife and Solicitor-General Wallace and his wife dined one day. And Johnson, of course, was on hand, in excellent form; and Arthur Murphy, as entertaining as ever. Fanny Burney was now sufficiently at ease to spar with Seward, and the D'Avenants added panache. Hetty was elegant these days, but still saucy, and her dapper husband had a hard time keeping her in order. Tom Cotton (very different from his sister, Hetty) was dependability itself — no style, but always ready to help. There was also young Fanny Browne from Wimbledon, a pretty, reckless, coarse miss, who was constantly being reprimanded by Johnson for her slovenly dressing. And this year too, of course, the incomparable Sophia Streatfeild was at Streatham.

Mrs. Thrale tried her best to see that everyone had a good time. She was here, there, everywhere, attentive to everyone. Her husband's attentions, however, were fixed on "S.S." As recorded in *Thraliana*:

Mr Thrale is fallen in Love *really* & *seriously* with Sophy Streatfield — but there is no wonder in that: She is very pretty, very gentle, soft & insinuating; hangs about him, dances round him, cries when She parts from him, squeezes his Hand slyly, & with her sweet Eyes full of Tears looks so fondly in his Face — & all for *Love of me* as She pretends; that I can hardly sometimes help laughing in her Face. (p. 356)

The holiday would soon be over, she went on to say, "& my poor Master . . . left to pine for his fair Sophia, till the meeting of Parliament calls him to London, & leaves him free to spend all his Evenings at her House . . ."[37]

With this in mind, and with anxious thoughts of herself, Mrs. Thrale wrote the last entry for the year 1778 — the last entry in The *Family Book*:

I think I am again Pregnant, I think I am; then let us conclude the Old

[37] This was in Clifford Street, but Thrale always left "his carriage at his sister's door in Hanover Square, that no inquirer might hurt his favourite's reputation" (Hayward, II, 36).

Year with humble Thanks to Almighty God for all his Mercies thro'
Jesus Christ our Lord, & most of all for the Health of my dear Children,
& for the Boon I hope *I have obtained by my Prayers & Tears ——*
That I shall never follow any more of my Offspring to the Grave ——
Amen Lord Jesus!

Amen!

if so — I will not fret about this Rival this S.S. no I won't.

III. THE DEATH OF THRALE AND REMARRIAGE OF HIS WIDOW

"I will close my first Volume of Family History," Mrs. Thrale wrote on the final leaf, by telling "how Susan and Sophy come home from School": but she could not stop with this. She proceeded to crowd the events of the last three weeks of December on to the back cover. The last sentence, a *cri de cœur*, written in tiny letters, is squeezed into a space below the bottom line. The book could not hold another word.

Mrs. Thrale intended to continue the record of her children, but she never had the heart to do so. Despite the attention of the best doctors of the time, she had lost Harry and Lucy (the two she loved the most) — and Frances, Anna Maria, Penelope, Ralph, and Frances Anna. Seven Thrale children had died in the twelve years she had been recording, a pitiful record, even by eighteenth-century standards. And the final hope that she had expressed in her journal was not realized.

The year 1779 was one of crisis. Thrale's brother-in-law, Arnold Nesbitt, who had been ill so long (for six years), died in the spring — insolvent. Thrale was one of the two executors. On 8 June, in apparently perfect health, he set out for the house of his sister, Susanna Nesbitt. Bateman Robson, the solicitor, was there to discuss the serious matter of the French annuities, which Nesbitt had purchased many years before. Soon after the purchase, he had needed money and so had sold the annuities at public auction, being permitted to do this by the Government on condition that security was offered for their payment. To provide for this, Thrale, who had been party to many speculations with Nesbitt, joined him in a bond. All this had taken place in 1760, three years before Thrale's marriage. Now, nineteen years later, Robson pointed out, if the Government should ever decide to press a claim for non-performance of contract, Thrale, as co-signer, would be responsible for two hundred and twenty thousand pounds. Thrale had never talked with his wife about this dreadful transaction which could mean bankruptcy for himself and for his heirs. He listened to Robson, stunned; and later, at his sister's dinner table, was seized by a stroke of apoplexy. The witless Susanna did not know what to do. She did not call for a doctor, and valuable time was lost. She finally drove Thrale back to his own house. It was seven o'clock when he was carried there and by that time he was incapable of recognizing anyone (*Thraliana*, p. 803). Mrs. Thrale called doctors, and took charge herself until they arrived. Her husband rallied, and responded to the treatment which followed, but from this day on — at fifty — his precarious health was the major concern of his family. Johnson was in Lichfield at the time of the stroke — Johnson seemed always to be in Lichfield when terrible things took place at home.

Thrale was watched carefully by his doctors during the summer of 1779, and his wife was also under close medical surveillance. In her last entry in the *Family Book*, she had said, "I *think* I am again pregnant." This was true, and once more she prayed for a son. It was a difficult pregnancy and her doctors advised extreme caution. Much of the summer she had been confined to the house, to her room for a good part of the time. By 10 August the child was expected any day, but problems had come up at the brewery, trouble with the clerks:

Mr Thrale wished me to go, nay insisted on it, but seemed somewhat concern'd too, as he was well apprized of the Risque I should run. I went however, & after doing the Business I went to do, beg'd him to make haste home, as I was apprehensive bad Consequences might very quickly arise from the Joulting &c. — he would not be hurried . . . no Pain, no Entreaties of mine could make him set out one *Moment* before the appointed hour — so I lay along in the Coach all the way from London to Streatham in a State not to be described, nor endured; — *but by me*: — & being carried to my Chamber the Instant I got home, miscarried in the utmost Agony before they could get me into Bed, after fainting five Times. (*Thraliana*, p. 401)

The tragedy of this day was great, for the stillborn child was a boy, full term, and perfectly formed. Thrale's inhuman behavior can only be accounted for by his illness. John Perkins, who was present at the scene in the brewery, said that Thrale seemed to be "*Planet-struck*" (*Thraliana*, p. 401, n. 2). By inaction Thrale lost what was to be his last chance to have a male heir.

Thrale was sunk in the lethargy of his own illness, and he showed little concern for the loss of his boy, or for the condition of his wife. She suffered her pain and disappointment philosophically; and in August wrote three imaginary dialogues (inspired by Dean Swift), showing how some of her family and friends would react to the news of her death: the characters in the first scene are Johnson, Burke, Pepys (William Weller), and Mrs. Montagu; in the second the Cators and Baretti; and in the third Seward, Dr. Jebb, Thrale, Queeney, and Lady Lade — extremely clever little dramas,[1] and with her natural resilience she probably felt better after writing them. In a short time Dr. Jebb advised that a change of place would be beneficial for both of the Thrales. They decided to go to Brighton, and to take Queeney with them and — in place of Johnson — Fanny Burney. This young friend was becoming a favorite of Mrs. Thrale, to the growing annoyance of Dr. Burney, who now felt that he rarely saw his own daughter. The Burneys, unlike the Thrales, were never happy unless the family circle was complete.

Under the present circumstances, however, Dr. Burney could hardly object, and the party set out for Brighton in October. On the way there was a stop at Sevenoaks and a visit to Tunbridge Wells, where Mrs. Thrale hoped that a little flirting with Sophia Streatfeild would dissipate her husband's gloom; this was not the case. The two "met with but little eagerness on either Side" (*Thraliana*, p. 409), and Thrale seemed relieved to move on to Brighton. The party stayed in the West Street house for six weeks but it was not a happy visit. It was October, the season was over, and most of the friends had departed. Queeney and Fanny wished they were in London. The weather was bad, Mrs. Thrale found the sea bathing too cold, and Thrale enjoyed nothing except voracious eating. This obsession was now a source of constant anxiety to his wife and to his doctors.

They were perpetually warning him, but he stubbornly maintained that he was perfectly well; nevertheless he drafted a will with Scrase's help and he discussed its provisions with his wife. She was to be an executor, and he asked her whom she wished to serve with her. Johnson of course, she said, and she would like to have William Weller Pepys as an executor; for "the softer parts" of management (her daughters' problems), his high principles, delicate understanding, and

[1] "Three Dialogues by Hester Lynch Thrale," edited by M. Zamick, *Bulletin of the John Rylands Library*, XVI:1 (January 1932), 97–114.

worldliness in the finest sense would be helpful, and he was after all a Master in Chancery, that department of government which supervised parentless children. (She told her husband that if *she* died, she would wish to have the girls under Pepys's supervision.)

For the harder parts of management (the business problems) she had to admit that her choice for a third executor was John Cator — Pepys's complete opposite. She wanted Cator, despite the fact that he was rough and vulgar, because he was an honest and loyal friend, "acute in his Judgement, skilful in Trade, and solid in Property." When asked if he would accept appointment as an executor for Thrale's estate, Cator said he would. But William Weller Pepys graciously declined this burden of responsibility. Mrs. Thrale was disappointed by Pepys's refusal, but she wrote in *Thraliana*, "I have at least given him a proof of my Friendship however, & the Comfort is He considers it as such" (p. 418).

In November the weather deteriorated further, and Thrale came down with a bad cold. It was time, Mrs. Thrale realized, for the party to return to London. They had a miserable journey; Thrale suffered a chill on the road and arrived home in a comatose state. Under doctors' care he improved, but he was totally listless, unable to attend to business matters of any kind. The brewery was now wholly managed by Perkins, Johnson, and Mrs. Thrale. She regretted having to sacrifice time with her daughters and she wrote in *Thraliana* (which was now taking the place of the *Family Book*) that she was hacking away at the trade. "I hate it heartily, yes heartily! but if living in Newgate [the debtors' prison] would be *right* I hope I should be content to live in Newgate" (p. 409). The Perkinses, incidentally, had a third child in December, a daughter, named Amelia, after Mrs. Perkins.

2.

On 21 February 1780 Thrale suffered a second stroke, but recovered sufficiently to go to Bath in late March with his wife and Queeney, and Fanny Burney was again along. In April Johnson wrote that if he could finish the *Lives of the Poets*, "I think to bolt upon you at Bath, for I shall not be now afraid of Mrs. Cotton. Let Burney take care that she does me no harm" (*Letters* 654). Fanny, who described Sidney Arabella Cotton in her diary as an ugly, proud old woman, certainly did nothing to injure Johnson's standing. Mrs. Cotton held him in higher estimation than he imagined; she even had a framed engraving of him hanging on her wall. This pleased Johnson, when reported, though he told Mrs. Thrale he was not at all sure how long his picture would remain in place (*Letters* 657).

By April it was learned that there would be a new election in the autumn and Thrale, despite all advice to the contrary, was determined to stand as a Member of Parliament for Southwark. Hearing this, Johnson urged Mrs. Thrale to return to London and work for Thrale's interests — but to come alone — her husband was in no condition to exhibit himself. This was certainly true. As Mrs. Thrale wrote to Johnson, every apothecary apprentice in Bath saw he was "*knockt down* like a *Cock at Shrove Tide*; & all by over feeding" (*Letters* 663A).

In May when Mrs. Thrale went to London, she left Queeney in charge of the household. Though this young lady was only fifteen (to Fanny's twenty-seven), she was the more competent manager by far. Fanny was good company but flighty and of no use in a crisis. In Southwark Mrs. Thrale and Johnson campaigned strenuously, and he reported to Queeney that her mother "has run about the Borough like a Tigress seizing upon every thing that she found in her way. I hope the Election is out of danger" (*Letters* 667.1). After a week Mrs. Thrale returned to Bath, and almost at once the Gordon riots broke out in London: a Protestant mob, led by Lord George Gordon, made violent and brutal attacks upon Roman Catholic citizens in the aftermath of the relaxation of penal provisions against them. Violence spread to provincial towns including Bath, where somehow a false rumor started that Thrale was a Papist. The household took great alarm and in the middle of the night of 10 June Mrs. Thrale removed everyone to Brighton and re-established the household there. She then went back to London to see what damage the Gordon mob had done to the brewery. Not so much as she had feared. Perkins with courage and sangfroid had saved the brewery by offering free beer and food to the mob.

Mrs. Thrale returned to Brighton, this time bringing Susan and Sophy with her. The family stayed by the seashore all summer, Mrs. Thrale keeping herself busy with the little girls, now nine and ten, tutoring them with lessons and watching them make verses, act plays, and swim in the sea.

Thrale took little interest in Susan and Sophy. He was, of course, not well — but even when he had been, he treated his children with considerable indifference. It was not that he did not love them; he was proud of them, trusting, kind, and generous. The greatest sorrow of his life had been the loss of young Harry and grieving for him had been the one show of emotion (though according to Mrs. Thrale he shed tears only once). Thrale was simply phlegmatic,[2] the complete opposite of his volatile wife, whose treatment of the children alternated between ardent affection and irascibility. Thrale treated them in an even-tempered, detached manner and Queeney and Susan responded in just the same way (Sophy had a somewhat warmer nature). "I am not sure," Mrs. Thrale said, "that his children feel much Affection for him" (*Thraliana*, p. 53). His affection for them was deeply felt but he was undemonstrative and not at ease with children. He had none of the delight in playfulness that Bennet Langton and Dr. Burney had. Nothing pleased them more than having all generations together noisily — but this has always been considered an unusual desire. The more normal kind of pleasure is association and enjoyment with one's contemporaries and in this Thrale revelled and found his greatest pleasure.

During the summer of 1780 he made a stubborn, fighting effort to carry on: he hunted, dipped in the sea, had friends to dine, dined out, played cards, attended assemblies — and concerts. The last were a special entertainment offered this year, particularly enjoyed by the ladies — singing and pianoforte concerts, given by the handsome Italian musician whom the Thrales had met two years before at the Burneys' evening party — Gabriel Piozzi.

At the beginning of September word was received that the Perkinses had yet another baby — one more fine boy — Frederick. And their two other sons were strong and healthy. Ironically, the clerk's fortunes were waxing in precisely the same measure that the brewer's were waning. Thrale no longer had a son and heir, and he himself was miserable and ill.

When the expected news came that Parliament was dissolved, Thrale obstinately insisted upon returning to Southwark to face his constituents. His appearance as a dying man did not help his chances for re-election, and at the close of the poll, he stood third on the list, far

---

[2] When the house of Lady Lade, his favorite sister, was on fire he never rose from bed. He told a servant to go to her assistance, turned over, and "slept to his usual hour" (*Thraliana*, p. 53).

behind the two successful candidates. Thrale's fifteen-year reign as an M.P. for Southwark was over.

The family stayed on for a while at Streatham after the election, but Thrale was depressed and restless — he wished to go back to Brighton. So he and Mrs. Thrale and Queeney returned to Sussex in mid-October. Fanny begged off, and Johnson came in her place this time. Just as the year before, the season was over and the weather bad. Thrale had little chance to exercise, and his compulsive eating was more alarming than ever. In less than a month, when Lucas Pepys returned to London, the Thrales followed him.

At Streatham Mrs. Thrale found the babies, Cecilia three, and Harriet two, fine and blooming. Cecy, she thought, looked like her husband's sisters, and little Harriet, plump and rosy, looked like Fanny Rice. On 15 December she had the two little girls inoculated against smallpox, not by Sutton the "quack." After the dreadful experience with Ralph, she felt safer with someone else, and she had Sharp, a "regular" surgeon, operate. He had recently taken care of Thrale's carbuncle with tenderness and skill (*Thraliana*, pp. 464–465).

Everyone in the family seemed well by Christmas time, and the houseparty, the droppers-in, and the entertainment were much like the last Christmas described in the *Family Book*, but with music added this year, for the Thrales arranged to have Signor Piozzi visit for a few days. He played and sang, to everyone's pleasure. This agreeable musician was to come often to the house now for he was giving Queeney singing lessons, a supplement to Dr. Burney's harpsichord lessons.

In January 1781 Perkins became something of a problem. He had the effrontery to talk to Thrale in terms of partnership. He offered to study "the operative part of the Business, & learn the Work," and since "he *must* not be deprived of his Wife &c . . ." he wanted "to fix himself in the House we are leaving — & tho' I never did anything but wish to leave it Since I lived in it . . . yet I hate to be *edged* out of it by Perkins" (*Thraliana*, p. 479 and n. 3).

This was how things worked out, however; the Thrales left Deadman's Place for Grosvenor Square, a furnished house which Thrale leased — something Mrs. Thrale had longed for years to do, but now there was little pleasure in the move because of Perkins' forwardness and the frightening state of her husband's health. He was either unnaturally animated or completely lethargic. He rushed all over London seeking company, he played the great host, he fell asleep at the dinner table.

Suddenly, Thrale announced that the trip to Italy — abandoned almost five years before — was going to take place! The party would be as they had planned before: he and his wife, Johnson, Queeney, and Baretti. Mrs. Thrale knew that any such excursion was madness. A man so ill could never survive the trip. And what of the burden of Johnson, also ill? How could she give a moment's attention to Queeney? The other girls could of course be left with Mrs. Cumyns. The only possible courier for this desperate trip was Baretti, and she would have to beg him to come, the man she hated most in the world, and who hated her most, she believed. These anguished questions, assumptions, and doubts she recorded on 18 March (*Thraliana*, p. 487).

Her husband, despite his bravado, must have had doubts of his own, for the day before, 17 March, in the presence of Bateman Robson and Christopher Norris, he signed a new will, replacing the one made in Brighton a year and a half before. At the same time though, plans for the Italian trip went forward. On Monday, 2 April, Baretti was at Grosvenor Square, discussing plans. And the Thrales were to give an elaborate concert on Wednesday the 4th. Miss Owen was on hand for this and Mrs. Byron as well.

On Tuesday, 3 April, after eating an enormous meal, eight things ("with Strong Beer in *such* Quantities! the very Servants were frighted"), Thrale retired to his room for a rest. A short while later Queeney found him lying on the floor; "what's the meaning of this? says She in an Agony — I chuse it, replies Mr Thrale firmly; I lie so o'purpose" (*Thraliana*, p. 489). Doctors Pepys and Jebb were summoned and came quickly but despite everything they could do, one apoplectic fit followed another, until all strength was gone. Henry Thrale died early in the morning of 4 April 1781 — aged fifty-two.

The funeral was on 11 April at St. Leonard's. There, Thrale's coffin was placed in the family vault, as he had directed, between his father and Mrs. Salusbury.[3] Mrs. Thrale did not attend the service; it was not the custom of the time for women to be present at funerals.

---

[3] Thrale and his wife had discussed their burial arrangements. This was his choice; hers was to be buried in the Salusburys' Tremeirchion Church in the Vale of Clwyd, and "he always promised to send me there" (Rylands 587.230). During the year after Thrale's death, a mourning tablet in his memory was placed on the south wall of St. Leonard's. The epitaph was composed by Johnson and the stone cut by John Flaxman. The young sculptor's charge was £31/13/4 (*Thrale Estate Book*).

The morning after her husband's death, she and Queeney went to Brighton:

where Mr Scrase . . . was a comfortable & useful Companion. There I had Time to collect my scattered Thoughts, to [review] my past Life, & resolve upon a new one. the best Consolation is the perfect Amity in wch we have lived 17 Years together, the few disputes or Subjects of Complaint either of us have endured from the other, & the Notion I always perswaded myself into, of having been an humble Instrument in the Almighty's hand — to turn the heart of my Husband towards heaven whither he is gone, & whither I hope one day to follow him. (*Thraliana*, p. 490)

3.

Dr. Johnson wrote to the widow in Brighton about the terms of the will: the contents of the houses in Southwark and Streatham were left to her outright; Streatham Park was to be hers until her death, after which it was to pass to her daughters; Crowmarsh Battle, the farm in Oxfordshire (which had been inspected on the way back from Wales) was left to Queeney. The two Brighton properties were not specifically mentioned, but it was generally assumed that the daughters shared in them equally.

Thrale's daughters were to receive equal legacies upon marriage (if this had the consent of their mother); or they would receive their legacies upon becoming twenty-one, whichever event came first. So long as the brewery was in operation, Mrs. Thrale was to receive £2,000 yearly from the profits and £150 for the maintenance of each daughter under fifteen (Susan, Sophy, Cecilia, and Harriet), £200 for those over fifteen but under twenty-one (Queeney). If the brewery were sold, Mrs. Thrale was to receive £30,000, the remainder (in equal shares) to be held in trust for the daughters.

There were five executors (and among them almost every decade from seventy through twenty was represented): Johnson, seventy-two; John Cator, fifty-three; Mrs. Thrale, forty; Jeremiah Crutchley, thirty-five; and Henry Smith of St. Albans, Thrale's cousin, twenty-five. The executors were appointed guardians of the children, and Thrale's will further directed that the daughters be made wards of the Court of Chancery.[4]

---

[4] This direction does not appear to have been carried out, which was not an unusual circumstance for the time. The eighteenth-century Chancery Court was ex-

Thrale bequeathed £200 to his executors (except for his wife, who was provided for in other sections of the will; Johnson received no other bequest). To John Perkins, chief clerk at the brewery, Thrale left £1,000, and to his head brewer, John Townsend, an annuity of £100.

Thrale's will stated that Henry Smith was to have "the chief acting management and superintendance" of the brewery, for which services he was to be paid not more than £200 annually. In this provision for his young Hertfordshire cousin (only eleven years older than little Harry Thrale would have been), lay the last hope that the brewery might continue as a family concern. Thrale had come in the end to realize that Perkins was indispensable, not only in present management, but also in future management. He therefore recommended "my said Trustees to continue my said clerk Mr. Perkins in the management of the said Trade as I have the greatest opinion of his Abilities and Integrity" (Thrale's will, Public Record Office, London).

Henry Smith of New House farm, near St. Albans, was now a barrister in London, and had chambers in the Harcourt Buildings, the Temple. He had no interest in becoming a brewer and made no effort to take up Thrale's challenge. And no one urged him. As for Mrs. Thrale, she was not tempted herself though she was of proper age and vigor, and wholly capable of carrying on the business. She had no desire to do so. She was tired of being "Lady Mashtubs," as her mother had phrased it. She wanted a different life for herself and her daughters, and there was certainly a risk for their fortunes if the major investment continued to be the brewery. Her adviser, Scrase, said it was madness to carry on with no boy to inherit, only five girls who needed security above all else. And he spoke from bitter experience; he had twice saved the brewery from bankruptcy. As for the executors,

---

ceedingly unpopular because of the dilatoriness and expense involved in the Court's proceedings, and because of the rigidity of the restrictions it imposed:

1) a ward must be kept in the care of a fit and proper guardian or guardians and he, they, or trustees were responsible for the fit and proper management of the child's property.

2) the ward must not be removed from the jurisdiction of the Court.

3) the Court insured that the ward was given a fit education and this included the child's being brought up in the religion appropriate to the family.

4) the ward was not allowed to marry without leave of the Court.

When Mrs. Thrale soon thought of taking the three eldest children to Italy, she knew that the Court of Chancery would not give permission. This doubtless gave her pause, and other requirements gave pause to her fellow executors.

QUEENEY THRALE AT SEVENTEEN
WATERCOLOR

Cator had no desire to be involved in a business he did not understand and Crutchley, always timorous, was for selling from the start. Johnson was the hard one to convince. He was enjoying business life and wanted to go on as before with Mrs. Thrale and Perkins. In the end, however, he recognized the great potential danger to the girls (and he inwardly appreciated the fact that he was over seventy and could not hope to be helpful much longer). Mrs. Thrale, by the end of April, recorded in *Thraliana* "I have pretty well cured him of his Wishes . . ." (p. 491). As for Henry Smith, he continued to be indifferent. Mrs. Thrale recorded that this "ductile Minded Creature took no Interest in the Affair . . ." (*Thraliana*, p. 499, n. 1). Thrale did not have the good fortune that his great uncle, Edmund Halsey, had had in establishing a young relation from St. Albans as a brewer.

Perkins was the strong man of the moment — fifty-one, vigorous, experienced, and eager to assume more responsibility. He had been with the Thrale brewery more than twenty years and, since his marriage to Amelia Bevan seven years before, he had been in comfortable circumstances. Money of hers could be called upon for part of the purchase, also money of her brother-in-law, Sylvanus Bevan, and two rich Quaker friends, David Barclay and his nephew, Robert Barclay (the last to head the firm with Perkins). The price for the brewery was £135,000, to be paid over four years. Perkins, the two Barclays, and Bevan were to have equal shares, and when Perkins had difficulty raising enough money, Mrs. Thrale came to the rescue, taking a bond for a loan that would fill out his quarter.[5] On 31 May 1781, less than two months after Thrale's death, these men signed the papers — John Perkins' signature as big and bold as John Hancock's.

According to the terms, the trade was to be carried on for four years under the name of H. Thrale and Company (during which time Mrs. Thrale was to be paid an annual sum of £100 for use of the name [6]). It was stipulated that the Perkinses' eldest son, John [7] (Mrs. Thrale's

[5] *Thrale Estate Book* and *Three Centuries, the Story of our Ancient Brewery* (London: Barclay, Perkins & Co., Ltd., 1951), p. 16.

[6] This annual sum was paid to Mrs. Thrale until her remarriage, at which time an agreement was made with Queeney for the use of the name until the brewery became Barclay and Perkins in 1796 (*Thraliana*, p. 499, n. 2).

[7] John Perkins, the younger, did not join the firm. At nineteen he eloped with the family governess and was disinherited (a happy marriage, however), and later John took a medical degree at Edinburgh and became a distinguished doctor in Brussels.

Two other Perkins sons, Henry and Frederick, did join the firm.

JOHN PERKINS
ATTRIBUTED TO RAEBURN

godson), should come into the firm. If he did not and if no other Perkins son joined the brewery in due time Robert Barclay would take over this quarter share of the company.

The Perkinses now took permanent possession of the Thrales' Southwark house and Mrs. Thrale presented them with all the furniture. The relationship between Perkins and Mrs. Thrale and Johnson was exceedingly friendly, and in the counting room, which was part of the house, Perkins (like Miss Cotton) hung on the wall a copy of Doughty's fine mezzotint of Johnson. One day when Mrs. Thrale and Johnson visited Perkins, she asked "somewhat flippantly 'Why do you put him up in the counting house?' he answered, 'Because, Madam, I wish to have one wise man there.' 'Sir,' (said Johnson,) 'I thank you. It is a very handsome compliment, and I believe you speak sincerely' " (*Life*, II, 286, n. 1). Perkins was an able man, and the brewery prospered under his management.[8]

4.

Mrs. Thrale hoped that after the brewery sale her life would become simpler and more agreeable. Her family, including Johnson, was established at Streatham, and all were enjoying the comforts of the fine house and the fresh air of the country, everyone well occupied. Dr. Johnson had philosophically turned his attention from business to education and was instructing Queeney in Latin; Fanny Burney was also an occasional pupil. Queeney, Susan, and Sophy were taking harpsichord lessons with Dr. Burney and singing lessons with Signor Piozzi. The former came often to Streatham, and the latter, as time

---

Alfred Thrale Perkins, born in this year, became a barrister at Lincoln's Inn. The last son, Charles Perkins, who was to be born in 1785, became a merchant in Birtley, County Durham.

[8] Barclay and Perkins continued a long and successful existence, in fact until 1955, when the firm merged with Courage Limited. At that time the "Dr Johnson" trademark, both face and full figure, on labels, letter headings, advertisements, and vans was replaced by the Courage cock.

The headquarters of the Courage Group remains at Deadman's Place (or more felicitously, Park Street, its present name) where the Thrale children once lived and played. The Thrale house most probably burned down in the great fire of 1832, which destroyed many of the brewery buildings. A print in *The Penny Magazine* for March 1841 shows no Thrale-Perkins house attached to the main entrance gate as it was when painted by Dean Wolstenholme about 1820. In its place is a brewhouse and brewer's office. These buildings remained until 1957, when work was started on a new bottling hall. When this was finished in 1964, it filled the whole of the Park Street frontage.

went on, was almost always there — he seemed to become part of the household as Johnson had become part of the family years ago. Everyone accepted the musician's presence; Johnson and all the girls liked him, even three-year-old Harriet talked sweetly about Piozzi in "her little soft voice."

Mrs. Thrale was having a hard time. She was nervous, depressed, had a rash, and her face was flaming red. She felt miserable, and told Johnson, "I fear I shall never be happy again in this world" (*Letters* 1788, II, 216–217).

In sorrow one is vulnerable and more than ever grateful for sympathy and assistance; and while Johnson was often stentorian, domineering, critical, and burdensome, Piozzi was always gentle and comforting, considerate, and cheerful — eager to sing or play the harpsichord to soothe her nerves, or to help her cope with household problems. Mrs. Thrale began to depend upon Piozzi and to have a special feeling for him during this period of quiet retirement. She was hardly conscious of what was happening, and no one in the family was the least bit observant.

What she talked about was her financial worry. She had not realized at first that maintaining Streatham in her new life was a very different matter from what it had been in the days of Thrale. On her much smaller income she could not run the house in the manner to which Johnson and her children were accustomed.

And soon, added to this problem, came the devastating news that she had failed in her lawsuit against Lady Salusbury. Thrale's lawyers had been able to keep matters pending for years, but now the court held that Lady Salusbury was entitled to the money which Sir Thomas long ago had given to pay off the mortgage on Bach-y-Graig. Mrs. Thrale had always been convinced that Sir Thomas never meant the debt to be repaid, but Lady Salusbury had documents to prove a legal obligation, and £8,000 was the Court's judgment. Cator thought that an appeal might be attempted, but Mrs. Thrale was afraid of this, for Lady Salusbury's lawyers darkly hinted that there were dormant claims, amounting to £10,000, and these would be brought forward if there were a rehearing. Lady Salusbury would settle, they said, for £7,500, and Mrs. Thrale, appreciating the relentless force of her opponent, was convinced that there was nothing to do but accept the compromise. But how could she raise the money? The only practical way seemed to be to borrow from her daughters' inheritance, at interest of course, and with the mortgage itself as security. The girls would be adequately protected in such a loan, all the guardians agreed. Even Crutchley (who himself lent Mrs. Thrale £300) thought so, but he told her insolently to "make a Curtsy to [her] Daughters for keeping [her] *out of a Goal* [sic] & the News Papers" (*Thraliana*, p. 561, n. 4), and he bade her make haste to repay them.

Mrs. Thrale had every intention of repaying her daughters as quickly as possible. She was already arranging economies: she would no longer take a London house for the winter season, and she would let Streatham for three years. She would live cheaply in Bath till the spring and then take Queeney, Susan, and Sophy to Italy. They would profit from travel and study abroad, and her money would go further in Italy than in England. Piozzi agreed to be the party's courier, and she felt that this was ideal; she was happy in his company and he could supervise and instruct the girls. Queeney approved of the scheme; she said (at almost eighteen) that she had no desire to form early matrimonial "connections" in England, and felt that she would greatly benefit from the trip.

The only problem was Johnson — for many years he had cherished the dream of a classical ramble, but now he was almost seventy-three — and ailing. Mrs. Thrale could not bear to leave him behind, and yet she could not bear to take him with her.

On 22 August 1782 she screwed up her courage and discussed the situation with him, explaining her financial difficulties, plans for economy, and the advantages the trip held for the girls. To her surprise, Johnson agreed without hesitation that a stay in Italy would be both practical and wise. He advised her to put the plan into speedy execution, and was not the least offended at not being included in the party. Though he did not admit it, he knew that he could not possibly keep up with the five energetic travellers. He wished them well and "seemed to entertain no doubt of living to see us return rich & happy in two or three Years Time . . ." (*Thraliana*, p. 540).

The other guardians were not enthusiastic about Mrs. Thrale's proposed trip, but Cator did not persuade her to abandon it, and neither did Henry Smith. Crutchley was the only one who expressed violent opposition, but Mrs. Thrale had strange ideas about Crutchley. She had never given up her fantastic notion that he was Thrale's natural son, and the serious attention this guardian was now paying to Queeney was only an added reason why the trip should be taken. She procceeded to make plans for departure in the spring.

Lord Shelburne had agreed to lease Streatham for three years. This distinguished gentleman, now Prime Minister, found Bowood, his country house near Bath, too far from London and wished to have a more convenient place. Mrs. Thrale was delighted to have so aristocratic and important a tenant (despite the fact that politically he stood for everything her husband had opposed). She was also pleased that Lord Shelburne was known to take remarkably good care of his properties, and she was confident that Streatham would be safe in his hands.

By the first week in October the Thrales were busy packing at Streatham. Johnson was with them, and on Sunday, the 6th, they attended services at St. Leonard's for the last time. They enjoyed a last meal in the dining room, and a last evening in the library.

On Monday morning they all went to Brighton. It was not a pleasant stay, nor were matters much improved when Fanny Burney came late in the month. Queeney was sullen; Johnson had a cold and was illhumored and so disagreeable that he was seldom invited out. At home, he felt neglected and bored — he was studying Dutch to fill the vacuity of his hours. He was irritated by Mrs. Thrale's lack of attention. She seemed utterly distracted for no reason that he could see. Others could. Both Queeney and Fanny now knew why Mrs. Thrale was not acting like her usual self — for the first time in her life she had fallen in love. Five years before, she recorded in *Thraliana*, with some self-satisfaction, that she had never been troubled with "the Tender passion." Love, she had said, was of three categories: first the emotion one felt for the members of one's family; second, that which one felt for favorite dogs and horses; and then, she supposed, "there *is* such a Thing as violent Love . . . suddenly excited, and sharply felt," making one defy all the world [9] (*Thraliana*, p. 110). Now, she was feeling just this way about Piozzi, who had been her constant and adoring companion ever since her husband's death.

One day, before the family came to Brighton, Mrs. Thrale had confessed to Queeney that she loved Piozzi — he was with them in the

---

[9] Dr. Johnson, in the abstract, acknowledged the existence of "violent love"; in conversation he once said: ". . . we must not ridicule a passion which he who never felt never was happy, and he who laughs at never deserves to feel — a passion which has caused the change of empires, and the loss of worlds" (*Anecdotes*, pp. 209–210).

room. After this, Piozzi and Queeney had talked together for a long time, but since that time Queeney would say nothing further on the subject. Mrs. Thrale had told her secret to Fanny Burney the same day at Streatham, and Fanny had been shocked and disapproving. Most of the stay in Brighton was endured in tense silence. Once, Mrs. Thrale showed Queeney and Fanny a page in *Thraliana*, describing her feeling for Piozzi. Fanny wept, she wept, and Queeney watched unmoved.

On 20 November the party came back to London, and the Thrales settled into a house on Argyll Street, where they planned to be until they departed for Italy in the spring. Mrs. Thrale soon discovered that her attachment to Piozzi had become public knowledge. Ever since Thrale's death, there had been gossip in the press, linking her name with a number of eligible suitors (and some ridiculous contenders). Now the one man named was Piozzi, most often described in sarcastic terms as a "fiddler." Society's reaction was outrage and disgust, that a woman of high birth and fortune, and with beautiful and accomplished daughters to bring up, would stoop to consider marriage with a paid entertainer, a foreigner, a Roman Catholic, an adventurer, who would rob her of her money (for a married woman's property belonged to her husband) — then desert her.

Before the end of January there was a terrible scene. Fanny begged Mrs. Thrale (now in a highly emotional state, and sick with nerves) to think of her reputation and of her children, their need for her now and their future prospects, which she would greatly damage. Queeney did not argue with her mother, nor make any attempt to understand her feelings. She simply "said coldly that if [she] *would* abandon [her] Children, [she] *must*: that their Father had not deserved such Treatment" — to have his children turned out "like Puppies in a Pond to swim or drown . . ." As for herself, she said she would have to "look herself out a Place like the other Servants." She knew, she said scornfully, that Piozzi actually hated her mother, except for her fortune. He would take her, she knew not where, and would abandon her. Susan and Sophy said nothing, but they had taught Cecilia and Harriet "to cry where are you going Mama? will you leave us, and die as our poor papa did? there was no standing *that* . . ." (*Thraliana*, p. 559).

Mrs. Thrale summoned Piozzi, and in an agonizing interview told him that she could not marry him. He was understanding and tender, and, realizing the impossibility of their remaining close to each other, agreed to leave England permanently. He returned all of Mrs. Thrale's love letters, not to her, but to Queeney (*Thraliana*, p. 564, n. 1).

5.

Mrs. Thrale did not discuss the matter of Piozzi with the guardians, she simply told them that plans for taking her three elder daughters abroad in the spring had been given up; she was going to take them to Bath instead, where she would establish a household, live economically, calm her nerves, and regain her health.

The departure from London was delayed because Cecilia came down with whooping cough, and Harriet with swollen glands, whooping cough, and measles. By early April, however, the two little girls were better and Mrs. Thrale thought it was safe to leave them. She could no longer turn to Mrs. Cumyns, for this reliable friend of many years had died of cancer, something Mrs. Thrale had dreaded and expected since 1779, when Mrs. Cumyns had showed her the cancer in her breast (*Thraliana*, p. 363). The school for girls in Streatham was now Russell House, a red-brick building opposite St. Leonard's Church, run by Mrs. Ray and Mrs. Fry. Arrangements were made through Mrs. Ray. Old Nurse was to have a place close to the school so she could care for Cecilia and Harriet, and Dr. Jebb and Dr. Pepys promised to attend them.

On 5 April Johnson wished Mrs. Thrale and the three elder girls a good journey to Bath, and he presented Queeney with a Latin grammar and a Virgil that she might continue her study. Little did he realize the finality of this parting from his family. Queeney was the only Thrale he would ever see again — and only once.[10]

On 6 April Mrs. Thrale took her three elder daughters to Bath, but she found little peace there, for within a few days she received alarming reports about Cecilia and Harriet; and on Good Friday, 18 April, a letter arrived from Cator, saying that "Harriet is dead, and Cicely is dying." She complained to Johnson (who had also sent the sad news) that Cator had told her not to "sit *philosophically* at Bath, but come to London — (I cannot guess for what) to see them buried I believe" (*Thraliana*, p. 563, n. 2).

In the middle of the night Mrs. Thrale left for Streatham where she arrived early on Easter morning, 20 April. To her relief, she found that Cecilia was out of danger. Harriet was buried at St. Leonard's.

[10] At Bolt Court, 14 November 1784.

Mrs. Thrale returned to Bath on 23 April and not one of her three elder daughters even said "how do you do." They avoided her company, showed no emotion over Harriet's death, and no concern for Cecilia's critical condition. They did not ask their mother if she had seen Piozzi, who was still in London (she had not). By "a sort of tacit Compact" his name was never mentioned. One day, when Mrs. Thrale inadvertently said that Pepys had lanced his throat ulcers, "Has he cut his own Throat?" asked Queeney, "in her quiet Manner" (*Thraliana*, p. 563).

The cheerless days passed slowly. Mrs. Thrale received calls from some of her friends, the most consoling from Mrs. Lewis, the recent widow of the Dean of Ossory. Mrs. Thrale refused to take her usual part in Bath society, much to Queeney's annoyance. She did not wish to show herself, and she saw no reason why she should provide social pleasure for three girls who were treating her heartlessly. She did, however, take the matter of their education seriously.

I have read to them what I could not force or perswade them to read for themselves. The English & Roman Histories, the Bible; — not Extracts, but the whole from End to End — Milton, Shakespeare, Pope's Iliad, Odyssey & other Works, some Travels through the well-known Parts of Europe; some elegant Novels as Goldsmith's Vicar of Wakefield, Voltaire's Zadig &c. Young & Addison's Works, Plays out of Number, Rollin's Belles Lettres . . . have filled our Time up since we left London for Bath . . . (*Thraliana*, p. 591)

Johnson wrote to Queeney toward the end of May telling her that he was not well. He was "writing," he said, "over the little garden. The poplars, which I have just now watered, grow kindly; they may expect not to be neglected for they came from Streatham" (*Letters* 839.1). Less than a month later he suffered a paralytic stroke and lost the power of speech. He was critically ill and without proper care but Mrs. Thrale made no effort to go to London to nurse him. He sent her long, pathetic letters, a virtual diary of his illness, but even these did not move her. By late summer when Johnson was better and able to travel she sent no invitation to rejoin his family. And in September when he stayed with William Bowles, a recent young acquaintance who lived near Salisbury, he was too proud to accept his host's suggestion that they pay a visit to Mrs. Thrale at the seaside. She was spending the summer at Weymouth, only some forty miles away.

By the end of September Johnson was back in London and Mrs. Thrale and her daughters had returned to Bath, where their dull life continued. Suddenly in November Sophy became ill, taken with fits, followed by lethargy, frighteningly reminiscent of her father's seizures. Sophy's attacks caused "an instant Cessation of all Nature's Pow'rs at once" (*Thraliana*, p. 580). The diagnosis of the Bath doctors, Dobson and Woodward, was "Attonitus," meaning the muscles lost their tone, became flaccid and limp. Sophy's fits, followed by loss of consciousness, suggest a cerebral irritation, a virus brain fever or a bacterial abscess of the middle ear. "I saved her in the first Attack," her mother recorded, "by a Dram of fine Old Usquebough [Irish whisky] given at the proper Moment — it reviv'd her, but She only lives I see to expire with fresh Struggles" (*Thraliana*, p. 580).

Onc dreadful time Mrs. Thrale rubbed her "while just expiring, so as to keep the heart in Motion: She knew me instantly, & said you warm *me* but you are killing *yourself* — I actually was in a burning Fever from exertion, & fainted soon as I had saved my Child" (*Thraliana*, p. 580).

Queeney and Susan were anxious and fearful during these days, and they tried to be helpful. They showed affection for their mother for the first time since the Piozzi crisis: "they see I love them," she wrote, "that I would willingly *die* for them; and I *am* actually dying to gratifie their Humour at the Expence of my own Happiness: they can *but* have my Life — let them take it!" (*Thraliana*, p. 580).

Mrs. Thrale was exhausted and distraught and soon suffered a complete nervous breakdown. Life in the household came to a standstill. Dr. Dobson, who attended her, at first did not understand the emotional cause of distress, but when he did he took charge of the situation. "We have no Time to lose," he said, "Call the Man home, or sec your Mother die" (*Thraliana*, p. 584). With great reluctance Queeney gave her consent for Piozzi's recall.

Mrs. Thrale, having quick powers of recovery, felt better at once, and she wrote to Piozzi to come back to England. Sophy, in appreciation for her mother's nursing, also sent a letter urging his return. But for months Piozzi did not make a move. At first, in the winter, traveling across the Alps was almost impossible but when April (1784) came there was no excuse for his not setting out on the journey. Queeney showed no surprise at his indifference, but Fanny Burney was amazed (the two were carrying on a secret correspondence on the subject). Piozzi's reluctance was wholly understandable. Mrs. Thrale's promise to him had been broken once, and it might well be broken again. He had no wish to come to England unless he could be sure of the outcome. He did not want to face hostility and humiliation all over again.

Mrs. Thrale's constant and impassioned letters finally convinced him that nothing this time would prevent their marriage. She was willing to live in Italy if that was what he wished. She was willing to defy the world, for she now saw her first duty as a wife rather than a mother. She had performed her duties to her children for many years, and she would gladly continue to care for them if they accepted her terms, but if not, her choice was for the man she loved.

Mrs. Thrale was acting the way her mother had when she married John Salusbury against solid family opposition, the way her niece, Fanny Plumbe, had acted when she ran away with Jack Rice, the way a girl of Queeney's twenty years might be expected to act — not a widow of forty-three. But in the Bath household everything was reversed. Queeney was the mature one, calm, detached, practical, and caustic. In early June when word finally came that Piozzi had started on his journey, she quietly informed her mother that she and Susan and Sophy would never consider going to Italy. (Mrs. Thrale was hoping they would wish to.) Queeney said scornfully that the guardians would never give permission, and in any case, she added, neither she nor her sisters wished to be in Piozzi's company abroad — or anywhere else — ever. Before he arrived in Bath, they wanted to go to their own house in Brighton. Mrs. Thrale could not very well deny this request, and she tried to locate a proper chaperone for the girls. She had considerable difficulty finding the right person, but in the end settled upon a mature woman of fashion, kindly but correct, Miss Jane Nicolson, a daughter of the Dean of Exeter who gave James Evans of Southwark as a reference.

On 24 June the long-awaited word reached Mrs. Thrale that Piozzi was in London and would soon come to Bath. The girls now "*must* move," though they were "very loath to stir" (*Thraliana*, p. 598). On the following morning Mrs. Thrale, Miss Nicolson, and the three girls drove to Wilton and Fonthill, viewing pictures and sights, and then on to Salisbury, where they parted, midway between their two destinations, so that no one later could accuse either party of desertion. Miss Nicolson and the girls proceeded to the West Street house in Brighton, and Mrs. Thrale returned to Bath, to await the arrival of Piozzi.

On 30 June, Mrs. Thrale wrote to the guardians, Cator, Crutchley,

Smith, and Johnson, informing them of the arrangements which she had made for her children, and advising them of her imminent marriage. Piozzi arrived in Bath on the first of July. "The happiest Day of my whole Life I think — Yes, *quite* the happiest . . ." (*Thraliana*, p. 599).

The reaction of all the guardians to Mrs. Thrale's announcement was violent disapproval. Johnson had doggedly refused to believe that she could ever make this degrading marriage. "Madam," he wrote:

> If I interpret your letter right, you are ignominiously married, if it is yet undone, let us once talk together. If you have abandoned your children and your religion, God forgive your wickedness; if you have forfeited your Fame, and your country, may your folly do no further mischief.
>
> If the last act is yet to do, I, who have loved you, esteemed you, reverenced you, and served you, I who long thought you the first of human kind, entreat that before your fate is irrevocable, I may once more see you . . . (*Letters* 970)

Queeney had sent a letter to Johnson which unfortunately does not survive. He answered her (1 July) the day before he wrote to her mother:

> My Dearest,
> I read your letter with anguish and astonishment, such as I never felt before. I had fondly flattered myself that time had produced better thoughts. I can only give you this consolation that, in my opinion, you have hitherto done rightly. You have not left your Mother, but your Mother has left you.
>
> You must now be to your sisters what your Mother ought to have been, and if I can give you any help, I hope never to desert you . . . (*Letters* 969.1)

The reaction of society was shock and condemnation. And the press and caricaturists were quick to subject Thrale's widow to malicious satire. Mrs. Montagu wrote to bluestocking Mrs. Vesey that their friend's behavior:

> . . . has taken such horrible possession of my mind I cannot advert to any other subject. I am sorry and feel the worst kind of sorrow, that which is blended with shame . . . I am myself convinced that the poor Woman is mad, and indeed have long suspected her mind was disorderd. She was the best Mother, the best Wife, the best friend, the most amiable member of Society. She gave the most prudent attentions to her Husbands business during his long state of imbecility and after his death, till she had an opportunity of disposing well of the great Brewery. I bring in my verdict lunacy in this affair. (Clifford, p. 229)

As for James Evans, the Rector of St. Saviour's and St. Olave's, he made great "Lamentation." [11]

Despite general opposition and outcry, Mrs. Thrale and Piozzi proceeded with their plans, and about a month after his arrival in Bath, on 23 July 1784, they were married in a Roman Catholic ceremony in London, and on 25 July they repeated their Church of England vows at St. James's in Bath.[12] She was forty-three, Piozzi forty-four (twelve years younger than her first husband).

The couple remained in Bath for the next six weeks, making plans for their wedding trip abroad; they ordered a special coach to be built, with a fitted place for a small harpsichord under one of the seats.

At the beginning of September, after "greater and longer Felicity than I ever yet experienced" (*Thraliana*, p. 611), Mrs. Piozzi and her new husband came up to London, and there Susan and Sophy called upon them. The little girls were warm and loving, but Queeney, who came on a separate occasion, was proud and reserved. They "parted coldly, [though] not unkindly" (*Thraliana*, p. 612). Mrs. Piozzi thought Fanny Burney was responsible for Queeney's lack of sympathy, and she crossed Fanny off her list forever — a treacherous friend.

The Thrale household in Brighton collapsed almost at once. Crutchley and Cator did not approve of Miss Nicolson, very likely because she knew Piozzi and took a sympathetic view of the marriage (*Thraliana*, p. 596). They went to Brighton and dismissed the woman.[13] The girls were adrift. Arrangements for them had not been made by the time the Piozzis were ready to start abroad, but this did not postpone their departure.[14] The newlyweds began their Continental tour as

[11] Mrs. Piozzi commented later (1786) that Evans' "Lamentation" was "from a mistaken regard to Mʳ Thrale; — He loved *him* exceedingly, & fancied I ought never to have left off crying when he died — Mʳˢ Evans did faint away from excess of honest Sorrow — & Gratitude seldom felt: my Husband gave them all they had to live on — poor dears!" (*Thraliana*, p. 663).

[12] Mrs. Piozzi maintained that her relationship to Piozzi had been entirely platonic until her marriage. The "wicked Insinuations" of prior intimacy were a charge "which those who make it do not themselves believe, and which is [as] false as cruel. God & himself — (I mean Mʳ Piozzi) *know* how false that Accusation is . . ." (*Thraliana*, p. 615).

[13] *Thrale Estate Book.*

[14] We "took our Leave of Britain on the 6ᵗʰ of September 1784 . . . & my heart rejoyced when I saw the Shores of England receding from my View" (Conway, I, 11).

"SIGNOR PIOZZI RAVISHING MRS. THRALE"

CARICATURE BY COLLINGS

planned in their custom-made coach, accompanied by a little dog, which sat in their laps by turns (*Queeney Letters*, p. 240).

6.

Early in September the Piozzis crossed the Channel from Dover to Calais, and from there drove to Paris, following a route much like the one the Thrales and Johnson had taken in 1775. From Paris the Piozzis made their way to Genoa and by November were in Milan, the city which he considered his home.

Here, they learned that the Cators had taken Queeney to live with them, both at Beckenham Place in the country and at the Adelphi in London. Susan and Sophy had been sent to Mrs. Murray's school in Kensington, Cecilia remained with Mrs. Ray in Streatham. The girls' aunts, so long entertained and assisted by Thrale, never thought of taking his daughters into their households, though Ann Thrale was well off and Frances and Susanna were both receiving annuities of £200 from their brother's estate.[15] The girls would not have been a financial burden for they had their own allowances.

The reaction of all Thrale's sisters to the Piozzi marriage was disgust and indifference. They were abusive in their talk but they made no effort to salvage the children. Plumbes, Lades, and Nesbitts were godparents: Susanna Nesbitt was godmother to both Queeney and Susan, so one might have expected particular kindness on her part, but "Nezzy" had remarried two years before, and was now the wife of one Thomas Scott, M.P. for Bridport, a bricklayer. She was occupied with her new life, and like Mrs. Plumbe and Lady Lade had no desire to become involved. None had any love for the girls.

As for the guardians, rough-mannered Cator was the only one who had assumed any responsibility, not remarkable, perhaps, for the other men were single. Henry Smith, however, had an established household, run by his cousin, Jane Hambleton, and they could have offered hospitality if they had wished to do so. And with a proper chaperone provided, Jeremiah Crutchley's fine house, Sunninghill Park in Berkshire,[16] would have been a delightful haven, but Crutchley, though he

---

[15] *Thrale Estate Book.*

[16] Sunninghill Park had been purchased in 1769 by Jeremiah. It was about five miles from Windsor, overlooking the Great Park; a 500-acre property, with luxuriant woods of its own and a fine lake. The seventeenth-century house, of considerable size, had been attractively altered by James Wyatt.

As for the later history of Sunninghill Park, it descended to Jeremiah's nephew,

BECKENHAM PLACE

RESIDENCE OF JOHN CATOR

FROM A DRAWING BY NEALE, ENGRAVED BY LACEY

SUNNINGHILL PARK

RESIDENCE OF JEREMIAH CRUTCHLEY

FROM A DRAWING BY NEALE, ENGRAVED BY TAYLOR

was always ready to protest and oppose, shrank now (and forever) from any kind of personal involvement. As for poor old Johnson, though he wanted to help, he was now too frail and powerless to do anything but to tell Queeney, when she called the one time at his comfortless house in Bolt Court, that he loved and admired her — and that he prayed she would carry on as head of the family.

Johnson died on 13 December 1784, while the Piozzis were enjoying a round of pleasure in Milan. They did not hear the news until some weeks later. "Oh poor Dr Johnson!!!" was all Mrs. Piozzi wrote in *Thraliana*, and she noted, on the same page, that she had received kind letters from Susan and Sophy. These "*should* compensate for the frigidity of their elder Sister" (*Thraliana*, p. 624). Sophy's health, she had recorded a little while before, was still not settled after the serious illness at Bath. She wished that Sophy could benefit from the air and exercise in Italy, "perhaps my personal Attendance too might be of use — but they would say I murdered *her* too if She died here; and my Heart tells me She will not live long" (*Thraliana*, p. 617).

The next year passed happily for Mrs. Piozzi as she and her husband ranged about Italy. Her letters to the "Miss Thrales," as she called them, were amusing and tactless accounts of new sights and experiences, of broadening horizons. Mrs. Piozzi, as ever defensive, stressed how well her husband was received and how aristocratic his friends were, and how they were both fêted and admired. The girls, who had been left to fend for themselves, could hardly be expected to revel in the Piozzis' pleasures and triumphs. But never throughout her life did she have the capacity to put herself in someone else's place.

In April 1785 the wedding trip continued to Venice; June and July were passed in Florence.[17] And when September came, and Queeney's

---

George Henry Duffield, who took the name of Crutchley. The property remained in the George Crutchley family until it was sold by Percy Edward Crutchley to Philip Hill in 1936. After Mr. Hill's death, Sunninghill Park was purchased by King George VI as a residence for Princess Elizabeth (Queen Elizabeth II) and Prince Philip.

Repairs and alterations were completed, and servants were to come into the house in a few days' time, when it burned to the ground. The fire was said to have been caused by a blow-torch left in the library by the workmen.

[17] The enjoyment of the wedding trip was marred upon arrival in Florence by Piozzi's having an attack of gout. Count Manucci visited his bedside, and as they chatted, Manucci asked how Mrs. Thrale was and if she had married again. When she appeared from the other room, Manucci exclaimed, "Ah Madame! quel Coup de Theatre!!" (Harvard *Piozziana*, II, 56).

GABRIEL PIOZZI IN ITALY
ARTIST UNKNOWN

MRS. PIOZZI IN ITALY
ARTIST UNKNOWN

twenty-first birthday, the Piozzis were in Pisa. Many of Queeney's birthdays had been noted in the *Family Book*, but this important one she had to manage by herself. She did. She signaled her majority by leasing a house at 30 Wimpole Street, Cavendish Square, and selecting her own chaperone, Mrs. Cochran, a respectable widow of about forty. Queeney's sisters came often to the house on Wimpole Street; frequently they all went to their house in Brighton, and sometimes they visited the Cators at Beckenham Place. The bond between the "Miss Thrales" was very close, and everyone thought of Queeney as Johnson had — as head of the family.

From abroad, the unwanted reports of the Piozzis' tour came at regular intervals; Queeney answered occasionally, cold letters, which gave little information. Susan and Sophy wrote frequently and fondly at first, begging their mother to return; but after the Piozzis left Milan in April 1785, there was hardly a word from any of the girls.

7.

The Piozzis returned to London in March 1787, and Queeney, Susan, and Sophy (now twenty-two, sixteen, and fifteen, respectively) made a polite and perfunctory call at their hotel. "I [kissed] Queeney's cold Face" (*Thraliana*, p. 708). During the rest of March and all of April Queeney called twice, and the Piozzis twice visited Susan and Sophy, who refused their mother's invitation for dinner. The reception of Mrs. Piozzi's friends and relations in London was not any warmer: there was no welcome from Mrs. Plumbe nor Lady Lade, nor "Nezzy" Scott, who had "never said an illnatur'd thing of any Person in her Life, *except* [now] *of Me*" (*Thraliana*, p. 755). No welcome from Henry Smith. And none from Mrs. Piozzi's relations, the D'Avenants and Tom Cotton. And none from the intimates of Streatham days: Reynolds and his sister, Frances, the Burkes, the Burneys, Seward, and Crutchley. None from Pepys (now Sir Lucas) and his wife, nor William Weller Pepys and his wife. Miss Burgoyne and her mother, Lady Burgoyne, were deeply offended by the marriage. And Mrs. Montagu rested on her verdict of lunacy, with which all the bluestockings agreed.

Mrs. Lewis, a confidante during the agonizing last months in Bath, was the only close woman friend who made an effort to be kind to the Piozzis. Mrs. Byron was loyal to her, but hated "the fiddler." Of the

men, Murphy remained loyal, Mr. and Mrs. Perkins civil and kind, and
Cator, the rough diamond, was still available when wanted.

Cator had been in charge of Streatham during the Piozzis' absence,
and had dealt with what now amounted to three tenants. Lord Shelburne had resigned his office in the government early in 1783, and after
that had little use for Streatham. The following year he was created
1st Marquess of Lansdowne and withdrew to Bowood, his house in
Wiltshire. Major-General Dalrymple followed him at Streatham for
a year, then Thomas Steele, Esq., of the Treasury. Steele signed a lease
in October 1786 (at £300 a year) to run through April 1790.

So the Piozzis could not reclaim Streatham Park till then, but for the
moment at least, a house in London was preferable because Mrs. Piozzi
was working on an edition of Johnson's letters for the publisher,
Thomas Cadell, and needed to be in London. Samuel Lysons, a clever
young antiquarian, was assisting her with the editing. As for business
matters, she was determined to discharge the Welsh mortgage payments to her daughters (her debt to Lady Salusbury), and she had been
able to save the money for this because Piozzi had managed expenses
well abroad. When she asked Cator the exact amount owed, she was
astonished to discover that no money had ever been borrowed against
the girls' inheritances. Cator had thought it a good investment and had
advanced the money himself. Mrs. Piozzi promptly settled with Cator
and repaid her loan from Crutchley. All was now even.

The Piozzis leased a house on Hanover Square,[18] and by the middle
of May were sufficiently settled to give a reception to welcome their
friends, and show off some of the fine furniture, pictures, and sculpture that they had brought back from Italy. "Miss Thrale & her Companion [Mrs. Cochran] were asked & refused: — pass'd my Door, &
looked insultingly up at the Window, as they went to Mortellari's
Benefit" (*Thraliana*, p. 681). Queeney had no desire for her mother's
company; neither did Susan and Sophy.

Little Cecilia, now ten, was the only daughter who showed the least
scrap of affection, and Mrs. Piozzi worried that:

. . . while She is at School [she] will honour us with her Visits no doubt,
but her Tenderness will end there I trust, as her Spirit is the same to that of
her Sisters. Well! never mind, my heart is vastly more impenetrable to their

---

[18] Their residence was on the south side of Hanover Square, at the corner of St.
George's Street. The building stood until after World War II, when it was pulled
down. Vogue House stands in its place.

unmerited Cruelty than it was when last in England. Let them look to their Affairs, & I shall look to mine: the World is wide enough I'll warrant it for Miss Thrales and Mrs Piozzi. (*Thraliana*, p. 680)

The older girls were doing their best to prejudice Cecilia against her step-father, and Mrs. Piozzi discovered that Henry Smith had "told that poor Baby Cecilia a fine staring Tale, how my Husband locked me up at Milan & fed me on Bread & Water, to make the Child hate Mr Piozzi: Good God! what infamous Proceeding was this? My Husband never saw the Fellow, so c^d not have provoked him" (*Thraliana*, p. 681).

Mrs. Piozzi still had legal control over Cecilia and was determined to bring the child back into her household. Queeney resisted these efforts strenuously, telling Fanny Burney that Cecilia would be corrupted by association with her mother. Fanny defended Mrs. Piozzi against this charge, and in so doing risked losing Queeney's friendship as well as her mother's. Despite Queeney's disapproval, Mrs. Piozzi brought Cecilia to Hanover Square:

I have got the Child home to us however, & Piozzi doats on her . . . if they steal her away from me now, I shall lose my life: 'tis so very comfortable to have *one* at least saved out of *twelve*. (*Thraliana*, p. 686)

She wrote a scorching letter to her eldest daughter, ordering her not to interfere. This caused a complete break in their relationship for the next six years.

In July (1787) the Piozzis made a trip to Wales, and not thinking Cecilia safe from Queeney if left in London, they took her with them. On their way, they stopped at Guy's Cliff, in Warwickshire, where they visited Bertie and Ann Greatheed, a charming couple they had met when in Florence. Greatheed (a grandson of the 2nd Duke of Ancaster) was a dilettante, with a keen interest in art and literature. He was at present writing a blank-verse tragedy entitled *The Regent*, scenes were read from this, and Mrs. Piozzi was asked to contribute an epilogue. Cecilia thought the Greatheeds were wonderful, and she adored their only child almost as much as they did, little Bertie, aged six — four years her junior. It was a joyous visit, and Cecilia hated to leave.

After Warwickshire, the travelers went on to Lichfield, where Mrs. Piozzi endeavored to obtain a few more Johnson letters for the edition. Queeney had refused permission to publish her considerable collection, and though Susan had surrendered five, and Sophy one, there were still not enough to fill both volumes. Mrs. Piozzi had a certain amount of good fortune collecting letters in Lichfield; but she had none in Ashbourne. Dr. Taylor was no longer cordial. He refused to give up any scrap of Johnson; he was thoroughly against the whole project.

The travelers continued on to Buxton and Chester, and into Wales, to the Vale of Clwyd. Sir Robert and Lady Cotton no longer lived there; they had moved to Combermere Abbey in Cheshire, having sold Llewenny in 1781 to the Hon. Thomas Fitzmaurice, younger brother of the Marquess of Lansdowne — and so far as the Piozzis' happiness was concerned, the Cottons' absence was fortunate, for Bob and Fanny were outraged by the Piozzi marriage, and this close family friendship was over forever. But the present owners of Llewenny, Sir Thomas Fitzmaurice and his wife (the Countess of Orkney in her own right), received the Piozzis graciously, and their young heir, Lord Kirkwall, played with Cecilia.

The stay in Wales was altogether agreeable, because Piozzi (unlike Thrale) was attracted to his wife's beautiful country. Cecilia, however, did not care for Wales. She said that she would marry Bertie Greatheed's little son when he came of age, and they would settle in Warwickshire, which she preferred to any place she had ever seen.

In November 1787 Mrs. Thrale was able to give Cadell finished copy for the two volumes of Johnson's *Letters*; and this accomplished, she and her husband and Cecilia went to Bath to rest and enjoy the waters and the entertainment. While there, Mrs. Piozzi took an interest in Cecilia's education. She tutored her, and the child showed marked improvement under her direction. Even so, it was apparent that Cecilia did not have the mental capacity of Queeney, nor of Harry — nor even of Susan and Sophy. As for Cecilia's appearance, she looked the way Susan had at her age, dark hair and very white skin. She was pretty and vivacious, but her disposition was no better than Susan's. She was not at all amiable — Piozzi was good-natured to put up with her (*Thraliana*, p. 708).

When the Piozzis returned to London the first week in January 1788, they stopped to visit their loyal friend, Charlotte Lewis, at Reading, and there Mrs. Piozzi "miscarried of a Daughter" (*Thraliana*, p. 704). The hostess was astounded; she could not believe that Mrs. Piozzi, within a few days of her forty-seventh birthday, was still able to have a child. The miscarriage was a bitter disappointment, for Mrs.

Piozzi longed to give her second husband a child. She reasoned, however, that things were not as bad as they might seem, for the baby had not been a boy,[19] and she was still "*capable* of bringing more Children" (*Thraliana*, pp. 704, 708). They could still hope for an heir.

On 19 February 1788, Mrs. Piozzi came across an old leatherbound book among her things at the Hanover Square house, "marked 1766 . . . a Register of my Children's Powers of Mind & Body beginning with the first down to the last." This was the *Family Book*:

> *It has lain by forgotten & neglected till now*, but I was glad to see it again for various Reasons, the Misses & their Adherents say I never cared for my Children — Ungrateful Girls! — let 'em look at this Book & blush for Shame — I cared for nothing else, twenty long Years together — The Book was locked up when I went abroad; and so mislaid that till today it has not appeared this Age, I made Cecilia look at it. (*Thraliana*, p. 709)

Cecilia must have had interesting reading.

Early in March Mrs. Piozzi's two volumes of Johnson's *Letters* appeared. Cadell had printed 2,000 copies and the edition was sold out within a few days. In the book Mrs. Piozzi had included a few of her own letters to Johnson at Cadell's insistence, and she noted that "My Letter to Jack Rice on his Marriage [to Fanny Plumbe] in the 1st Vol. seems the universal Favourite: the Book is well spoken of upon the whole . . ." (*Thraliana*, p. 711).

On 29 March 1788 the play which had interested the Piozzis so much during the summer, Bertie Greatheed's *The Regent*, opened in London. Mrs. Piozzi pronounced the tragedy an overwhelming success but judging from critical reports the play was a failure (*Thraliana*, p. 713, n. 2). The leading roles were taken by John Kemble and Sarah Siddons. (The latter had taken Johnson's place as the eminent person in Mrs. Piozzi's life.) The stars gave brilliant performances, and Mrs. Piozzi was delighted by the reception of her "Epilogue" — applause at the theatre and publication later in *The World*.

When summer came the Piozzis and Cecilia went to Devon. They settled down at Exmouth, in a charming house on the Strand "with the Water quite washing yᵉ Wall on one Side, & a smart little Garden on

---

[19] Recording this event in William Augustus Conway's copy of her *Journey through France, Italy, and Germany*, Mrs. Piozzi wrote that she "vexatiously miscarried at Reading in Berkshire of a dead boy in the house of dear Mrs. Lewis" but this statement was written thirty-one years later; the contemporary *Thraliana* record has the better claim to truth.

t'other, I shall sit down to work with much Chearfulness & Comfort"
(*Thraliana*, p. 718). Mrs. Piozzi was now turning her travel journals
into a book, and she established a strict daily routine: in the morning
work on the book; in the afternoon sea-bathing and Cecilia's tutoring;
in the evening more work, reading, or quiet diversion. The child
(now eleven) found this regime exceedingly dull, but in October the
Piozzis went to Bath, and life there was more to her taste. By 10
November 1788, Mrs. Piozzi had a finished manuscript of her *Journey
through France, Italy, and Germany*; and soon thereafter the family
returned to London.

The house in Hanover Square was pleasant and comfortable, but
Piozzi wanted very much to return to Streatham when Thomas Steele's
lease would terminate the following year (1790):

> I wonder [Piozzi wishes] to fix there, for if I were to dye, he must turn out
> directly; and the Girls perhaps would not let my Body stay till it grew Cold,
> before they kick'd *me* out: at least their *present* Conduct gives Room to ex-
> pect no better from their *future*: so it *may* be no Loss. Were some great
> Windfall to drop in, I would coax my Husband to buy a House in London,
> & build a Cottage on [Tremeirchion] Hill: the Situation is demidivine, and it
> would be *his own*. Pulling down Bachŷgraig would make us hated in the
> Country, and no Money could render it habitable: Streatham does very well
> for a Summer Villa, but the Consciousness that one should hate to *dye* there,
> would make me *live* in it with a kind of odd Anxiety one knows not how to
> describe — *like being abroad*. (*Thraliana*, p. 708)

Despite her qualms, the Piozzis made plans during 1789 to re-estab-
lish themselves at Streatham. They also thought of going to Italy in
the spring, but the problem of Cecilia's custody made an excursion out
of the United Kingdom impossible. And if they left her behind, they
were sure that Queeney would seize her; a journey to Scotland and
Wales seemed wiser. Mrs. Piozzi wished to include Ireland in the
itinerary, but Cecilia and Piozzi were both afraid of the sea (*Thraliana*,
p. 749).

They started out for Scotland in June, but before this, three events
occurred which bear recording. One evening in March Miss Nicolson
(the chaperone who had been with the girls briefly in Brighton) came
to a concert the Piozzis gave at the Hanover Square house, and she
pleased them by saying that they both looked ten years younger than
when she had seen them last, at the time of their marriage. She further
pleased Mrs. Piozzi by saying that it was hard for her to believe that
Queeney, Susan, and Sophy were able "to resist the Vortex which

brings every one beside them to our Feet!" (*Thraliana*, p. 735). The second event took place one night in April: Mrs. Piozzi ran into Sophia Streatfeild at an assembly and the beautiful lady was all confusion.[20] The third happening was the death of Baretti on 5 May. This enemy of Mrs. Thrale had written three spiteful articles concerning her treatment of her children. They had appeared in the *European Magazine* in May, June, and August 1788 — and more were promised. Early this year, 1789, he had published a play on the subject, entitled *The Sentimental Mother*, a cruel satire in which she was portrayed as Lady Fantasma Tunskull and her second husband as Signor Squalici. Now, Baretti's persecution was over. "Poor Baretti!" she wrote in *Thraliana* (p. 745).

When the Piozzis started out for Scotland they passed through Scarborough, Durham, and Newcastle, arriving in Edinburgh by early July. There they met and enjoyed a fellow traveler, the London banker poet, Samuel Rogers, in his twenties, not a physically attractive man, but a delightful companion, intelligent and cultivated. For his part, Rogers formed a high opinion of Piozzi and his vivacious wife, and he was captivated by twelve-year-old Cecilia — thus, she too made an early and interesting conquest of the heart, just as Queeney had.

On their way home from Scotland, the Piozzis stopped at Sizergh, a fine old castle in Westmorland which belonged to Mrs. Strickland, the friend who had been in France with the Thrales in 1775 and had done so much to make that journey pleasant. Mrs. Strickland was no longer a widow, though her name was unchanged. In 1779 she had married Jarrard Strickland, her first husband's cousin, and now, added to her three grown-up children, were George, not quite nine, and Jarrard Edward, seven.

Mrs. Strickland now looked much older than Mrs. Piozzi, for she was lame (since the birth of young Jarrard) but despite her difficulty in getting about, she was as full of drive as ever. She seemed extremely happy with her second husband. The Piozzis liked him — and fortunately the Stricklands liked Piozzi.

[20] Sophia Streatfeild's powers of attraction were still considerable, though not so great as they had been when she was irresistible to Mr. Thrale. At that time she had herself been in love with the unhappily married Mr. Vyse, but this did not prevent her from accepting the attentions, not only of Thrale, but those of the Bishop of Chester and also those of Alexander Wedderburne (created Baron Loughborough, Lord Chief Justice in 1780) — and later the attentions of Dr. Burney.

Many men ran mad for Sophia, but none ever chose her as a wife.

Mrs. Strickland proudly showed her visitors the alterations she was making in the castle (not all in good taste, but certainly with a feeling for modern fashion and comfort). And she showed them the fine garden — including her chestnut trees, grown from the chestnuts she had carried home from Versailles.

Mrs. Strickland was enchanted to see how well her namesake was maturing. As for Cecilia, she liked Mrs. Strickland very well, also the young Strickland boys, but she still preferred the Greatheeds "to all people and Things" (*Thraliana*, p. 749).

After going on to Wales and having a pleasant stay there, the Piozzis and Cecilia returned to London; and by December they were settled again in the Hanover Square house. There was no particular news of the "Miss Thrales," though shocking news concerning a guardian — Henry Smith had died in September, only thirty-three years old. So ended the life of the young man in whom Thrale had placed his hopes.[21]

During the winter the Piozzis were much concerned with Streatham plans, and in April they took back the house. There had been a great deal of damage during the seven and a half years it had been rented: "General Dalrymple's *Hogs*, and Mr. Steele's *Goat*" had ruined many things, but at least the fruit trees which Mrs. Salusbury had planted, and which Baretti had wanted to cut down (to prevent Harry's constant falls) had been spared and were more beautiful than ever. The house was filled with memories, and Piozzi was very tender about his wife's feelings; he "changed the furniture of every Room that convey'd black Ideas, & perpetuate[d] the remembrance of every Circumstance likely to please . . ." To enjoy her mother's fruit trees the more, she chose "Dr Johnson's old Room, (new furnished for the Occasion) to be [her] Bed Chamber . . ." (*Thraliana*, p. 767).

The Piozzis worked hard during the spring, putting the place in order, and they spent more than £2,000 on restoration. By the time of their sixth wedding anniversary (25 July) they were ready to have a proper housewarming — to welcome their friends and show off

[21] Henry Smith left Jane Hambleton, the cousin who kept house for him, an annuity of £40; and he made bequests of £1,000 to Joseph Stevens of Ely Place, London, and £1,000 to James Trower of Lincoln's Inn. His joint executors were Trower and William Smith (son of his cousin, Ralph Smith). In a codicil he left his house and the residue and remainder of his estates and effects to his cousin, William Smith. Bateman Robson and Christopher Norris, witnesses to Thrale's will, were also witnesses to his. Will of Henry Smith, Public Record Office, London.

Streatham Park in its renewed splendor. This was one of Mrs. Piozzi's finest parties: "not less than a Thousand Men Women & Children might have been counted in the House & Grounds . . ." (*Thraliana*, p. 775). Needless to say, the "Miss Thrales" did not attend. "I never knew so rancorous a Hatred," Mrs. Piozzi recorded. If the daughters would only marry, that "might perhaps soften their Hearts, but I hear no likelihood of such an Event" (*Thraliana*, p. 768).

Old Nurse, incidentally, had made sly visits to Streatham over the years, and never without carrying something away. According to Mr. Steele, she had even brought a locksmith upon one occasion and broken into a chest. Piozzi threatened to have her arrested, but Queeney rose to the defense, and the Piozzis let the matter drop "lest old Nurse should swing on a Gallows — or take a Trip on a new Discovery to Botany Bay" (*Thraliana*, p. 761).

All went well at Streatham. Piozzi was a good manager, and on Mrs. Piozzi's £3,000 a year he found no difficulty in maintaining the house in style. She, however, continued to be uneasy about the future. Sreatham was enjoyable only in the summer months, and she was haunted by the knowledge that the house could never be Piozzi's home if she died. Soon, they would be wise to live in Wales in the summer, and Bath in the winter, where it was easy to get about and doctors were readily available. The sensible thing to do, was obviously to enjoy Streatham while they were still strong enough to manage the place; but she insisted that they should keep thinking about Wales for their final retirement. This winter they made a visit to Bath, and Piozzi surprised her by drawing some pretty plans for a cottage on Tremeirchion Hill.

8.

In February 1791, while they were in Bath, surprising and disturbing news came. According to someone called Charles Gilbert, a lawyer in Lewes, and Steward of the Brighton court:

the three eldest Thrales were unjustly possessed of their Father's Estate in Sussex, which of right belonged to his *youngest* only — meaning *Cæcilia*, by the Custom of Brighthelmstone Manor: a Circumstance we none of us ever dreamed on; but which proves upon enquiry . . . [to be] strictly true: and all they have received from that Estate whether much or little, — must be refunded to the youngest Sister. (*Thraliana*, pp. 805–806)

Everyone had always considered the house in Brighton as belonging jointly to the four girls. This was certainly what Thrale intended, but during his lifetime he and Scrase had not taken the necessary steps to make the property descend according to his will. Queeney and Susan and Sophy felt very hurt and had great resentment against the law — fortunately not against Cecilia.[22]

During the autumn of 1792 the Piozzis were in Wales; they had a land survey made of their building site on Tremeirchion Hill, and construction began on the cottage. As so often happens, the plans became more and more elaborate, and the cottage soon grew into a villa. "Belvedere," they had first thought of calling it, because of the beautiful view of the Vale of Clwyd, but "Brynbella," half Italian, half Welsh for "beautiful hill," was the final choice.

The Piozzis stayed in Denbigh, at the Crown Inn, and went daily to supervise the work. It was frustrating how little progress was made on the house during their visit (building was to continue throughout 1793 and 1794). And their two young charges were a great worry: Cecilia, now fifteen, and her guest, Sally Siddons, seventeen (a beautiful daughter of Sarah). The girls amused themselves by riding their horses around the countryside and attracting the local swains. The

[22] As we have seen, there were two Thrale properties in Brighton — a cottage originally purchased by Ralph Thrale in 1755 and the substantial house which Henry Thrale acquired in 1767 (see XXIV, 147, 150–151). The disposition of these properties ought to have been completed within a short time of Thrale's death in 1781, but it took more than 10 years. The explanation is possibly the sheer dilatoriness of eighteenth-century legal procedures.

As far as the main house was concerned, it has already been noted that this was never "surrendered to the use of Thrale's Will" (see XXIV, 151, n. 10). On Thrale's death, therefore, this property could not pass according to his will, but had to go to his "heir according to the Custom of the Manor." Since the Custom of the Manor of Brighthelmstone was descent to the youngest son or, failing sons, youngest daughter, Cecilia inherited it. It is obvious that Thrale never intended this result and failure to carry out the proper legal procedures was a bad mistake on the part of his attorneys.

Ralph Thrale's cottage also went to Cecilia, but here both the Manorial Court and the family attorneys seem to have blundered, because the Court Roll for 26 August 1760 clearly shows that this property *was* surrendered to the use of Thrale's will soon after he inherited it from his father. A possible explanation for this extraordinary mistake is that everyone had forgotten that the two properties had been acquired separately and assumed that what applied to one applied to the other.

The family never realized the mistake or, at any rate, it was never corrected and Cecilia kept both properties. Mrs. Piozzi did not seem to know that, as Thrale's widow, she was entitled to possession of the main house for her lifetime, notwithstanding her remarriage, because this was also the Custom of the Manor of Brighthelmstone.

Piozzis fussed about the friendships they made, and they were alarmed when both girls became ill, Sally with a frightening attack of asthma, and Cecilia with so bad a cold that they feared her lungs were affected, and that she was consumptive. They made rapid preparations to go home and were grateful when every member of the party was safely back in London.

In 1794 Mrs. Piozzi faced a serious personal problem. She was now in her fifties and, even with her indomitable spirit, she could no longer hope to have a child — an heir for her husband — but a boy was offered them by Piozzi's favorite brother (fourteen years her husband's junior). This brother, who greatly resembled him in appearance, had been kindness itself when the Piozzis had been in Italy, following them everywhere. Some while after the Piozzis returned to England, they heard from Giambattista that he had married a young woman named Teresa Fracassi,[23] of an "excellent" Venetian family. The couple had had three children: two boys, Pietro and Giovanni Maria, and a little girl, Cecilia Margarita, named in honor of Cecilia Thrale. And in 1793 they had a fourth child, a boy, whom they named John Salusbury to please Mrs. Piozzi. Now, a year later, Giambattista wrote from Brescia, asking if his brother and his wife would like to have John Salusbury Piozzi for their own — this was obviously a gesture of sympathy for the fact that they had no son, but also a desire on Giambattista's part to improve the chances his child might have in life. The Napoleonic campaign in the north of Italy had left the family destitute.

The prospect of a baby arriving at the moment was too much for Mrs. Piozzi to face, she was having problems enough with Cecilia — her admirers and her illnesses — and she was striving for a reconciliation with Queeney, Susan, and Sophy. After six years they had finally come forward and visited Streatham. This was no time to introduce the infant John Salusbury Piozzi — but she wanted the boy. She wrote to Giambattista, saying that she and her husband could not send for him now but arrangements would be made in a few years to bring John Salusbury Piozzi to England.

Meanwhile, she turned her attention to Cecilia. This seventeen-year-old had become a Bacchante girl, beautiful, delicate, and wild. She could be sweet-tempered when not thwarted, but if she were, she became disrespectful, irresponsible, and violent. She loved horses and

[23] Conway, II, 8.

dogs, preferring animals to humans, she said, but nevertheless she had a few close human female friends and a crowd of suitors. Cecilia was a born coquette and was pursued by whoever was introduced, young bloods in Wales, titled Italians (Count Garzoni and Count Zenobio — among others), and certain highly respectable friends of the family, such as Samuel Rogers, faithful since meeting her in Scotland; Sammy Lysons, the antiquarian who had helped her mother with her Johnson books; and William Makepeace Thackeray, the scholarly young Chester doctor (a great-uncle of the novelist), who prescribed for Cecilia's colds and coughs, and Piozzi's attacks of gout, which were now coming every few months, with increasing severity.[24]

When Cecilia was fifteen the Piozzis had rescued her from James Drummond, a bank clerk, with whom she fancied herself in love. Drummond was an insolent, persistent suitor and an impostor — altogether a very disturbing episode. As Mrs. Piozzi put it, Cecilia:

. . . by dint of Intriguing Lovers teized my Soul out before she was 15; when [at 18] she *fortunately* ran away; jumping out of the Window at Streatham Park with Mͬ Mostyn of Segroi[t]. (Conway, p. 3, at back of Vol. I)

Cecilia had met John Mostyn in Wales and they had been inseparable during the summer and autumn of 1794 when the Piozzis came again to supervise the building of Brynbella. Their intention was to go to Bath in late autumn, but as the time approached Piozzi was stricken with a long and painful attack of gout, and this kept the family at Denbigh all winter. Tall, handsome, dark-haired John Mostyn was always on hand, and it soon became clear to Mrs. Piozzi that she had not only the serious illness of her husband to contend with, but also the serious romance of her daughter. When questioned, Cecilia said casually that of course John Mostyn was in love with her, and she thought she was in love with him too, and they might get married. This was not to be tolerated — they were both under age.

Fortunately, Piozzi was able to travel at the time of crisis, and both he and his wife agreed that the only thing to do was to take Cecilia

[24] Ironically, for almost any disease other than gout Piozzi would have been better off in the United Kingdom than elsewhere but France offered a possible cure. Colchicine, an organic alkaloid, was used in treatment there with dramatic effect. In England this "poison" was banned.

Benjamin Franklin appreciated the effectiveness of colchicine and introduced it into America. It is still used in the treatment of gout, though no one yet knows why it is so effective.

back to Streatham. They returned there and immediately John Mostyn appeared. He continued to press his suit ardently, and in a short while Mrs. Piozzi found herself unable to resist the romantic appeal of the courtship. John would reach his majority in August of the next year (1796), and for any time after that date she tentatively gave her consent for their marriage (a necessary condition under Thrale's will). John promised to make a binding settlement as soon as he could.

All seemed reasonably under control, but this was not so. Cecilia and John were too impatient to wait a year and eloped to Scotland. They were married at Gretna Green on 8 June 1795. On their way back to Wales, they stopped in Westmorland to give their news to Mrs. Strickland. She was delighted. They made a very handsome couple, she wrote to Mrs. Piozzi: Cecilia seemed radiantly happy, and she liked the good-looking John Mostyn, who seemed to adore his bride.

The Mostyns' elopement left the whole question of their marriage settlement unsolved. Cecilia was only eighteen, John not twenty. Technically, until Cecilia came of age, her sisters were heirs to her fortune of £50,000 and though Mostyn now gave impassioned promises, none of them were binding. Mrs. Piozzi feared difficulties with Cecilia's sisters, particularly the eldest. She herself was already in conflict again with Queeney, this time over Crowmarsh Battle Farm.[25]

Despite all the Mostyn problems, however, Mrs. Piozzi could not help but feel relief that Cecy's impostor, Drummond, was now shaken off for good (Piozzi had always thought that romance would be revived[26]). Now the girl was settled with Mostyn, and there was much good to be said about him. He was not a fortune-hunter, for he owned Segroit Hall, a fine property on the outskirts of Denbigh, and he had a personal income of £2,000 a year (*Thraliana*, p. 919). Furthermore, the Mostyns were a distinguished Flintshire family; John's grandfather had been an intimate friend of Mrs. Piozzi's father. On the whole,

[25] Thrale had willed Crowmarsh to Queeney, but had failed to revoke the clause in his own marriage settlement, which stated that £400 a year from Crowmarsh should go to his widow upon his death (*Thraliana*, p. 491, n. 1).

[26] Drummond was not a faithful lover. By the next month he had married someone else, a "Miss Castell" (*Thraliana*, p. 934, n. 3).

Years later (1815) Mrs. Piozzi wrote of him, "I hear the other day that Cecy's Cast-off Lover James Drummond is come from abroad rich & Prosperous; & is married to Lady Emily Murray the Duke of Athol's Daughter . . . I suppose Miss Castle — his first Wife who went with him, soon died" (Rylands 588.256).

though it was not the brilliant match she would have liked, she was satisfied. And she was pleased that Cecilia was to live in Wales. Cecy had always said that she hated Wales, but her mother was sure that the changeable girl would soon love this country as much as she did.

As for the reaction of Queeney, Susan, and Sophy, though they deprecated their younger sister's hasty marriage, they felt little else could be expected of Cecilia, with their mother setting such a horrible example of marrying for love. It was too much to expect, to have her make a prudent choice. They had known all along, they said, that something like this would happen. They accepted Mostyn, and soon began to play him off against his mother-in-law.

Throughout the summer the Piozzis stayed at Streatham; various friends were entertained, and Arthur Murphy was their guest for some eight weeks. The Piozzis enjoyed their fine house and were undecided whether or not to let it after they took over Brynbella. In the end, they determined to keep Streatham Park, to use whenever they wished to be near London.

In September 1795, they set out for Wales and when they arrived were pleased to find that it was possible to live at Brynbella, though workmen were still in the house. The cottage which turned into a villa had regrettably cost £20,000 (*Commonplace Book*, under Piozzi) but it was beautiful. Cecilia and John Mostyn stayed with the Piozzis at first, while renovations were being made for them at Segroit. And in October, according to their promise, made earlier in the year, Queeney, Susan, and Sophy came to the Vale of Clwyd for a visit of inspection. Queeney, at present her mother's heir to this property, was no more impressed by what she saw than she had been twenty years before, and it was clear that she did not love Wales any more than she had then. Nevertheless, this visit in the autumn of 1795 was a joyous occasion for Mrs. Piozzi, because she was surrounded by all four of her children for the first time in a long while — no greater happiness — and her sweet husband trying so hard to oblige them all.

This pleasant state of affairs did not continue long. Her three daughters returned to London, and the year 1796 arrived and passed without John Mostyn making a marriage settlement. His attitude toward Cecilia had changed; he was no longer her abject slave, but her constant adversary. There were endless arguments, flares of temper, and irresponsible actions on both their parts. "Cecilia's Regard for Mr Drummond the Lover, & Mr Presto the Lapdog, & Mr Mostyn the

Husband was all of the same Kind," Mrs. Piozzi commented bitterly, "She could set them *all three* to *snap* at, and *bite* her Mother, *for her Sport*: That Game done, She *has* already turned off the *two first*, and I suppose the 3ᵈ will *follow*" (*Thraliana*, p. 985). The Mostyns' whole way of life was incomprehensible to Mrs. Piozzi. Cecilia had shied away from physical love, and now her own maid, Mason, was pregnant by her husband. Cecilia's reaction to this situation was what she called "modern," that is to say, total indifference. But though Cecilia might not care, the Piozzis were shocked, outraged, and mortified. They became vindictive, demanding a proper settlement from John, and when he hesitated, they pressed charges against him for all the expenses they had borne for Cecilia from the time she had come to live with them until her marriage — eight years of charges. Mrs. Piozzi wrote to Cator, demanding an accounting for Cecilia to present to Mostyn. Cator replied that he was working hard toward a settlement with the young man but could do nothing further until he had an order from the court. He advised Mrs. Piozzi not to be violent and vengeful. This wise counsel only served to infuriate, and to turn her against Cator. She vowed that Murphy from now on would advise her and that she would never have anything further to do with Cator; it was an unfortunate decision to sever all connection with Cator, for he had been a very valuable friend over the years. And he remained a loyal friend to the Thrale daughters. He now worked with Cecilia and John. All communication between Brynbella and Segroit ceased.

Mrs. Piozzi felt overpowered with problems — and one of them was Streatham. This available, unoccupied house was being used all the time, with and without permission, by relations and friends; it seemed to be everybody's house. The Mostyns were bad offenders, shocking even Murphy by their casual behavior while in residence (and they departed without paying a large wine bill). Murphy himself was an offender; he felt free to stay at Streatham for weeks at a time. Upon one occasion he asked if persons *not* even known to the Piozzis, but friends of their neighbors, the Daniel Macnamaras (he was agent to the Duke of Bedford) might be put up in the house. Mrs. Piozzi was much annoyed by the request and refused, which Murphy resented. She felt that he took altogether too much for granted. Once, in 1797, he invited the Prince of Wales (later George IV) to come to Streatham to meet the beautiful "Miss Thrales." Susanna had already attracted the Prince's attention in Brighton (*Thraliana*, p. 921, n. 3).

Mrs. Piozzi saw no moral purpose being served by her girls receiving a royal visit from the thirty-five-year-old roué, even though her daughters could more appropriately be called spinsters than girls (Susanna, the belle, was twenty-seven, Sophy twenty-six, and staid Queeney, thirty-three). Nevertheless, Mrs. Piozzi did not trust their good sense and promptly rescinded the invitation, which was a great rudeness to His Royal Highness. Murphy never quite forgave her, and she never forgave him.

As for the relationship between Cecilia and John Mostyn, the year 1797 brought improvement — she was pregnant — a baby was expected in August. When the time came, Mrs. Piozzi was not called upon to assist at the delivery. She was much disappointed and Piozzi was indignant. The person honored with an invitation to be present at the accouchement was Queeney, certainly less qualified by experience. Queeney "cross'd the Country hither to attend Cecilia, 285 Miles from the Coast of Sussex, with no Companion, no female Servt — nothing but a Groom & Saddle Bags: all the way on one Horse, as People travelled in Days of Yore. They are astonishing Girls" (*Thraliana*, p. 974). On 28 August, after three days of tortured labor, Cecilia brought forth a dead boy. From the report, Mrs. Piozzi blamed incompetence; she was sure that a "London Hospital would have saved this Child" (*Thraliana*, p. 974). Cecilia did not wish to go into the matter with her mother and refused to see her, even after the baby's death. The whole neighborhood discussed the incident in full detail for some time.

In the next year, 1798, the Piozzis decided to give up Streatham. They had hardly used the house themselves, and it was nothing but an harassment as matters stood. Mrs. Piozzi offered the house to "the ladies," rent free. But Queeney, Susan, and Sophy had no desire to be responsible for taxes, tithes, and dilapidation. It was their mother's duty to take care of these burdens during her lifetime, after which the house belonged to them anyway. They promptly refused.

Mrs. Piozzi thereupon leased the house for £550 a year to a rich corn factor, Mr. Giles, a coarse but sweet-tempered man. His lease was to run until 1801 (*Thraliana*, pp. 985, 1013). The papers were drawn up in the spring of 1798, and soon after they were signed, the Piozzis departed for Wales.

Cecilia was expecting another child this August, and again Mrs. Piozzi hoped to be called, but, as before, Cecilia wanted no help from her mother. This time all went well, the baby was born, and named John Salusbury Mostyn. Three months passed, and still Mrs. Piozzi had not been asked to see her first grandchild. She only met her daughter "one Night by Chance at [the] Denbigh Assembly" (*Thraliana*, p. 990, n. 2).

9.

The indifference of her own children made Mrs. Piozzi determine that the time had come to take on her husband's nephew, the little Italian boy. She wrote to Giambattista Piozzi that they would now like to have his son. Early in December 1798, the five-year-old John Salusbury Piozzi arrived in England. He was met by Robert Ray, son of the Streatham schoolmistress. Ray was now Mrs. Piozzi's lawyer (she had turned against Robson and Norris as accomplices of Cator).

Ray took the lad, who spoke no English, to Reynold Davies, and they had a rough time of it, with sign language, for the better part of a month. Davies' school had taken the place of old Dr. Thomas' in Streatham. Davies was curate of St. Leonard's and had put up a school building on the Piozzis' land. "Streatham University" was the title he gave to his academy in light-hearted conversation. It was for young boys under twelve.

The Piozzis seemed to be in no hurry to see their nephew, for it was not until Christmastime that Robert Ray was instructed to bring him to Bath. The boy was short and stocky, with black hair and dark skin. He was shrewd, mischievous, and affectionate. Mrs. Piozzi thought he was a dear little thing, but she had no idea of changing her own way of life for Salusbury (this is what she wished him to be called). He would spend holidays with his uncle and herself, and the rest of the time he would be at Davies' little "University." And it would be up to Davies to teach him English and the manners and customs of the country before beginning formal instruction. Mrs. Piozzi had no intention of tutoring the boy herself. She had felt too old for this with Sophy — over twenty years ago. With Salusbury, there was no question. She would count upon others to make him a fine scholar, a good Christian, and an English gentleman.

As can be imagined, the taking on of Piozzi's nephew astonished the four Thrale sisters. They felt embarrassment, as well as anxiety about their inheritance. His intrusion into the family put an end to any hope of a true reconciliation between Mrs. Piozzi and her daughters.

In April of the next year, 1799, Mrs. Piozzi wrote from Brynbella to Penelope Pennington, a friend she had made some years earlier in Bath.[27] Susan, she said, had been to Streatham "on purpose, I fancy, to gratify hers and her family's curiosity. So she saw a little boy with my *name*, and my husband's *face* . . ." (Pennington, p. 172). Mrs. Piozzi hoped that the name, John Salusbury, which her only grandchild also carried, would be a happier appellation for them both than it had been for her father. "*That* never *yet* has been a *lucky* Name" (*Thraliana*, p. 993).

In November 1799, Mrs. Piozzi received word that Cecilia had had a second son, whom she named Henry, in honor of her father and her brother. The baby was born in London, and a report soon reached Mrs. Piozzi that Cecilia had gone out to dine with the Macnamaras in Streatham when the child was only "eleven days" old (Rylands 592.43). Her horrified hostess had sent her home to bed.

Mrs. Piozzi often thought of Cecilia and worried about her, as she carried on with her various projects. She and her husband were restoring the Salusbury family house, Bach-y-Graig, built as has been said by Richard Clough, second husband of Catherine Tudor, heiress of Berayne (Mrs. Piozzi was having a portrait of this famous ancestress painted to hang at Brynbella). Piozzi was generously paying for the restoration of the house, also paying for the restoration of the Tremeirchion Church and the Salusbury family vault, and paying a £7,000 mortgage on the Welsh property as well.

Bach-y-Graig had been in a sad state when the Thrales had seen it with Johnson over twenty-five years before, but by the time the Piozzis moved to Wales it was a virtual ruin. Piozzi's rebuilding was being carried out with his usual taste and sensitivity. He was even placing the Salusbury lion on the roof top again:

. . . [and the place was now] inhabited by comfortable Tenants, & the Curate lodges with them in old Cathcrine de Bcrayne's Apartment with the Fleur de Lys . . . and we are putting little [Tremeirchion] Church in order; paving, glazing, slating, painting it &c and we give them a new Pulpit, Desk, & Cloths besides — with a brass Chandelier. — It *was* a Place like a Stable you know;

[27] Penelope Weston had become a friend in 1780. They enjoyed each other's good talk when they were together, and good letters when they were apart.

On 27 December 1792 Penelope Weston married William Pennington, an American loyalist, ruined by the War of Independence. The Penningtons now lived at Clifton, where he held the office of Master of Ceremonies at the Clifton Hot Wells.

and we have made a Vault for ourselves & my poor Ancestors, whose Bones were found by digging under the Altar; Dear Grandmama's Skull had a black Ribband pinned tight round it with Two Brass Pins — Old Lucy Salusbury — A Brass Plate over her, & one or two of her Sons. There was no Flannel Act [28] then, so I suppose they buried her in the Cap & Knot She wore."
(Bowood Papers, HLP to Queeney, 20 September 1803)

While her husband was busy with his work, Mrs. Piozzi was starting on a new book. He could never understand why she found pleasure in driving herself to exhaustion by writing when there was no necessity for the effort — but he was always gentle, polite, and very sympathetic — he never interrupted. Her book, which she called *Retrospection*, was to celebrate the coming of the nineteenth century, an abridgment of world history for 1800 years, for the general reader. She wanted her book to appear on New Year's Day 1801, which she considered the beginning of the new century, and this deadline was met, though the final rush of reading proof-sheets left many errors in the thousand pages.

In the excitement of publication day, her husband and others persuaded her to send one of the inscribed copies to her old enemy, Lady Salusbury, who was in London at the time. Mrs. Piozzi wrote a letter to accompany the book; this present, she hoped, would be accepted from the "Girl with whom She once was pleased" and a "Woman with whom She once was offended. But since Time's Wing has swept away all which stood between them 40 Years ago, let it in Gods Name sweep away all Remembrance of Offence too . . ." (*Thraliana*, p. 1014, n. 5). Lady Salusbury was now eighty, but relentless as ever. She refused to accept the book or the letter and sent both back by a servant.

During the first year of the new century there was gratifying news from another quarter. John Mostyn at last received an honor, he was made High Sheriff for Denbighshire, that is to say the chief officer of the Crown in his county, an office both of great honor and of great expense. In July happy tidings came again from Segroit that a third

---

[28] Three Acts of Parliament "For Burying in Woolen" were passed in the reign of Charles II (in 1666, 1678, and 1680). They were designed to encourage the English woolen cloth industry and to discourage the importation of foreign silks and other materials. Burial of corpses in any other stuff was subject to a fine of £5. The Acts were repealed in 1814 (54 George III c.108).

Mrs. Piozzi was wrong therefore, in saying that there was no Flannel Act at the date of Lucy Salusbury's death in 1745, but perhaps the Acts were not much enforced in the remoter parts of the country.

Mostyn son had been born, Thomas Arthur Bertie (the last name honoring Cecilia's childhood friend, little Bertie Greatheed [29]). After this, good news stopped and bad reports reached the Piozzis, that John Mostyn was deeply in debt and that he was drinking heavily and treating his wife abominably, and that her beauty was fast going, almost gone. There was continual wrangling at Segroit, a good deal of the argument being over money. Cecilia and John were hopeless in handling their affairs and John's appointment as High Sheriff proved a crippling blow. The office is a one-year tour of duty and it is significant that in 1802 the Mostyns sold the Brighton properties inherited from Henry Thrale.[30]

In October 1804, Mrs. Piozzi wrote to Queeney that Cecilia had miscarried of a girl child as a result of a tumble but, said Cecilia, " 'tis no Loss &c. — was on Horseback the third Day and galloping about as usual" (Bowood Papers, 12 October). Shortly after her miscarriage, there was a reconciliation of sorts with the Piozzis, and Cecilia paid a three-day visit at Brynbella. She was studiously agreeable, and the Piozzis were tactful, but none of them gained much pleasure from the meeting. Discussion of John Salusbury Piozzi was carefully avoided.

[29] Bertie was now twenty, as close as ever to his adoring mother and father. They had removed him from Eton after "observing the bad effects upon the morals which unavoidably result from public education" (*Gentleman's Magazine*, 1804, p. 1236). Thereafter, they assumed the responsibility of his education themselves, laying special stress upon literature and the arts. Bertie became an accomplished amateur painter.

In 1797 the Greatheeds took Bertie to Germany to acquaint him with the arts of that country, its manners, customs, and language. A similar family Grand Tour of France took place in 1802.

There was to be one more trip — to Italy in 1804. This time the Greatheed family was enlarged, for not only were there Bertie's parents, but Bertie had married in France, and was now accompanied by his wife and infant daughter.

While the party was in Vicenza, Bertie became ill of an inflammation of the lungs. He died there on 8 October 1804, aged twenty-three.

[30] Thrale's Brighton properties had been owned by Cecilia (under her mother's guardianship) for four years, and now, jointly by Cecilia and John Mostyn for seven years. In April 1802 they sold Ralph Thrale's old cottage (the Howell property) to James Charles Mitchell, and the West Street house (the Dornford property) to Robert Chatfield.

The fine house on West Street, held by various owners, was demolished in 1866, to give place to "the Grand Concert Hall" (*Southern Weekly News*, 14 November 1931). This building later became Sherry's Dancing Saloon.

THE THRALES' WEST STREET HOUSE, BRIGHTON, 1865

The next year, 1805, Cecilia and John Mostyn separated; and two years later, in May 1807, gangling, lazy, sullen, showy John Mostyn died of tuberculosis — not quite thirty-two years old. He died intestate, and Cecilia coped as well as she could with his tangled affairs, his debts, and the responsibility of the children. Salusbury was eight; Harry, seven; and Bertie, five. Segroit now legally belonged to Salusbury, but Cecilia continued to live there, for all three boys were at Davies' school in Streatham, where their fifteen-year-old "uncle," in a manner of speaking, Salusbury Piozzi, had recently been. (This young man had moved on to "Enborne Cottage" near Newbury, in Berkshire, where, with a few other boys, he was being tutored by Charles Shephard, a Gray's Inn lawyer in whom his aunt and uncle had every confidence.)

Mrs. Piozzi would have liked to give comfort and help to her youngest daughter in her troubles, but no assistance was requested by Cecilia. Like the other "Miss Thrales" her relationship to her mother was consistently cold, just as the sisters' relationship to each other was consistently warm — they had depended on each other ever since their mother had abandoned them. And it was their sympathy that Cecilia appreciated now.

Life for Queeney, Susan, and Sophy had been going along comfortably — if uneventfully. None of them was married, but this was not from lack of opportunity, for though the social life of Henry Thrale's daughters was not as brilliant as their mother could have made it if she had provided the proper background, it still had considerable luster. "The Ladies" were handsome and rich, and society respected them. The Wynns had wanted Susanna for their William (*Thraliana*, p. 841), and Sammy Lysons had courted her (as well as Cecilia), and in 1794 Lady Deerhurst (Peggy Pitches) talked to Mrs. Piozzi of nothing but Lord Peterborough's passion for Susan and their approaching nuptials (Bowood Papers, 3 January 1794). Apparently Lord Peterborough's passion cooled, or else he did not please Susan sufficiently, for nothing came of the romance. Susan was not easy to please. She wrote to her sister, Cecilia, from Brighton in March of the next year, that *"there was not a tolerable Man* left in the County of Sussex" (*Thraliana*, p. 914).

Sophy had taken a long time to find the right man, but at thirty-six she made the excellent choice of Henry Merrik Hoare, a year her senior. Merrik was a handsome, high-principled, cultivated man, gen-

SOPHIA THRALE HOARE
PASTEL, THOUGHT TO BE A SELF-PORTRAIT,
OR A PORTRAIT BY PRINCE HOARE

HENRY MERRIK HOARE
ATTRIBUTED TO WOODFORDE

tle and understanding. He was a banker, and since 1794 had been a partner in the family bank. He was a direct descendant of the seventeenth-century founder, a grandson of Sir Richard Hoare, Lord Mayor of London in 1745, and the fourth son of Sir Richard Hoare, Bt., of Stourhead. He grew up at this beautiful place.

Sophia Thrale and Merrik Hoare were married on 13 August 1807 at the church of St. Mary le Bone in London, the date purposely set at a time they could be sure that the Piozzis would be in Wales. As a bachelor, Merrik had lived at the Adelphi with two of his brothers, but now he took up residence with his bride at 31 York Place, just off Regent's Park. Their house was one in a handsome row between the Turnpike (now Marylebone Road) and Paddington Street, a substantial brick building, dignified without and comfortable within.

Before her marriage, Sophy had shared a house with Susan, but when the Hoare wedding plans were being made, Susan (thirty-seven) made less conventional arrangements for herself. In June 1807, two months before her sister's wedding, she joined a forty-three-year-old watercolorist, William Frederick Wells, at his house, "Ashgrove Cottage," near Knockholt in Kent. It was a pretty place of some twenty acres, once part of the Stanhope property. (Susanna's and Wells's names were given as "joint occupants" of "Ashgrove Cottage" in the tax roll of the following year.) It is apparent that Susanna's family was not happy about this action, for nowhere in the known Thrale correspondence is there mention of Wells's name. The only veiled reference to him is in a letter from Mrs. Piozzi to Queeney, at the time Susan went to Knockholt:

> Susette leaves [London] tomorrow if I am right, and consummates her Marriage with Mʳ Ashgrove: If like Many Modern Couples they should be soon tired of the binding Words *to have & to hold*, She may get a Divorce any Day: — Those beautiful Places within 20 Miles of Town, are incessantly changing Possessors; and her Comfort may arise from the Reflexion that her Money will be paid her again . . . (Bowood Papers, 8 June 1807)

A drawing instructor to young aristocrats, and a respected artist in his own right, Wells had exhibited at the Royal Academy, and in 1804 had made a successful sketching tour through Norway, Sweden, and Denmark. On his return, he busied himself with the promotion of art, founding the Society of Painters in Watercolours. He was its current President.

Wells was a delightful man, fine-looking, cheerful, and imaginative.

31 YORK PLACE, 1807, RESIDENCE OF MERRIK HOARE
DRAWING BY FELIX KELLY

He was well-informed and a good talker, an avid reader and a fine musician. He liked to be surrounded by friends, and was a wonderful host. He loved to give parties at "Ashgrove Cottage" or at his London house, 33 York Buildings (the latter very near the residence of Sophy and Merrik Hoare).

One of Wells's closest friends was his protégé, William Turner, thirty-two at the time Susan came to "Ashgrove" in 1807. And on an October visit that year, Turner noted that there is not a quality, endowment, faculty, or ability, which is not in a superior degree possessed by women. "Vide Mrs. Wells." [31] One wonders whether this compliment referred to Susan, who was there at the time, or whether it was a reference to Wells's wife, Mary, who had died on 7 February 1807. Wells was generally thought to have been devoted to his wife, and to have enjoyed a happy family life. They had had nine children; two died in infancy, and there were now seven, ranging in age from twenty to five. Susan must have had deep feeling for the children — as well as for their father — to have taken on such a responsibility.

When she came to "Ashgrove" in June 1807 no legal tie prevented Wells from marrying, but either he did not wish to take a second wife, or else Susan chose this informal relationship, preferring perhaps to handle a Piozzi situation in her own, more modern way.

When her turn came to choose a partner, Queeney, as might be expected, followed the rules of society. In November of the same eventful year, 1807, she wrote to her mother that she would soon be marrying Admiral Lord Keith — a name known throughout the kingdom. This was a brilliant match, though somewhat unusual in the matter of age. Queeney was forty-three and Keith was sixty-two. He had served the Royal Navy with distinction for forty-six years. Throughout the War of Independence he was in American waters, and in 1781, at Charleston, South Carolina, he led his men ashore, a strategy which helped to effect a speedy capture of the city. General Clinton commended Keith highly for this action.

In the French war, Keith's sea and land strategy was again successful in effecting the surrender of Toulon in 1793, for which achievement he was awarded the Order of the Bath. Next year Keith was promoted to Rear Admiral, and the following year to Vice Admiral. In 1796 he effected the capture of the Cape of Good Hope (by the same amphi-

---

[31] *The Old Water-Colour Society Club*, 46th annual volume (London 1971), p. 13.

SUSANNA THRALE
MINIATURE BY COSWAY

WILLIAM FREDERICK WELLS
BY BRIGGS

ASHGROVE COTTAGE, KENT

bious tactics), and with the prize money from this conquest he was able to purchase Stonehaven, an estate in Ireland, and Tullyallan, a vast property in Scotland, in Perthshire, close to the place of his birth.

In 1797 he was created Baron Keith (an Irish title), and in the following year he joined the Mediterranean Fleet as second-in-command. Upon the Earl of St. Vincent's resignation in 1799 he became Commander-in-Chief of the Mediterranean Fleet (Nelson was one of the officers serving under him). In 1801, the British title of Baron Keith was bestowed, and in 1803 Admiral Lord Keith was appointed Commander-in-Chief of the North Sea.

Keith did not achieve the fame of a great naval hero for he never had the good fortune to have a dramatic victory at sea, but through long years of steady employment, expert administration, and performance of duty he "made a bigger fortune by prize money than any other naval officer has probably ever earned."[32] By the time Keith asked for Queeney's hand, he had, besides Stonehaven and Tullyallan, a fine London house in Harley Street, also Purbrook Park in Hampshire and Banheath in Dunbartonshire.

He had met Queeney in 1791, four years after the death of his first wife, Jane Mercer, an heiress, to whom he had been married but two years. Their only child, Margaret, was three, when Keith first came to know Queeney. Over the years, Margaret, a beautiful, talented, headstrong girl, treated Miss Thrale with polite respect, as did the Admiral's sisters. And Keith pursued his courtship with reserve, good taste, and tenacity; Queeney, characteristically, responded with steady decorum and a full display of her virtues. She had strengthened her mental faculties by studying perspective, fortification, mathematics, and Hebrew. In the letters which the couple exchanged, besides the discussion of these subjects and matters of national and naval interest, much space was given to the details of their health — the joint complaint of poor digestion being a favorite topic.

During their courtship of sixteen years, Queeney had never introduced Lord Keith to her mother, and since he was punctilious in matters of etiquette, he was now obliged in December 1807 to write a letter to an unknown person, about to become his mother-in-law. "The approbation of a parent," he said in his stiff communication, "is a matter of essential consequence to the General comfort of such a

<hr>

[32] *The Keith Papers, Selected from the Papers of Admiral Viscount Keith*, ed. Christopher Lloyd, III (1955), xi (*Publications* of the Navy Records Society, XCVI).

Union." He would, he assured Mrs. Piozzi, devote his declining years to making her daughter comfortable. Mrs. Piozzi thought Keith's letter very sensible, and found him "a *good* Man for ought I hear, a rich Man for ought I am told, a brave Man we have always heard — and a wise Man I trow *by his Choice*" (*Thraliana*, p. 1087).

Mrs. Piozzi would have liked to be present at the wedding of Lord Keith and the daughter she admired so greatly, but Queeney wished no risk of embarrassment and, as her sister Sophia before her, saw to it that her wedding took place at a time when her mother and Mr. Piozzi were safely ensconced at Brynbella. The ceremony was held on 10 January 1808 in Kent, at Ramsgate. There was little more than five years' difference in age between the bridegroom and his father-in-law.

Piozzi and the Admiral never met. The former's health was failing rapidly, and during the next year he and his wife were forced to remain close to Brynbella. In 1808, Salusbury Piozzi, now fourteen, spent his summer holidays with them there; Cecilia Mostyn and her boys sometimes called; and Mr. and Mrs. Hoare arrived in July for a visit; but the Keiths found no opportunity to come to Wales.

Autumn and winter were dismal seasons at Brynbella, for Piozzi's seizures of gout were now unremitting and agonizing. For weeks he wavered between life and death, his only relief coming from opium and brandy. On 30 March 1809, Mrs. Piozzi wrote on the final page of the sixth little volume of *Thraliana*, "Every thing most dreaded *has* ensued, — all is over; & my second Husbands Death is the last Thing recorded in my first husband's Present!" (*Thraliana*, p. 1099). Piozzi was buried beside his wife's ancestors in Tremeirchion Church, down the road from Brynbella, the church which he had restored at his own expense, six years before, as a tender show of his devotion. "Every day dismal," "Blank-Sorrow" was all his widow could write in her pocket diary.

QUEENEY THRALE
BEFORE HER MARRIAGE TO ADMIRAL LORD KEITH
MINIATURE

IV. THE THRALE DAUGHTERS AND THEIR CHILDREN

The Thrale daughters responded to their mother's bereavement after a fashion: Cecilia made calls from Segroit, and Queeney, Susan, and Sophy wrote kind letters. Piozzi's nephew, John Salusbury Piozzi, and Charles Shephard, the boy's tutor, came to stay at Brynbella for a time, doing all they could to be helpful.

In mid-April, Mrs. Piozzi made a trip to London; there she saw her daughters and also saw something of Merrik Hoare and Admiral Keith, but she did not visit either family. She was not urged to do so and she found it better in any case to be on her own in a central location (first a hotel on Manchester Square, later in lodgings). Susan, the Keiths, the Hoares, and Cecilia and her boys were extremely attentive. Sir John Lade visited her, as did Sir William Pepys, Mrs. Siddons, the Deerhursts, and Davies, the Streatham schoolteacher. There were innumerable calls every day. There was also business to take care of, and Charles Shephard was on hand to help with this.

The first matter was the proving of Piozzi's will. He had left everything to his widow, with the exception of £4,000, which he wished to have given to his relations in Italy. Mrs. Piozzi was in hearty agreement with this bequest, and wanted payment made at once, despite the generally depressed state of securities. Shephard arranged matters to her satisfaction, though it cost her £6,000 to settle the claims without delay. Family relationships were not improved by this action. Merrik Hoare, her banker son-in-law, was highly critical of Shephard.

The second matter of business, formal adoption of John Salusbury Piozzi, subjected Shephard to even fiercer attack from her family. Mrs. Piozzi, however, was determined, and Shephard was simply carrying out her wishes. He prepared a Memorial, and by this instrument, Piozzi's sixteen-year-old nephew was adopted and his name was legally changed to Salusbury — John Salusbury Piozzi Salusbury. Denization papers were prepared and John Salusbury became a British citizen, entitled to the full privileges of English birth and inheritance.

All this was achieved by mid-June, after which Mrs. Piozzi returned to Brynbella, where she hoped soon to have the full attention of the young gentleman for whom she had done so much. But human nature being what it is, Salusbury was not of the same mind. "Pug," as he was known at Enborne, was happiest when he could be with his classmate, Edward Pemberton, and visits now to Pem's house in Shropshire had an added interest, in the person of Pem's fifteen-year-old sister, pretty, auburn-haired Harriet Maria, five months Salusbury's junior.

However, in spite of the attractions of the Pembertons, Mrs. Piozzi enjoyed a good deal of Salusbury's company during his holiday (and she saw to it that he was confirmed by the Bishop of St. Asaph on 8 August). And Cecilia, though not at all pleased by the adoption of Salusbury, was more cordial than usual this summer. She was an amusing companion though her mother observed with disappointment that Cecy's mental powers had not increased with maturity. She was still a lightweight — her philosophy in general being that everything and everybody was ridiculous. She lacked Queeney's forceful character and general knowledge. Nevertheless, Cecy did have a talent which her elder sister lacked, an extraordinary artistic ability; she could do anything with her hands — draw, paint, bind books, even fashion shoes — and she had a flair for collecting things, any old thing, without discrimination. The effect she created was enchanting. She had made Segroit "a little Nutshell of a House," and "tricked out her Pleasure Ground" with great taste (Rylands 585.34).

During their holidays Cecilia made her boys come to Brynbella; Salusbury Mostyn (called by some "White Face" as opposed to "Black Face" John Salusbury) was sent to read with his grandmother, and Harry and Bertie tagged along. These boys were the tallest children for their respective ages (now eleven, ten, and eight) that she had ever seen, complete giants, particularly Salusbury, like "something at a fair." Unfortunately they were not handsome and more unfortunately they were not healthy. They were "old men," always sick; they had every possible childhood disease and constant colds. As for their intellect, Davies, the Streatham schoolmaster, told her that the boys were sharp and would do well in their studies except for the fact that they were constantly being distracted by their mother. Cecilia would

CECILIA THRALE MOSTYN

SEGROIT HALL

RESIDENCE OF THE MOSTYNS

WATERCOLOR

never leave them alone. "Mrs. Mostyn & Mr Davies live in a constant Quarrel" (Rylands 585.12).

Mrs. Piozzi reported one dreadful story to her nephew: that her grandson Salusbury and a schoolfellow at Streatham "sit up at Nights & drink 5 Bottles of Strong Ale when the Masters are asleep" (Rylands 585.31). She was grateful that next year the boy would be sent to Westminster, where she was confident he would be properly disciplined.

Mrs. Piozzi worried about all the young Mostyns, not only when they were in school, but when they were on holiday as well, for Cecilia would not let them stay in one place. She was forever taking them somewhere else — always taking Harry to the seaside. She wanted him to have a future in the Navy, and she was pestering Queeney and Admiral Keith to have him admitted to the Royal Navy College at Portsmouth.

Queeney was a good aunt, genuinely solicitous about her nephews' schooling, and about their health (often bringing them from Streatham to her house in Harley Street when they were ill). At the moment, however, her greatest concern was for herself as she was expecting a child at the end of the year. Cecilia, her mother commented, was selfishly praying that the baby would *not* be a boy.

As the time of confinement approached Mrs. Piozzi fretted about the dangers Queeney faced, having her first baby at forty-five. She offered many cautions by letter, and hoped to be asked to come to London at the time of the delivery, but Queeney had no more desire to have her mother with her than Cecilia had had.

Georgina Augusta Henrietta Elphinstone, a name to "fill up a letter," her grandmother commented, was born in her parents' Harley Street house on 12 December 1809. Her sponsors were His Royal Highness the Prince of Wales (whom Keith had served as secretary) and His Royal Highness the Duke of Clarence (who had once been an officer on Keith's ship the *Warwick*, and whom the Admiral had later served as treasurer) — two future Kings of England. Mrs. Piozzi was never considered as a sponsor, and she did not see this grand baby until the following April, after which meeting she recorded in her diary that Augusta, as she was called, was "very pretty indeed — like the Mother exactly" (Rylands 1810 Diary).

2.

Mrs. Piozzi regretted not having closer relations with her four grandchildren; she was no more intimate with them than with their parents. It had not mattered so long as there was Piozzi — her life with him was complete and happy. Even when he became ill, caring for him had given purpose to her existence, something every person craves. But now she was alone. None of her children or grandchildren gave any indication of needing her, nor any desire to share experiences, nor indeed to communicate with her at all — they were totally indifferent. The only relation who showed affection was John Salusbury, and he soon became the focus of her life. She began to concern herself deeply with his studies, which had now reached an interesting point. She checked on his progress, writing to him at Mr. Shephard's every few days: "My dearest Boy — my dearest Friend," "Son of my Soul," "Only Friend," "Dearest Angel," "My best Beloved," "Joy and Pride of my Heart," "I am thinking always of you and me." Her letters were full not only of affection, but also of advice on behavior, honor, and virtue, and the importance of studying hard (her heart was set upon Salusbury's going to Oxford). Her letters were also filled with corrections of his spelling, philosophic observations, puns, foreign phrases, discussions of her financial problems, and adult confidential gossip — hard going for Salusbury — and it was small wonder that his replies were always tardy.

For Mrs. Piozzi, the happiest event of 1811 was Salusbury's acceptance at Christ Church, Oxford; there he went in October. His aunt's pride, however, was short-lived for the young man was no scholar, despite Mr. Shephard's heroic efforts to make him one. Salusbury hated Oxford, and by the following spring, 1812, he was making a poor record and begging his aunt to let him come home. He wanted to live at Brynbella and to farm.

Mrs. Piozzi was sadly disappointed to have Salusbury's "fiery trial" at Oxford end in failure. It was humiliating to her pride. But, she rationalized, there were things she did not like about Oxford herself, and probably Salusbury was making a judicious decision. "Oxford is indeed a dreadful Place for Body, Soul and Purse," she wrote to him, and added, "glad at heart shall I be when you quit it" (Rylands 586.139). A little later she said, "You are the best of all wise Boys . . .

in wishing to leave Oxford, and come home with poor Aunt — to take Care of her" (Rylands 586.146). She imagined the happy times they would have together at Brynbella, and she promised that she would plan for his future.

She was not at first aware of the fact that the chief reason Salusbury wanted to settle down in Flintshire was that he was in love with Harriet Pemberton. He wanted to marry her and bring her to Brynbella. When Mrs. Piozzi realized this, she considered the matter philosophically. She did not know Harriet nor her parents, but the Pembertons were a good Shropshire family. Salusbury's chum, "Pem," had visited at both Brynbella and Bath. She was devoted to him and sure that his sister must be a fine person. In principle, it was a satisfactory match; the only drawback was Salusbury's age — he was only nineteen. When the lad, however, promised that he would not marry until he came of age, his aunt became wholly sympathetic.

Salusbury's love of Wales, his desire to live there and to raise a family, made a strong emotional appeal, and in time she decided to do something which was very foolish from her own point of view. When Salusbury became twenty-one she wished to give him all her Welsh property. She talked to Charles Shephard, her "dear Oracle" she now called him. (He had replaced Robert Ray as her legal adviser.) She wished to make a Revocation Deed, for her property was willed at present to Queeney. Shephard warned her that Queeney would resent being disinherited and also that such a large gift in Mrs. Piozzi's lifetime might well be impoverishing, for Streatham was a liability and she had only a little capital, a few investments, and a small income from Crowmarsh. Most of her income came from Wales. She would lose this and she would lose Brynbella. She had built this house to give her second husband a safe home for old age, and now, Shephard told her, she was giving up the same security for herself. He told her to think of King Lear. She did not wish to — she took a romantic pleasure in making a great sacrifice — she trusted her "best Beloved." She told Shephard to proceed with the Revocation Deed, and he drafted it for her.

He also drafted a new will, which she signed on 19 April 1813, bequeathing everything she possessed to John Salusbury, his heirs and assigns. Sir Walter James of Bath and Sir John Williams of Flintshire were her executors, and until Salusbury came of age (9 September 1814) they were to serve as his trustees and guardians. If Salusbury

should die before reaching his majority, her eldest grandson, John Salusbury Mostyn, was to become her sole heir. She did not wish to compli-
cate the will by adding special bequests; thus, on the same day she
signed it she wrote her nephew a letter specifying certain objects she
wished him to give to the Thrale daughters. She hoped that Lady
Keith could have the Zoffany portrait of Mrs. Salusbury, also the Reynolds of Henry Thrale, and the picture of her great-great uncle
Edmund Halsey "with a Dog." The Baskerville Bible, with the record
of family births and deaths, she would like Mrs. Mostyn to have;
Queeney's cabinet, the gift of Dr. Johnson, to Lady Keith, and "if refused, give it Mrs. Mostyn." (Why Queeney's present was not already hers is not clear.)

"Mrs. Mostyn likes any old odd Stuff of that Sort," the letter to
Salusbury continued, "& I think you don't care about it. You should
present her with the Chest at Brynbella . . . Thraliana should be
hers — or burned . . ." (Rylands 587.161). For Susan and Sophy no
specific objects were mentioned but Mrs. Piozzi hoped, if one of the
ladies wished, that she might have her earliest writing desk, inherited
from her grandmother, Philadelphia Lynch Cotton.

Salusbury was naturally agreeable to the requests and pleased by
what his aunt told him of her will. His life was altogether more enjoyable than it had been at Oxford. A date was set for his marriage to
Harriet Pemberton — 7 November — two months after his twenty-
first birthday.

For a year Mrs. Piozzi had been carrying on an animated correspondence with Salusbury's fiancée, and though they had still not met, she
had come to appreciate Harriet as a lovely, sensible young woman.
Mrs. Piozzi was confident that she and Salusbury would be happy and
that they would have a big family ("dear uncle" Piozzi had been one
of fourteen children).

Both Salusbury and the Pembertons were insistent that Mrs. Piozzi
come to Shropshire for the wedding, and she wanted very much to be
with the "son of her heart" — she had never been invited to a daughter's wedding — but now, alas, she could not afford the trip. Streatham was devouring her money. The place had become run-down and
the last tenant had gone bankrupt. When she had wanted to cut a little
timber on the grounds to pay for repairs (Charles Shephard advised
her to do this), her daughters, the eventual owners of Streatham, were
as incensed as she had once been at the thought of losing her trees at

JOHN SALUSBURY PIOZZI SALUSBURY
BY JACKSON

HARRIET PEMBERTON, LATER MARRIED TO JOHN SALUSBURY
ARTIST UNKNOWN

Bach-y-Graig. Even the trees close to the house, which were filling up the drain pipes and causing damage, they would not let her take down. Lady Keith and Mrs. Hoare made their husbands threaten legal action, and in the end Mrs. Piozzi was forced to pay almost all her capital — £6,500 — for fronting the house, fencing the whole 100 acres, repairing the unused stables, outbuildings, barns, and hothouses (on the last of which she paid a triple tax annually). She wrote to Harriet Pemberton on 13 August, begging to be "Let . . . off [her] Wedding Visit . . . [for] neither [her] Purse nor Person" (she was now seventy-three) could "bear the Journey" (Rylands 592.24). Salusbury refused to accept her excuses, and, as ever, he was able to wheedle his aunt into doing what he wished.

She came to Condover Park, loved the bride at first sight, and loved her family as well. At the wedding reception, she danced animatedly with Papa Pemberton and charmed everyone present.

3.

After this happy interlude, Mrs. Piozzi drove back to Bath and faced reality. Instead of the usual fine house on Pulteney Street or some other fashionable place, she took cheap lodgings at 17 New King Street — a miserable hole, but she was determined to economize. Sir Richard Colt Hoare (half-brother of Sophy's husband) found her there and was shocked by the poor accommodation. So was Mrs. John Perkins, widow of Thrale's one-time chief clerk.[1] Mrs. Piozzi said of the visit that her old acquaintance "behaved very prettily" but "great was her amazement indeed at my small apartments and contracted situation" (Broadley, p. 64). It was now Mrs. Perkins who had a fine house on Pulteney Street for the season.

So far as Mrs. Piozzi's social life was concerned, it made no difference where she lived; she had a legion of friends, eager to seek her out wherever she was. And in every gathering she found herself the center of attraction — she had never ceased to be a show child. All her life she had retained an innate sense of drama and her powers remained undiminished. She did not actually seem old. She had none of the disabilities associated with age — defective faculties and ill-temper. Her hearing was good, as was her eyesight (though she needed spectacles

---

[1] John Perkins had died in 1812, at eighty-two, struck down by a man on horseback at the Brighton races.

for reading). She was agile as a young girl, always "run, run, run" —
and she still loved to dance. She was animated, witty, and extremely
entertaining.[2] She was attractive in appearance, stylish in dress, straight
as a ramrod, diminutive, and trim in figure. She ate sparingly; she had
determined not to be fat and lose her looks as Sophy Hoare had.

Mentally, Mrs. Piozzi was more alert than most of the young, and
better informed about what was going on in the world. She had little
of the pessimism of old age — that the good days are past and the best
people dead; she was still passionately interested in the present and insatiably curious about the future. She had more enthusiasm for life than
any of her daughters except Cecilia — the others were pure Thrale.

A source of Mrs. Piozzi's strength, apart from her strong constitution, was her deep religious faith. This was a constant support, and so
was her confidence in her own judgment. She never suffered, as
Frances Reynolds had, from indecision; when an important issue arose,
she acted impulsively, and if her decision turned out to be wrong, she
accepted the consequences with good humor and made another decision. She never lost her resourcefulness nor her hope that things would
soon be better. She was a romantic and a realist as well — one with a
sense of humor. All these qualities helped her to handle difficult problems. And two other qualities were also useful, her extraordinary
capacity to keep herself amused (she was never bored) and her unique
power to make substitutions. If she lost an important person in her
life, she immediately found someone else to fill the void.

After Piozzi's death Salusbury had been the person who needed her
and to whom she devoted herself. But when he married she quite
properly relinquished her possessive hold and established a new relationship in which Salusbury and Harriet shared her affection. Harriet liked
her aunt and was not only affectionate but attentive. She wrote to her
often and performed many labors of love, one of which was to paint
a watercolor of Brynbella (Rylands 588.248). This, Mrs. Piozzi framed
and hung on the parlor wall, showing it to all visitors. She loved her
Salusburys and was extremely proud of them, but she made no attempt
to interweave her life with theirs. They were too far away — independent, and self-sufficient.

She accepted this fact and turned elsewhere to make an agreeable

[2] Very different from her one-time intimate, Fanny Cotton, widow of her cousin
Robert. Fanny now lived in Bath and was civil enough at last but she was sick and
looked a hundred years old (Rylands 585.55).

BRYNBELLA

WATERCOLOR BY HARRIET SALUSBURY

new life for herself (an impossibility for most lone ladies in their seventies but not difficult for Mrs. Piozzi). She busied herself by writing a new book. Work absorbed much of her time, and her large circle of friends provided the audience, the caressing attention, the flattery and sympathy which she required. For the close and affectionate relationship, the sentimental friendship that was also required, she chose two persons from her circle of admirers. They were much younger than she, but very willing friends nevertheless, for though Mrs. Piozzi was incapable of gaining the affection of her own children (who stood in constant dread of what their competitive, undignified, un-dying mother would do next to embarrass them) she was always able to attract the friendship and confidences of contemporaries of her children, men and women who had no responsibility for her actions. They found her captivating — a blithe spirit — seemingly immortal.

Her first "cavalier" was Edward Mangin, whom she met in 1815, an Oxford man, later ordained in the Irish Church, a miscellaneous writer, a charming widower of means (forty-three, a year younger than Sophy). Mangin was well-read, a fascinating conversationalist, and clever at impromptu verses (a number of these Mrs. Piozzi copied into her *Commonplace Book*, which had now replaced the completed volumes of *Thraliana*).

Mangin took a kind interest in a manuscript which she had ready for a publisher — if one could be found. *Lyford Redivivus, or a Grandame's Garrulity*, Mrs. Piozzi called her book. It was a sort of dictionary — some thousand proper names for men and women — derivations, anecdotes, biographical notes on famous bearers of the names, quotations in Italian, French, Latin, Greek, Hebrew, Celtic, and Saxon.[3] The idea was interesting but the text was complicated, ostentatious, and dull. The printing of *Lyford Redivivus* was constantly discussed by Mangin, but what he really enjoyed were the stories Mrs. Piozzi told of her past life and her close association with Johnson and the Streatham Circle. (Some twenty years later Mangin was to publish his recollections in *Piozziana*, the first book to be written about her.) She had, he said, given him "so many delicious hours of life" (Mangin, p. 163).

Her other cavalier Mrs. Piozzi had also met at the beginning of 1815, Sir James Fellowes, just retired as a Naval doctor, forty-four, exactly

---

[3] This was suggested by a seventeenth century volume, Edward Lyford's *True Interpretation and Etymologie of Christian Names*.

Sophy's age. Sir James came from a venerable Army and Navy family. He had attended Cambridge, where he had also received his medical degree. He had seen service in Santo Domingo, Cadiz, and Gibraltar. His treatment of yellow fever in these places had saved many lives, and he had been knighted in 1809 for his excellent service. Sir James was not only a good doctor, but an extremely cultivated man, a linguist and a raconteur — an enchanting companion. Like Mangin, he took an interest in trying to find a publisher for *Lyford Redivivus* (neither of them succeeded and this ponderous effort is still in manuscript only). Also like Mangin, Fellowes delighted in Mrs. Piozzi's stories of her past literary life. He became deeply attached to her.

Soon they were seeing each other daily, and if separated they wrote letters. She annotated copies of her books, wrote him a short biographical sketch of her life, and when he asked for her picture, had Roche, a talented artist, paint a miniature for him. Sir James was very proud of his little portrait, and all her friends "adored" it.

She discussed her financial embarrassments with Sir James at length; he was sympathetic and gave good counsel. She discussed the problems of her will with him. She wished to give everything to Salusbury and his heirs, but was worried about her most recent will, made in 1814, while visiting the Pembertons at Condover Park, at the time of Salusbury's marriage. He and his father-in-law were the executors. Now she felt that this might give the appearance of undue influence (Rylands 588.256). She asked Fellowes if he would serve as co-executor with John Salusbury. Fellowes agreed and a new will was drawn in Bath, and signed on 9 March 1816. (This was the will which was to prevail.)

Mrs. Piozzi told Fellowes that her greatest problem at the moment was what to do with Streatham Park.[4] Count Lieven, the Russian Ambassador, had taken the beautifully renovated house for three years at

---

[4] Mr. Giles, who had taken the house in 1801 at £500 per annum (with the Piozzis paying the taxes), was a good enough tenant, despite his vulgarity and the fact that everyone in the house was drunk every night, but he gave up his lease in 1807, unwilling to pay an increased rent to offset higher taxes.

Mr. Abram Atkins agreed to take the house for seven years at a rent of £500 and pay all the taxes except the property tax (*Thraliana*, p. 1013, n. 1). At the end of this time there was so much dilapidation that Mrs. Piozzi had had to undertake extensive repairs.

After these had been made, she thought all would be well, when the distinguished Count Lieven leased the house.

£600 per annum (*Thraliana*, p. 1013, n. 1), but he was an impossible tenant. He had broken a great deal of furniture and his coach had torn the coach-house to pieces. He was in financial trouble, had not paid his rent — and wished to cancel his lease. He had put in a sub-tenant, a Mr. Anderdon, once an apothecary, a rich man, but crude. Anderdon said in June 1815 that he was willing to take the house himself on a three-year lease at £450 a year. Mrs. Piozzi finally said she would accept this reduced rent if he would pay taxes, tithes, and dilapidations, the responsibilities which were ruining her. Anderdon said he would pay the taxes, but he would have nothing to do with the tithes; these came to £100 a year and the present rector of St. Leonard's, the Reverend Mr. Hill, was threatening to take the haystack (Rylands 587.210). Anderdon also refused to assume any responsibility for dilapidation, the most burdensome charge, particularly in his case, for Mrs. Anderdon was a second wife, with a raft of young children. Mrs. Piozzi's best bedchamber (Johnson's old room) was being used for the nursery, and her dressing room for the children's eating place. Her mother's needlework carpet had been badly damaged (Rylands 588.283); and in all their bedrooms her nice mattresses had been ruined by Mr. Anderdon's little babies and her walls defaced by the bigger babies (Rylands 588.292). Alexander Leak, her loyal steward, felt so strongly about the Anderdons that he threatened to leave if they took over as tenants in their own right.

The whole history of leasing Streatham had been a disaster, and Mrs. Piozzi now made a desperate last effort to persuade the Keiths or the Hoares to purchase the property for £6,000. She had heard reports, but nothing directly, that both Queeney and Sophy were interested in having the house. Though seventy-four and not feeling well, Mrs. Piozzi came to London in July 1815 and took a room at Blake's Hotel. The day after her arrival she went to see Sophy at York Place. Sophy was out of town, but she found Merrik alone at dinner. She stayed with him for two hours, pleading for Streatham. Merrik was not responsive, but he was civil, and at the end of the interview he walked his mother-in-law back to Blake's. The "Bargain" of Streatham, he told her, was "so good a one that if *he* had the Money He would purchase immediately" (Rylands 588.278), but he did not have the money and all he could do was write to Lord Keith, who was at Plymouth. It is understandable that the Admiral had little time to be concerned about Streatham. His business in Plymouth was to dispatch Napoleon to St. Helena.[5]

By the end of July Mrs. Piozzi received her letter of refusal from Keith, "cold, civil, and steady" (Rylands 588.281). He had no interest in Streatham. Now, with final victory over his great enemy, the Admiral was retiring from the Royal Navy. The Keiths would live henceforth in Scotland, where he wished to develop his vast estate of Tullyallan (he was soon to employ the fashionable country-house architect, William Atkinson, to build a Gothic castle).[6] Keith no longer wished to own properties south of the Tweed; he planned to sell everything in England.

With flat refusals from the Hoares and Keiths (the other daughters did not have enough money to be considered) Mrs. Piozzi realized that nothing could be done except to auction what belonged to her, that is to say, the contents of Streatham Park, and then to sell her life interest in the property. Fellowes agreed with this decision and helped her with the depressing task of making arrangements for the auction at the place where she had been "queen and mistress" in splendor for over fifty years.

During the course of their talks, Fellowes revealed the fact that he was going to be married in March, to Elizabeth James of Adbury House, near Newbury. Mrs. Piozzi's reaction to her cavalier's announcement that he was going to marry a pretty heiress was characteristic. She accepted her own great loss with grace and proceeded to involve herself in the romance.

She insisted that Streatham Park serve one last happy purpose, that Fellowes and his bride spend their honeymoon there. This was not a good idea financially, for having inhabitants in the house meant extra taxes. But romance prevailed. The Felloweses came to Streatham with their complaining servants (who did a great deal of damage). Mrs.

---

[5] Since 1812 Keith had been Commander-in-Chief of the Channel Fleet, and in June of 1815, even before receiving news of Napoleon's defeat at Waterloo, he had drawn a line of his cruisers along the French coasts.

On 15 July 1815 Napoleon boarded the *Bellerophon*, hoping he would be allowed to go to America. The ship proceeded, however, to Plymouth, and there Admiral Keith, representing the Government, informed General Bonaparte that he was being sent to St. Helena.

[6] Atkinson, who excelled in the baronial style, had already built a number of Gothic houses, including Scone Castle in Perthshire for the Earl of Mansfield, and Rosebery in Midlothian for the Earl of Rosebery — and after Tullyallan, among many other commissions, he was to complete Abbotsford for Sir Walter Scott.

Piozzi visited, and she and the bride and groom worked on the sale catalogue. There was constant trouble with Leak, the steward, who felt the Felloweses were too demanding, and they in turn endured hardships which should not be part of a honeymoon. Despite all these trials, however, the friendship of the Felloweses and Mrs. Piozzi survived.

Before the sale there was of course an exhibition, and crowds of fashionable people came to examine the lots to be sold. Mrs. Piozzi stayed away from the scene, in Bath, but there she gathered as much news as she could. She heard that Merrik and Sophy Hoare were "in the croud every day; Lord and Lady Keith occasionally!!!" (Rylands 589.322). The sale began on 8 May and continued through the 13th; £3,921/7 was realized, nearly half this amount coming from the famous Reynolds portraits in the library, only two of which Mrs. Piozzi had held back, the pictures of her first husband, Thrale, and of Murphy, faithful friend through both her marriages. Her "life interest" in Streatham was sold after the auction to a Mr. Elliott, a rope-maker, who contracted to pay her £260 a year, as long as she lived, for the bare house and grounds. Elliott was to assume the responsibility for taxes, tithes, and dilapidations — at last she was free of these terrible burdens. But the entire amount realized from the sale was little more than half of the money that Mrs. Piozzi had put into the renovation of the place only two years earlier.

4.

She was grateful, nonetheless, to have anything for herself, free and clear, and it was enough to settle her debts and to take on a small, pretty house in Bath, 8 Gay Street (designed by a well-known architect, the senior John Wood). While her new house was being painted and decorated she took the opportunity to make a visit to her family in Wales. This she had been promising to do since the time of Salusbury's wedding.

There were two babies at Brynbella now, the first having been born on 25 August 1815. In the spring of that year, when Harriet had written that they were expecting a child, Mrs. Piozzi had suggested "Hester Maria," her mother's name (if it should be a girl), and her choice had been accepted. Mrs. Piozzi was asked to join the Pembertons as godparents. To share in naming a child, to have a part namesake, and to be a godparent were honors no Thrale daughter had bestowed.

The second baby, Angelina, had been born on 27 July 1816. Mrs. Piozzi found both little girls adorable. She thought that Hester Maria ("Missey," as she was called) would be "brighter" but tiny Angelina would be the beauty — her resemblance to her father she found charming (Rylands 592.45, 49). In every way the visit began well. Salusbury seemed delighted to see his aunt, and Harriet enjoyed her Bath chit-chat. Cecilia sent an invitation to come to Segroit. The grounds were beautiful now, and Mrs. Piozzi was pleased to find that her tall grandsons had become quite handsome. But she was saddened by the fact that Cecilia was letting the house and going abroad — by autumn Cecy would be in Switzerland.

As the days passed in the Vale of Clwyd, Mrs. Piozzi became more and more depressed. The weather was abominable and her house, Brynbella, was no longer pretty and well-kept. It was not even comfortable, and Salusbury's poor management was visible everywhere on the farm. She wrote in her diary: "the Hay spoil'd — or else *uncut. No* Newspapers, & *no* Company: *no* Books, and *no* Conversation. Sun never shines." [7]

However, despite depression and discomfort, Mrs. Piozzi was tactful and put on a cheerful front. After all, the Salusburys were happy and they were young and she reasoned that in time things would be better.

There was hope for Brynbella, but the fate of her old family house nearby, Bach-y-Graig, seemed hopeless. It was in a miserable state (after all the money Piozzi had put into its repair in 1800); and Salusbury was cutting timber on the property. The condition of "Poor Llewenny" was even more distressing. Lord Kirkwall, Cecilia's childhood friend, had inherited the place at fifteen and at twenty-four (1802) had married Anna Maria, the lovely eldest daughter of Lord de Blaguiere. Next year the Kirkwalls had had a son, and the birth of other children followed — the great house seemed in strong hands — but what had begun so well was ending tragically. Kirkwall had separated from his wife and was about to divorce her. He had sold Llewenny (1810) to the Reverend Mr. Edward Hughes of Kinmel, owner of the Parys copper mine in Anglesey, and Hughes had "pulled down the venerable mansion built 1000 years ago." Mrs. Piozzi's "heart bled to see its ruin . . ." (Mangin, p. 29). [8]

[7] Diary, 1816, in possession of James L. Clifford.
[8] The property, now spelled "Lleweni," was bought in the late nineteenth century by Mr. Jack Watson Hughes (no relation to the Hughes of Kinmel). It was sold

When Mrs. Piozzi came home to Bath, she sent presents to Missey and Angelina and gave friends a full account of her Brynbella stay. The Salusburys promised a return visit to Gay Street in March, and she eagerly anticipated the opportunity of introducing them to her circle. A new member had recently been added to this, for in July Edward Mangin (after being a widower for fifteen years) had taken a new wife, Mary Nangreave. Mrs. Piozzi thus lost her second cavalier, her "Patron" as she often called him. Mangin had not been as close or as important to her as Fellowes, still he had been a source of constant strength and entertainment. She responded to Mangin's marriage in the same good-natured way that she had to Fellowes' — she took delightful Mary Mangin to her heart, and Mary, like Elizabeth Fellowes before her, became a devoted friend.

In the summer of the next year (1817) the Mangins went to Ireland for an extended stay. They took with them a Roche miniature of Mrs. Piozzi, a copy of one the artist had painted earlier for Fellowes. This was to be their "substitute for sunshine" on the journey, Mangin said. Mrs. Piozzi urged the Mangins to visit Brynbella on their way to Dublin and she wrote to Salusbury asking him to be sure to show them the portrait of her ancestress, Catherine of Berayne, and also the "Pedigree" of the Salusbury family which she had painstakingly written out for her heir.

On 4 March, several months before the Mangins left Bath, Mrs. Piozzi had dined at the house of George Gibbes, her favorite doctor (he was a literary charmer as well), an Oxford graduate and a fellow of the Royal College of Physicians. While at Gibbes's house, one of her servants arrived and called her back to Gay Street; Salusbury had appeared without warning. She hurried back to her house, and there she learned to her disappointment that the long-anticipated family visit this month was not going to take place. Though he did not say in so many words, it was clear that Salusbury did not wish his wife to be spoiled by the social pleasures of Bath. He had come now only because he had urgent personal business to discuss. He had been made High Sheriff for Flintshire and was to carry an address from his county. With "proper consideration" he would be knighted. Mrs. Piozzi's diary for 5 March records, "Gave Salusbury £200 — he went away directly" (Rylands 1817 Diary). Salusbury came back on 17 April, and again

by him in 1947 to Mr. Reginald Field Glazebrook, and is now (1975) part of Mr. Glazebrook's large farm.

on 24 April — at which time she noted in the journal, "Sir John Salusbury returned."

His aunt hoped that the knighthood could be made an hereditary baronetcy by a further "consideration," so his "Boys at College would know who they belonged to, and the Girls would walk in and out of a Room with a more determined Step" (Rylands 589.355). She endeavored to see how things could be arranged and, through a Mr. Cathron of the College of Heralds, she discovered that 5,000 guineas was probably the necessary payment. Unfortunately, this was more than she could afford, but during the summer Cathron wrote that 3,000 guineas might possibly be sufficient. Negotiations were under way by the autumn, but in November the tragic death (in childbirth) of Charlotte, only daughter of the Prince of Wales, forced a postponement of all such business.

Apart from the abrupt calls of Salusbury, there were no visits from other members of Mrs. Piozzi's family, though she received a few letters from them, and learned through Bath gossip of important events, such as the fact that Queeney's step-daughter, Mercer Elphinstone (almost thirty), was determined to marry "a Monsieur God knows Who: one of Bounaparte's ferocious Officers . . . it will deeply grieve the old Admiral" (Rylands 589.360). This was the Comte de Flahault ("pronounced 'flow' "), some ten years Mercer's senior. Mrs. Piozzi wrote to Salusbury that "It would be hard to find . . . a Man more cruelly mortified than Lord Keith. His Title & his first Wife's splendid Fortune devoted to enrich & to ennoble an Enemy of the King & Country he has been serving for ½ a Century — the Bastard of Tallyrand, the Aid de Camp of Bounaparte" (Rylands 589.367). To Harriet Salusbury, she wrote that it was a "national calamity." [9]

---

[9] In July 1817 Admiral Keith wrote a Deed of Trust together with a will (which was to prevail). The marriage of his daughter Mercer to Count Flahault, he wrote, was "most repugnant to my wishes, and I am convinced to her true interest, as I previously repeatedly intimated and declared to her in the most explicit terms . . . I am now fully resolved and determined . . . she shall be excluded from all interest in or benefit from my Estates . . . her children only, shall be allowed to succeed" (p. 54). And the Flahault children were to succeed only if their father and grandfather were barred from any connection with management, administration, or counseling, and also, reiterated many times, only if they were Protestant, educated in the United Kingdom, and under no allegiance to any foreign power (Admiral Keith's Deed of Trust, Scottish Record Office, Edinburgh).

Admiral Keith's enmity toward his son-in-law was understandable, but his daughter's love for Comte Flahault was also understandable. He was a cultivated

As for less world-shaking family news: Susan and Sophy had made a trip to Paris. Where Cecilia was, her mother wished she knew — Cecy had been living abroad for more than a year. Her eldest and youngest sons, Salusbury and Bertie, had been sent to Westminster in 1810. Salusbury had done well in his studies but Bertie was the lowest boy but three in his form. Mrs. Piozzi was half ashamed at this and distressed by the lack of discipline in the school. She had expected a great deal on that score, but both boys had been allowed far too much freedom, had done wicked things, and run up shocking debts, "such is the Credit given to Babies" (Rylands 587.228). With guidance from Admiral Keith, Salusbury was sent "to finish his Studies in Edinburgh, where less Money will be spent, and more Literature gained, and more Vice avoided — than in the heart of London . . ." (Rylands 587. 223). His grandmother still fancied that "the eldest Mostyn will be something of a Scholar, & the other two good Officer-like Fellows: — I hope so" (Rylands 588.290). By 1817 Salusbury was a Lieutenant in the East India Service in Bengal.

Harry was the favorite of his uncle and through Admiral Keith's influence he was sent to the Royal Naval College at Portsmouth. He was a student there from 1813 to 1816 and made a fine record, winning five coveted prizes — a good omen for the future.

At the beginning of 1814, Admiral Keith had placed Harry's younger brother, Bertie, in the hands of his friend, Captain Nash, aboard the *Saturn*, a 74-gun man-of-war. "Lord Keith's Kindness is *unbounded*," Mrs. Piozzi wrote to her nephew (Rylands 587.205). He had sent Bertie on "a 3 Year's Cruize to seek a sight [of] these fierce Americans . . ." "Rough Service for such a Youngling" (Rylands 587.216). Bertie was only twelve.

Rough service indeed, for the *Saturn* was a fighting ship engaged in the War of 1812. Hostilities between Britain and the United States had begun on 1 June of that year and the violence of the conflict was steadily increasing. The *Saturn*'s orders were to intercept all American shipping along the Atlantic seaboard from Block Island to Cape May. With her superior power, it was not difficult for the *Saturn* to pursue and to capture any vessel she encountered. Nash would confiscate the cargo and then, if he did not fire the ship, would commandeer it, dis-

---

man (educated by Edmund Burke, Mrs. Piozzi noted in her *Commonplace Book* under "Mrs Grant"). The Comte was charming and he was able. Under the Second Empire he served as the French Ambassador to the Court of St. James's.

patching the vessel, now under the command of his officers, to the British base at Halifax. Bertie's sight of "fierce Americans" was limited to that of the prisoners he saw aboard the *Saturn* or on the prize ships.

Obviously the *Saturn* never entered an American port, so it cannot be claimed that a grandson of Mrs. Piozzi visited the United States, but Bertie viewed the country's shores from close range as his ship lay at anchor off such places as Block Island, Fishers Island, New London, New Haven, Gardiners Bay, Montauk Point, Sandy Hook, and Cape May. And in November 1814 Bertie was able to visit the part of North America which had close association with his great-grandfather, John Salusbury, because for over a month, from 10 November to 15 December, the *Saturn* was moored in Halifax Harbor.[10]

On Christmas Eve 1814, peace came with the Treaty of Ghent, and the length of time originally set for Captain Nash's cruise was shortened. The *Saturn* was back in Plymouth by the end of March 1815. Bertie came through the rigors of his voyage very well. He was fortunate, for during the past September another ship's boy, William Dodge, had been "committed to the deep."

Bertie's brother, Harry Mostyn, received a signal honor in February 1816; he was chosen as one of the Portsmouth midshipmen to accompany Lord Amherst and his embassy to China aboard Captain Murray Maxwell's *Alceste*. Lord Amherst and his delegation were being sent on a mission to the Emperor of China to present a list of grievances, wrongs which British subjects were suffering under his rule. Mrs. Piozzi was proud of Harry's connection with the mission, "a most desirable advantage certainly; & will be of lasting Benefit . . ." (Rylands 588.305).

The first part of February 1816 the *Alceste* left England and in Madeira, at Funchal, the party found the *Phaeton* with Sir Hudson and Lady Lowe aboard. Lowe was bound for St. Helena to be Napoleon's new guardian.

At the beginning of March, the *Alceste* crossed the equator, and by the 21st reached Rio de Janeiro. The ship proceeded around the Cape of Good Hope, into the Indian Ocean and on to Java, thence to Hong Kong and through the straits of Formosa. Captain Maxwell cast anchor at the mouth of the Hai River on 28 July. At this point Lord Amherst and his embassy left the ship and, carrying their gifts, proceeded by land for their meeting with the Emperor.

[10] The log of HMS *Saturn* is in the Public Record Office in London.

Lord Amherst and his mission did not fare well. Amherst refused to "kow-tow" to the Emperor (to strike his forehead nine times on the ground before approaching). Thus he never had an audience with the Emperor. The expedition was a failure. The *Alceste* set sail for home.

Mrs. Piozzi was indignant when she heard of the total waste of time and money. "By non-Compliance with the Rules of the Court" Lord Amherst "will subject us to drink *coarse* Tea, I suppose, & pay a *fine* Price for it — You might just as well insist on shaking hands with the Regent . . ." (Rylands 589.359). This letter to her nephew Salusbury was written in March 1817, and already complete disaster had overtaken the expedition — on 18 February 1817. But it was not until July (it took news this long to travel) that the dreadful report reached England of the wreck of the *Alceste*. In the Straits of Gaspar, off Sumatra, the ship had struck on an uncharted reef.

Captain Maxwell was able almost at once to dispatch Lord Amherst and his embassy on the ship's barge to Java, but it was nineteen days before anyone returned to help those who had remained behind. These men had managed to reach the closest land, but it was a marshy island, without fresh water, and infested with ants, scorpions, and snakes. They had been able to salvage some stores from the mastless *Alceste* when the tide was low. But soon Malays came to plunder the ship, and they were followed by Battas, cannibals, who pillaged further and then burned the wreck.[11]

Mrs. Piozzi was sure that Harry Mostyn was dead, and she wrote to Harriet Salusbury, "my Heart is bleeding for that little presumptuous Puss Cecilia Mostyn . . . & to know nothing of her, where She is, or how She bears the news" (Rylands 593.67). In August old Davies, the Streatham schoolteacher, was able to tell Mrs. Piozzi that Harry was not lost; the lad was safe and in England, though he had never thought of informing his grandmother of the fact. Captain Maxwell had not lost a man in the shipwreck.

In October Cecilia asked Admiral Keith if Harry could be ordered to Leghorn so that she might see him. And Harry came, just as she hoped he would.

---

[11] See *Narrative of a Voyage in his Majesty's Late Ship Alceste* . . . by John M'Leod, ship's surgeon (London: John Murray, 1817); also the 1817 log of the *Alceste* in the Public Record Office, London.

5.

Mrs. Piozzi, despite her concern for Harry during this year, did not forget the Salusburys in Wales, and at Christmastime she made up her box for Brynbella: "2 Babies Dresses, 4 lb. of fine Tea, 2 Shawls and my own miniature" (Rylands 1817 Diary, 23 December). This miniature was the second copy of Fellowes' portrait, for "dear Lady Salusbury" who had "fallen in love with the likeness."

Early in January 1818 the joyful announcement came, which Mrs. Piozzi had been awaiting for three years: the Salusburys had a son, John Owen, born on 7 January 1818. Mrs. Piozzi was asked to be the boy's godmother, and the Salusburys wrote that the christening would be postponed until July, the best time for her to travel. She accepted the invitation with pleasure and promptly bought a christening robe and cap for Owen.

During the spring of 1818 Mrs. Piozzi received word from a friend that Harry Mostyn was still with his mother in the Mediterranean — and that Salusbury Mostyn was with her as well. By June Mrs. Piozzi imagined that Cecilia must be in Naples. Queeney and Sophy wrote that their husbands were unwell, and Harriet complained of Salusbury's health. He was greatly depressed — much fatigued "from Race Balls, late Dinners etc." (Rylands 593.91). It was hard for his aunt to understand how any able-bodied man of twenty-five, with a splendid wife and three adorable babies, including a fine, healthy heir, could possibly be depressed.

When summer came, Mrs. Piozzi was true to her word. Though seventy-seven years old, she did not hesitate to make another journey to Brynbella and there she stayed for six weeks (it was to be her last visit). The christening of John Owen, in the fine robe and cap she had given him, took place on 25 July, the thirty-fourth anniversary of her marriage to Salusbury's "dear uncle." It was a joyous day, and as a remembrance, she was given a lock of Owen's hair for a ring, which she promised "shall never come off my Finger" (Rylands 592.96). She felt well loved by the Salusburys; and all members big and small were affectionate with each other. A happy family was everything, she felt, and this consoled her somewhat about Brynbella. Her lovely house was in even more shocking condition than it had been two years before. Salusbury had not improved as a manager. Nothing on the estate was maintained, and much more timber had been cut. On 19 August, Mrs. Piozzi wrote in her diary:

We walked to poor old [Bach-y-Graig] . . . I felt low spirited — but the Children took up my attention and diverted Melancholy Thoughts. The wood is gone, but young trees are growing.

Next day was Missey's birthday, "3 years old; company to dinner 14 people sat down — a very cheerful Day." One night while she was at Brynbella Mrs. Piozzi "looked out poor old Thraliana, could not sleep . . ." (Rylands 1818 Diary, 28 August).

In September Mrs. Piozzi returned to Bath and was relieved to be comfortable again. She appreciated the amenities which this town offered. Edward Mangin had once described them as "good pavement, frippery shops, adulation, curative springs, Doctors divine & medical . . ." (Rylands 595.9). Four months later glad tidings again arrived from Brynbella: a second Salusbury son had been born, Thomas Henry, on 26 January 1819, one day before Mrs. Piozzi's seventy-eighth birthday.

For the third time she was asked to be godmother (her record was becoming almost as constant as Mrs. Salusbury's had been). She was happy to accept, but made it clear that she could not consider an excursion to Wales this year, even if Tom's christening could be postponed until summer. She was saving money for a special purpose, and was determined to content herself with pleasures close at hand.

Letters were her only tie with friends and family who were far away. Cecilia's reports from Italy were particularly welcome. They were frequent, lively, and amusing. Cecilia was the only daughter who had inherited her mother's talent for letter-writing. Her long account of a visit with the Giambattista Piozzis in Brescia was especially entertaining; how she had made everyone laugh by saying that not one Piozzi in Italy was as handsome as Salusbury. (Her hostile attitude was softening with time.) Giambattista adored Cecy, and she promised to visit his family again (Rylands 593.112, 120).

In October Mrs. Piozzi read in the newspaper that Susan (now forty-nine) and in "decaying health" was at Malvern, some fifty miles distant, trying the waters. Her mother was disappointed that Susan had not considered coming to Bath instead where they could have had a visit. These waters, she thought, were superior and the counsel of Dr. Gibbes could not be matched (he attended the royal family when they were in town). But Susan avoided her mother, and Mrs. Piozzi accepted the neglect without complaint.

News came during this month that Cecilia was in Florence, "making good sport of her Cavaliere Servente, the Marchese (sic) Garzoni" (Pennington, p. 279). It was Garzoni who had written a proposal of marriage to Cecilia in 1795, after he returned from London to Florence, not realizing that she had eloped with John Mostyn. Mrs. Piozzi had commented when the letter arrived, "a Goose Cap! . . . had he spoke a Year ago [before he left], 'tis Odds but he might have succeeded: — What a Mercy 'tis that he did *not*!" (*Thraliana*, p. 938, n. 6).

Cecilia was obviously enjoying life abroad, and her mother wondered if she would ever come home, surely not by 27 January of the next year. That was the all-important date in Mrs. Piozzi's mind at the moment, and she wished that every member of her family could be with her on that day. For over a year she had been living as frugally as possible because she was determined to celebrate her eightieth birthday with fanfare (actually 27 January 1820 would be her seventy-ninth birthday, her eightieth year, but that was the way she and Johnson and others figured their age). Throughout her life, she had marked significant occasions with parties, and this time she intended to make a proper farewell bow. She planned to give a fête — a combined concert, banquet, and ball. Her friend, Mrs. Pennington, feared that such a celebration would be enormously expensive if held in Bath, and she and Mr. Pennington were sure that it could be given for much less where they lived, in Clifton, which was only fifteen miles away. A similar party had been given there recently, she wrote, "*very handsomely*, at half a Guinea per head, *wine included*: for after all there is very little drank at a Supper where women are the half, or larger proportion of the company" (Pennington, p. 297). Mrs. Piozzi did not listen to this advice. Bath was her spiritual home, and she was determined to have her final triumph there, regardless of cost. Also, she rationalized, the fête was not entirely self-indulgence for it would benefit Salusbury as well. Her friends would come to know and appreciate her nephew, and Sir John's welfare was "really very near [her] heart" (Pennington, p. 291).

Preparations for the party went on throughout the year 1819. Many of her friends were helping with the plans — the Felloweses, as might be expected, and also the Mangins, now home from Ireland. The Salusburys agreed to come, and Susanna Thrale and Sophia Hoare "prom-

ised *their* Attendance" (Rylands 590.450). The Keiths declined —
and no grandchildren showed interest.

The time came for the fête. Sir John and Lady Salusbury arrived a
few days early, and Mrs. Piozzi saw to it that they met William Augustus Conway. He had become her new cavalier, "Chevalier," the title
this time. Conway was a handsome giant, star of this year's Bath theatre
season — only four years older than Salusbury, over whom he towered.
Conway had elegance and grace, fine manners and a captivating voice.
His conversation was informed and entertaining, and his attention to
Mrs. Piozzi was tender. (She had had a lovely miniature of herself
painted for him by Jagger, a Bath artist.) Conway came to dine with the
Salusburys and they saw him play Mark Antony. Harriet thought the
actor superb in beauty, voice, and action, but Salusbury did not care for
him at all.

On Thursday, 27 January 1820,[12] Mrs. Piozzi's birthday fête took
place in the Lower Assembly Rooms at Bath. More than six hundred
guests attended: they began to arrive at nine o'clock, the concert commenced at ten sharp, and was followed at midnight by a sumptuous
banquet.

At this there was a head table for three persons only: Mrs. Piozzi,
with a renowned British admiral on either side (both outranking the
absent Keith). At two in the morning the ball began. Mrs. Piozzi, in
an elaborate white dress, with a white plumed headdress (the only time
she had not worn black since Piozzi's death), led off with Sir John
Salusbury, and as Mangin remarked, she danced with "astonishing elas-
ticity." After formal dances there were quadrilles and country dances
which continued until five in the morning. Yet, by ten o'clock, Mrs.
Piozzi was up again, receiving calls in the Gay Street house, "mirthful
and witty as usual" (Pennington, p. 299).[13]

At the ball and at every other occasion during his visit Salusbury
had a chance to see that his aunt was a beloved celebrity; it chagrined
him to discover how large a circle of admirers she had, and he could not
help showing jealousy. He complained to Mrs. Pennington at the ball

---

[12] The date of Mrs. Piozzi's birthday was fortunate, for two days later King
George III died, and had this event taken place earlier, there would have been
national mourning and no party.

[13] Salusbury's old tutor, Charles Shephard, read about the fête in the newspapers and
wrote a letter of congratulation to his "favourite Lady." He had gone to the West
Indies in 1814 and was now the Honorable Charles Shephard, Chief Justice of the
Island of St. Vincent (Pennington, pp. 319–320).

MRS. PIOZZI AT HER EIGHTIETH BIRTHDAY FETE
AFTER HOPWOOD, ENGRAVED BY THOMSON

WILLIAM AUGUSTUS CONWAY AS HENRY V, 1814
BY DE WILDE

about his aunt's "*increased* acquaintance," to which she complacently replied that "[*her*] claims in that line were prior to his own" (Pennington, p. 303). He disliked Mrs. Pennington, some ten years younger than his aunt; and he disliked a Miss Willoughby even more, an outspoken woman, young enough to be Mrs. Piozzi's daughter, high-spirited and independent (she had thrown over a suitor, Captain Vollopra, a few months before). Miss Willoughby was a bad influence altogether, with advanced ideas and radical political opinions (she was a natural daughter of Charles James Fox).[14] As for Conway, the actor, Salusbury resented his gallantries and the obvious affection he showed for Mrs. Piozzi — the fact that many other ladies in Bath, including Mrs. Pennington and Miss Anne Fellowes, Sir James's sister, seemed infatuated, did not lessen his aversion. He hated Conway and so did Miss Willoughby. It was their single point of agreement.

For his part, Conway was devoted to Mrs. Piozzi, and he was enjoying her literary reminiscences as much as Fellowes and Mangin had before him. And like them, he had made her his confidante in matters of the heart. He had been jilted by a young lady in Bath, and Mrs. Piozzi was advising her Chevalier and consoling him as well. So was Mrs. Pennington. We "are, alas! something fallen into 'the sere and yellow leaf,' and cannot cope with these summer blossoms," Mrs. Pennington wrote to Mrs. Piozzi. "If however not downright *scarecrows* to the young, 'the beautiful, and brave,' we may at least be useful land-marks and monitors, if they will permit us" (Pennington, p. 292).

Mrs. Piozzi's attachment to Conway was inspiriting, effusive, and somewhat silly — but platonic, a fact of which John Salusbury, with the scorn of youth, was fully aware. This did not prevent him from feeling indignant. He resented Conway far more than her two earlier cavaliers, and one strong reason for this was his anxiety that he might lose some of his inheritance. Conway was poor, in contrast to Fellowes and Mangin, who were well-off.

Salusbury had a miserable time in Bath, worrying about his aunt's favors to Conway and the attraction she held for his wife. Harriet was caring too much for Bath society. When a message arrived saying that Mr. Pemberton was gravely ill at Condover Park, Sir John instantly removed his Harriet to Shropshire, "glad to carry little Wifey far from that widely spreading influence which . . . throws an attractive halo

[14] So says Mrs. Piozzi in her *Commonplace Book*, under "Princess."

round us all: which *she* feels among the rest," Mrs. Piozzi wrote to Mrs. Pennington, adding that "Sir John's chagrin won't kill him: and he says he will perhaps come again — *by himself* . . ." (Pennington, pp. 306–307).

In June he did return. Mrs. Piozzi had left Bath, but he followed her to Clifton, where she was staying with Conway's mother. Salusbury knew that his aunt had accumulated some £6,000 and he wished to take no chance of losing any of this money to Conway. Sir John revived the subject of his baronetcy; Cathron this time reported that the price would be 5,000 guineas — and that there was a good chance Salusbury could be included in the Coronation List of the new King, George IV. On 16 June Mrs. Piozzi noted that she and Salusbury had "had a long Business Talk, unpleasant of Course," and on the 18th she wrote, "my poor 6000£: gone — Addio!" [15] Next day Salusbury left Clifton.

6.

Once again Mrs. Piozzi was in straitened circumstances through unwise generosity. On this occasion, however, thoughts of the benefit she was conferring upon Salusbury and his children helped her face the necessary economies. She had let the comfortable Gay Street house, [16] and after the few weeks in Clifton, went on to Cornwall, to Penzance, where she knew she could find inexpensive lodgings and have good sea bathing, still the therapy which she felt was most beneficial. She was accompanied by her faithful maid, Bessy Bell (who had been in her service for almost twenty years) and Bessy's little boy, Angelo,[17] a favorite of Mrs. Piozzi's, along with Sir James, Mangin, and Conway — and hence another worry to Salusbury.

None of Mrs. Piozzi's family offered to visit in Cornwall, but Miss Willoughby astonished her by arriving in October and staying in Penzance through the winter. The appearance of this buoyant younger woman made life much more cheerful. Miss Willoughby was popular with everyone; she played for country dances, thought up charades, and won at whist (Pennington, p. 356).

[15] Diary, 1820, in possession of James L. Clifford.

[16] Number 8 Gay Street has passed through many hands. Before World War I and for some time thereafter it was owned by Dame Edith Sitwell. It now houses an insurance company.

[17] Angelo had been born at the Gay Street house on 9 October 1817. He was one of her many godchildren.

Sir John fretted about the presence of Miss Willoughby in Cornwall, and feared (unnecessarily) that she had designs upon his inheritance. He never considered giving his aunt the pleasure of a visit, he simply worried about the expense of the long journey to Penzance if she should die there. He now thought about her mainly in terms of death. And Mrs. Piozzi herself was constantly thinking about death — when would she die? — and from what cause? The whole melancholy subject now occupied her mind as completely as the joyous plans for her birthday celebration had occupied it the year before.

News from Brynbella reached her in January 1821: on the 19th another Salusbury son had been born, Edward William, named after Harriet's brother, Salusbury's dear friend, "Pem," and this time Mrs. Piozzi was not asked to be godmother. It was as if she no longer existed.

In February an unusually kind letter came from Sophy Hoare, and Mrs. Piozzi wished there were some way to show her gratitude, but "What *she* wants is out of my power, — children to enjoy hers and her husband's fortune" (Pennington, p. 362).

By March Miss Willoughby had left Penzance and Mrs. Piozzi could stand the place no longer. She set out for Clifton, with Bessy and little Angelo. On the way, the party stopped at Exeter for the night (Saturday, 10 March). And as she tried to climb into the high inn bed, she suffered a fall; she wrote to Sir James Fellowes and others, describing the injury to her leg, "a cruel bruise and a slight tear" (Broadley, p. 264). Despite the accident, however, she was able to attend services at the Cathedral on Sunday morning, and later continued on to Taunton for the night.

The party arrived in Clifton the following day; the house which Mrs. Piozzi had arranged to take for the next few months was not yet prepared for her, so she went back to Conway's mother, who cared for her tenderly during the next fortnight, urging her among other things to eat, for she would hardly touch food. On 25 March, though she was weak, Mrs. Piozzi was able to attend Conway's benefit of *Mirandola*,[18] something she had been anticipating for some time. He gave a brilliant performance and appreciated her being with him. The Felloweses entertained at a party after the theatre — she and Conway were the center of admiring friends. A flaming night.

The affection of her Bath friends was in heartwarming contrast to Salusbury's continued neglect. He had not seen his aunt since the pre-

[18] A tragedy by Bryan Waller Procter (Barry Cornwall, his pseudonym).

vious June when he had taken away her £6,000; possibly he was afraid to face her, for he had spent the money on things other than the baronetcy. He did not write and he showed no concern for the state of her health. Neither did the Thrale daughters.

Gibbes and the other doctors in attendance were satisfied with the condition of Mrs. Piozzi's leg; in fact, after a short while it healed, "it was *perfectly cured*" (Pennington postscript, Broadley, p. 74). Her general debilitation, however, was worrying. The doctors insisted that their patient eat more, but she "either *could* not eat enough to support nature, or had brought herself to it from a mistaken system" (Pennington, p. 369). On 23 April, a seemingly slight inflammation of the intestines set in, "over which medicine had no power" (Broadley, p. 74) and she herself had no strength to combat. She was as alert as ever, cheerful, interested in everything happening around her, but she grew steadily weaker. The comfort of her devoted friend and priest, Edward Mangin, would have meant much during these days; unfortunately he was out of England at the time, unaware of her danger. But Mrs. Pennington stayed close by her bedside, and when the doctors could no longer hold out hope, it was she who summoned Queeney, Susan, Sophy, and Salusbury — Cecilia was still in Italy, too far away to reach. Queeney arrived on 1 May, and Sophy a little later the same day. "On hearing of their arrival [Mrs. Piozzi] is reported to have said, 'Now, I shall die in state'" (Hayward, I, 363), but this is probably apocryphal, for according to Mrs. Pennington she was unable to articulate some time before this.

Susanna arrived on 2 May, joining her "weeping" sisters by the bedside. As Mrs. Pennington wrote to Miss Willoughby, the ladies behaved with great tenderness and propriety; ". . . *more* charming women I know not," she wrote to another friend. "Oh! what a sum of happiness did she throw from her, through the *misapprehensions*, etc., which separated her from them!"

Shortly before nine o'clock on 2 May, Hester Lynch Salusbury Thrale Piozzi died. She had had her wish: "never to live to support the mere *dregs* of life . . ." (Pennington, p. 369).

Sir John did not arrive in Clifton until the night of 4 May and the next day Sir James Fellowes read the will. All Mrs. Piozzi's property, money, securities, and personal effects came to Salusbury and his heirs. There were only four bequests: to Fellowes £200; to her faithful agent Leak (who had died before her) £100; to his son, Alexander Piozzi

MRS. PIOZZI

MINIATURE BY SOPHIA HOARE, AFTER A MINIATURE BY BENNETT

Leak £100; and to her maid, Bessy Jones Bell £100. After the reading, "Lady Keith and her two sisters present, said they had long been prepared for the contents and for such a disposition of the property, and they acknowledged the validity of the Will" (Hayward, I, 364).[19] This made no mention of personal gifts, but for these there were written requests to Salusbury and Fellowes.

According to her wishes, Mrs. Piozzi was buried beside her second husband in the Tremeirchion Church. She had not dared to travel out of the United Kingdom after Piozzi's death, for fear she might die abroad and her body would not be brought home and placed beside his; her "rendezvous," her "last appointment," was the way she often referred to this final journey. Her burial wishes were carried out, but none of the children, not even the adopted "son of her heart" at nearby Brynbella, went to the trouble and expense of erecting a memorial. The tablet which is now seen on the wall of the Tremeirchion Church was placed there in 1909 by a grandson of Sir James Fellowes.[20]

At Mrs. Piozzi's death Streatham Park became the property of the four Thrale daughters, but the strong feeling they had shown for the place during their mother's lifetime was no longer manifest. The property was sold in 1825 and thereafter passed through the hands of a number of different owners, the last being a Mr. Phillips, who did not reside there, and allowed the house to become such a ruin that no builder would repair it. The house was demolished in 1863, at which time *Punch* magazine made the macabre suggestion (with the industry of Shakespeare's mulberry tree in mind), that the "timbers of the walls which used to reverberate with Johnsonian thunder . . . be cut up

[19] Two days before her death, Mrs. Piozzi gave Conway a draft for £100. He returned this to Sir James Fellowes on 7 May, with a note, saying he had received much kindness from his revered friend during her lifetime, and he felt this benefaction more properly belonged to her heirs. A true gentleman.

[20] In 1909 numerous tributes were paid to Johnson on the two hundredth anniversary of his birth. Mr. O. Butler Fellowes believed that Mrs. Piozzi should also be remembered by "some slight memorial," and he proceeded to raise a subscription fund. He was the major contributor to this but among other participants were the 5th Marquess of Lansdowne and Mr. Peter Hoare.

The inscription on the wall tablet to "this remarkable woman" was composed by Fellowes:

"Witty, vivacious and charming,
    In an Age of Genius;
She ever held a foremost place." (Fellowes ALS to Peter Hoare, 29 May 1909).

into no end of snuff-boxes, relics of the immortal SAM, and if MR. PHILLIPS wishes to do a handsome thing, he will send one of them to *Punch's* office" (Broadley, p. 288).

7.

Mrs. Piozzi's death made no change in her daughters' lives. They received no inheritance from her — their fortunes had come long ago from their father — and since they had avoided their mother for over thirty years, they did not miss her company.

Queeney and Admiral Keith continued to be fully occupied at Tullyallan (which Mrs. Piozzi had never been invited to see). The construction of the castle had been completed in 1820. It was an impressive building of about a hundred rooms, including fine state apartments. And the landscaping of the property was remarkable for its beauty. Keith had a special interest in this aspect of the plans and was well supported by his architect, for Atkinson was a keen horticulturist. Besides the park, formal gardens, and pleasure grounds, there were vegetable and cutting gardens, an orchard, hothouses, stables, and a magnificent octagonal dairy. There were three lochs on the property, moors, forest, and farmland; over twenty miles of roads conveyed one through the several thousand acres. Streatham Park was a small remembrance in comparison to Tullyallan.

Life here represented all the qualities of happiness which Queeney had sought as a young girl — dignity, comfort, and serenity. An indoor staff alone of thirty took care of the small family. The old Admiral was punctilious and considerate, and their child was a pleasure. Augusta (eleven at the time of Mrs. Piozzi's death and her only granddaughter) was a lively and pretty young girl, with fine manners. As for her studies, she was not encouraged to be an intellectual prodigy like her mother and grandmother — quite the reverse — she was given an education "suitable to her rank and station" and urged to make riding her greatest accomplishment.

The Keiths enjoyed fifteen years of quiet companionship, before the Admiral died at seventy-seven (two years after Mrs. Piozzi's death). He was mourned by friends and neighbors, who respected his upright character. He was also mourned by the nation, and his long and distinguished career entitled him to a hero's final resting place. Keith, however, had made other provisions. On his property, a few miles

Sophia Merrik Hoare, CAUSE CAUSED IT fecit 1816.

ADMIRAL VISCOUNT KEITH
WATERCOLOR MINIATURE BY SOPHIA HOARE,
AFTER A PORTRAIT BY SANDERS

VISCOUNTESS KEITH
WATERCOLOR MINIATURE BY SOPHIA HOARE,
AFTER A PORTRAIT BY SANDERS

TULLYALLAN CASTLE, RESIDENCE OF ADMIRAL VISCOUNT KEITH

from the castle, he had created a family mausoleum. Here he was buried, in a pretty little building in the Gothic style, situated on the crest of a hill where he had often ridden or walked. It was a peaceful spot and beautiful, with a sweeping vista up the valley of the Forth toward the Highlands. The view was a panorama of his life and its achievements — from the small place of his birth to Tullyallan castle.

The management of Tullyallan, together with the other properties — baronies, farms, dwellings, fishings, mills, ferries, patronages, and rents — Keith left in the hands of four trustees, his brother-in-law Merrik Hoare, his brother-in-law William Adam, and his friends David Erskine of Cardross and Petersham and James Loch of Lincoln's Inn. These men were to dispose of the lands not yet sold "in that part of the United Kingdom called England" [21] and to make substitute purchases in Scotland.

Keith wished to entail his estate and having no male heir he empowered the trustees to carry on until such time as his married daughter Mercer produced a son and this son (provided, as previously stated, that he was a Protestant, educated in the United Kingdom, and beyond foreign influence) had reached the age of twenty-one.

If Mercer failed to produce a son, the succession was to pass to the son of Augusta. Failing sons by both Mercer and Augusta, their daughters would inherit, the daughters of his elder child, Mercer, having precedence. Failing grand-daughters, Keith had proceeded to list, as his possible successor, sixteen relations (to be followed by male heirs), and he had further stipulated that if at a later time he named anyone else to inherit, that person should do so. His successor was to take the surname and arms of Elphinstone. The Scottish Record Office copy of Keith's trust instrument fills 134 pages.

Since the Comtesse de Flahault had no son, Augusta Elphinstone (thirteen) continued at live at Tullyallan in the company of her mother. Keith's will made provision for Augusta's expenses and for an annuity for his widow.

As for the Harley Street house, Viscountess Keith was to give this up whenever it was "convenient" for her "to accommodate herself with another dwelling house not exceeding twelve months after my decease." The new London house in which Queeney established herself was 110 Piccadilly (now part of the Park Lane Hotel). It was

---

[21] Admiral Keith's Will, Scottish Record Office, Edinburgh.

more modest than the Harley Street house, but pleasant, facing Green Park and still close to York Place where the Hoares lived. Queeney depended greatly upon Sophy and Merrik.

He, together with Keith's brother, William Elphinstone, and Queeney were guardians of Augusta and were a congenial triumvirate, with Queeney naturally the dominant member. She was determined that her daughter should be given the supervision and the advantages of which she believed herself to have been deprived — above all, Augusta was to have a proper and easy background to facilitate a good marriage when the time came. The other guardians were in complete agreement with Queeney on this matter, and so was Sophy. Indeed she always agreed with Queeney on important issues. Sophy was her most comforting companion in bereavement.

It was a sudden and cruel stroke of fate that Sophia Hoare (at fifty-three) should die the next year (8 November 1824) only twenty months after Keith's death. For Queeney this was a tragic loss and for Merrik a devastating blow. The Hoare marriage had been extremely happy except for the one thing — their lack of children. It is not known whether Sophy's serious illness at twelve (the last autumn the girls had been with their mother) had anything to do with the problem, but Sophy was never a robust person after this long siege. She was able within two years to resume most normal activities but she was never able to lead a strenuous life.

In her twenties Sophy had become the beauty of the family. She was a lovely person, sociable and charming, and she had a greater single talent than any of her sisters — her ability to draw and to paint. Her efforts were considered unusual when she was a child, and in the years after her marriage, possibly guided by the fine painter, Prince Hoare, a connection of her husband, she became an extremely competent artist. The watercolor miniatures which Sophy painted of members of her family and of friends, kept in a dark-red velvet album, entitled "Souvenirs de l'Amitié," are more than fine amateur productions — they are exquisite studies of professional quality.[22]

As a memorial to Sophy, Merrik commissioned John Flaxman (sculptor of Henry Thrale's wall tablet and now a celebrated artist) to make

[22] Sophy's miniatures include portraits of her husband and her sisters, Susan and Queeney, also one of Admiral Keith — and a miniature of her mother, painted a year after Mrs. Piozzi's death. In each case Sophy's portraits are taken from those of other artists.

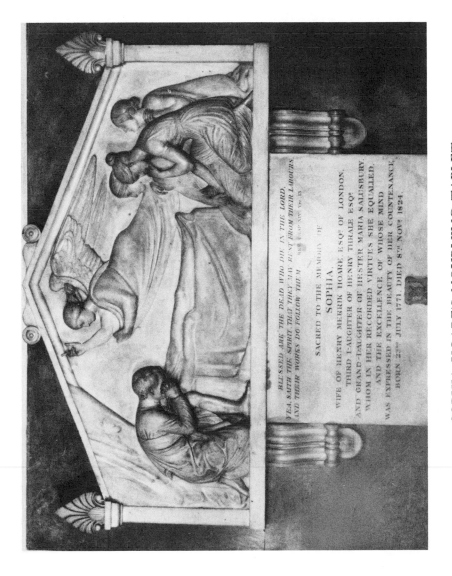

SOPHIA HOARE'S MOURNING TABLET

BY FLAXMAN

a monument in St. Leonard's.[23] Sophia's mourning panel is a beautiful example of Flaxman's work, and one of the last, for he died shortly after completing it. The tablet has the added interest of being a family portrait, for Queeney, Susan, and Cecilia are shown (in classical dress and idealized form), kneeling at the foot of their sister's bier. Merrik, grief-stricken, kneels at the head, and an angel hovers above. Sophia's epitaph compares her to her virtuous grandmother, Mrs. Salusbury, and states the fact that she was the "third daughter of Henry Thrale, Esq." — but mention of Mrs. Piozzi was carefully avoided.

Flaxman wished to have Sophia's monument erected in the spot occupied by Mrs. Salusbury's tablet so that his "Basso Relievo" would show to better advantage. He urged Merrik Hoare to take action in the matter, assuring him that the rector, Mr. Hill, had no objection. Flaxman's letter is preserved at the Hoare Bank, but no change in position of the tablets was made.

Sophia Hoare is commemorated by another tablet and a benefaction in Streatham — the Thrale Almshouse.[24] This building was erected "as a home for four women who, being indigent, shall have attained an honourable old age in this parish." The almshouse was given in 1832 by Queeney, Susan, and Cecilia — with Merrik Hoare making Sophy's contribution so that she might be counted with her sisters. Merrik remained loyal to Sophy's memory; he did not marry again though he outlived her by over thirty years. He never left their house at York Place.[25]

8.

By 1827 Cecilia, the rambler, had returned from abroad and decided to live in England. At first she spent some time in London and some in

[23] Flaxman's charge for this monument was £200. Flaxman MS Account Book (1809–1826), Montgomery Collection, Rare Book and Manuscript Library, Columbia University Libraries. In the inscription (Plate LIV), "Merrik" is spelled correctly; many printed works on the Thrales give it *incorrectly* as *Merrick*.

[24] The Thrale Almshouse, pictured in Broadley (facing p. 286), stood on the High Road, next to the Police Station until 1930, when it was pulled down. A new Almshouse was erected on Polworth Road, enlarged first to take care of eight old ladies, and now of ten. The Thrale tablet, with its inscription, is still to be seen on one of the walls.

[25] York Place is now a continuation of Baker Street but the row houses still stand. Number 31 York Place is 109 Baker Street. Several business offices occupy the building.

Brighton. After a while she decided to settle in the latter place. She took lodgings, and Bertie, her youngest son (now twenty-six), came to live with her.

Harry was pursuing a distinguished career in the Navy. Five years before (1822), as an Acting Lieutenant, he had navigated HMS *Termagant* from India to England. In January 1823 (at twenty-four) he had been made a Lieutenant, and in 1830 he was to be advanced to the rank of Commander. Harry was the successful member of the family.

The giant, Salusbury, was the failure. His scholarly inclinations, to which Mrs. Piozzi had referred with high hopes when he was sent to Edinburgh, never developed. And the Army life which he chose proved too strenuous for his delicate constitution. He had an inherited weakness of the lungs, and heavy drinking from schooldays on had not helped matters. Now, though Salusbury owned property in Wales, the climate was too severe for him to live there. He stayed by the sea, at Worthing, near Brighton. He was idle and sick, and in August 1827 he died at twenty-nine — a bachelor and intestate.

Cecilia sorted through Salusbury's possessions and added some of his sentimental trifles to her "things." With the passing years she had become an even more passionate collector than her mother had described. Cecilia was indefatigable in her efforts to acquire objects, and indiscriminate in her choice — treasures and trash — remembrances from childhood and married life, family memorabilia, journals, notes, magazines, newspapers, cuttings; and from her years of recent Continental travel, books, prints, souvenirs, paintings, sculpture, furniture, all manner of bits and pieces.

On 27 November 1827 Cecilia wrote a letter to Sir John Salusbury, thanking him for a tiny *Book of Common Prayer* which she said she would cherish. She had asked Sir John for something which had belonged to her mother and she was delighted with the little book he had sent. She remembered it well, the binding was in straw work, beautifully made for her mother by the poor, divorced Lady Kirkwall of Llewenny. Cecilia's letter was cordial — she was at last well disposed toward Sir John. She apologized for not having thanked him for the locket containing her mother's hair, which had been given by Sophy before her death, "I did not understand it came from you or of course [would] have written to thank you at the time." Cecilia wrote also that she was "glad to hear that you and [Harry and Bertie have] met and hope it will always be with friendly feelings toward one another."

The three had seen each other in the Vale of Clwyd. Harry, as heir to his elder brother, had inherited Segroit and though he had now reached the rank of Captain in the Navy, he resigned his commission and began a new life as a country squire. His brother Bertie had been visiting him. "Harry regrets that you are leaving [Brynbella]," Cecilia said, "and Bertie tells me that you have a large family and talk of its being an [increasing] one . . . Bertie & I shall always be happy to see you" (Rylands 572.33).

Sir John replied on the instant, saying that "Few occurences of my Life have afforded me greater gratification than the receipt of your kind Letter." He added that he was indeed sorry to be quitting Brynbella "Saturday next" to live permanently in Chester, but he and his wife wished to be close at hand to supervise the studies of their two girls and seven boys (Rylands 572.34). Mrs. Piozzi's strong feeling about the importance of a good education had not been forgotten by Salusbury.

Since his aunt's death four children had been born, all boys: George Augustus, in 1822 (eventually Sir John's heir); Charles Arthur, in 1823; Frederick Octavius, in 1825; Augustus Pemberton, in 1826.[26] The child on the way, mentioned by Cecilia, was to be Caroline Mary, born in May 1828. Another girl, Harriet, the eleventh child, was born in January 1831, but this infant died a few days later and her death was followed after three months by that of her mother, who was only thirty-eight years old.

Harriet Pemberton Salusbury, the pretty, warm-hearted Shropshire girl, had not journeyed far nor experienced much variety in life. She had married her first sweetheart, her brother's best friend, the saucy, ardent Italian boy. John Salusbury Piozzi Salusbury was not clever, nor ambitious — not an easy husband. He was often moody, he was

---

[26] It would have pleased Mrs. Piozzi to know that though Salusbury had failed at Oxford two of his sons were to be successful there: Charles Arthur at Jesus College, B.A. 1846 (later rector of Stretton, Shropshire); and Augustus Pemberton at Exeter, B.A. 1840, M.A. 1853 (thereafter curate of St. Paul's, Halliwell, Lancashire, and vicar of Netley and Wrockwardine in Shropshire).

George Augustus went to Cambridge, matriculating at Magdalene in 1846 at the advanced age of twenty-four. In 1849 he was ordained deacon at Chester; later he was curate of Hinstock in Shropshire, and from 1852 until his death he was rector of Westbury, near Shrewsbury.

slow, lazy, humorless, unimaginative, and jealous. But Salusbury had many compensating good qualities: he was a loving husband and a devoted father. He was kind, gentle, unaffected, determined, and high-principled.

And he was loyal. In the long years after Harriet's death, Salusbury remained faithful. Like Merrik Hoare he did not remarry, he carried on by himself — but unlike Merrik he had little money and a great many children, which combination gave him more affection but created many more problems. Sir John did exceedingly well by his children [27] but he failed in almost all other endeavors. He never secured his baronetcy, he was never an effective public servant nor a successful farmer. He simply struggled on, and as he did he kept a tight hold on all of his aunt's papers. Like the Thrale sisters he had an obsessive fear of any publicity concerning her — in particular any publication of manuscripts, diaries, or letters. Sir James Fellowes, as joint literary executor, got nowhere with any plan to publish.

9.

Salusbury never found the time nor the money to make a visit to Cecilia — a pity, for her life was agreeable in Brighton. She bought an attractive house on Sillwood Terrace in 1833, the year the row of houses was built in "the furlong next the west fields" and close to the sea. Number 9 was Cecilia's house and she called it Sillwood Lodge.[28] She needed the many high-ceilinged rooms for her growing collection,

[27] Of his sons who reached maturity, three, as noted above, attended university. The other two became army officers. Edward William served in Bengal and was killed during the insurrection at Kabul in 1841; Frederick Octavius also served in Bengal, later returning home. He lived until 1905.

"Missey," Mrs. Piozzi's namesake, in 1841 married the Reverend Mr. Arthur Downes Gardner (M.A. and Fellow of Jesus College, Oxford), vicar of Holywell, Flintshire. Four years earlier, Angelina, her younger sister, the beauty of the family, had married John William Hardern, barrister of the Inner Temple. The last child, Caroline Mary, married the Reverend Mr. Watkin Williams, rector of Nannerch. She died in 1908.

[28] Sillwood Lodge still stands (1975), the various floors divided into flats, and its name changed to "Sillwood Mansions," which title is painted in large letters on the house façade. In the entrance hall is a framed statement telling of Cecilia Thrale Mostyn's connection with the property.

From the forlorn and dilapidated appearance of the building and of others adjacent, this east row may soon be claimed by the bulldozer. The north and west rows of Sillwood Terrace have already been replaced by square white blocks of flats.

and she brought the hundreds of items into the new house with Bertie's help. Bertie himself moved into Sillwood Lodge and made a dependable and good-natured companion for his mother.

Harry was the only one of the brothers who married. In November 1832 Susanna Townshend became his wife, an attractive woman, three years his junior, daughter of John Stanislaus Townshend of Trevallyn, a large country house near Rossett. Harry and Susanna were warm and hospitable and popular in the countryside. Harry was a good citizen and an ardent churchman; he founded St. David's Church in Denbigh in 1838.

In business matters Harry was fair and able and managed his property well. Segroit was a happy place — but not for long — Harry died, "suddenly snatched away, at almost a moment's warning" [29] before he was forty-one (29 July 1840). He was buried in the parish church of Llanrhaiadr and greatly mourned. He and Susanna had had no children, and according to his will Segroit Hall was given to the use of Susanna for her lifetime. Only after her death was Segroit to pass to his surviving brother.[30] Bertie, however, had inherited Llewesog Lodge (which had come into the family through Major Wynne, his Mostyn grandmother's second husband). Though he spent part of the year in Wales, Bertie continued to stay for long periods of time with his mother at Sillwood Lodge. The house was fast becoming a museum.

In 1857, the *Brighton Herald* (7 October) referred to Sillwood Lodge as containing "our best collection of literary and artistic nickknackeries . . . a sort of cabinet stuffed full of rare and curious things." The report went on to say that much of the interest of the collection derived from Cecilia herself, who had made it the labor of her life. Her recollections of past events, particularly literary anecdotes, were extremely engrossing. And a visit to Sillwood Lodge, presided over by Mrs. Mostyn, was one of the most spellbinding experiences

---

[29] *A Sermon Preached on Sunday, the 9th of August 1840 in St. Hilary's Chapel, Denbigh, on the Lamented Death of Captain Mostyn RN* [by John Jones]. Denbigh: Thomas Gee, 1840.

[30] Segroit never passed to Bertie, for Harry's widow, Susanna, outlived him by thirteen years, not dying until she was eighty-seven (1889). Upon her death, the estate came into the hands of her nephew, Robert Townshend Wickham, a Chester estate agent. In 1920 he sold Segroit to Pryce Edward Story, a local brewer. Story died in 1931, leaving a life interest in the estate to Mrs. John Hooson. The property, now called Segrwyd Hall, is owned (1975) by her nephew, David Hooson, a Denbigh solicitor, and his wife, Eirlys Whitford Hooson.

SALUSBURY FAMILY SILHOUETTE
ANNOUNCING THE ENGAGEMENT OF ANGELINA IN 1837
BY EDOUART

FROM LEFT TO RIGHT: CHARLES ARTHUR (14); HESTER MARIA (22); CAROLINE
MARY (9); JOHN HARDERN AND ANGELINA (21), HIS FIANCÉE; GEORGE
AUGUSTUS (15); AUGUSTUS PEMBERTON (11); FREDERICK OCTAVIUS (12);
EDWARD WILLIAM (16); AND SIR JOHN SALUSBURY

CECILIA MOSTYN'S SILLWOOD LODGE, BRIGHTON, 1975

that could be imagined, for Mrs. Mostyn was a last connecting link between Dr. Johnson and the Thrales and Brighton; between literature and art of the eighteenth and nineteenth centuries. Cecilia, in her old age, became a minor celebrity in Brighton, just as her mother had been in Bath.

Cecilia was headstrong to the last. In May 1857, when she was eighty and in delicate health, her doctor forbade her to go to London. She made the trip by train regardless, and upon her return collapsed and died in the Brighton railway station. In October, the contents of Sillwood Lodge were auctioned. The sale lasted for eight days — two days longer than the Streatham Park auction.

Three months before Cecilia's death, Queeney, Viscountess Keith, died at her Piccadilly house in London (21 March 1857), at the great age of ninety-two. She had been a widow for thirty-four years and for two decades had led a quiet life, withdrawn from society. Her greatest pleasure was to be with Augusta.

When Augusta made a fine marriage at twenty-one, Queeney had continued her possessive watch, and Augusta, when she was widowed at thirty-eight, had returned without hesitation to live with her mother in London. Tullyallan was to pass to a Flahault.[31]

Warm affection had united Mrs. Salusbury and her daughter; it had been conspicuously lacking in the relationship between that daughter and those of her children who survived childhood, but now the pattern of the earlier generation recurred. Cecilia was devoted to her boys, and there was a close attachment between Queeney and her only daughter.

[31] It passed to Emily, eldest daughter of Mercer Elphinstone and the Comte. There was no de Flahault son, and Augusta never had issue.

In 1843 Emily became the second wife of the 4th Marquess of Lansdowne, and in 1895, upon Emily's death, the castle was inherited by the 5th Lord Lansdowne. Seventy-two years after Admiral Keith's death his wish for a male heir was realized, but Tullyallan was not long to remain in the family.

In 1904 the 5th Marquess sold the castle to Sir James Sivewright. And at this time Lord Lansdowne removed the family papers to Bowood House, his principal residence. This explains the existence there of the material connected with the Keiths, the Thrales, and Johnson.

In 1924 Tullyallan was purchased by Colonel Alexander Mitchell. And in 1934 it was inherited by his son, Sir Harold Mitchell, Bt., M.P., who during World War II placed it at the disposal of the King of Poland.

In 1948 Sir Harold Mitchell sold Tullyallan to the Government for the establishment of the Scottish Police College. This institution now flourishes at "Tulliallan" — this being the spelling favored today.

Queeney was buried in the Keith Mausoleum. Her commanding memorial tablet

10.

In November 1858, the year following the death of her two sisters, Susanna Thrale died at Ashgrove Cottage in Knockholt; and the next month Sir John Salusbury died at Cheltenham, aged sixty-five. Brynbella and Bach-y-Graig [32] passed to his fourth son, George Augustus. Owen, Tom, and Edward — all the boys who had been born during Mrs. Piozzi's lifetime — had died before their father.

Susanna was the last of the Thrale daughters to go. Her life, after the giddy flutter in her twenties, became quiet and settled. She was a resident at Ashgrove Cottage from the time she first came there in 1807 until her death. Her connection with the co-owner, William Wells, lasted only a few years, but while it did, Susanna took a keen interest in his children and other children in the neighborhood. It was she who founded the village school in a barn at Ashgrove.

By 1819, if not earlier, Susanna had taken over Ashgrove Cottage for herself, and Wells had bought a house of his own in Mitcham, Surrey,

is high on the wall, center back, and it bears the curious misstatement that she was "Born 1775" — eleven years later than the actual date. One wonders how this error was made.

During her long widowhood, the prospect of eternal rest in this idyllic spot must have comforted Queeney, to whom the beauty and importance of material things meant so much. She was to be surrounded by Keiths, in the solitude and privacy of her husband's great park.

That was in 1857; now (1975) a melancholy change has occurred. The approach is a morass of overgrown and fallen trees, weeds, briars, and nettles. Water seeps from a quarry which is within sight. Dust fills the air and there is the sound of heavy machinery and the vibration of power lines. Pylons tower over the mausoleum, and cables cut across the sky.

The little building itself, with the date-stone of "1822" over the door, is derelict. The door has been prized open and hangs on its hinges. The mausoleum has been vandalized. Queeney's tablet is covered with graffiti and Admiral Lord Keith's stone is broken; his grave is an open hole, sobering testimony to the vanity of human wishes.

[32] Brynbella and Bach-y-Graig were inherited, after George Augustus' death, by his son, Major Edward Pemberton Salusbury. At the end of the nineteenth century Major Salusbury sold Brynbella to Mrs. S. K. Mainwaring (Edith Sarah Williams, daughter of Sir Hugh Williams of Bodylwyddan). The house passed to her son, Col. Sir W. R. K. Mainwaring, who sold it in 1944 to Mr. R. F. Glazebrook, who now (1975) lives at Brynbella.

Bach-y-Graig passed from Major Salusbury to his widow, and from her to their daughter, Rose Salusbury Colman, who sold it in 1919 to Robert Roberts. It is now owned by his son, Clwyd Roberts.

a more convenient location as he was a drawing master at nearby Addiscombe College. Wells died in 1836.

Mrs. Piozzi visited Ashgrove Cottage on several occasions and Mrs. Pennington came in 1824. She had promised the "three charming" Thrale daughters at the time of their mother's death that she would come to see them. She "spent ten delightful days" with Susan at her "beautiful Villa in Kent, surrounded by Nobleman's Seats, which we visited in our daily morning drives" (Pennington, p. 376).

Susanna enjoyed Ashgrove for over fifty years. A visitor, who saw her there late in life, described her as a "stout easy comfortable old lady, full of good works and alms, and one who, as she has no love for books, or very little, does not care to talk about Dr. Johnson and still less about her mother" (*Johnson and Queeney*, p. xxiii). Susanna proved the truth of her commitment to good works by leaving bequests to two orphanages, two London hospitals, two religious societies, and one institution for the blind. But her purchase of Dr. Johnson's summerhouse,[33] when Streatham Park was sold, also proved that she still retained warm feelings for Johnson and the early Streatham days, even though she might not choose to talk about them.

Susanna, the sickly infant whom no one (except Johnson) had expected to survive, reached the age of eighty-eight, outliving everyone mentioned in her mother's *Family Book*. Of the twelve Thrale children, only she and three other daughters reached maturity, but the combined ages of these four — Queeney, Susan, Sophy, and Cecilia — equalled 313 years, a striking example of the survival of the fittest.

II.

At the time of Susanna's death only two Thrale grandchildren were alive, Bertie Mostyn, fifty-seven, and Queeney's daughter, Augusta, forty-eight. These cousins were devoted friends and were both fond of their Aunt Susan; it was they who proved her will, saw that her

---

[33] Johnson's summerhouse remained at Ashgrove until the 1960s, when it was moved to the Streatham Common. After a brief stay there, it was taken to a place where it would be more appreciated and better protected. It can now be seen in Hampstead, in the garden of Kenwood, a property owned in the Thrales' time by Lord Mansfield.

Ashgrove Cottage now (1975) belongs to the Derek Chittocks, a couple of whom both Wells and Susanna would have approved. He is an artist, and her world is the theatre.

wishes were carried out, and made arrangements for her to be buried at St. Leonard's. Her coffin could not be put in the Thrale vault, for burial within churches was no longer permitted, but her grave, on the northwest side of the church, is close to the location of the vault.[34] The inscription on Susanna's stone, like Sophy's and Cecilia's (the latter erected by Bertie) proclaims her to be a daughter of Henry Thrale, but no mention is made of Mrs. Piozzi.

After Cecilia's death, Bertie acquired a residence in London, part of the house at 41 St. James's Place, not far from Augusta in Piccadilly. The cousins were often together.

Bertie was now increasingly well off, for he had inherited from his mother and had received Crowmarsh Battle from his aunt, Viscountess Keith. The farm came to him because, according to Henry Thrale's will, the property was to descend (after passing to the eldest son or daughter) to the eldest son of any of the daughters. Bertie managed Crowmarsh efficiently and made visits of inspection there. He also maintained Llewesog Lodge and other land in Wales. He even remained loyal to Streatham, making a donation of £866 for the charities of St. Leonard's in 1860.

Before Bertie died at seventy-five (in 1876),[35] he had made a request to be buried at St. Leonard's in the same grave with his aunt, Susanna Thrale. Presumably Augusta attended to this, but she was not very efficient in supervising the stonecutter, for in adding Bertie's name under Susanna's, the man mistakenly described him as her "son." This he tried to correct to "nephew," but he was not entirely successful. Both words are now equally visible. If this slip was Augusta's fault, and also the wrong date on her mother's tablet, she was doubly careless.

---

[34] During the time of the Thrales' residence at Streatham Park the family vault was below the south aisle, directly beneath their pew, but when much of St. Leonard's was rebuilt in 1831–32 the Thrale coffins were moved to what is now their vault, number 7, below the north aisle.

Burials within churches were not permitted after the passing of the Public Health Act of 1848.

[35] Llewesog Lodge passed to Anna Maria Mostyn Mainwaring. This house, now called Llewesog Hall, is owned (1975) by William Renallt Williams, who farms its thousand acres.

Crowmarsh Battle passed to Augusta and upon her death to Emily (Flahault), widow of the 4th Marquess of Lansdowne. Upon Emily's death (1895) the farm came, like Tullyallan Castle, to her son, the 5th Marquess of Lansdowne.

Crowmarsh was sold by him in 1910 to F. P. Chamberlain, father of P. C. Chamberlain, who continued to farm the property (1975).

But she made up for her errors, at least in part, by seeing that Bertie's name and correct dates were added to his mother's tablet at St. Leonard's on the wall of the south aisle, just above the memorial to Henry Thrale.[36]

Augusta, the youngest Thrale grandchild, was a spirited, attractive, and accomplished woman. She was small in stature, though not so small as her grandmother. She was agile and dauntless and from "her earliest days," as her Flahault cousin, the 6th Marquess of Lansdowne said, "she was devoted to riding . . . one of the first women to invade the hunting field, which had previously been almost exclusively patronized by the stronger sex" (*Johnson and Queeney*, p. xxxi).

In 1831 she had married the Hon. Augustus John Villiers, a son of the Earl of Jersey. After Villiers died in 1847, Augusta had returned to live with her mother, and in 1870, thirteen years after Viscountess Keith's death, Augusta married again. She was sixty by this time — her husband sixty-six, a brother of the Duke of Leeds, William Godolphin Osborne. He added "Elphinstone" to his surname.

The Osborne Elphinstones enjoyed eighteen years together before Lord William died at eighty-four (1888). He was buried in the Keith mausoleum, which now contained, besides the graves of Admiral and Viscountess Keith, those of the Admiral's maiden sister Mary; Sarah, the younger de Flahault daughter who had died unmarried at twenty-six; and Sarah's mother, Margaret Mercer, Comtesse de Flahault, who died in 1867. (The Comte, who outlived her by three years, is buried in France.)

In 1892, thirty-five years after Queeney Thrale's death, Augusta Osborne Elphinstone died at eighty-two in the Piccadilly house which

---

[36] Bertie Mostyn was the last member of the Thrale family to be buried at St. Leonard's, and the fate of this church, which was so much a part of the Thrales' lives, was even more tragic than that of the Keith mausoleum.

On the night of 5 May 1975 St. Leonard's burned to the ground. In the early evening there had been a brush fire in the old rectory garden; this was thought to have been extinguished by the Streatham fire department, but shortly after eight, flames broke out on the roof of the church. There was a gale wind from the east and the fire was soon out of control. Within a few hours nothing remained of St. Leonard's but the tower and spire, charred walls and bits of the stained-glass windows.

The Thrale monuments survived the fire, but a few days later, when the walls cooled and contracted, and damp set in, the tablets fell to the ground. They are shattered, and Cecilia's and Bertie's tablet no longer exists.

AUGUSTA GEORGINA HENRIETTA ELPHINSTONE VILLIERS

BY GRANT

had been her mother's home and hers for so many years. She was brought to Scotland to lie beside her second husband, and her grave completes the number in the mausoleum.

Augusta was the last of the Thrales.

Anecdotes	*Anecdotes of the Late Samuel Johnson, LL.D. During the Last Twenty Years of His Life*, by Hester Lynch Piozzi. London: T. Cadell, 1786.
Baretti	*Easy Phraseology for the Use of Young Ladies, Who Intend to Learn the Colloquial Part of the Italian Language*, by Joseph Baretti. London: G. Robinson and T. Cadell, 1775.
Bowood Papers	Letters from Mrs. Piozzi to her daughters, 1793–1821. (*Manuscript*: Lansdowne)
Broadley	*Doctor Johnson and Mʳˢ Thrale*, by A. M. Broadley. London: John Lane, 1910. (This includes the Welsh journals of both Dr. Johnson and Mrs. Thrale. Dr. Johnson's is also in *Life*, V.)
Burney	*Diary and Letters of Madame D'Arblay* [Fanny Burney], ed. by her niece. 7 vols. London: H. Colburn, 1842–46.
Clifford	*Hester Lynch Piozzi (Mrs. Thrale)*, by James L. Clifford. Oxford: Clarendon Press, 1941.
Commonplace Book	New Commonplace Book. Jottings kept by HLP after the completion of *Thraliana*, begun at Brynbella in 1809; last entry 1820, at Penzance. (*Manuscript*: Hyde)
Conway	Biographical Memoir of Hester Lynch Piozzi for William Augustus Conway, May 1819. Bound into the two volumes of Mrs. Piozzi's *Journey through France, Italy, and Germany* (London: A. Strahan and T. Cadell, 1789). (*Manuscript*: Hyde)
European Magazine	*The European Magazine, and London Review* (1782–1826): Three Baretti "Strictures," May and June 1788 (vol. XIII) and August 1788 (vol. XIV).
Evans	The K. M. Evans Thrale–Piozzi–Salusbury Papers. (*Manuscript*: National Library of Wales, Aberystwyth)
Fellowes	Biographical Memoir of Hester Lynch Piozzi for Sir James Fellowes, 1815. Bound into two volumes of Johnson's *Letters* (1788). (*Manuscript*: Princeton University Library)

Harvard *Piozziana*	Biographical material written out for John Salusbury Piozzi Salusbury by HLP (1810–1814), much of it paralleling entries in *Thraliana*. Formerly Mainwaring *Piozziana*. (*Manuscript*: Harvard College Library)
Hayward	*Autobiography, Letters and Literary Remains of Mrs. Piozzi (Thrale)*, by A. Hayward, 2nd ed. 2 vols. London: Longman, Green, Longman, and Roberts, 1861.
Johnson Diaries	*Samuel Johnson, Diaries, Prayers, and Annals*, ed. by E. L. McAdam, Jr., with Donald and Mary Hyde. New Haven: Yale University Press, 1958.
Johnson and Queeney	*Johnson and Queeney, Letters from Dr. Johnson to Queeney Thrale from the Bowood Papers*, ed. by the Marquis of Lansdowne. London: Cassell, 1932.
Journals	*The French Journals of Mrs. Thrale and Doctor Johnson*, ed. by Moses Tyson and Henry Guppy. Manchester: Manchester University Press, 1932.
Letters	*The Letters of Samuel Johnson, with Mrs. Thrale's Genuine Letters to Him*, ed. by R. W. Chapman. 3 vols. Oxford: Clarendon Press, 1952.
Letters 1788	*Letters to and from the Late Samuel Johnson, LL.D.*, ed. by Hester Lynch Piozzi. 2 vols. London: A. Strahan and T. Cadell, 1788.
Life	*Boswell's Life of Johnson*, ed. by George Birkbeck Hill and L. F. Powell. 6 vols. Oxford: Clarendon Press, 1934–1950.
Mangin	*Piozziana; or, Recollections of the Late Mrs. Piozzi, with Remarks*, by a Friend [Edward Mangin]. London: Edward Moxon, 1833.
Memoirs	*Memoirs of Doctor Burney*, arranged . . . by Madame d'Arblay. 3 vols. London: Edward Moxon, 1832.
Miscellanies	*Johnsonian Miscellanies*, ed. by George Birkbeck Hill. 2 vols. Oxford: Clarendon Press, 1897.
Pennington	*The Intimate Letters of Hester Piozzi and Penelope Pennington, 1788–1821*, ed. by Oswald G. Knapp. London: John Lane, 1914.
Perkins	The Perkins Genealogy Book, compiled by Charles Alan Carlos Perkins and George Algernon Perkins. 1936. (*Typescript*: Courage Ltd.)
Queeney Letters	*The Queeney Letters: Being Letters Addressed to Hester Maria Thrale by Dr. Johnson, Fanny Burney, and Mrs. Thrale-Piozzi*, ed. by the Marquis of Lansdowne. London: Cassell, 1934.
Rice	Thrale-Rice Correspondence: 23 letters, 1773–1776, some undated. (*Manuscript*: Hyde)

Rylands

Manuscript Archive of Hester Lynch Thrale Piozzi at the John Rylands University Library of Manchester.

St. Leonard's

The Heritage of St. Leonard's Parish Church, Streatham, by H. W. Bromhead and Mrs. Arundell Esdaile. London: Hatchards, 1932.

Thrale Estate Book

Accounts of the Estate of Henry Thrale, also Guardian Accounts with the four Thrale daughters. (*Manuscript*: Hyde)

Thraliana

Thraliana, the Diary of Mrs. Hester Lynch Thrale (Later Mrs. Piozzi) 1776–1809, ed. by Katharine C. Balderston, 2nd ed. 2 vols. Oxford: Clarendon Press, 1951.

INDEX

Abbreviations: HLS: Hester Lynch Salusbury; HLT: Hester Lynch Thrale; HLP: Hester Lynch Piozzi; Q: Hester Maria Thrale (Queeney); JSPS: John Salusbury Piozzi Salusbury; SJ: Samuel Johnson